PEP CONFIDENTIAL

INSIDE PEP GUARDIOLA'S FIRST SEASON
AT BAYERN MUNICH

PEP CONFIDENTIAL

INSIDE PEP GUARDIOLA'S FIRST SEASON
AT BAYERN MUNICH

MARTÍ PERARNAU

BackPage Press
World-class sports books

First published in Great Britain in 2014 by
ARENA SPORT
An imprint of Birlinn Limited
West Newington House
10 Newington Road
Edinburgh
EH9 1QS

www.arenasportbooks.co.uk

Published in association with
BACKPAGE PRESS
www.backpagepress.co.uk

Copyright © Martí Perarnau, 2014
Translation © Louise Hunter, 2014

ISBN: 9781909715257
eBook ISBN: 9780857908179

First published in Spain in 2014 by Rocca Editorial as *Herr Pep*

9 8 7 6 5 4 3

British Library Cataloguing-in-Publication Data
A catalogue record for this book is available on request from the
British Library.

Designed and typeset by Polaris Publishing, Edinburgh

Printed and bound by Clays St Ives

ACKNOWLEDGEMENTS

Thanks go to Lufthansa and the Munich U-Bahn (Metro) for getting me there on time.

And to the security guards at FC Bayern, led by Heinz Jünger, who sheltered me from the heat and the cold.

A huge thank you is also due to everyone at Munich's Hotel Wetterstein, where I spent much of last year and felt very much at home.

Thanks also to Markus Hörwick, FC Bayern's very able director of communications, and to his team Nina Aigner, Cristina Neumann, Holger Quest and Petra Trott.

I am enormously grateful to all the FC Bayern players, and in particular to Thiago Alcántara, Jerôme Boateng, Dante Bonfim, Pierre-Emile Højbjerg, Philipp Lahm, Javi Martínez, Manuel Neuer, Rafinha, Franck Ribéry, Arjen Robben and Bastian Schweinsteiger, for their collaboration and the kindness they have shown me.

Thanks also to Paul Breitner, Roman Grill, Jupp Heynckes, Jürgen Klopp, Alexis Menuge, Christoph Metzelder, Stefen Niemeyer, Manuel Pellegrini, Daniel Rathjen, Ronald Reng, Karl-Heinz Rummenigge, Xavier Sala i Martín, Christian Streich, Julien Wolff and Mounir Zitouni, who have all made interesting contributions to this book.

To Matthias Sammer, for all his passion and his German language tutorials.

Thanks also to Isaac Lluch, a young, talented journalist whose vital support for me, in every sense of the word, knew no bounds.

Sincere thanks to Guardiola's technical team, Domènec Torrent, Lorenzo Buenaventura and Carles Planchart, without whose direction and advice it would have been impossible to understand the team's training regime and playing style.

And to Manel Estiarte, the key that opens every door. It is impossible to express the enormous debt I owe him for all his help and support.

And finally, to Pep Guardiola, the man who gave me this opportunity to understand in depth the workings of an elite football team, for all the generosity he showed me even through the blackest moments of the season.

PART ONE

TIME, PATIENCE, PASSION

'We need patience.'
KARL-HEINZ RUMMENIGGE

* * *

'We need passion.'
MATTHIAS SAMMER

* * *

'We need time.'
PEP GUARDIOLA

DINNER WITH KASPAROV

New York, October 2012

TAKING A LAST bite of salad, Garry Kasparov shook his head and muttered irritably: 'Impossible!'

For the third time that night he tried to fend off Pep Guardiola's relentless questioning. The Catalan was determined to understand why Kasparov would not even *consider* the idea of competing against the young maestro, Magnus Carlsen, the world's most promising chess player.

Until then, the atmosphere over dinner had been perfectly congenial. Indeed, since meeting Kasparov a few weeks before, Pep had made no attempt to conceal his fascination for the great champion.

Kasparov embodies the qualities Pep prizes above all others: resilience, intelligence, dedication, persistence, inner strength and a healthy streak of rebelliousness. It had therefore been an absolute delight to meet up over a meal or two. So far the conversation had covered a range of topics from economics and technology to, inevitably, sport and competition.

Guardiola was a few months into his sabbatical from the elite of world football. He had promised himself a year of tranquility in New York and was just starting to enjoy it.

He had spearheaded a triumphant era at FC Barcelona, the most successful period in the Catalan club's history – achievements which may never be matched. During his four years in charge he won a formidable total of 14 trophies out of the 19 available, including six titles in 2009 alone. Yet, despite all of the brilliance and passion, the experience had left him drained and exhausted. Increasingly dispirited, he had decided to leave Barça before the damage became irreparable.

New York represented a fresh start. He wanted the chance to switch off, forget the past and discover new ideas. This was an opportunity to recharge his batteries and top up the reserves of energy that had become so depleted. He was keen to spend time with his family, whom he had neglected under pressure of work.

There would also be time to touch base with old friends. One of those was Xavier Sala i Martín, professor of economics at Columbia University, who had been director of finance at Barça from 2009 to 2010, during Joan Laporta's final term as president.

Sala i Martín, a renowned economist with an international reputation, is a good friend of the Guardiola family and has lived in New York for some time. His presence there was an important factor in overcoming the family's misgivings about moving to the city. The children had not yet mastered English and Cristina, Pep's wife, would have to leave her own job in the family business in Catalonia.

Initially, none of them was particularly enthusiastic about Pep's proposal, but Sala i Martín persuaded them to give New York a go and so far the whole experience had proved much better than expected.

Sala i Martín also counts Garry Kasparov as a close friend and one autumn night was forced to decline a dinner invitation to the Guardiolas' New York home: 'Sorry Pep. I can't make it tonight. I'm having dinner with the Kasparovs.'

He then suggested that his Catalan friend accompany him to the meal, an idea which delighted not just Pep but Kasparov and his wife, Daria, too.

During what was a fascinating evening, the conversation flowed despite the fact that neither chess nor football was mentioned. They talked about inventions and technology, about the value of breaking pre-established paradigms and the virtue of remaining steadfast in the face of uncertainty. Most of all, they talked about passion.

Central to the discussion was Kasparov's rather bleak assertion that technological potential is being directed to the world of entertainment more than anything else. In his view, current technological advances lack the transcendence of their predecessors and this has helped contribute to worldwide economic stagnation.

According to the former world chess champion, even the birth of the internet can't be compared to the transformative power of the invention of electricity, which resulted in authentic worldwide economic change. It gave women access to the workplace and doubled the total volume of the world economy. In other words, he believes that the economic impact of the internet in terms of market production rather than pure finance, is vastly inferior.

Citing the example of the iPhone, whose processing potential is far superior to that of the Apollo 11 computer, the AGC (Apollo Guidance Computer), which had 100,000 times less RAM memory, he pointed out that whilst ACGs were used to put men on the moon, now we use mobile phones to kill little birds (a reference to the popular game *Angry Birds*).

Sala i Martín observed the encounter with some admiration.

'It was fascinating to spend time with two such clever men and be privy to their discussions about technology, inventions, passion and complexity.'

The mutual fascination was such that a few weeks later they made a date for a second meal. Sala i Martín, who had left for South America, was unable to attend, but this time Cristina Serra, Pep's wife, joined the group.

On this occasion the subject of chess was definitely on the agenda.

Guardiola was surprised by Kasparov's intransigent attitude towards the Norwegian Magnus Carlsen, whom he predicted would be the new world champion (Carlsen did indeed become champion a year later in November 2013, when he beat Viswanathan Anand 6.5 to 3.5).

Kasparov was unstinting in his praise of the great young maestro (then 22 years old), whom he had secretly trained in 2009. But he also pointed out the weaknesses Carlsen would have to overcome in order to dominate the world of chess.

It was then that Guardiola asked Kasparov if he felt capable of beating the emerging Norwegian. The response surprised him: 'I have the ability to beat him, but in practice it is impossible.'

The answer struck Guardiola as little more than political correctness.

It was, he assumed, an attempt by the impetuous Russian to be as diplomatic as possible. 'But Garry,' he insisted, 'you have the ability, so why couldn't you beat him?'

For the second time, the rejoinder was an emphatic 'Impossible!'

But Pep Guardiola is a stubborn man and Kasparov had, after all, allowed him to open this particular can of worms. He was not going to let the matter rest. The Catalan stood his ground and repeated his question for the third time.

This time Kasparov seemed to visibly retreat into the protective shell he had developed in his chess playing days. Eyes fixed on his plate, as if defending a particularly tenuous position on the chessboard, he snapped: 'Impossible.'

A change of tactic was in order and Guardiola decided to wait for another opportunity to explore the reasons for Kasparov's stubbornness – not out of idle curiosity but because he sensed that, somewhere within, lay the answer to a key question for Guardiola: Why had he been so worn out by Barça? And, above all, how could he avoid repeating the same mistake in the future?

If I had to define Pep Guardiola I would describe him as a man who questions everything, not through insecurity or fear of the unknown, but in the search for perfection. Although he recognises it as an impossible goal, it is nonetheless the force that drives him. As a result, he is often left with a pervading sense of unfinished work.

Guardiola can be obsessional in this respect and believes that the ideal solution can be found only after examining all the available options. Rather like a master chess player who analyses all the possibilities before moving his next piece.

When he sits down to prepare his game plan he does not spend time thinking about his team's general approach. His players will be going out to get the ball, play attacking football and win the match.

The basic strategy never changes but there is still room for nuance, for the application of a range of different options all of which he examines in the week before a match. He goes over and over the line-up in his mind, analysing the contribution of one player with respect to another and examining how their opponents will affect what his players can do. He wants to be sure of the level of synergy between playing partners as well as how the different lines in his team will work together when under attack.

No matter the opponent, his preparation never changes and he will not rest for a second until all the variants have been dissected and assessed. Then, when he has finished, he goes over it all again. This is what Manel Estiarte, his right-hand man at Barça and Bayern, calls 'the law of 32 minutes'. The term refers to his often-fruitless attempts to persuade Pep to disconnect from football. From time to time Estiarte will use all the resources at his disposal to curb the coach's obsessional behaviour. Experience, however, has taught him that Pep cannot be distracted for much longer than 30 minutes at a time.

'You invite him for a meal in a restaurant, hoping that he'll forget about football, but 32 minutes later you can see his mind is already wandering,' Estiarte explains. 'He starts staring at the ceiling and, although he's nodding as if he's listening to you, he's not looking at you. In actual fact he's probably thinking about the opposition left-back, the marking scheme for the midfielders, how much the wingers can support the inside-forwards… the guy can only manage half an hour and then he goes straight back to his mental contemplation.'

The stress caused by this constant need to analyse will be much easier to cope with at Bayern, as long as the players and management are behind him.

In fact, Estiarte now insists on him leaving Säbener Strasse, Bayern's training ground, from time to time and going home to disconnect. On these occasions Pep does indeed go home. He plays with his kids and then, at about the half-hour mark, goes off to a little alcove at the far end of the hall and returns to his analysis. His 32 minutes are up and, for the fourth time that day, he sets about exploring all the options from every angle.

This is why Kasparov's response had become so important to him. This is why Pep had to decipher the enigma.

Why would a legend like Kasparov, himself an amazing talent, consider it impossible to beat an opponent?

In the end, it was the female members of this New York gathering who provided the answer. Bringing the conversation back to the concept of passion, Cristina and Daria began to discuss the pressures and emotional exhaustion involved.

'Perhaps it is an issue of concentration,' suggested Cristina.

'That's it!' Daria agreed. 'If it were just one two-hour game Garry could beat Carlsen, but in reality the match would go on for five or six hours and Garry just doesn't want to go through the pain of so many hours with his brain on overload, calculating possibilities. Carlsen is young and isn't aware yet of what that does to you. Garry understands the impact only too well and wouldn't want to go through that for days on end. You would end up with one player who can concentrate for five hours and another who can manage only two. It would be impossible for him to win.'

That night Guardiola managed very little sleep. He was too busy reflecting on everything he had heard.

2

'I NEED TO KNOW EVERYTHING ABOUT THE CLUB, AS QUICKLY AS POSSIBLE.'

Munich, June 24, 2013

IT'S THE FESTIVAL of San Juan, Pep's first day at Bayern, and it is raining. It does not seem to bother him. He is radiant, almost to the point that he has to contain the feeling of pure joy that threatens to overflow at any moment.

There are no nerves. What he feels is pure elation and he has no intention of hiding it. He is delighted to have returned to football; he feels like he is standing in the starting gate, confident in the knowledge that his ride is fast, spirited and eager to be off. Everyone at Bayern shares the same excited anticipation. This is the day of Pep's presentation and emotions are running high. It is as if they have just added yet another title to the treble won in the season just ended – or else made the first conquest of the new season.

This is a day that will go down in the club's history books. The celebrations are, however, low key.

Two hundred and forty seven journalists have been invited to the press conference – the biggest number ever to have been given accreditation for an event like this at the club. The atmosphere in the Allianz Arena is extraordinary, as if Pep's arrival represents not a simple presentation, more an accession. Enthusiastic noise fills the Munich stadium and there is tension in the air as a solid mass of journalists cram themselves into the press room.

Pep is delighted to be back in the saddle. No longer the exhausted figure we watched walking away from Barça; today there is a gleam in his eye, and he looks rejuvenated. He is doing what he loves once again. Working with a ball at his feet.

'I love football,' he declares. 'I liked it even before I started to play it. I still like to play it, I like to watch it, I like to talk about it. I'm going to shut myself up in Säbener Strasse so that I learn everything I need to know about the club as quickly as possible, right down to the youngsters in the youth system.'

Karl-Heinz Rummenigge, president of the executive committee, starts off by announcing the club's objectives: 'For us, the most important title is the Bundesliga because it represents 34 matches. The highest prize as always is the Champions League, but it is a competition where there are no guarantees and the things you take for granted in domestic football don't always work.

'I am really looking forward to finding out what Pep will change in the team.' The coach waves his hands as if to say he intends to change very little, although I have the feeling that this is his natural diplomacy rather than anything else. His technical team, standing just a few metres away from him, seem to agree.

Manel Estiarte, who prefers to work quietly behind the scenes, will be his right-hand man, the person who will tell it like it is, regardless of whether the news is good or bad. Domènec Torrent shares the post of assistant coach with Hermann Gerland. Gerland is a Bayern man through and through, and has worked with players such as Thomas Müller, David Alaba and Philipp Lahm.

Lorenzo Buenaventura is sitting amongst the journalists. Buenaventura is the physical trainer whose dedication to Guardiola is such that he dropped everything to follow him to Barça, and has now joined him in Munich.

Carles Planchart is next to Buenaventura. Planchart will be responsible for scouting, as well as the tactical analysis of rivals and, still more importantly, their movements on the pitch.

Cristina, Pep's wife, and Maria, his eldest daughter, are in the sixth row of the hall. His brother, Pere, has also come along today, accompanied by both Evarist Murtra, the director who initially suggested that Pep become Barça coach, and Jaume Roures, the impresario who controls Spanish football's broadcast rights.

The coach's agent, Josep Maria Orobitg, is the last of the small group of family and friends who have made the trip to be here today.

Bayern welcomes Guardiola as if they have just found the final piece of their puzzle. Pep represents everything they need to make that final leap to the highest echelons of the sport.

Rummenigge puts it into words for us: 'We have made up a massive amount of ground on FC Barcelona but remain in second place despite the great successes of this last season. I am delighted to have signed someone like Guardiola. It is a privilege for Bayern.'

Guardiola tries to quieten the crowd and temper their growing enthusiasm: 'It would be presumptuous to say that Bayern is about to embark on a new era. We have to take it step by step. Expectations are very high and it isn't going to be easy. I'm actually a little nervous.'

To everyone's surprise, he speaks in very accurate German. He has a go at complex grammatical constructions and correctly uses the demonstrative pronoun 'diese' as well as the difficult word 'herausforderung' when he talks about the challenges he faces.

In his first few weeks in charge the German press will make a fuss of his mastery of their language but, as the months go by, it will become a normal part of their interactions, even if he has to ask them to slow down from time to time.

Everyone wants to know what he intends to change. Should they expect the kind of revolution he initiated at Barça in 2008 when he showed Ronaldinho and Deco, the supremely talented but wayward Brazilians, the door?

Pep shakes his head: 'There is very little in the team that has to change. Every coach has his own ideas but, in my opinion, any team that has won four titles [including the 2012 German Super Cup] doesn't need much of an overhaul. Bayern are doing brilliantly and you have an excellent team. I hope to maintain the same level of success as Jupp Heynckes. He is a first-class coach and I admire him enormously not only because of his most recent triumphs, but for the work he has done throughout his whole career. I hope to meet him again soon because I value his opinion. It's a great honour to be his successor and I have the greatest respect for him.'

It is as if the club and its new coach are starting afresh. Pep won 14 titles in four years at Barcelona, the Munich club gathered seven titles in the same period; but for today they have forgotten their past successes and are thinking only of this new beginning.

Uli Hoeness, the club's president, confesses that he had to pinch himself when Guardiola indicated an interest in joining them: 'Initially, when Pep said that he could imagine himself coaching here one day, we couldn't believe it!'

With almost childlike enthusiasm, big hopes and high expectations, they are embarking on this new journey together. But there is also an element of fear. In football everyone starts from zero with every new season. You are only as good as your last game.

Pep: 'When a club like Bayern calls you have to respond and I am ready to face the challenge. My time at Barcelona was fantastic, but I needed something new and Bayern has given me this opportunity.

'There is going to be lots of pressure but I'll just have to put up with it. As Bayern coach you are expected to play well and keep winning.

'I want to reiterate that a team as successful as this one won't need too many changes.'

The speech is very different to the one he delivered back in 2008, when he took over at Barça. Back then Pep promised to struggle, to run and to fight until the last whistle of the last minute of the last game. Here, the effort is taken for granted and the huge pressure that Guardiola will impose on himself and others will be considered much like the rain or the beer in Munich, just another normal part of everyday life.

Right now he is anxious to explain his football philosophy: 'My football is simple: I like to attack, attack and attack.'

Then everyone makes their way down to the Allianz Arena pitch so that Guardiola can sit on the coach's bench for the first time. One of the Catalans present quotes Cavafy's famous poem 'Íthaca' – a favourite of Pep's. 'May the journey be long,' he wishes Pep on this fresh Munich morning. Guardiola turns to him and adds: 'Let's hope it's a good journey, too!'

Pep has spent as much time as he could endure away from football.

Some weeks previously, Manel Estiarte was taken aback when the Catalan asked him to have his office in Säbener Strasse ready from June 10.

'What on earth are you going to do there at that time of the summer?' he demanded. 'There won't be anyone about! Enjoy your holidays, because very soon you won't have any free time at all.'

Pep is back where he wants to be. Pursuing his passion.

But what about Bayern? Why the change? Why would a treble-winning horse decide to change its rider?

Por qué?

Warum?

Why?

To understand the reason for Bayern's decision to appoint a new coach just as they were enjoying such success requires an understanding of the realities of a modern football club, and the role of the directors in an industry which combines the tangible with the intangible – mixing goals and roars in equal measure.

Bayern could boast a proud history, financial clout, innate self-confidence and a strong fan base. After a glorious run of successes, the future looked bright. They had built their excellence on the virtues that best represent the German character: endurance, unshakeable belief and an iron will. What they lacked was a playing philosophy.

Hoeness and Rummenigge were no longer interested in just winning titles, now they wanted a clear identity, an enduring hallmark which would establish their dominance once and for all. They wished that, in due course, the Bayern brand wouldn't simply be related to effort, courage, power and victory. They wanted more. In this quest, Pep was the chosen one.

Perhaps the real stroke of genius on the part of the Bavarian club was to start making changes at the peak of their success. After all, nobody would have complained had they continued with Heynckes and his staff after their treble win.

Under Guardiola, the club hoped to take a quantum leap forward and achieve the kind of consistent and enduring success they craved. They understood that none of this would be easy. Heynckes had set the bar very high.

All of this has led to this moment. Here, today, on June 24, 2013, in the Allianz Arena.

On the pitch Guardiola's eyes meet those of Matthias Sammer, Bayern's technical director, the man on whom he'll come to rely in the coming months.

Pep's expression seems to hint at the paradox he is accepting. His climb starts here, at the summit. His mission is to climb higher still.

In Munich it rains for about 134 days a year. Just one more thing Pep will have to get used to.

3

'I COULD SEE MYSELF COACHING HERE ONE DAY.'

New York, October 2012

'PREPARE YOURSELF, MANEL. I've chosen Bayern!'

In Pescara, in the north-east of Italy, Manel Estiarte smiles. Hard though it had been for his old friend to close one chapter of his life, the decision about his next step had obviously been an easy one. Their destination would not after all be England, but Germany.

The exchange is taking place five months after Pep's departure from Barça. In this time, he has been flooded with offers: Chelsea, Manchester City, Milan and, of course, Bayern. In reality, they are not job offers, but love letters, project proposals for this most illustrious of coaches.

The departure from Barça had been long and difficult and Guardiola had shared his plans with his friend Estiarte before speaking to the club, or even to Tito Vilanova, his deputy and successor. The reason was pretty straightforward. After four years at maximum intensity, Pep was drained. He had no more to give.

This was not the only reason, of course.

Over his four-year tenure, Pep had been expected to act as coach, club spokesperson, virtual president and even travel co-ordinator. During that time he had also struggled to remain on good terms with two successive presidents.

He had found in Joan Laporta a dynamic but pushy man, who possessed volcanic energy and who could be supportive one minute and undermining the next. Electric, contradictory – occasionally lewd.

Sandro Rosell was different and Pep quickly discovered that the new president's smiling demeanour concealed the cold, treacherous heart of a bureaucrat. Guardiola balanced the at-times hysterical behaviour of Laporta with his own calm sobriety. He coped with Rosell's sanctimonious posturing by injecting an overdose of his own energy.

Relations with neither president were simple. Pep managed to deal calmly and quietly with Laporta's histrionic outbursts. Although the two men were not close, the coach appreciated the opportunities the president had given him. Laporta had initially appointed Guardiola as Barcelona B coach and Pep had been hugely successful there, bringing the team up from the tough Third Division, an achievement he still considers one of his greatest successes. His gratitude to Laporta was absolutely sincere and also extended to the sports director, his old colleague from Johan Cruyff's Dream Team, the elusive winger, Txiki Begiristain.

The triumphs of Laporta's period in charge, however, concealed the struggles and skirmishes going on behind the scenes.

At times Pep felt like the captain of a ponderous ocean liner as he fought to steer the team in one direction whilst the club pulled in the other. No decision was straightforward, whether it involved transferring training sessions to the new training ground, making sure his technical staff had the same sponsored cars as the squad, organising publicity shots or agreeing the club's official position on any issue. FC Barcelona was a vast machine that moved to a rhythm and leadership style that had little to do with the way Guardiola managed his team.

However, by early 2010 Guardiola sensed that things were about to take a turn for the worse. Presidential elections were looming that summer and Sandro Rosell was the favourite to win. Rosell had been vice-president from 2003 to 2005, until disagreements with Laporta forced him to resign.

Under Laporta, the Catalan coach had won all six titles: La Liga, the Copa del Rey, the Champions League, the European and Spanish Supercups and the Club World Cup.

Rosell won the elections with an overwhelming majority and his arrival added a sense of animosity and resentment to the already complex bureaucratic difficulties which plagued life at the club.

In private, the new president referred to Pep as the Dalai Lama. Believing his coach to be a Laporta devotee, he was slow to trust him and resented the fact that the team had peaked too early by winning the six trophies during his predecessor's reign. The gulf between president and coach became unbreachable when Rosell persuaded the club's general assembly of members to vote in favour of taking legal action against Laporta. Rosell was smart enough to abstain from the vote himself, but for Guardiola it was the beginning of the end.

For four years, Pep demanded unstinting effort from his players. Nothing but their best would do and at times his exacting standards caused friction within the group. Many of the players were unfazed by the relentless work rate, but some felt they had earned the right to relax a bit. They were the elite of world football, after all, and they had the trophies to prove it. More than one of Pep's men were now interested in contesting only the important games and they began to make excuses to avoid the kind of grim, uninspiring winter matches which were played on cold, inhospitable pitches. To add to Pep's woes, one new signing in particular was failing to live up to expectations.

Despite the team's continuing success, Pep knew that his time at Barça was nearing its end. 'The day I see the light go out of my players' eyes, I'll know it's time to go.'

By early 2012, some eyes were already a little less bright.

People around FC Barcelona have often claimed that Pep's decision to leave was influenced by Sandro Rosell's lack of support for his plans to make drastic changes to the squad. Plans which apparently included selling players like Gerard Piqué, Cesc Fàbregas and Dani Alves.

The Catalan coach flatly denied this when we spoke: 'It's just not true. I left Barcelona because I was worn out. I explained how I felt to the president in October 2011. There was no change of heart after that. So it would have made no sense at all for me to start changing the squad. I knew I was leaving!

'The facts of the matter are that we won four titles that year and were playing better than ever, with the 3-4-3 we used against Real Madrid and the 3-7-0 I opted for in the Club World Cup. We were playing brilliantly but I was on my knees and had no new tactical ideas left. That was why I left. There was no other reason.'

Having gone to New York in search of some peace and quiet, Pep nonetheless still had to cope with a certain amount of parting shots aimed at him from Barcelona.

During his sabbatical year the job offers poured in. His ex-colleague Txiki Begiristain, the director of football at Manchester City, was very insistent. He also met up in Paris with Roman Abramovich, who was prepared to do anything to lure Pep to Chelsea.

Bayern, too, were anxious to register an early interest and a delegation from Munich attended Pep's last game with Barça, the final of the Copa del Rey against Athletic in Madrid on May 25, 2012. The Catalan club won 3-0 that day.

In the event the Bayern delegation did not get a chance speak to Guardiola, but they made their interest clear during a meeting with his agent. It was just six days since the Munich team had suffered a painful defeat to Chelsea at home in the Champions League final, a game they had lost on penalties. It was another heavy blow for the Bavarian club at the end of a bitterly disappointing period. One week earlier, they had lost 5-2 to Borussia Dortmund in the DFB-Pokal [the German cup] final in Berlin. Their opponents had just won their second consecutive league title after a brilliant campaign, beating Bayern by eight points.

In the space of a few weeks Bayern had lost three titles: the Bundesliga, the DFB-Pokal and the Champions League. After enduring the agonising Champions League defeat, Heynckes promised his wife that he would only go on for one more year. The directors of Bayern felt the same way. A substitute had to be found.

From the start Pep was well disposed to the overtures from the Bavarian club.

A year before, in late July 2011, not long after a resounding 3-1 victory in the Champions League final against Manchester United at Wembley, Barcelona competed in the Audi Cup in Munich. Pep liked the set-up at Säbener Strasse, despite the fact that it was smaller than Barça's training ground and had fewer technical facilities. The Catalan was impressed and told Manel Estiarte privately: 'I like this place. I could see myself coaching here one day.'

Estiarte was not too surprised by the comment. Pep had said something very similar a few months before, at Manchester United. The day after beating Real Madrid in the Champions League semi-final, Guardiola and Estiarte travelled to Manchester to watch their next opponent in action. It was May 4, 2011, and the pair sat together in the stands of Old Trafford watching Sir Alex Ferguson's team beat Schalke 4-1. Once again Pep had turned to his friend and said: 'I like this atmosphere. I could see myself coaching here one day.'

Guardiola has always felt a deep admiration, almost veneration, for the legendary teams and players of Europe. Estiarte knows this and was therefore not surprised by Pep's eagerness to meet up for a chat with Uli Hoeness and Karl-Heinz Rummenigge in June 2011. The four had a quick coffee together and it soon became clear that his feelings of admiration for the two Germans were reciprocated in equal measure.

Bayern had just appointed Jupp Heynckes to manage the second phase of their project, the initial stage having been overseen by Louis van Gaal. Guardiola, fresh from winning another Champions League title with Barça, was still totally committed to the Catalan club. At that moment none of them could have imagined how closely linked their destinies would become.

There is no truth in the rumour that Pep gave the Germans his phone number that day. This was a man who had won every trophy imaginable and whose football philosophy was admired the world over. He had no need to scribble his details on a scrap of paper.

'It didn't happen the way it has been portrayed in the press. We were there for a friendly against Bayern and we met Kalle [Rummenigge] and Uli [Hoeness] for a chat. I told them how much I admired both their current team and Bayern Munich as a club. It has always been one of the great clubs of European football. But I had never given a thought to coaching there. Nor was I thinking about it then. I was certainly not offering them my services. The fact that I ended up signing for the club a few years later was just a twist of fate. It wasn't something I was planning or proposing that day.'

Indeed, as we now know, the situation would have changed dramatically by the spring of 2012. With four more titles (the Spanish and European Supercopas, the Club World Cup and the Copa del Rey) under his belt, an exhausted Guardiola was bidding a weary farewell to FC Barcelona.

Over in Munich meanwhile, the indefatigable Hoeness and Rummenigge knew that Heynckes had only one year left and had started to look for a replacement. The Copa del Rey final was the ideal opportunity to register their interest.

Within a few months, in October 2012, Pep would be giving Estiarte the news during one of their regular *FaceTime* chats.

'*Prepare yourself, Manel. I've chosen Bayern.*'

These two men are well matched and had both been first-class global sportsmen and Olympic champions.

Guardiola was an extraordinary footballer who preferred to go unnoticed on the pitch. He positioned himself far from the opponents' goal and played a pivotal role in driving the flow of the game. He was a player who was constantly planning his next move as he played the ball and everything he did was designed to open up spaces and support his team-mates. For Guardiola, success meant organising the team around him.

Estiarte was an exceptional athlete. Known as the Maradona of water polo, he was a prolific goal-scorer who possessed a killer instinct. He won every honour and trophy available, earned 578 caps, scored 1,561 goals for Spain and played in six Olympic Games. For seven consecutive years, from 1986 to 1992, he was voted No.1 in the world in his field.

The ease with which he seemed to single-handedly change the course of every game also earned him comparisons with Michael Jordan, the greatest basketball player of all-time, and he was the top goal-scorer in four consecutive Olympic Games, as well as in all the other competitions he competed in. Despite this success, one thing still eluded him. Winning Olympic gold for Spain.

In the end it would take a change in philosophy rather than athletic prowess to secure this final prize. Having met and befriended Guardiola, Estiarte began to reflect upon his own approach to sport. He began to understand that while his individualistic playing style and single-minded determination to score had won him plenty of honours, only effective team-work would help him to secure that elusive gold medal. Estiarte decided he needed to make some changes.

Already a harsh self-critic, he examined every aspect of his own game and saw that his egotistical ideas had to go. Working co-operatively with his team-mates, he began to play a more supportive, enabling role. Almost inevitably, Estiarte lost the top spot in terms of goals scored, but his sacrifice changed the fortunes of the whole team and Spain won Olympic gold and the World Cup consecutively.

Working first at Barcelona with Pep and now assisting him at Bayern, Estiarte prefers to keep a low profile. He understands more than anybody the difficulty of reconciling personal ambitions with the needs of the collective.

Nowadays, the Maradona of water polo is known most of all for his intelligence and intuition. Always ready to offer players the benefit of his own experience, his primary role is to support and protect Pep as much as possible, rather like a gifted midfielder making a well-timed pass to his striker.

Pep told me how important Estiarte is to him: 'Coaching a football team is a lonely job and that's why I value loyalty above all else. When you hit the inevitable rough patch, you need to know who you can trust. Manel helps me enormously in a host of practical ways and is always happy to take on some of the more irksome parts of my job. All of that is vital to me, but more than anything it is his loyalty and emotional support I prize. When I'm going through a difficult period, maybe even struggling with self-doubt, he is there for me. And he's there to enjoy the good times as well of course. It's wonderful to have someone I can chat everything over with. He was an elite athlete himself, the best in his field, and although we come from different backgrounds, as sportsmen we have a lot in common. Manel has an unerring instinct. He knows immediately if things are going well or not. He is quick to sense the slightest change in atmosphere and can tell me with absolute certainty whether or not the players are behind us. If there's a leak he'll know about it. After five years working together he has learned to filter what he shares with me and I leave it to him to decide. I regularly say to him, 'Manel, what's your take on this?' and can always rely on getting an honest, intelligent response. He interprets body language brilliantly, too, and knows exactly what a particular look or gesture means. The true greats all share this quality, this intuition. Other sportsmen do things mechanically, but to be truly great you need this extra special ability. And Manel has it in spades. That's why I need him here working with me – all of that and the fact that we're good friends as well. This is the Maradona of water polo, who has achieved everything in his chosen profession and yet still he is the first to roll up his sleeves and get on with the task in hand, no matter how trivial.'

It is October 2012 and in New York, Maria, Màrius and Valentina, Pep's three children, are still struggling to learn English and adjust to life at their new school. The Catalan coach's phone is ringing off the hook with job offers.

Txiki Begiristain's Manchester City are still keen, and very insistent. Abramovich is deploying all his charm. He wants Pep and is prepared to mould the team to his specifications. The Germans, too, are determined, although their pitch is slightly lower key and to the point.

'*Prepare yourself Manel. I've chosen Bayern*'

Choosing Bayern does not mean signing the contract immediately, however. It is just the first stage in the negotiations about financial terms and footballing philosophy.

Hoeness promises Pep from the start: 'Don't worry, we'll find the money.'

Bayern prefer to avoid debt and their policy is to ask their club members and sponsors to foot the bill for any new investment. In this case everyone is happy to invest in Pep.

They discuss their preferred playing styles and the kind of players the club will need. Not a lot more needs to be said. Pep, Uli and Kalle are on the same wavelength. The conversation goes so well it's almost as if the three of them have a ball at their feet. They discuss Mario Gómez, Luiz Gustavo and Anatoliy Tymoshchuk, and Pep insists that he wants to hold onto Toni Kroos.

By December they are ready to sign the contracts, and president Hoeness meets Guardiola at his home in New York. Guardiola then informs Manchester City, Chelsea and AC Milan that he is going elsewhere and before long Sky Italia breaks the news. Bayern's hand has been forced and on January 16 the club hastily issues a statement. Unfortunately they also, rather insensitively, fail to inform Heynckes first. The incumbent coach feels badly let down. His friends Hoeness and Rummenigge had told him they were looking for a replacement, but not who it was going to be.

Over in Barcelona tongues are wagging and Pep's critics accuse him of taking the soft option. Little do they know that back in Munich Jupp Heynckes' metamorphosis from coach to living legend has just begun and that he is about to lead his team through a jaw-droppingly successful treble, setting the bar tremendously high for his successor.

4

'THEY WILL BE AT THE VANGUARD OF EUROPEAN FOOTBALL FOR THE NEXT FIVE YEARS.'

Munich, June 25, 2013

'THE REJUVENATION OF Bayern Munich's football is still ongoing. Phase three begins here.'

Paul Breitner, a Bayern and Real Madrid legend, is speaking from an office on Säbener Strasse. The conversation ranges from the late 1970s onwards as he outlines each stage of the regeneration project.

'When Kalle [Rummenigge] and I played for Bayern under coach Pal Csernai, we used a certain system. And we stuck to that until 2008. Whether you call it 4-1-4-1 or 4-2-4 or 4-4-2 doesn't really matter. The tactical ideas were the same. It was just that some of the moves were different. But that system is ancient history now. This is the 21st century and all of that should be consigned to the past.'

It was clear that things had to change at Bayern, but nobody knew exactly how to go about it. That is, until the arrival of Dutchman Louis van Gaal.

'We knew that in the modern game you only win titles by playing the kind of football Barcelona espouse,' Breitner points out.

'Barça had started to play like a basketball team. They moved much more, kept circulating the ball and altering positions. They were aiming for high possession and liked to keep changing the rhythm of their game. It always felt like they had produced five hours of possession, when they had in fact only played for 90 minutes. That's what modern football is all about. It's what we need to be doing now and perhaps even for another decade. At least until another new idea comes along. But how were we going to bring our antiquated system up-to-date? Louis van Gaal was the answer we came up with and, happily, it was the right one because he completely transformed our football.'

For Breitner, Van Gaal represented the key to the first phase of the rejuvenation of Bayern's game.

'He changed a few positions and introduced possession-based football. We swapped Bayern's traditional style for this high-possession game. But there was still no flexibility in terms of players' positions and everyone had to stick rigidly to his own area. No one was allowed to wander out of his specified sphere of influence and we began to play one-touch football. We had to focus on passing the ball to each other. In some matches we ended up with 80% of possession, but there was no real rhythm or pace. After half an hour, everyone in the Allianz Arena would be yawning at this display of constant passing. I bet all of the 71,000 spectators could predict our every move. Our game was well executed but very, very predictable.'

Phase two would be in the hands of Jupp Heynckes.

Breitner: 'He maintained Van Gaal's system, but tinkered with this idea of constant possession. He pointed out that the basic idea was sound. What we lacked was speed and regular changes of rhythm. It took two years for him to fully implement his ideas and he was rewarded in the second half of season 2012-13, when we topped the league with a record number of points. In the first half of the season, between August and December he was still working on some moves but, by the beginning of the second half, in January and February, the team was already displaying the desired rhythm and was producing a completely different game.'

Now Pep will oversee the execution of stage three.

'That's it exactly. Heynckes continued to opt for fixed positions. He wanted a high-speed game that would produce a lot of goals. That was the key. It wasn't just about possession; we wanted lots and lots of goals. Now, under Pep, we're changing to more flexible positioning. We'll be circulating the ball more and aiming to produce non-stop fluid movement, very much in the image of what Barça were doing two or three years ago, when they were at their peak.'

Breitner is speaking after he has just presented Guardiola as the club's new coach. As such, his words speak of hopes and aspirations, rather than actual reality. Bayern, let's not forget, have gone through seven different coaches in just 10 years. From Ottmar Hitzfeld to Guardiola. Seven. Not the most convincing evidence of rock-solid stability, even if Breitner's words do go some way to justify the thinking behind their last three appointments.

It is a day after Pep's presentation and people are already asking the inevitable question: 'Is this the start of a new era in European football? Are we seeing the beginning of Bayern domination?'

In the Biergarten, a traditional Bavarian tavern in Munich's Viktualienmarkt, three Catalan journalists address this very question. Ramon Besa of *El País*, Marcos Lopez of *El Periódico* and *Ara*'s Isaac Lluch are not convinced.

'It could happen, but it's by no means inevitable. Barça are showing no signs of deterioration. In fact, they're strengthening all areas of their game. There's no reason to believe that we're witnessing the birth of the new dominant force in European football, the successor to Team Pep. We don't as yet see Guardiola's Bayern as the great new European dictator.'

Mounit Zitouni, a journalist with the German magazine *Kicker*, points out how important emotional intelligence will be to the success of Operation Guardiola. 'Pep has a plan and the players will have to alter some of their current ideas. We journalists will also have to make an effort to understand what he's doing. It's vital that the players change their game and embrace this new style of football. But Pep, too, needs to adapt. This is going to be about everyone making some compromises in order to get the right results. These are quality players, but it is emotional intelligence that's needed here as much as anything else.'

All over Germany, supporters gather in the great football cities to exchange views over a few beers. There are journalists and bloggers around and tonight we're dining with one particular group active on Twitter using #tpMuc. One of their number, Stefen Niemeyer, a supporter who follows Bayern wherever they go, endorses the club's decision. 'In December 2012 we had lost our way in the Bundesliga, the DFB-Pokal and the Champions League. At that moment everyone was saying that Bayern were the perfect team, but that wasn't the case. One of Bayern's great strengths is that we never stop looking for ways to improve and move forward. They did it with Heynckes and now they're doing it with Pep. Obviously Heynckes has left a very special legacy, but there are still things to aim for. We have a score to settle with Mourinho's Chelsea in the European Supercup for example and it would be great to get a second consecutive Champions League title. Despite their unquestionable talent, our players could still improve certain areas of their game. There are still lots of things to work on, let's put it like that. And Pep is the man for the job. This is a win-win decision.'

Making such a significant change when things are going so well would generally be considered the high-risk option in the world of football. 'It actually makes complete sense to me and I'm right behind this decision,' insists Niemeyer. 'Up until last year Guardiola was considered the best coach in the world, for a whole host of reasons. This was a great opportunity for Bayern to take a leap forward and they took the right decision. Everyone benefits from this: Bayern Munich, the fans, Guardiola and German football as a whole. I think that his plan is to broaden his knowledge of the football played in other parts of the world and learn about different sporting mentalities. He'll then apply that knowledge to the kind of game he learned at Barcelona, a game that comes pretty close to perfection. That's why he's been so keen to work abroad – to improve his own style, change his ideas and perfect his tactical approach. Pep has had a lot of time to study Bayern and I don't think he'll try to imitate the Barcelona game. He'll set out to improve our football by making changes here and there, and then he'll be off in three years, to study football in another country.'

Christian Seifert, chief executive of the Bundesliga, agrees. 'Everyone in Germany is delighted with his appointment and there has been no hint of anger or jealousy. We all see Pep as a real godsend, someone whose contribution will benefit the whole Bundesliga. This is a very popular choice and things can only improve now.'

But back to Paul Breitner for a last word on the reasons for Pep's signing. 'For Bayern, Pep was the only suitable candidate. He was our future, the only possibility. All we had to do was work out how to get him.'

The Bayern board's decision took courage. They were, after all, making changes to a winning formula. Breitner is keen to correct this notion. 'That doesn't reflect the facts of the situation. Even before the start of the 2012-13 season, Jupp Heynckes had told Hoeness and Rummenigge that it would be his last year. We knew that he was leaving and that we'd have to find a replacement and the board started to discuss Pep. In fact they had already been considering him well before we won the treble.

'Then in March and April people began to challenge our plans. Heynckes was winning everything and the team was on top form. Why on earth were we going ahead? Because Heynckes had already taken the decision in June 2012 of course! Pep's appointment wasn't high risk. Everyone was absolutely convinced that he should be our next coach.'

'So are we going to see Bayern dominating Europe just as they did in the 70s and as Barça have done in recent years?' I ask next.

'They'll be at the vanguard of European football for the next five years, even without winning the Champions League every year,' he assures me. 'In reality you don't have to win it every year to be considered the best. Bayern are about to embark on the same kind of golden era Barça enjoyed for five years. There is no doubt in my mind at all.'

I press him further. 'Would you agree that it's a little ironic that the Bayern of Franz Beckenbauer has signed the 'son' of Cruyff to secure success?'

Breitner refutes this suggestion. 'Not at all, not at all. We have huge respect for Dutch football and Johan Cruyff has been both a friend and a worthy adversary in the past. He is, moreover, a fine person and was a first-class coach when he was at Barça. There is definitely nothing ironic about this situation.'

Beckenbauer and Cruyff, emblematic players for Bayern and Barça respectively as well as national icons in Germany and Holland, faced each other in the 1974 World Cup final in Munich. Now their heirs have come together in pursuit of the same objective: the domination of European football.

On this particular chessboard, Pep's pieces are all in red.

5

'I'M DESPERATE TO WATCH TRAINING – I WANT TO SEE WHAT PEP DECIDES TO CHANGE.'

Munich, June 26, 2013

IF PEP GUARDIOLA had to go into battle, Lorenzo Buenaventura is the man he would want by his side. A natural early riser, Buenaventura is happy to get up at 6am for a breakfast meeting to discuss that afternoon's training session.

It is June 26. Day One.

Pep has known for a few days now exactly what the inaugural session will involve. It will take place in the Allianz Arena, and not the Säbener Strasse facility, because the club is expecting a sizeable crowd. Up until now the two men have needed very little discussion to plan the work of the first seven weeks. With Pep in New York and Lorenzo in Cadiz, they have limited themselves to exchanging a few ideas and organising their diaries. The club has planned a dozen matches before the start of the Bundesliga on Friday, August 9. The matches include both a DFB-Pokal game and, more importantly, the German Super Cup in Dortmund against no less a rival than Borussia. Later Bayern will organise a friendly in aid of the victims of the floods which have recently devastated Bavaria.

On May 14, Guardiola emailed his colleagues a five-line action plan for the first seven weeks. His objectives were straightforward: do well in the German Super Cup and begin the Bundesliga in good shape. His proposals, written in both German and Catalan, included organising pre-season training in Italy. Everyone was delighted with the idea, which for Pep would be a real treat after the gruelling pre-season tours of Asia and North America he had endured with Barça. Buenaventura is also pleased.

In his first 45 days in Munich, Bayern's new head fitness coach will have to co-ordinate 13 matches (10 friendlies and three official games) as well as 45 training slots, of which 12 will be double sessions in the morning and evening. An agenda of this kind would have been impossible at Barcelona.

At Bayern, the training and matches combined mean that the players will complete 60 sessions in only seven weeks. By the standards of modern clubs it is an absolute luxury and Buenaventura has a permanent grin on his face. He does not speak German, just English, but has no problem at all communicating with his new colleagues.

Considered one of the foremost fitness coaches in the world, Buenaventura was trained by Paco Seirul.lo. Although originally from an athletics background, Seirul.lo became a brand name in the fitness training of footballers and professionals from other team sports. He used his own methods when he worked with Johan Cruyff's Dream Team and spent 25 successful years keeping Barça players fit and healthy.

Buenaventura uses Seirul.lo's 'structured microcyle' approach which involves short training cycles over three to five days, focused on one area. It might be strength – resistance, elastic strength or explosive force depending on the player and the particular stage in the season. Training sessions simulate the technical and tactical aspects of the next game and the ball is always used. In other words, the players train in the same way they play. Guardiola's principles underpin every aspect of training and before the session he and Buenaventura agree the day's tactical and technical objectives. These then become the focus of the session. One day it might be bringing the ball out from the back, the next they'll work on pressing the opposition from the point at which the ball is lost, and so on. Consequently in this, Bayern's first session, the ball will play a starring role.

Rummenigge has already told me how excited he is: 'I'm desperate to see training. I want to see what Pep decides to change in the team.'

Matthias Sammer views this first session differently: 'This is the opportunity for Pep and the team to get to know each other. This is where we start to work together as honestly and as openly as possible.'

In the event, the day holds a few surprises for Rummenigge, Sammer and, of course, the players. There is no jogging, no long sprints, no weight lifting. They do not do any circuit training and there is no single exercise that focuses on athleticism. In fact, all that awaits the players as they arrive is a mountain of footballs.

Over breakfast in Munich's Westin Grand Hotel, Pep goes over his plans for the day with his team and at 7.30am they set off for Säbener Strasse. The players have come in early for medical checks and Pep wants to say 'hi'.

Out on the grass of the stadium's training ground, the new arrivals meet the veteran technical staff who have remained with the club since Jupp Heynckes' departure. Hermann Gerland who, along with Domènec Torrent, will be Pep's assistant coach, is here along with Toni Tapalovic, who has been goalkeeping coach since he arrived with Manuel Neuer in 2011. Andreas Kornmayer and Thomas Wilhelmi, the fitness coaches who will work under Buenaventura, are also ready to start the day.

By four in the afternoon Buenaventura and his two assistants are in the Allianz Arena preparing for the training session. Three members of the youth team come with them. They will be briefed on the day's exercises so that they can then demonstrate to the first team. Meanwhile, some 7000 fans stream towards the stadium, all of them more than happy to hand over five Euros in aid of the flood victims despite the arduous journey they have had to endure. Maintenance work in the Munich subway system has forced them to disembark at Alte Heide metro station instead of the much more convenient Fröttmaning stop. Stoically, they leave the metro and board a slow bus to the stadium.

In the normal course of events the citizens of Munich prefer to travel in silence. Travellers are to be found reading or typing into their mobile phones, but telephone conversations are rare – a phenomenon which can catch the rather more expansive Mediterranean visitor unawares. The only exception to this rule is the very occasional whispered conversation. On match days, however, all of this changes. The silence is shattered by the jubilant roars of fans pouring into the carriages, usually cheek-by-jowl with their rivals. Together they turn the journey into a chanting competition.

Today things are a little different. This is the first chance to see Pep. He is here at last and whole families have come along to celebrate. There is a festive atmosphere on the long trek to the Allianz Arena.

Pep decides not to share the season's objectives with the players today. He will save this crucial information until the whole squad is together. Several key personnel are still absent for one reason or another. Javi Martínez, Dante and Luiz Gustavo will not be here until July 15. Arjen Robben, David Alaba, Mario Mandžukić, Xherdan Shaqiri, Daniel Van Buyten and Claudio Pizarro are due to join the team in Italy in seven days' time and Mario Götze, Bastian Schweinsteiger and Holger Badstuber are nursing injuries which, in Badstuber's case, will plague him for the rest of the season.

It has been 398 days since Pep last ran a training session and he is itching to get back to work in his natural habitat, the football pitch.

At exactly one minute to five he trots out onto the grass with about 20 players following him. Many of them are youth team players. They gather round him and he keeps his instructions short and to the point: 'I need just one thing from you. Keep running. I don't mind if you miss a pass or mess up a move, just keep running. If you stop that's it. Kaputt. You're out.' Training has started.

The first team-talk is just as brief. Two hours later, Jan Kirchhoff, one of the new Bayern signings, will comment: 'We thought he'd stick to English, but all his instructions were in German.'

The session starts with some warm-up *rondos*. The players are divided into three groups. In each group, six players form a circle. Their aim is to pass the ball to each other as quickly as possible whilst their two team-mates inside the circle try to stop them. Today the Bayern players are much less fluid than their Barcelona counterparts who have been doing this since they were kids. In fact, the champions of Europe appear a little slow and clumsy as they struggle through the exercise. Pep scratches his head. Apparently his players have come here expecting athletics training and here they are kicking a ball about.

The lower sections of the stands are packed but quiet. On match days the faithful flock to their footballing cathedrals, ready to sing themselves hoarse, but right now they have come to watch training and a respectful silence is the order of the day.

The warm-up concludes with two eight-minute *rondos*, a couple of drinks breaks and a few stretches. Up until now the focus has been on general ball work but the next exercise is more specific. This time it is about resistance work, which they do in three lines. Pep and Buenaventura have to keep correcting the players who are struggling to understand. They use the youth team players to demonstrate again and again. Pep is worried. He is still scratching his head.

Buenaventura explains: 'The players work in an area 70 metres long. They run the first leg slowly, practising three different technical-tactical exercises. Then they sprint back. It takes about six minutes to complete both legs and they will actually be covering about 4 km in the 150-metre space. It involves resistance exercises, but also requires them to work co-operatively. The idea is that they'll then transfer these skills to their game. Each exercise incorporates an aspect of Pep's footballing philosophy. One is looking for the third-man move, the second, 2v1 exercises and the third is a passing drill.

'The players start off working together in threes and then move on to individual exercises. It's all completely new to them. In the past, resistance work like this would have involved continuous sprints of 800 to 1000 metres, or longer-distance running.

'What we do is get them using the ball and we also introduce concepts like inter-co-operation at this stage.'

Matthias Sammer and Bastian Schweinsteiger watch intently from the bench. *Basti* is still recuperating from an operation on his right ankle on June 3. Initially the doctors predicted a 10-day convalescence, but more than double that time has passed and he is still not fully fit. From the stand Badstuber and Götze are also watching their team-mates. Badstuber will have to undergo another operation on his right knee in September. He was injured during a match against Borussia Dortmund and needed cruciate ligament surgery, but the injury had flared up again by mid-May. Beside him, Götze is rubbing his thigh. On April 30 he damaged the hamstring area of his left leg during the Real Madrid v Borussia Champions League semi-final. Anxious to play in the final, the player returned too early and his leg collapsed again. Almost two months after the original injury, Götze is still out.

All three players are taking much longer than anticipated to recover full fitness. Guardiola scratches his head once more.

Out on the pitch the basic exercises, supervised by Lorenzo Buenaventura, have finished. The players have been sprinting faster than necessary and have made technical mistakes as a result. This may be because so many youth team players are here today but it will take 10 more training sessions for Pep's men to perfect this exercise.

Now there are four rounds of positioning games, lasting four minutes each. These exercises in holding possession are a vital part of Pep's arsenal. Four players form a rectangle, four more position themselves within it and there are three wildcards. The ball circulates with the first touch and the coach shouts from time to time, 'Drück! Drück! (Press! Press!)'

What we are seeing are the first signs of what Pep wants Bayern to become: a team that circulates the ball quickly and applies intense and constant pressure. Two players are singled out for special attention. The first is Toni Kroos, who needs help to get his body into the ideal position for greater fluidity and the non-stop circulation of the ball. One of Pep's basic axioms is that every player should be thinking ahead to his next move as he passes the ball. As a player, Guardiola was always a second ahead of everyone else. He spends a long time with Kroos, whom he sees as the future conductor of this Bavarian footballing orchestra. He shows him that it is not enough to pass the ball. It must be done anticipating the next move, so that he can then position himself correctly. It is vital to offer immediate support, at the new base of a triangle of players, so that the ball movement can continue without slowing down and so that the team can both dominate and control the play. That way his team-mates will have more options. It is all about passing and then making yourself available. Sometimes that means moving, at others, staying put. Effective passing is about thinking one step ahead of everyone else. Kroos seems to grasp the point easily and starts to apply the advice as he carries out the exercises.

Then it is Jérôme Boateng's turn. The coach sees him as a real talent who just needs a little bit of guidance. As the season progresses, Pep's attention to Boateng will reach almost obsessional levels as he works to eradicate the player's three weak points. Pep will ask him to work on holding his position in the defensive line, defending with power and avoiding loss of concentration.

From day one Pep moves the defensive line several metres higher up the pitch than the team is used to. The objective is better marking and anticipation of opposition forwards, plus a faster, bolder and more aggressive defence. He wants his defenders playing much further forward and Boateng's input could be crucial whenever Javi Martínez is missing. Training is over for the day – 80 minutes of short, intense exercises which have allowed the players to work on various tactical aspects of the game. It will be like this for the rest of the season and Pep will continue to lead short sessions of 90 minutes, during which he will demand 100% commitment.

Pep still wants a private chat with two of his players. The first is Pierre-Emile Højbjerg, a midfielder who made his debut for the first team in April 2013 aged only 17. Albert Celades, a former Barça and Real Madrid player and currently the Spanish Under-21 coach, has prepared a detailed report on the youngster for Guardiola, in which he describes Højbjerg as a diamond in the rough. Guardiola has watched the player carefully during this first session and at the end puts a hand on his shoulder. The coach intends to invest time and effort in refining and correcting the young Dane's performance. This will start with intensive sessions over the next four weeks and then more sporadically throughout the season. He will set about teaching him all the tricks of the trade which he himself, having played in the same position, learned as a youngster.

During the stretching and proprioception exercises which mark the end of the session and are combined with some gentle abdominal work, the players sit around the centre circle. Pep grabs the opportunity to have a one-to-one with Franck Ribéry. Today's exchange sets the tone for the rest of the season and their mutual admiration is immediately obvious. Pep is impressed and fascinated by the attacker's talent and the Frenchman believes that under Pep's guidance his own professional development is about to take another massive leap forward. It is not just that the two men get on well. They dazzle each other. Despite this it will be months before the two begin to actually understand each other. And not just because of the language barrier. Today, as the rest finish off their stretching exercises, Pep asks Ribéry if he would be comfortable playing in central attack. Ribéry does not understand. The Catalan coach has become accustomed to Leo Messi playing in the 'false 9' position. A striker who does not only prowl the penalty box but plays much deeper and who improvises when to arrive around the edges of an attack. One who attacks the zones in which the opposition centre-halves work, but without them being able to patrol him. For Guardiola the ideal striker doesn't work permanently in the box, instead he arrives there at the culmination of a collectively-constructed attack.

Pep intuitively understands that Ribéry has the potential to become a formidable presence down the middle, but the French winger cannot yet visualise what his coach wants. It will take both time and passion before Ribéry mutates into the central attacker Pep is looking for.

Guardiola may not have much time to spare these days, but no one could doubt his passion. It is there in his face as he signs hundreds of shirts for fans the length and breadth of the Allianz Arena, patently surprised and moved by the warmth of their reception. He is back. Football is coursing through his veins once more and no problem seems insurmountable. At his side, Domènec Torrent speaks in English and Hermann Gerland responds in German. Over the coming months it will be vital for the two men to understand each other.

As the day draws to a close, Lorenzo Buenaventura is the last to leave. For the rest of the season he will make it his business to arrive first and leave last and the sight of him strolling from the pitch as the lights go out will become a familiar one here at Säbener Strasse.

6

'LEO, IT'S PEP. CAN YOU COME OVER? NOW, PLEASE.'

Weiden in der Oberpflaz, June 29, 2013

WEIDEN IN DER Oberpfalz is a small town in the Palatinate region of Germany near the border which separates Bavaria and the Czech Republic. It is also the location of Guardiola's first match as Bayern coach.

It's midday on Saturday, June 29. So far Pep has had to content himself with just four training sessions, in which several of his youth team players have had a starring role. He has had no choice but to use the youngsters as he waits for the rest of the European champions to join him at pre-season training in Trentino. Only 13 of the squad's main players will contest this match and the rest of today's line-up are drawn from the young hopefuls.

It is going to be an easy game. Every season Bayern play a 'fantasy football' fixture, known locally as a *traumspiel*, against one of the 3600 supporters clubs in the country. Today the honour has fallen to Weiden–Bayern. It is a huge event for the 41,684 inhabitants and around 11,000, more than a quarter of them, have turned out. It is going to be one big party.

Despite the festive atmosphere, Pep sees this as an opportunity to make his first declaration of intent.

His team will be playing with a sole holding midfielder. One of the many reasons for Jupp Heynckes' success at Bayern was his use of the double-*pivote* (*doppelsechs* in German) partnership of Bastian Schweinsteiger and Javi Martínez. The two played in the area normally reserved for the No.6 and their role was to close down spaces and break up opposition attacks. Together they were a formidable force and a key part of the team's treble-winning season.

One of Pep's first decisions upon arriving at the club was to dispense with this system. During his own playing days, Guardiola played as a sole holding midfielder, positioning himself in front of the defenders and organising the team from there. The position is known at Barça as the No.4. The Argentines call it a 5, and the Germans a 6.

In Spain this position tends to be called the *mediocentro*. It's the player who takes the ball directly from the defenders or the keeper and, with the whole of the pitch open in front of him, elects how his team's play re-starts. He's also the guy charged with cutting out the opposition's final pass – the one who can avoid the back four paying the consequences of an unstoppable counter-attack. His defensive qualities are essential.

Back in the late 1980s, Guardiola – lean, slow and lacking the powerful physique of a defender – was struggling to make it as a youth team regular when he caught the eye of Carles Rexach, Johan Cruyff's assistant.

'Guardiola isn't getting a game, but he is the best of the youngsters,' Rexach told his boss. Sure enough Pep, who was already a natural in attack and would quickly evolve into a gifted playmaker, was soon playing for the first team.

On joining, Guardiola was given the No.4 shirt, little knowing that he was about to define that position – that number – at Barça.

Cruyff saw him as a crucial part of his nascent Dream Team, whose mesmerising football would sow the seeds of Barça's ascendancy for decades to come.

Conscious of his own failings, Pep set out to maximise his talents. Lacking speed himself, he would ensure that the ball circulated at a pace that no player could ever match. Unwilling to risk too many physical tackles, he used his devastating passing to cut through the opposition. As a young player, Guardiola was already forming the football philosophy he would later implement so successfully as a coach; high-speed, attacking football as the best form of defence; effective passing and ball control, and as little hard tackling as possible.

We sat down together one December day in 2013, just after training.

'Do you think I would have lasted 11 years at Barça if all they were looking for was speed, strength and the ability to score goals?' In the 385 games he played for Barcelona, Pep scored just 13 goals.

To survive in the jungle of the football world he had had to foster and exploit the natural skills he possessed, rare as they were at that time. He used his personal training regime to develop not just physical strength but technical prowess and was happy to play a supportive role, distributing the ball with deadly accuracy. Pep prided himself on his ability to anticipate the next move even before he had the ball at his feet and delighted in using his passing to trick his opponents and break through their lines.

'If I had a line of five rivals in front of me, as usual, they'd want to make sure that we could only circulate the ball in a U-like circular movement in front of them – searching from wing to wing for space via the midfield, but never getting any depth or creating any danger. This line of five midfielders would inevitably be tightly pegged to the four defenders behind them – there would be no space between the lines. These two compact lines of opposition obliged me to use space wide in order to avoid danger. I'd use two wingers – making themselves available on each touchline and capable of going deep when it was the right time. The other attackers needed to move between the two lines. To achieve that I had to lead the line of five astray – move it about, shake it up, introduce disorder, trick it into thinking that I was about to go wide again and then – boom! – split them with an inside pass to one of the strikers. And that's that. They are turned inside out, suddenly having to run towards their own goal. Basically, that's how I separated my team from others during my career.'

All of this is exactly what Pep wants from his holding midfielder. At Barça he found it in Sergio Busquets and here in Weiden in der Oberpfalz, in late June 2013, it is the young Pierre-Emile Højbjerg he has in his sights.

Pep heard good things about Højbjerg before coming to Bayern and it has taken just a couple of training sessions for him to fall in love with the player who, having started in April under Heynckes, clearly has a dazzling future ahead of him. Højbjerg reads the game brilliantly and has an astonishing ability to break through five players with a single pass. Pep thinks that he may just have found the Busquets of Bayern, although at 17 the young player has a bit of maturing to do. In fact Højbjerg is the only one of the 23 to play the full 90 minutes of this friendly. The game ends with a 15-1 victory and, as expected, their rivals have given them very few problems.

Guardiola's debut XI consists of Neuer; Lahm, Kirchhoff, Can, Contento; Højbjerg, Schöpf, Strieder; Markoutz, Müller and Rankovic.

But let's leave Weiden in der Oberpfalz for a moment to talk a little about the idiosyncrasies of football terminology. Every country in the world seems to have its own terms to describe what happens on the pitch. We've already seen that a player in the same position will be called a 6 in Germany, a 5 in Argentina and a 4 at Barça, where he will also be known as a *pivote*.

Something similar happens in the numerical sequences which try to indicate the specific positioning of a given player on the pitch.

Guardiola has no time for these schematics and dismisses them as 'lists of telephone numbers'. One of his mentors, Juanma Lillo goes further: 'You'll never see players in those positions, not even when they first come out onto the pitch.'

However, for our purposes and to better explain the point, I'd like to refer to these formations now. Pep's 4-3-3 in Spain would be a 4-1-4-1 to a German. Two distinct ways of presenting the same formation: four defenders, an organising midfielder, two attacking midfielders, two wingers and, at the point of it all, a striker.

Of course, no match plan could ever convey the complexity of the organisation of a football team. For our purposes, however, when I talk about Guardiola's Bayern team I will often refer to the 4-3-3 formation.

As expected, Pep played a sole midfielder in his first game. As a player he disliked playing as part of a double-*pivote* because it limited his space on the pitch, and neutralised the effect of his ability to anticipate the next pass. He felt lost and ill at ease and as a coach is reluctant to impose that system on his players. Over time, however, he would rethink this attitude and eventually come up with his own particular version of the position.

Today, Højbjerg plays very well and Guardiola sees something of himself in the young Dane. He likes the way he positions his body when he gets the ball and then feints one way while actually intending to move in the opposite direction. He is convinced that he has indeed found a diamond in the rough. His job will be to polish the player over the next three years (the length of his current contract with Bayern).

Everyone in Weiden is enjoying the celebrations, despite the final score. The young Austrian, Oliver Markoutz, scores the first goal of the Guardiola era, 10 minutes into the game. At half-time the scoreboard shows 0-3, but in the second half the men from the supporters' club collapse. Bayern's line-up has some changes. It's now Starke; Rafinha, Wein, Boateng, Schmitz; Højbjerg, Weihrauch, Kroos; Weiser, Ribéry and Green. In the second half Toni Kroos steals the show, although all the photo opportunities are provided by two youngsters: Patrick Weihrauch, who performs brilliantly and scores four goals, and Julian Green, a lethal presence on the wing, who puts three away. Kroos plays a compact, fluid game and seems as comfortable playing on the left, his preferred side, or the right.

There is no serious opposition, but Pep nonetheless uses the 45 minutes to watch and assess his players. Even before taking over and certainly from the very first training session, Pep's instincts have told him that Toni Kroos will be a vital part of the motor that drives his team.

Today Franck Ribéry plays as a false No.9. It's his debut in a position Guardiola developed for Leo Messi and which helped turn the Argentine into the world's deadliest player. Pep would not claim to have invented the position, but it is one he cherishes and he was certainly responsible for giving it a new lease of life.

The false 9 existed in football as far back as the days when the Argentine Adolfo Pedernera was playing for and leading Máquina de River Plate (1936-1945), although the first player to really make it his own was the Hungarian Nándor Hidegkuti, known for his great exploits in the Hungarian national team of the 1950s, the Magical Magyars. Players such as Alfredo Di Stéfano, Michael Laudrup and Francesco Totti had all been great exponents of the same position but it had fallen out of fashion until May 2, 2009, when Pep Guardiola revived it. The venue was the Santiago Bernabéu stadium, Barcelona against Real Madrid. The two teams were battling it out for the Spanish title (the first of the three consecutive leagues won by Pep with Barça). The scene was set for the Catalan to unleash his secret weapon.

Ten minutes into the game, with the score at 0-0, Pep gave the nod to Messi and Samuel Eto'o. The two players had to swap positions. Eto'o, usually a centre-forward, moved to the right wing and Messi, a right winger, took up position in the centre of the field – but playing deeper, more like an attacking midfielder than a striker. Christoph Metzelder and Fabio Cannavaro, the Madrid centre-backs, were lost. They had no idea how to counteract the change.

Whilst researching this book I had the chance to meet Metzelder over dinner in Dusseldorf in November 2013. That astonishing day was still fresh in his memory. 'I think it was that day that Pep first used the false No.9. He put Eto'o on the right and Messi in the centre. Fabio [Cannavaro] and I looked at each other. 'What do we do now? Do we follow him to the midfield or stay deep?' We didn't have a clue what to do and it was impossible to catch him.'

Barça's historic win was a vital victory in the race for the title, but it also marked an unheralded period of glory and prestige.

The false 9 would go down in history as one of the more extraordinary of Guardiola's innovations, not because he invented it but because he was able to redefine the position through an exceptional player like Messi. How then did Pep come to resuscitate the memory of this type of player?

It was the day before the match – a holiday Friday, May 1, 2009.

Guardiola had stayed at the stadium to study his opponents. This was a well-established routine for him, which he continues today at Bayern. He spends two days analysing the team they are about to face, looking for strengths and weaknesses. He reviews entire matches as well as sections of the videos his assistants have picked out for him. Domènec Torrent and Carles Planchart, who are now at Bayern, provided this kind of information for him back then, too.

The day before the game, he shuts himself in his office, puts on some gentle music and thinks about his approach to the match. Where should they attack their opponents? What is the best way to dominate? He is seeking inspiration; inspiration which comes only now and again. Pep put it into words in Barcelona in September 2011, when he was awarded the Generalitat de Cataluña's gold medal.

'Before every match I lock myself up in an office I've set up myself. I sit down with pen and paper and watch two or three videos. I take lots of notes. That's when that flash of inspiration comes – the moment that makes sense of my profession. The instant I know, for sure, that I've got it. I know how to win the match. It only lasts for about a minute, maybe 80 seconds, but it's the moment that my job becomes truly meaningful to me.'

When he talked about this moment of magic he was probably thinking back to May 1, 2009. To that wonderful moment when he showed the whole world that he had found a new way to beat Real Madrid, who at that point were on a 17-game unbeaten run. Having watched a previous match between the two great teams, Pep noticed how much pressure the Madrid midfielders Guti, Fernando Gago and Royston Drenthe put on his own players, Xavi and Yaya Touré. He also noticed the tendency of the central defenders, Cannavaro and Metzelder, to hang back near Iker Casillas' goalmouth. This left a vast expanse of space between them and the Madrid midfielders – a vast, empty space.

It was 10pm and Pep was alone in his office. Everyone else, including his assistants, had gone home. He sat in that dimly lit room imagining Messi moving freely across that enormous empty space in the Bernabéu, having shaken off the Madrid midfielders. He saw him face-to-face with Metzelder and Cannavaro, the two players frozen on the edge of the box, unsure whether or not to chase the Argentine. The image was crystal clear and he picked up the phone. He wasn't calling his advisors, or even Xavi, the brains of his team. Instead, Guardiola dialled Messi's number.

'Leo, it's Pep. I've just seen something important. Really important. Why don't you come over. Now, please.'

At 10.30pm there is a gentle knock at Pep's office door and a 21-year-old Leo Messi comes in. The coach shows him the video, pausing it to point out the empty space. He wants his player to make that space his own. From now on it will be 'the Messi zone'.

'Tomorrow in Madrid I want you to start on the wing as usual, but the minute I give you a sign I want you to move away from the midfielders and into the space I just showed you. It's the same thing we did last September in Gijón.'

In Gijón, on September 21, 2008, in trouble after having lost their first league match against Numancia and drawn the second against a weak Racing de Santander, Guardiola's future as Barça coach hung in the balance. He decided to send Eto'o to the right wing and play Messi in the space between midfield and defence, as a false 9, just as the young Argentine has done many times in the youth teams. It was a resounding victory for Barça (6-1) and marked the start of Pep's dominance in European football. Now, seven months later, the coach explains his ideas to the player who will implement the strategy again.

'The minute Xavi or Andrés [Iniesta] break between the lines and give you the ball I want you to head straight for Casillas' goal.'

It was a secret between the two. Nobody else would know about the plans until Pep explained to Tito Vilanova the following day in the team hotel. Just minutes before kick-off on May 2, Guardiola took Xavi and Iniesta to one side and told them.

'When you see Leo in the space between the lines down the middle, don't hesitate. Give him the ball. Like we did in Gijón.'

That day in May 2009, the strategy worked perfectly and Barça destroyed Real Madrid, winning by six goals to two. Messi had become a false No.9 and Pep was happy. From that day to this, Guardiola has stuck to this system. Today it's the debut of his Munich false 9, Franck Ribéry.

Pep took the time to explain his idea during their first training session in the Allianz Arena, but the Frenchman still hasn't quite got it. Having learned his trade on the streets of his home town, all Ribéry's instincts tell him to get the ball on the wing, make a dribbling run and get it to the box before passing it for an assist. It's tough for him to understand that he can take a qualitative leap forward as a footballer if he quits the wing and plays in the middle; if he drops a bit deeper, gets the ball in space, behind the defensive midfielders, and runs at the central defenders in search of a goal.

Guardiola believes that he has three or four players in the squad who could adapt to play as a false 9: Mario Götze, Ribéry, Arjen Robben and Thomas Müller. He has made a start with the Frenchman, although so far it's not working particularly well.

Ribéry starts off on the inside and plays well alongside Kroos, Weiser and Weihrauch. However, gradually he drifts towards the left wing, his natural habitat, where he feels most comfortable, even though the white line hems him in. Guardiola lets him be, for the time being. But the coach won't forget his plans.

Everyone enjoys the party at Weiden in der Oberpfalz, despite the huge goal difference, or perhaps because of it. The Bayern fans have seen their star players up close – these treble winners who have now been joined by that apparently invincible coach, Pep Guardiola. However, whilst the fans make the most of this opportunity to see their idols, the coach leaves the pitch lost in thought. Højbjerg and the lone midfielder; Kroos and the rhythm of the team; Ribéry and the false No.9.

There is a lot to think about.

7

'DO YOU SEE LAHM'S POTENTIAL?'

Regen, June 30, 2013

IT IS STILL four days before Borussia Dortmund's pre-season training starts and Bayern are already contesting their second friendly. This time they are up against TSV Regen.

A table overflowing with buns, pastries and drinks awaits them in the dressing room and a few of the players immediately tuck into the chocolate tarts. This is the second match in a row they have been treated to a similar spread and Guardiola is taken aback. With an hour-and-a-quarter left before kick-off he takes a minute to ask Kathleen Krüger, the team manager, why both TSV Regen and Weiden in der Oberpfalz felt it was appropriate to provide his players with pastries and she reassures him that it was Bayern themselves who originally established the custom.

Regen is near the border between Germany and the Czech Republic, an hour-and-a-half from Munich. The local team, TSV, plays in the German seventh division and was founded in 1888. This game will mark the club's 125th anniversary. Seven thousand spectators are crammed into the tiny stand and they applaud wildly when Daniel Kopp opens the scoring for the home side with the first goal of the game. It is a sunny day and Guardiola has chosen a line-up that is reminiscent of the teams he fielded during his final days as Barça coach. He has gone for a 3-4-3 formation, with Emre Can, Jérôme Boateng and Diego Contento as the only defenders. The Catalan journalist Isaac Lluch, who will cover Pep's entire first season at Bayern, highlights this in his match report for the newspaper *Ara*: 'With this 3-4-3 Guardiola brings the German champions to quench their thirst at the Cruyffist fountain he carries within.'

As a player, Guardiola was well used to the 3-4-3 formation that Cruyff employed so successfully during his time in charge of Barça. Later as coach, the same formation would help Pep find a way to integrate Cesc Fàbregas into his line-up after the player's return to Barcelona. Playing with three defenders can be a high-risk option, but Pep's insistence on tactical precision meant that his team could use it time and again with outstanding results. One of the most memorable moments came during a Real Madrid game in the Bernabéu when Jose Mourinho's team took the lead after only 27 seconds with a goal from Karim Benzema. In response, Guardiola, who had started with a 4-3-3 formation, took just 10 minutes to reorganise his team into a 3-4-3 which, in the end, resulted in a 3-1 victory for Barcelona.

This is the formation he opts for in the first half of today's game in Regen. His objectives at this stage of the pre-season are simple. He wants to try things out and watch his players' reactions. He wants a deeper understanding of their capabilities. His own analysis will be much more penetrating than a superficial scouting exercise. He wants to test their limits.

One of the common misconceptions about Pep's time as Barça coach was that he planned to duplicate every position in his team, giving him two right-backs, two left-backs, two centre-forwards and so on. In fact, he wants footballers who can play in at least two, if not three positions. He is looking for men with the talent and flexibility to play as central defenders, defensive midfielders or central midfielders. Players like Sergio Busquets. Or as central defenders, full-backs on either side and midfielders, like Javier Mascherano.

Ultimately, Pep would prefer a much smaller squad. His ideal would be no more than 20 players in total with each player, except for certain key posts like the goalkeepers, excelling in three different positions. Guardiola knows that he already has players in the squad who fit the bill. Javi Martínez, for example, has shown at both Athletic Bilbao and Bayern that he is equally comfortable as a defensive midfielder, central midfielder or a central defender.

But Pep wants more. He wants to find out exactly how far he can push each of his players. Right now, during this pre-season period, before his men face any serious competition, he has the perfect opportunity to do exactly that. And this is why he has started training so early.

Ribéry may have been the hero of Weiden, but here in Regen it is Philipp Lahm who steals the show. Isaac Lluch writes: 'The evergreen captain of Bayern and Germany approached the game with determination and resolve and, in his position in midfield, breathed new life into the game with his attacking flair. His was the main innovation of the day.' Today Lahm has played in the *pivote* position, a role until recently occupied by Højbjerg.

Bayern win their second friendly game 9-1. On the way home, Guardiola tells Sammer that they need a nutritionist. He doesn't want any more pastries. For Pep, the players' diets, and in particular their post-match nutrition, are a vital component of their professional life and need to be closely controlled. His requirements are far from radical, but they are demanding.

Sammer wastes no time in carrying out Pep's wishes and, within a week, leading nutritionist Mona Nemmer will join the Munich expedition to Trentino. There will be no more buns for Bayern.

On the same bus journey home, Pep's mind is wandering. He's thinking about Lahm. The conversation between Guardiola and Domènec Torrent, his assistant coach who is sitting beside him, lasts the whole journey. It focuses on one subject.

'Do you see Lahm's potential? Have you seen how well he anticipates the next pass? Have you seen how he turns and protects the ball? He can play on the wing or in the middle of the field.'

It is clear that he has just made one of the season's biggest discoveries.

8

'THIAGO'S COMING.'

Arco, July 6, 2013

HALF THE POPULATION of Europe seems to descend on the airports and roads. The sheer volume of tourists catches me unawares. I had forgotten that it is already the first weekend in July, the start of the holiday season. To add to my woes, I take the wrong route. Instead of driving up the eastern shore of Lake Garda, I opt for the western side. It is a lovely journey through pretty little villages ablaze with colourful flowers, but the speed limit is 40 kilometres an hour as I drive through Salò, Boglisco, Gargano, Campione and Limone sul Garda. It takes me a while to reach Trentino.

For the fourth consecutive year, Bayern have come to this part of northern Italy for their pre-season training. The Munich club is a big draw and the regional authorities are happy to pay a significant amount of money, as well as subsistence costs, to guarantee the team's presence here. I can vouch for the club's pulling power. Trentino is bursting at the seams, and not just with German tourists. Guardiola and his men attract crowds.

I've come along too because, with the initial period of intense work in Munich behind him, Pep has promised to have a coffee with me so that we can talk about this book. In Trentino things are a bit calmer and he has some time to spare.

My arrival at Bayern's training camp in Arco brings two surprises. The first is that Saturday's session will be closed. There will be no access for the public or the media. During his four years as Barça coach, Guardiola insisted on closed training sessions and it was perhaps to be expected that that he might take the same approach at Bayern.

President Uli Hoeness initially requested an open-door policy to give supporters as much access as possible to the players throughout the season, but he has agreed that his coach need open up only post-match training. The rest of the squad's preparation will remain private.

There are two reasons for Guardiola's approach. He prefers to work with as few distractions as possible and he is also keen to avoid his techniques becoming public knowledge. His training sessions don't focus solely on tactics for the next game; they are part of an ongoing, season-long teaching process. He'll introduce a specific move or key aspect of his game into every training session and allow the players to practise it. He'll then revisit the move with them at a later stage. The idea is that his men will refine and eventually master a variety of plays which he can then use whenever strategically necessary. It is not always the next game he has in mind as he takes his men through the moves he wants them to perfect. He wants as much privacy as possible and when he gets back to Munich he fully intends to block off Säbener Strasse's main pitch.

The second major surprise is that Pep has decided to grant me a first-hand, in-depth insight into the team's work. I had hoped that a controlled level of access, the odd cup of coffee with him, and limited attendance at training sessions would give me enough material for the book. But Guardiola's unexpected offer changes all my plans. Free access means that I will be privy to everything that goes on. I'll be able to observe his coaching methods up close and witness the decision-making and planning process as it happens. Essentially, I will be spending months at the heart of this elite team with complete access to an enormous amount of internal information. Not even in my wildest dreams could I have imagined that the champions of Europe and the most successful coach of the decade would grant me such a privilege.

Pep asks for only one thing in return: my total discretion during the season.

'You can write about everything you see and be as critical as you like in the book but during the season please don't talk to the outside world about what you witness inside.'

I am enormously grateful despite the fact that my journalistic skills will have to be put on hold for a while. For one year I will live through all of the team's vicissitudes. The highs and lows, the injuries, the tactics, the line-ups, the periods of sickness, the good behaviour and bad, the jokes, the praise, the worries, the transfer plans ... I will know it all, yet the journalist in me will have no voice until the day I pour everything I have learned into this book.

So, the doors of the Arco stadium are closed for the training session today, Saturday, July 6, 2013. It has been two days since Bayern arrived in Trentino and Guardiola has used their rest time this morning to show his players a video about pressing the opposition. They are images taken from the first seven training sessions and the coach explains to his men that he doesn't want long runs. He doesn't want to see Ribéry and Robben running 80 metres in every game as they attack the opposition defence. Pep wants attacking runs that last 'four seconds at peak performance'.

The afternoon training session focuses on pressing, too. The defenders and one midfielder start things off, working together at the back, and the forwards try to get the ball from them using fast, aggressive pressing.

Neuer's skilled footwork stands out and Mandžukić's Eto'o-style aggression also impresses. The coach shouts his instructions to his players as he directs their efforts.

'It's four-second pressing only. I don't want to see Ribéry chasing his winger the length of the pitch. He needs to make it into the centre and stay put. What I need is for them all to press together for just a few seconds. That way they'll get the ball back high up the pitch.'

At the end of the session, Pep sits down on the bench in the heat of the afternoon and shares his ideas: 'We need intense, precise work. If all we were interested in was one-on-one man marking, all this effort wouldn't be necessary. I could just sit back and that would be enough. But we are aiming at a very specific style of play and must therefore work extremely hard to perfect every single move.'

There is no middle ground. If the players want to play his brand of football, they will have to give it all they've got. 'We have to train with the maximum intensity. It's just like the *rondos*: you do them with 100% effort or you don't do them at all. If the players don't like them then they're welcome to go mountain running, but in that case we'll never achieve our potential.'

Zonal defending rather than man marking; four-second pressing with the nearest player in position to press the man who's about to receive the ball; moving calmly into the middle to create and use space; working in a co-ordinated way. Pep breaks down his fundamental ideas about the game for me.

'This team just needs to slow down a bit. They've already got everything else down pat. They need some deceleration in the centre of the field. Neuer makes a clean pass and they move together to penetrate deeper – completely co-ordinated. I want intricate passing as they move forward, not too fast initially, so that none of our men ends up in the wrong place. A highly-organised advance until they reach the centre and then, boom! We trample them underfoot!'

Kroos possesses this ability to slow down, as do Schweinsteiger and Götze. And Thiago.

'Thiago's coming,' Pep tells me.

I have to ask him several times: 'Which Thiago? Thiago Alcántara? Thiago from Barça? Are you talking about the pearl of the Barça youth system?'

'Yes, that Thiago,' he replies.

Bayern are hoping to transfer Mario Gómez to Fiorentina and, since the striker is happy to make the move, the deal looks set to go through. The club will then buy Thiago, whom Barcelona have been trying to transfer since the summer of 2011, a year before Guardiola left the Catalan club.

Mario Gómez is a committed professional with a strong work ethic. He continues to train as hard as his team-mates despite the fact that his transfer to the Italian team is about to go through. In other circumstances, Pep would be quite happy to keep him because he values the player. In reality, however, he would struggle to find a role for the German striker alongside the other centre-forwards, Mandžukić and Pizarro, in the false 9 system his team will play. Pep already relies on Mario Götze and Frank Ribéry to fulfil this role and Gómez's departure is therefore inevitable – which must mean that Thiago's arrival is imminent.

In fact Thiago is interested in signing only for Bayern, and the deal is done without any difficulty. Despite claims by some sections of the media that he is considering Manchester United, the eldest of the Alcántara brothers is desperate to be reunited with Guardiola. For the time being he is holed up in a little holiday house in Begur, on the Costa Brava, where he barely has any means of communication with the outside world. He has even had to buy a special antenna to get an internet connection. Thiago will spend several tense days waiting for Gómez to sign with Fiorentina and for Rummenigge, Bayern's chief executive, to close the deal with Barça. In the end it will be eight long days before negotiations are completed, on Sunday, July 14.

Guardiola and his staff are extremely happy at Bayern. As a nation the Germans are renowned for their efficient, if at times overly rigid organisational skills and the Bayern press department certainly lives up to this reputation. They have established a press centre here in Trentino which would be the envy of any World Cup media centre.

The people at Bayern treat Guardiola and his staff with the greatest of care. Nobody doubts for a moment that he is second only to the president in terms of importance and everyone works together to ensure his ideas and plans are fully implemented. People are already commenting on the efficiency of the member of staff responsible for logistical organisation, as well as the impressive work of the team manager, Kathleen Krüger, a young woman who until recently was a midfielder in the successful Bayern women's team. Kathleen is responsible for all first-team administration issues and she carries out her duties with assured efficiency.

A few days ago Pep stopped taking German lessons. His teacher, a Borussia Dortmund fan, stayed in New York. Pep believes that he now knows enough to carry out the daily interactions with players and press. 'Our language on the pitch is all about giving instructions. I use the imperative a lot: *drück* (press), *schwingen* (balance), *sehr gut* (very good). With this type of language I think I have enough for the moment.'

After the session, which has focused on pressing, Stefano, who looks after the Arco stadium, offers us a refreshment. Sweltering in the evening heat, we are only too pleased to accept. Stefano is a cultured man who explains, to our amazement that, despite being situated in the north of Italy, near the Austrian Tyrol province, Trentino is home to no fewer than 450 different fruit species, some as heat reliant as the avocado. It seems that Arco and Riva del Garda have their own special ecosystems with the kind of microclimate which supports this amazing natural phenomenon. Here, in the shadow of the mountain range, lies an abundant fruit garden.

Stefano knows a lot about nature locally as well the culture and geography of the area. He also has a nose for football. 'Guardiola is the third Bayern coach I have known in four years. Van Gaal directed with his eyes, with facial expressions and silence. Heynckes was a coach who moved a bit more and gave a few instructions to his players. But Guardiola! He's a whirlwind of energy, a volcano.'

9

'THE IDEA IS TO DOMINATE THE BALL.'

Riva del Garda, July 7, 2013

THERE ARE CURRENTLY no guests staying at the Lido Palace in Riva del Garda – except for the Bayern party, who have reserved the whole hotel. On this, the first Sunday of July, two guards patrol the steel fence that rings the lakeside building, which is accessed via a long wooded path. Here, thousands of birds welcome the newly-arrived traveller. Their unceasing chorus is an ad man's dream and if right now there is a place of tranquility and calm in the world, this is it.

Pep is on the terrace of the Lido Palace going over yesterday's training session on his laptop. He is obsessed by football, obsessed by work and revels in the hours of detailed, methodical analysis. He will, from time to time over the next 12 months, reproach himself for this meticulous, demanding attitude and is aware that there are those in football who take a more light-hearted, less fastidious approach, preferring to put their faith in good luck and raw talent. However, the whispered tones in which he tends to express these sentiments suggest that in his heart of hearts, he's happy as he is.

Inside, on the other side of the window, Domènec Torrent, his assistant coach, is also studying the previous day's training on his computer. It's a curious situation. Pep is outside and Domènec inside. Both men are reviewing yesterday's 'four-second pressing' exercises but they choose to do it separately.

'I prefer watching it without Pep so that I can make my own evaluation and then swap notes with him later,' the assistant coach tells us.

He shares his own take on his boss's first few weeks at Bayern:

'Pep is off to a flying start and is more motivated than ever. I keep telling him that we have to go *piano, piano* though. We don't want to overwhelm the players with too many new concepts. These guys are switched-on tactically and they have welcomed our training model which involves a lot of ball work and no continuous running, but we have to take into account that all of this is like a whole new language to them.'

This concept of language learning will come up in conversation again and again this season. Guardiola uses it to describe a particular way of understanding football, both in terms of match strategy and training methodology. The coach makes a clear distinction between the notions of 'the core idea', 'language' and 'people'.

For him, 'the core idea' is the essence of a team and its coach. More than a single concept, it is the synthesis between a particular belief system and the group's stated mission. It can be summed up in a phrase often used in Pep's playing days by Johan Cruyff, the man who has been like a father figure to him in the course of his career: 'The idea is to dominate the ball.'

'Language' is the way in which the core idea is expressed on the pitch and is the culmination of a training regime which uses a range of systems, exercises and moves to reinforce understanding and mastery of the basic concepts.

And finally, 'people'. The quality of the ideas and the complexity of the language are of no consequence if your players are reluctant students. Essential though it may be, it is not merely sheer talent that matters here. The player must also be completely open to learning the secrets of the language, to practise them and make improvements where necessary. They must have complete faith in this process.

In Guardiola's view these three concepts, the 'core idea, 'language' and 'people' are fundamental parts of any playing model and can determine a coach's chances of success or failure.

To Guardiola, his job at Bayern Munich presents far greater challenges than those he encountered at Barça. There is a simple explanation for this. At Barça, the language of the game is taught from a very young age. Thousands of children pass through La Masia, the club's youth academy, where they are taught the Barça language as defined by Johan Cruyff more than 25 years ago and implemented by a serious of great coaches since then. They learn the specific details of this unique and precise language. By the end they will have mastered this particular brand of football so that by the time a player has made it into the first team he will have accumulated more than 10,000 hours of practice and training in this single playing model. As such, he has become a fluent speaker of the language.

There is no equivalent at Bayern, at least not with the same level of uniformity either in terms of the language or the machine which teaches it – and this has a major impact on Pep's plans. Domènec Torrent explains: 'It's like we're showing them the numbers first, then the days of the week, then verbs, etc. This is a huge departure for them and we need to be flexible and cautious. In the past they were taught about man-marking and now we're talking in terms of covering a whole area, for example. We don't want them to mark a player and abandon the positions we've assigned them, because all it takes is a long pass, and the opposition will ruin our organisation. It will take time but they are assimilating everything well. Yesterday's pressing exercises were well executed, particularly considering it was only the second time they had done them.'

I am struck and rather surprised by the way the players interact with Guardiola. I don't sense any of the usual hierarchical barriers between players and coach. This morning, with the sound of bird song in the air, the coach seems like just another one of the lads. Boateng and Alaba go out to the terrace to share a joke with him. Schweinsteiger interrupts and sits with him for a while as he says his goodbyes. He's going back to Munich, along with Doctor Hans-Wilhelm Müller-Wohlfahrt, to continue treatment on his ankle which was operated on at the start of June. There are fewer of the necessary resources in Trentino than in Munich and his recovery has been slow. This worries Pep. He wants *Basti* to play a key role in implementing his playing model. He sends the player off with good wishes for a speedy recovery: '*We need you, Basti.*'

Lorenza Buenaventura arrives. He has spent the morning overseeing a strength-building workout for the youngest players, as well as an induction session for Arjen Robben, who has recently joined the team. 'We gave Robben the same basic training the others had in their first day in the Allianz Arena, the three initial exercises and the work on developing compact defensive cover. He assimilated it all brilliantly, and quickly.'

Guardiola is particularly interested in the Dutch forward's work. 'Splendid, Pep, absolutely splendid,' reports Buenaventura. 'He worked really hard.'

Robben will be one of the surprises of the year. Guardiola's appointment had barely been confirmed in January 2013 when people began to question whether the new coach would want to keep the Dutch player on. The doubts persisted even after Robben scored the goals which were so decisive in the club's Champions League victory. But the player's attitude on his arrival in Trentino has been just right and the man responsible for the winning goal at Wembley has approached his work with all the hunger of a youngster desperate to win a place in the team. Robben will continue to apply this same work ethic, in the process earning the support and admiration of his coach.

When I spoke to Robben, he explained: 'I started the season with an open mind and was happy to try new ideas.'

Maintaining an open mind is essential for anyone hoping to learn this new footballing language. Pep's players are quick to demonstrate that this is one quality they all share. If the boss has gone to the effort of mastering German, the least his players can do is learn the language of the man from Santpedor. The players' initial unfamiliarity with the *rondos*, the *Kreisspiele*, soon changes to positive enthusiasm. Toni Kroos, who is delighted with the new regime, is sure that the ball will become a good friend to him. 'The ball moves very fast,' explains Daniel Van Buyten, 'and that means we have to play and think just as fast.'

Lorenzo Buenaventura takes the chance to share his impressions of the coach: 'Pep is obsessed by work but he's also a revolutionary.

Bayern had just won the treble when he took over and 99% of coaches would have come here and not changed a thing. If it ain't broke, don't fix it. But he wants to transcend the mundane and ordinary. He is trying to introduce new concepts to football and he likes to see it evolving year by year. There have been several key periods in football in the last 25 years: [Arrigo] Sacchi's era, the era of the Dutch and the era of Barça.'

Months later, during the Christmas holidays, Fabio Capello will say something similar: 'Guardiola's era is one of the three greatest legacies in the modern history of football: the Dutch school, Sacchi's Milan and Guardiola's football.'

But let's get back to Riva del Garda. It is already clear that the players' adaptation to Pep's new game will not be easy. Or fast.

Lorenzo Buenaventura: 'It isn't the same as speaking to Xavi and Iniesta, who have spent 20 years at Barcelona. They learned all of this there and have put it into practice a thousand times. It's another thing entirely to do it here with any speed. Pep always starts well. He goes slowly at the beginning as he explains A, B and C. But then there will be this sudden acceleration when you least expect it and before you know it, he's on to Z and is revising the entire alphabet. In reality you can't expect super-quick results from this kind of immersion.'

Outside on the spacious terrace, Pep's ears must be burning because, despite the birdsong, he seems aware of everything we're saying. He comes in and joins the conversation, waving his hands about animatedly.

'That's all well and good, but if we lose two consecutive games everyone will say it's because of all the *rondo* training we're doing instead of spending the pre-season doing 1000-metre runs or sprinting up Trentino's mountains,' he laughs as he gives Buenaventura a friendly shove. 'The players won't say it and people like Toni Kroos will insist that he loves training with the ball, but there's no doubt that if we start losing some journalist will blame it on the way we train.'

Buenaventura laughs at this vision of doom. 'I've worked with around 30 coaches. Lots of them were very good and all of them left me with something, some detail I could later use. But Pep, he's the whole package. He possesses something which is vital in sport: a willingness to take risks. It is like that high jumper [Dick Fosbury, 1968] who one day decides to jump backwards and break all known records. How many football professionals are so willing to break the mould and dispense with tradition? People say, 'There's nothing new under the sun'. Well, I beg to differ. Pep is capable of coming to a new country, assessing what's being done and working out how to respond. He is confident enough to take risks and introduce innovative ideas.'

Mona Nemmer has joined Bayern as the team nutritionist and today is her first morning at work. She is also sitting out on the terrace, surrounded by the hotel chefs, with whom she is planning the menu for the next few days. She is 28 and has worked previously in the youth sections of the German national team. Bayern listened to Guardiola's request. The players' post-match meals were already carefully planned by the club. The team bus has its own kitchen, where the players get their post-match ration of freshly cooked pasta, salad and meat or fish, prepared, as is all of Bayern's catering, by well-known chef Alfons Schuhbeck. These meals are vital for their physiological recuperation. Despite this however, Pep felt that there was room for improvement and now Mona, who will closely monitor the players' nutritional intake, has joined the staff.

Buenaventura agrees that this is vitally important: 'Like all big teams, Bayern plays a game every three days, and that affects the way we prepare. Medical studies in Italy have shown that the speed of post-match recovery depends entirely on the players' diet. If they eat properly then they should have recovered 80% of the glycogen in their muscles within three days. Only 80%! Just imagine what it would be if they ate unhealthily! And after four consecutive matches in cycles of three days, the risk of injury increases by 60%.'

In order to cope with the demands of these three-day cycles, players must be rotated. Playing so often means that the players never recover more than 80% of fitness, injuries occur more frequently and dips in performance are common.

'In Barcelona, players like Messi, Busquets, Xavi, Alves and Pedro would play up to nine or 10 games [in three-day cycles] and every so often one of them played 12. The only exception was when they were called up to play for Spain, but of course that meant that they were still playing games. This is terrible for the players because, as well as the risk of injury, it can mean a sudden, brutal downturn in performance. That's why it is important to have a full squad which allows you, from time to time, to leave a player out of a game and give them a little rest cycle of five days training,' explains Buenaventura.

In Bayern, life is likely to be less demanding. 'The fact that there is no tour of Asia in the summer is already a blessing. And this pre-season training gives us a real advantage because we have a series of complete five-day periods during which we can work without interruption. In those five-day slots we do six or seven training sessions, but without the usual physical exertion. Later in the year we also have the very welcome winter break.'

Over the next few months, Lorenzo Buenaventura will talk at length about the benefits of the winter break but today he simply says: 'Having 14 days of rest at Christmas and two weeks of preparation afterwards is a huge competitive advantage.'

Guardiola and Torrent compare notes as the morning draws to a close, after each of them has fully reviewed yesterday's training exercises.

Out on the shores of Lake Garda the birds are still singing as the coach's thoughts turn to Schweinsteiger's ankle problems, whilst the player himself wends his way home to Munich.

10

'WE DON'T HAVE A MESSI OR A RONALDO – BUT WE HAVE THE RIGHT COLLECTIVE MENTALITY.'

Arco, July 7, 2013

THEY HAVE BEEN training like beasts.

As Pep Guardiola approaches the bench he shouts: 'This is how Barça trained that first year!'

He opens his arms wide and waves them about, the way we've seen him do so many times during a match. He shouts again: 'That's how they trained that first year, like beasts.'

We are sitting on the bench next to Arco's tiny training pitch. Bayern are preparing for the great battles of Guardiola's first year as successor to the treble-winner, Jupp Heynckes.

Matthias Sammer, the club's sports director, is seated on the same bench, chatting about what Guardiola is instructing his men to do out there on the pitch. The team is playing a game of 10 v 11 and the coach wants to see his forwards pressing hard and his defenders and midfielders marking tightly. Guardiola is running up and down, all the while shouting instructions whilst his players work with formidable intensity.

Sammer smiles: 'We're going to have some fun.'

'We have two objectives,' Sammer will tell us this Sunday afternoon. 'We want to establish ourselves at the top level and then set about building an era of repeated and consistent success.'

Some months before, in January 2013, when the treble was still a distant dream, a senior executive from one of the world's biggest sports goods companies put it to me like this: 'In Munich they aren't happy with the playing style of the team. The directors have a modern vision of management and believe that the team should be playing differently. At the moment they're doing well and are very focused on winning, but

Hoeness and his colleagues haven't forgotten that this team has lost two Champions Leagues in three years, two Bundesligas in a row and has been trounced in the DFB-Pokal by Dortmund. They want to win, but they want to play in a more consistent way which will avoid all the highs and lows.'

So it was that Guardiola was brought in to spearhead what Paul Breitner called the 'third phase' of Bayern's plan.

When he was still in New York, Pep had already begun to envisage his ideal Bayern line-up. We've never managed to find the time to chat about it but I reckon that at that stage, before he had the chance to get to know the players, his team would have looked something like: Manuel Neuer in goals. A defence of Philipp Lahm, Javi Martínez, Dante, David Alaba; Bastian Schweinsteiger as *pivote*; Mario Götze, Toni Kroos in midfield; Thomas Müller and Arjen Robben either side of the false 9, Franck Ribéry. His ideal would probably have been to have Götze and Ribéry alternating as false 9s, but if this was what he jotted down as he sat in New York planning his line-up, events would prove that a team is a living organism. It grows and develops, suffers setbacks and has to overcome obstacles. Over time, expectations are created and the team improves some areas of its performance but deteriorates in others. In other words, it evolves and usually in ways that you could not have planned for. In the end, it never turns out quite as you imagined.

In any case, neither Javi Martínez nor Dante are in the Trentino group, vice-captain Schweinsteiger has gone back to Munich because his ankle injury has been so slow to heal and Götze is still restricted to an exercise bike in the gym, despite it already having been two-and-a-half months since his hamstring injury. Robben has trained only once and Thiago still hasn't signed for Bayern. If he did once have visions of his optimal line-up, Pep has discovered that the reality is very different and his main preoccupation at the moment is whether or not Thiago will arrive in time for the German Super Cup final in Dortmund. If not, he'll have to consider exposing young Pierre-Emile Højbjerg to the Borussia sharks.

Alaba, Daniel Van Buyten, Mario Mandžukić, Xherdan Shaqiri, Claudio Pizarro and now Robben have been re-united for this pre-season training camp, whilst seven youth team players make the return trip back to Munich after working with the veterans for 10 days.

Pep spends a lot of time chatting one-to-one with his players. He finds in Jérôme Boateng a player who readily assesses and corrects his own performance and in Neuer someone whose obvious potential inspires complete trust. From day one he discovers his football alter ego in Toni Kroos and over time his chats with Lahm will reveal a prodigious and unexpected tactical intelligence. Højbjerg, too, receives individual attention. The youngster gets a private masterclass on positional play – taught how to move the ball forward, find the right passing lines and push his team forward. From now on Pep will protect his young protégé. He sees in him the makings of a great footballer.

The main activity of this Sunday afternoon training session in Arco is a 40-minute game which has two objectives. Pep wants the forwards to work on their penetration and he also wants to see how co-ordinated the other players can be in pressing the opposition. To achieve this first objective, Mandžukić and Müller, supported by Ribéry or Shaqiri, have to press and punish the opposition defenders until they have them absolutely hemmed in on one side. Once again Pep is pleased with their performance.

'Their pressing is brutal. If you ask Müller to make a 40-metre diagonal run to the other wing, he'll do it at full speed, regain his position and do it a hundred times more if necessary.'

But Pep also makes it clear that pressing of this ferocity around the opposition penalty area won't be the norm in the coming season. 'We'll need to work this hard on the pressing only against a team like Barça and perhaps one or two more. Every other team ... well, the second or third time we press them hard they'll just resort to kicking the ball long and gifting us possession. We'll have other preparatory work to do – against teams who want to put the ball long over the heads of our defence to make them have to turn, and in defending the second ball when a team mounts a counter-attack.'

Lorenzo Buenaventura explains why Guardiola insists on perfecting this exercise when it isn't something he plans to use frequently.

'He doesn't like to leave anything to chance and is the kind of coach who makes sure his players understand every manoeuvre, even the ones they'll use only three times a season maximum. He wants his men to have a range of tools at their disposal. The majority of teams won't play out from the back when they face the greats like Bayern, Barça, Arsenal, Madrid or Manchester City.

'Therefore, knowing how to press the keeper and his full-backs via strikers who are pushed as high up the pitch as possible is a resource we'll need rarely. But we must know how to do it. That's why Pep likes to explain it and keep on explaining it throughout the year.'

The second objective of this training session focuses on ensuring players combine and co-operate to press the opposition (wherever on the pitch) and on marking. When the central defender goes out to press the opposition striker, the organising midfielder must drop back and fill his space. If the full-back moves up to press the winger, then the central defender must move to cover and, once again, the *pivote* midfielder must drop back to cover the central defender. If they succeed in pressing the winger then the full-back, central defender and organising midfielder will each have been crucial in robbing the ball back.

The Bayern players go over these moves again and again. From time to time Pep stops the game and corrects them, especially Boateng and Højbjerg. He wants them to get to the point that co-ordination between them becomes instinctive. 'It has to be instantaneous. If Jérôme moves up to challenge, Højbjerg, you cover his position. If Lahm runs, Jérôme covers him and Højbjerg covers Jérôme.'

Pierre-Emile Højbjerg, like Sergio Busquets, the linchpin of Barcelona, has a natural sense of position. It is an innate skill and something he has never needed to work on. At just 17 he does most of the right things automatically. He has also come along ready and willing to learn, unlike another promising young player who seems to react badly to Guardiola's corrections.

A team is a living entity. Some players develop and improve, like Shaqiri, who is impressing the coach with his work, or Højbjerg and Boateng, who seem to soak up every little detail. But there are also others who disengage, either in terms of performance or their attitude. A team is not a homogenous group.

If he had been there, Rummenigge would have enjoyed the training session, but he has still not arrived in Trentino. He is tying up the loose ends of Mario Gómez's transfer to Fiorentina and once he closes this deal he will get on with that of Thiago. The player has already reached an agreement with the Munich team and is not interested in going anywhere else. No one from Bayern anticipates any opposition from Barça, who have for some time been very open about their wish to sell the player. When Guardiola was still coaching Barça, in the summer of 2011, the club was already testing the market. Later, they agreed to include an escape clause in the player's contract, which detailed that if Thiago played less than a stated minimum number of minutes per year, his rescission fee would drop hugely, to €18 million instead of the prohibitive €90 million figure in his original contract. Later, having won the Spanish league, nobody at Barça was interested in changing the team dynamic just so that Thiago could reach the target amount of playing time and it seems unlikely that the club is going to reject a reasonable offer now.

At the end of today's training session Arjen Robben will explain what he sees as Bayern's main virtue: 'We don't have a Messi or a Cristiano Ronaldo, but we do have the right collective mentality. We also have quality players, players who stand out. When we attack, we are always looking for the next goal and our defence is compact and co-ordinated. That is our strength.'

Guardiola approaches the bench, visibly pleased with the team's work.

'That's how Barça trained that first year! That's how they trained that first year, like beasts,' he repeats. 'It just isn't possible to always be at the top of the mountain. [Usain] Bolt, [Roger] Federer ... we thought they would never stop winning, but it's not possible, it's just not possible.'

His response evokes that of Garry Kasparov in New York: 'Impossible!'

Despite being champions, Bayern are hungry. Desperately hungry. It's as if they have not yet made it to the top of the mountain.

'Right now we are all hungry. The players, because they have a new coach and new concepts to learn and they want to win playing a little bit better than they have in the past; me, because I want to win with a different set of players. Let's see if we can do it.'

11

'WHO ARE OUR UNSTOPPABLE GUYS? RIBÉRY AND ROBBEN.'

Arco, July 8, 2013

PEP NOW HAS a clear mental picture of the line-up with which he would like to start the season. Neuer in goal, with Lahm and Alaba supporting him as full-backs, although Rafinha is also performing very well in training and will be a great alternative; Javi Martínez, Boateng and Dante are the three players who will have to share the two central defensive positions.

In front of them, Schweinsteiger will slot in as the only dedicated holding midfielder. While it's certainly true that he did his best work last season as part of a double *pivote* partnership, Guardiola thinks that his vice-captain is fully capable of performing at the same level solo. Beside him, he'll have Kroos and Thiago, two attacking midfielders with tremendous creative skill. Thiago, of course, has not even signed yet. If, in the end, he doesn't make it to Bayern, then Götze could take his place. In attack, Guardiola has a number of options, although all of them, of course, include Ribéry. In the coming months, however, Pep will come to appreciate the massive gulf between the line-up he is considering now, in early July, and the reality of events as they unfold.

Amongst other things, within the next six months, by the end of 2013, the team will have suffered a virtual epidemic of injuries. Only four players will make it to Christmas injury-free; reserve goalkeeper Tom Starke, midfielder Boateng, defender Van Buyten and the forward Thomas Müller. The 20 remaining players will all have fallen victim to injuries. Some of them, such as Neuer, Mandžukić and Alaba will get off lightly, but for Schweinsteiger, Thiago and Robben, the damage will be far more serious. And that's without even mentioning Holger Badstuber, who will find himself spending his second year trying to recover from injury. This situation will ruin Guardiola's plans, oblige him to reinvent players to cover certain positions and force him to change many tactical decisions. All of this will make it much more difficult for his players to assimilate new game plans. Things will move much more slowly as a result.

The coach is anticipating none of this as he sits here on the bench in Arco, having just completed another work session, and explains how he envisages his Bayern will play. In this respect he is spot-on. Slowly but surely, Bayern will produce the football Pep intends them to play. And on July 8, 2013, Guardiola anticipates that Bayern's future success will be driven by what happens on the wings.

At first glance this may seem surprising, because in his days as a player and coach at Barça the team's game was driven from the midfield. Think of the Barcelona midfield from the 2011 Champions League final against Manchester United: Sergio Busquets, Xavi, Andrés Iniesta, and even Lionel Messi dropping back from his false 9 position. Maintaining superiority in the central area was always part of the Pep brand. Could he dispense with this at Bayern? In reality, no. He is trying to explain that he still wants that same superiority in the centre, but now he wants to go one step further and redouble the team's efforts on the wings.

At Barça, Guardiola had Leo Messi, whom he calls 'the beast,' 'the animal'. Messi was the perfect solution for Barça. His team-mates would outnumber and overwhelm the opposition in the midfield, give him the ball and then he'd do the rest. There would be no Messi at Bayern. Pep would have talented players such as Mario Götze – able, elusive, intelligent and a prodigious goal-scorer – and Mario Mandžukić, another superb striker and a tough, efficient warrior. But Messi was in a different dimension.

So, under the hot Italian sun, Pep unveils his playing idea. As ever he wants his players to establish numerical superiority in midfield, but to also cause the opposition chaos in the wide positions. At

Barça, Iniesta and Xavi dominated down the middle, where Messi would then destroy the opposition defence. At Bayern, Guardiola sees things slightly differently.

'Who are our unstoppable guys? The wide guys – Ribéry and Robben. We have to use that weapon. We have to be superior down the middle of midfield, but open up the width with diagonal passes. That means we have to push the whole team upfield in order to release Robben and Ribéry, because they can't be dropping deep to start the play.' He will explain this over and over again.

Within just two weeks of arriving, it has already become the coach's obsession – Ribéry and Robben must no longer be making 80-metre runs up and down the wing to attack, defend and re-start the play. 'If they are the ones re-starting the play so deep, they'll have both the opposition midfielder and full-back in front of them to get away from. That makes it really difficult. However, if we set a really high line and establish our central defenders where the midfield would normally be, then it will limit our opponents' scope to double up on the wingers. We will convert each play into a one-vs-one situation. In that type of situation our guys are the very best and I'd back them to get goals. They can also cross excellently and we've got top-quality finishers to put those chances away. At Barça, Messi did the destroying down the middle of the pitch – at Bayern it will be Ribéry and Robben – but from the wings.'

These then are his plans in the month of July. It will take him more than six months before all his men are available and he will need all his creative powers to solve the difficulties ahead.

However, it isn't enough to explain how he wants them to play. This is something that has to be worked on day in, day out. As Lorenzo Buenaventura explains: 'Pep has told me that we will put much more emphasis on the wide positions than we did at Barcelona. Why? Because there are different ingredients in the recipe here. Across five Barça matches how many times will our full-back get up and cross into the opposition box? Perhaps four times per match – at most. Because when Messi played wide, at the beginning, he'd always try to get by his man with a dribble, rather than cross. If Dani Alves reaches the byeline then normally he'll cut the ball back, rather than cross. Moreover we didn't have so many goal-scorers, so four crosses per match would be a high number. But at Bayern there'll be games where we cross more than 20 times, because we simply must feed Müller and Mandžukić. Obviously, if you've got the ball out wide and you see these two penalty-box predators arriving then the normal thing is to get the ball into them. Bayern are infinitely more equipped to take advantage of the ball into the box than Barça were – better than most, in fact. Pep's big challenge is to successfully create chances from wide positions, but still keep order in the middle of the pitch to protect against the opposition's counter-attack – to be aware of where the ball will drop if it's cleared from a cross and, thus, attack the second ball too, not just the first cross.'

The Bayern fitness coach, who is also a qualified football and swimming coach, will put extra care into supporting this part of Pep's strategy. He'll create special training routines to re-create this complicated pattern that Pep wants to achieve: establishing superiority in midfield, opening up the wings for the guys who can destroy the opposition, finishing on the volley inside the penalty area and at the same time being properly placed to cut out a counter-attack.

Some weeks later, at the end of September, Buenaventura will, over coffee on a non-training day, recall this conversation in Trentino and explain further: 'A few days ago we trained in the headquarters of the bank that sponsors Bayern [HypoVereinsbank]. The main exercise involved three men playing the ball out from the back – sometimes with the full-back tight with them, sometimes pushed forward; in front of them, the *pivote* and two attacking midfielders, plus three forwards. The attacking moves need a diagonal pass, breaking through one opposition line. At the end of the move, our attacking midfielder should be on the edge of the box. We'd place one of the dummies from the free-kick walls in the place we wanted him to end up, so that any counter-attack could be snuffed out. It was a curious routine to stage.'

After a few days, Pep explained to the players why they had done the exercise: 'Do you remember that day that you did this and you were meant to end up positioned next to the dummy? Well the reason was...'

Buenaventura continues: 'All of this is the result of the analysis Pep carried out on German football: who played counter-attack football, how, and how to protect against it. It meant reaching the opposition penalty box in numbers and all at the same time, and always vigilant not to suddenly be caught on the counter. If it's already tough to co-ordinate a good, effective, balanced attack, imagine how hard it is to add in the fact that we needed to have half our minds on what would happen if the attack broke down and how to be prepared for the opposition counter-attack! This is the 'extra' that Pep has: to be capable of analysing how they play in any given country, to not renounce his own strengths [in this case the wide play in which Bayern excel] but to be prepared to protect ourselves against the breakdown and the counter, all at the same time. And every day introducing another small detail of his own plus one or two about the opposition team.'

Let's go back to Trentino. On the morning of July 8, Mario Gómez bids a brief but elegant farewell to his team-mates after breakfast. It has been a month since Matthias Sammer, the sports director, told him that Bayern wanted to transfer him. Gómez, who had lost his place to Mandžukić, on goal difference, accepts. 'I love Bayern and I will always belong to Bayern,' the player tells his team-mates today. And he packs his bags.

Many kilometres away from Lake Garda, Thiago is also keen to start packing. He has made his deal with Bayern and all that remains is for Rummenigge to call Sandro Rosell, the Barcelona president. Thiago has had three weeks' holiday and has just started to train by himself. He is nervous about some last-minute detail unravelling the whole deal. The other thing that worries him is that there are only three weeks to go before the German Super Cup final against Borussia Dortmund, and he is desperate not to miss it.

12

'THEY'LL CLIMB THAT MOUNTAIN 10 TIMES IN A ROW.'

Arco, July 9 2013

GUARDIOLA HAS NEVER considered himself a creative genius, an inventor. Instead he has defined himself as an 'ideas thief', someone who, as a footballer, experimented but most of all learned, and when he decided to be a coach kept on learning. When he reached the top as a coach, he still felt he had more to learn, so he studied the strategies of the best. 'Ideas belong to everyone and I have stolen as many as I could.'

His influences include all the ones you might expect. First and foremost, Cruyff, his coach at Barcelona and his mentor. But also Arrigo Sacchi, whose Milan team won back-to-back European Cups. He was influenced by contrasting footballing visions, such as those of César Luis Menotti, Argentina's World Cup-winning coach in 1978, and Sacchi's heir at Milan, Fabio Capello. The Dutch, the Italians, the fierce competitiveness of the Argentinians, the innovation of the Hungarians, the hunger for centre-pitch dominance of Barça, the perfectionism of Marcelo Bielsa, the analytical clarity of the Spanish coach Juanma Lillo (more or less unknown at the top level) and the passion of the Scots.

If he is a football revolutionary it is thanks to the way he deconstructs ideas. The false 9 position he used with Messi is a good example. As a player, Pep was a team-mate of Michael Laudrup in Cruyff's Dream Team. Laudrup was an immense false 9. This team, which won four consecutive Spanish leagues and gave Barça their first European Cup, played for a long time without a centre-forward. Cruyff left the centre-forward's zone empty and used Laudrup as a 'man without a zone'. The rival defenders would get all tangled up, not knowing what to do with him. Before they knew it, Laudrup would be long gone from the penalty box, having left the way clear for his team-mates to arrive suddenly and put the ball away. Guardiola was both witness and protagonist during this era. Later, he continued to study the evolution of the false 9 position in the work of Adolfo Pedernera in the 1930s and 40s, Nándor Hidegkuti and Péter Palotás of the great Hungary side of the 1950s, the legendary Alfredo Di Stéfano, Laudrup and Francesco Totti, the modern-day Roman icon.

He extracted the essentials from everything he'd learned and then broke down and reconstructed the position for Messi.

What is the true essence of the false 9? Leaving a normally occupied zone empty. Teams put a centre-forward in the main part of the penalty area, bang in the middle, the area where, if you strike the ball you're more than halfway to scoring. It was about clearing space in the central part of the most attacking zone on the pitch. Pep saw that Messi possessed the tactical ability to understand it. He wanted to give the best area of the pitch, the centre-forward's space, to his best player. But he planned to do it by leaving it free, unoccupied. The area would be his, he told Messi, but only on condition that he didn't use it except to finish a chance. He needed to get into the zone for the final shot, but he shouldn't stay there. And of course, we all know how well his ideas turned out.

It was exactly this type of creativity he was looking for with Franck Ribéry and Arjen Robben in telling them to limit their runs to a maximum of 40 metres. It meant eliminating the deficiencies of a movement and reconstructing it using different principles, whilst still maintaining its core purpose. He still wanted a penetrating attack down the wing, quick and direct, but it would be more brief, more intense and starting from a greater point of advantage. However, first he'd have to ensure that the team were moving as a group toward the middle of the pitch.

'We'd like Ribéry not to drop back any further than the centre line,' confirms Manel Estiarte on the morning of July 9.

The Bayern players are training hard despite the fact that they are due to play Brescia in a fairly important friendly this evening.

'Ribéry is totally committed to Pep's cause. Maybe there are things that he would prefer to do differently, but he puts 100% into everything. He's a terrific guy, who has taken on board all the strengths of the German game. His will and energy are absolutely limitless. We want to harness that energy. We don't want him running 80 metres across the pitch 20 times a match. We need him concentrating his efforts on shorter bursts which will actually be more productive.'

The morning training session is brutally intense, as all of this season's training will be. Its purpose is to train the team in defensive organisation, correcting them where necessary. Pep is passionate about improving the team's defensive skills. This is one of his main characteristics. Guardiola is no romantic idealist when it comes to football, nor is he an aesthete, as has been claimed. He is a single-minded pragmatist. Above all else, Pep wants to win.

If he's working so hard on the defensive organisation, it is because he wants to attack. One day in Säbener Strasse, I said to him: 'You work on defensive strategy most.'

His response was short: 'Because it's absolutely essential if I want to attack a lot. Defensive organisation is the cornerstone of everything else I want to achieve in my football.'

Throughout the season there will be dozens of sessions like the one he has just finished in the Arco Stadium, during which the team has practised facing crosses from full-backs and defending against corners. They have also covered how to cope with the long ball down the middle to the penalty box and how to defend when the opponent attacks in greater numbers.

His players have trained well and Estiarte is delighted. 'They work like Trojans and their attitude is just outstanding. They're ready to learn and are willing to have a go at anything we ask. If we asked them to climb that mountain [he is looking out to Arco Castle], they would climb it 10 times in a row.'

Guardiola, as always, is more circumspect: 'It won't be easy. At the start we're going to find it hard because we're going to have to play with great intensity whilst, at the same time, thinking about the new concepts, and it isn't easy to play and think simultaneously. It's pretty difficult to spend 90 minutes concentrating and playing well, whilst thinking about the moves you have to make or where you have to be.'

The coach warns that there are difficulties on the horizon, now that everyone is predicting a happy and straightforward future for the team: 'It won't be easy,' he insists. 'They are finding it difficult to assimilate some concepts because they have always defended man-to-man in all areas of the pitch, but now I am changing it so that they leave no gaps or positions uncovered.'

He is also missing a bit of nous in the centre of the pitch. He has Toni Kroos, an astonishing talent who moves the ball precisely and sharply, but Pep wants him to increase his control of possession. This is why he is so desperate for Thiago to arrive, although he has not yet fully realised the important role Philipp Lahm will play in this area of Bayern's game.

'The physical side we already have down, and the pressing too. It comes as standard with these players. I have to add a few tactical touches without letting them lose this level of pressing or the fitness they have achieved. They just lack that little bit of 'pause' in the play. Iniesta is a good example of that. At Barça he had it. He took the ball and it suddenly seemed as if time stood still and there was order all around him. Here, right now, we don't have that ... yet.'

When Thiago arrives the coach reckons he'll have 16 'starter' players – the precise figure he likes to manage in his teams. Pep doesn't like to have more than 20 players in his squad if he can help it. It helps him manage them without tensions getting in the way. He hates that moment when he has to tell two or three guys, in the hours leading up to a match, that they'll be sitting in the stands and won't even make the bench. For that reason he likes a small group, within which about 15 or 16 of them can feel like they are, or should be, starting players. This is a real 'Pep' characteristic, which doesn't necessarily mean it is a virtue.

During his four years with Barça he often had to patch things up in order to make his small-squad idea function properly. Of course the majority of the time things worked out, like when he won two Champions League finals with improvised back fours. But a lot of patching up had been done for those two games nonetheless.

Both Pep and his backroom staff firmly defend this idea. All of them reckon that agreeing to a larger squad, say 25 players of similar ability, wouldn't necessarily avoid some patching up during the season. In any case, virtue or defect, this is what makes Guardiola comfortable.

Right now, he's pondering the subject. 'I've no idea what I'm going to do when all the players from the Confederations Cup come back [Javi Martínez, Dante, Luiz Gustavo]. Plus there's Götze and Schweini too…'

Negotiations to sell Luiz Gustavo are already in place, but even so Pep is still going over and over the possible player combinations in his ideal Bayern team. On paper there just isn't room for all the players in his squad. However, reality is just about to bite and rid him of these particular preoccupations. When the injuries hit, Pep's problem won't be how to use all his players but how to piece together a competitive team. Not once in the whole of 2013 will all his first-team players be fit or available at the same time. It's the downside of managing a 'short' squad.

At the end of this training session a single image attracts the attention of Pep and his staff. Ribéry and Robben are knocking the ball back and forwards, away from everyone else, as if they're hanging out on the beach. Someone mentions that only a few months ago, in spring 2012, they came to blows in the Allianz Arena during the Bayern-Real Madrid Champions League semi-final. Now they are laughing and joking on the Trentino pitch.

Guardiola and Estiarte get involved in a debate about the best moments of Barcelona's recent golden era. For Estiarte the absolute peaks were: 'The first half against Arsenal at the Emirates [March 31, 2010. 2-2] and the first half against Chelsea in the Champions League semi-final of 2012. We never played better than those two days.'

Guardiola disagrees. 'The performance against Chelsea was fabulous but I think we played better in the final of the World Club Cup against Santos. That was our all-time peak.'

Later that afternoon the Bayern players appear to have lead in their boots as they take on Brescia from Italy's Serie B. The morning session, coming on top of all the training they've done up till now, has robbed them of their fluidity.

Pep picks his best XI from his current squad; Neuer; Lahm, Van Buyten, Boateng, Alaba; Højbjerg, Müller, Kroos; Shaqiri, Mandžukić and Ribéry.

The pre-match team talk is short and to the point but it sets the tone for the next few months. He wants them to use nous when they play the ball up to the middle of the pitch and tells them that they must get there in a tight group. From the moment they're on the pitch they must represent the traditional Bayern play: vertical and direct. Be shrewd up to the middle of the pitch – and then all-out attack.

In the event they won't manage to comply with his instructions. During the first half Pep will keep issuing orders. Boateng should hold the defensive line better; Kroos should impose the tempo of play more firmly; Shaqiri should widen the pitch right out to the touchline and use his runs to add depth. Against a tough but not excessively dangerous opponent, Bayern win 3-0 (with goals from Müller, Kroos and Kirchhoff) but Guardiola will be far from satisfied and will end the game even clearer about all the work he'll have to do if they are to realise his aspirations.

That same night Mario Götze will go back to Munich. Up till now he's been doing only bicycle work in the gym but the moment has come to advance his recuperation. His return to match fitness, however, still seems far off.

13

'I TOLD ROSELL I WOULD BE GOING 6000km AWAY FROM HIM.'

Munich, July 25, 2013

PEP STILL HAD some doubts as he left Trentino for Germany. Pierre-Emile Højbjerg was ready to play as a midfielder in the German Super Cup final in Dortmund although it would be an enormous risk. But what alternative did he have?

After spending nine days in Italy Pep now knew that he could not count on Schweinsteiger, Götze, Javi Martínez, Dante or Luiz Gustavo and would have to go up against their great rivals with the players who had been training morning and evening in the shadow of Arco Castle – unless Thiago got here in time.

He had dedicated more time to Højbjerg than to anyone else, showing him the right way to position his body when he received the ball so that he could move it on immediately as effectively as possible. He had taught the player how to place himself in between his two central defenders in order to re-start a move. He had encouraged him to be bold in his penetration of the opposition lines, either with the ball at his feet or with a long, low pass. He had given the player hours and hours of almost non-stop obsessional attention, at times apparently oblivious to time and place.

Pep felt like Cruyff would have when he was teaching the young Guardiola how to be Barcelona's No.4 and he set out to take Højbjerg through the entire manual relating to the position of the organising midfielder. However, he wasn't sure that it would be reasonable to put the lad to the test in these circumstances. Dropping him into Westfalen Stadion without a parachute. Facing a strong Borussia Dortmund desperate to have revenge for their defeat in the Champions League final wasn't exactly the best time to use a kid of 17 who clearly had an exciting future ahead of him. He would be too exposed and the whole experience could end up having terrible consequences for that promising future.

In the two friendlies they had played in Trentino against the Paulaner Dream Team (13-0) and against Serie B's Brescia (3-0), the coach had used Højbjerg as a midfielder, but during that trip back from Verona to Munich he decided that it would be unwise to put the young Dane through a baptism of fire in Dortmund. He would consider a different option.

Immediately after their return from Italy, on July 14, Bayern played a friendly in Rostock. It was a benefit match for Hansa, an ancient and historic German club which was struggling with serious financial problems. A year before, Uli Hoeness had agreed to the fixture as a fundraiser to help Hansa renew their federation licence which qualified them to play in the German third division. The fundraising exercise was a success and 28,000 fans turned up at the DKB Arena, contributing almost a million Euros to the Rostock club's funds.

Out on the pitch, Pep had chosen Toni Kroos as his organising midfielder. It was a declaration of intent. He was looking for alternatives to Højbjerg so that the youngster could be spared the ordeal of going up against Borussia. Kroos would be a good first choice as long as he had the right kind of support, and in Rostock it was Philipp Lahm who once again provided that back-up. The captain had played as a midfielder in their second friendly against TSV Regen and in the third, against the Paulaner Dream Team, and Pep liked the way he managed things in the middle of the pitch. Bayern won 4-0 and for the next five days were able to work continuously in Säbener Strasse for the first time since Guardiola's arrival. As he was leaving Rostock stadium Pep had received a text: 'We've signed Thiago.'

Days before, just as he was about to leave Trentino, Pep had insisted: '*Thiago oder nichts*'. Thiago or nobody.

Rummenigge had responded by making a formal offer to Barcelona. As far as the Catalan club's management was concerned it was the perfect deal. Not only did it meet their price but it also allowed them to sell the pearl of Barça's youth academy, the jewel of La Masia, without attracting too much flak. This way they could argue that Guardiola had stolen the player. The leaked news of the potential deal had not come from Bayern, nor from Thiago himself, who was still holed up on the Costa Brava. Pep knew that it could only have come from the club selling the player, which meant that the agreement was well on the way.

That day in Trentino the German journalists had asked him if Bayern were interested in the player. The coach's emphatic response left them in no doubt. 'Of course I want him.' For a few moments the press room in the hotel annex lapsed into a surprised silence. The newsmen had not been expecting such a direct reply, although the need for transparency was not Pep's primary concern at that moment. His intention was to give a helping hand to the negotiations which were already underway. By making his wishes public in this way he would, he hoped, help bring things to a satisfying conclusion. If Barça had decided to leak the news then Guardiola played his role by making his personal interest in the signing crystal clear. He also announced that there would be no more signings. '*Thiago oder nichts.*'

On July 11 Guardiola did much more than confirm his interest in Thiago, however. He also took the opportunity to launch an attack on Sandro Rosell, then president of FC Barcelona.

Rosell had insulted Cruyff by withdrawing the title of honorary president from him, and he had taken his predecessor, Joan Laporta, who had appointed Pep as coach, to court. And in March 2011 he had also dealt with serious accusations of doping against the club with a surprising lack of enthusiasm.

If, during Laporta's time in charge, Pep had been forced on several occasions to act as the club's official spokesperson (the Catalan media sometimes called him the 'virtual president'), then under Rosell's mandate he had increasingly sensed a creeping, progressive alienation which became only too apparent during Pep's last season.

Pep had decided to speak out at last and opted to do it in Trentino:

'During my sabbatical I told president Sandro Rosell that I would be going 6000 kilometres away from him. All I asked was that he leaves me in peace, but he has chosen not to do that. He has broken his promise. I did my time and then I left. It wasn't their responsibility. I was the one who decided to go. And I went 6000 kilometres away. Let them get on with their own business now. I hope they're happy with the players they've got and with the things that they're doing. I wish them all the luck in the world because in some small way their success is my success. I don't need to tell you what that club means to me, but this year they have crossed the line too many times.'

Attacking someone as devious as Sandro Rosell was not a great strategy and Guardiola knew it. He was just unwilling to contain himself for any longer.

As his friend, Sala i Martin, explains: 'Pep just needed to get it all out that day. He had put up with so much abuse and had just taken it in silence. It was inevitable that he would have a blow-out eventually.'

In fact, he had probably chosen the wrong way and the wrong place to explode because the German journalists had no real understanding of the details. Not only because Pep was speaking in Catalan, but because it was too difficult for them to understand the context: what he had put up with over the years; the grievances he had dealt with; the manipulation of the last year and the financial and editorial influences in Barcelona. It was all too complicated and all the German press really understood was that Guardiola was furious with Sandro Rosell because of the way he had treated him once he knew the coach was leaving. In fact, this would end up being a pretty good summary of what actually happened.

A few days later Thiago arrived in Munich and on July 17 he took part in his first training session. He had come with very little physical preparation. Just a month before he had scored a hat-trick as Spain beat Italy in the final of the UEFA Under-21 European Championship. Since then his personal training regime had been restricted to mountain biking and hill running with his younger brother Rafinha, who had been loaned to Celta de Vigo by Barça.

Thiago was delighted to have made it to Munich. 'It's an amazing feeling that someone of the calibre of Pep has so much confidence in me. When the best coach in the world calls you, you don't have to think twice.'

Guardiola had propelled Thiago through the youth ranks, promoting him to the B team at 16 and then to the first team aged 18. He had complete confidence in the player and, just as he was doing now with Højbjerg, had spent many hours honing this rough diamond. With Thiago he had focused on defensive concepts.

The player himself tells me over coffee in Munich shortly after his arrival: 'Pep told me I had to get rid of some aspects of my game. Things like the way I celebrated. I am Brazilian after all! I often got really annoyed with him because he was always telling me to calm down. Whenever we were winning he'd try to impose a bit of order and stop us getting too carried away. He got rid of a lot of the things I used to do, probably all the superficial stuff, but in exchange he taught me much, much more important concepts. I reckon that's a pretty good deal.'

Thiago arrived ready for anything. 'Now I need to express myself. I'm going to use everything Pep has added to my game and at the same time try to express who I am as a player.'

The Brazilian would soon get his opportunity to do that – three days later he was in the starting line-up for the Hamburg-Bayern game which kicked off the Telekom Trophy tournament. Bayern won easily and Thiago played well as the single organising midfielder with Kroos to one side of him. Pep's plans for the Dortmund final were beginning to emerge. If Thiago held up physically he would be the starting *pivote* in the Super Cup.

The next day, July 21, the coach repeated this strategic approach for the tournament final although this time he added one more piece. With Thiago as *pivote*, Lahm and Kroos took up the other two midfield positions. The captain brought defensive power whilst Kroos added his creative flair. The trio played brilliantly and Bayern destroyed Borussia Mönchengladbach 5-1. As long as Thiago stayed fit, Pep had his line-up for the Dortmund match in a week's time.

However, in the meantime Bayern had to face Barça in the Allianz Arena. It wasn't a match Guardiola was looking forward to. He had been everything to the club: La Masia graduate, ball boy, player, captain, coach, spokesperson and ultimately the symbol of Barcelona. He would never be comfortable having to play against them.

The friendly had been fixed for Wednesday July 24, three days before the German Super Cup final, another reason for Pep's reluctance. But this was Uli Hoeness' cup. The president, patriarch, the father of Bayern, as he was affectionately known ... so Pep just had to put a brave face on it and get on with the game.

Nobody at Barcelona was particularly enthused by the prospect, either. Those members of the squad who played for the national team were still on holiday and the club was still reeling after the terrible news of coach Tito Vilanova's relapse in his fight against cancer. It was five days since they had heard that he was ill again and would have to resign as coach of the club he had just led to victory in La Liga.

On July 23 Gerardo 'Tata' Martino had been appointed as the new coach, but he would not be in Munich in time for his new team's debut match. Jordi Roura, who had been interim coach whilst Vilanova recovered in New York in early 2013, would be on the Barcelona bench. The team was returning to the scene of its most recent nightmare. Three months had passed since the Champions League semi-final in which Jupp Heynckes' Bayern had beaten them 4-0 before winning 3-0 at the Camp Nou.

Thiago, supported by Lahm and Kroos, was Bayern's new midfielder. All the pieces for the team that would face Dortmund had fallen into place.

In the event, the friendly was completely straightforward. The consequences were, however, anything but. Bayern won 2-0 by denying Barcelona barely any chance to develop their game, but on Thursday morning Guardiola learned the cost: Neuer and Ribéry were injured. The goalkeeper had some pain in his abductor muscle and the striker had taken a painful kick to his leg. Neither would make the Dortmund game.

Now, on July 25, Guardiola is to be found scowling and cursing the Barça friendly. He hadn't wanted to do it, had always believed that playing it three days before a final amounted to disastrous timing. To make matters worse, the game has left two of his most important players injured. He will have to do without his No.1 goalkeeper and his most devastating forward. Guardiola is furious. He is going to have to play his first official fixture with too many men missing.

He spends the whole night studying Jürgen Klopp's Borussia, as he always does before a match. For two-and-a-half days he analyses his opponents down to the last detail and looks for weaknesses he can exploit. His analytical approach is similar to that of Magnus Carlsen, world chess champion who likes to study the thinking behind every chess move without using a computer. He then reaches his own conclusions and instructs his assistants to find alternatives using powerful computers. In just the same way, Pep prefers to scrutinise the information himself before consulting his assistants, Carles Planchart and his team of analysts. Only once he has examined his rival in depth does he exchange ideas with the technical team. The final conclusions are usually a combination of both parties' work. When I pointed out the similarity with Carlsen, Pep seemed pleasantly surprised with the comparison: 'I'm getting more and more interested in chess.'

He has doubts. Pep always has doubts. He goes over everything a thousand times. How to attack opponents, his line-up, the instructions he needs to give individuals and the whole team. He's missing Neuer and Ribéry, Javi Martínez and Dante, Götze and Luiz Gustavo and Schweinsteiger is still limping about. He decides to go on the attack.

He still has doubts and swithers between Rummenigge's words – 'We need patience' – and Sammer's – 'We need passion.'

Patience and passion. Guardiola's two main weapons. Which credo will this first appearance of the new Bayern reflect?

He opts for passion. When in doubt, go back to basics: attack, attack, attack. He's going to move Philipp Lahm from the midfield and return him to right-back. He will play in Dortmund with as many forwards as possible. But it is going to be a huge risk.

14

'BORUSSIA DESERVED TO WIN.'

Dortmund, July 27, 2013

PEP HAS VALENTINA in his arms. The little girl hugs her dad tightly. She seems to sense the gravity of the situation. The Bayern players are already on the team bus, waiting for their boss, his white shirt bathed in sweat, to come aboard. Temperatures in Dortmund are Mediterranean – 38 degrees centigrade and Guardiola has just lost his first official match. After a 4-2 win, the German Super Cup belongs to Borussia. Ten metres away, Jürgen Klopp, the victorious coach, goes by triumphantly, as volcanic as ever.

Every single ticket in Dortmund's Signal Iduna Park has been sold for this one-off match, as they usually are for games in almost every stadium in the country. 195 countries are televising the final and both coaches have spruced themselves up for the occasion. They wish each other well at this, the start of a long and friendly rivalry.

No glory without pain. For Guardiola this is the most difficult opponent against whom he could have begun his new career. Klopp and Guardiola, together; Borussia and Bayern head-to-head in the fight for another title and it's only late July. It is a wonderful way to begin this journey. The two men make beguiling dance partners, perhaps because they evoke Pep and Mourinho in the days when they created the tactical solutions to help their respective teams, Barcelona and Real Madrid, achieve excellence.

Will Klopp become the German Mourinho? I am talking here in terms of tactics and strategy, of course – not collateral damage. Guardiola puts enough pressure on himself that he doesn't need an external incentive to come up with his innovative ideas. However,

Klopp has a similar character and the pair are like two skilled fencers who will thrust and parry to unpick football's enigmas.

Dortmund, a city proud of itself and of its yellow-and-black Borussia, gives Pep a brutal welcome. This is the real Bundesliga, where even in the month of July the jet-fuelled rockets of the Champions League runners-up are ready and waiting. The home team has made only one change to its line-up since the Wembley final, 63 days ago. Nuri Şahin replaces the injured Łukasz Piszczek in the centre of the field. Dortmund's line-up, playing their traditional 4-2-3-1, is: Roman Weidenfeller; Kevin Grosskreutz, Mats Hummels, Neven Subotić, Marcel Schmelzer; Nuri Şahin, Sven Bender; Jakub Błaszczykowski, İlkay Gündogan, Marco Reus and Robert Lewandowski.

In contrast, Neuer, Dante, Schweinsteiger, Javi Martínez and Ribéry are all missing from the Bayern team that won the Champions League. Out on the pitch there's Thiago as the sole holding midfielder, with Kroos and Müller as attacking midfielders; Robben and Mandžukić play on the wings and Shaqiri at centre-forward. The formation is 4-3-3: Starke; Lahm, Van Buyten, Boateng, Alaba; Thiago, Müller, Kroos; Robben, Shaqiri, Mandžukić.

Having swithered between patience and passion, the coach has decided to go straight on to the attack. He restores Lahm to the back four, but the starting XI signifies that Pep's team will play the majority of the game in a 4-2-4 formation, specifically thanks to Müller's tendency to join the forwards. There is no escaping the fact that he's a striker. From here, Guardiola knows in his bones that he can't use this guy in the midfield because his basic instincts impede him being sufficiently disciplined to hold a key position in the middle of the pitch.

Pep has fallen victim to his own ambitious plans and although Bayern do succeed in penetrating Borussia's defensive lines, they struggle to dominate such a strong counter-attacking team. Given the state they have arrived in, Pep's team could have done with Lahm's vital defensive discipline in the centre of the pitch, but he has chosen to jump in without a lifebelt and attack. He pays a high price for the decision.

It's all sufficient to confirm that Dortmund remain rock-hard at home. Notwithstanding the fact that they get a gift from the visitors after barely five minutes. Neuer's replacement, Tom Starke, is the guilty party and the 1-0 lead signifies that Klopp's team can dig in, switch to 4-4-2, allow Bayern the ball, try to channel them wide – then wait for the opportunity to counter-attack.

In just a few years, Jürgen Klopp has created a killing machine. Borussia are runners-up in the Champions League, Bundesliga champions in 2011 and 2012 and this stadium appears unassailable.

The humidity in Dortmund is stifling, much like it is in Barcelona, perhaps to remind Pep of his roots. The players sweat their way through the match and there is a refreshment break or *Trinkpause* in each half. The coaches decide when they take place. Klopp calls the first one in the 24th minute with the score in his team's favour. Whilst his players have a drink and rehydrate the Dortmund coach gathers his defenders together to give them their instructions. A few metres away Guardiola is talking to his forwards and it is this contrasting image that provides the perfect symbol of the two rivals' different strategies.

Borussia don't mind not having the ball. On the contrary, they are quite happy to bide their time and then pounce. They don't need the ball at their feet because of the fact that they dominate available space so intelligently. They're not embarrassed to appear over-run – the more they are forced back the better they seem to defend.

It's eight men back, with Gündogen and Lewandowski left in the centre circle to pick up the scraps or spearhead the counter. Thus Bayern set up camp in the Dortmund half and seek out the chinks in their armour – but it's a hard shift and rarely successful.

Klopp goes into the dressing room looking like he thinks he's planned things better than Guardiola.

After half-time the Bayern coach switches his attacking players. He sends Robben to the left, Mandžukić to the centre of attack and Shaqiri to the right. This apparently minor adjustment changes everything. Thiago and Lahm start to turn the tide and the equaliser comes from an intricate pass from Thiago to his captain, who crosses for a Robben header. Bayern have equalised. They seem to have reached a turning point at last, but the illusion is short lived. In barely 180 seconds the scoreboard goes from 1-0 to 3-1, leaving the men from Munich humiliated and emotionally broken.

Kroos is slow and Van Buyten is distraught after he scores an own goal to make it 2-1. Gündogan, a prodigious midfielder, puts the third goal away almost immediately and suddenly it's all become very tough for Bayern. Guardiola could not have imagined just how hard the game in Dortmund would be.

Despite everything, Bayern fight on and three things happen: Robben scores and narrows the margin; Müller hits the crossbar, and Borussia continue to punish Bayern whenever they lose their shape.

Thiago's game symbolises this tension. He makes wonderful passes in attack and then loses the ball when he's defending. His passes result in a goal and Bayern hitting the post. But the one he gives away becomes Dortmund's fourth goal. The paradox is bittersweet for the player who is trapped in the battle between those who dominate the ball and those who dominate space.

This same battle is raging all over the football world and it is clear that the ultimate winners will be those teams who manage to find a balance between the two approaches. In Germany, Bayern and Dortmund represent the two models. Guardiola wants his players to play calmly and with a bit of nous towards the centre circle, and then unleash a rapid attack.

Finding the right combination of different rhythms will be vital for his team's future but at the moment they are not getting it right. Thiago's game sums up the challenges that await them. In this Super Cup final he exploits the cracks in his opponents' defence brilliantly but fails to protect his own team.

The defeat is even more of a blow for Guardiola than it is for the club. This was the first of the six titles Bayern have set their sights on this season, determined to build on Jupp Heynckes' successful campaign, which the Catalan coach is keen to honour every time he speaks in public.

The match has been played with a passion and intensity hard to match anywhere else in Europe at this stage of the season and the result has people asking if today marks the start of a new champion's reign.

One year ago, in the summer of 2012, Heynckes' Bayern hosted Klopp's Borussia to compete for the same Super Cup title. At the time Bayern had just missed out on two Champions League titles, two consecutive Bundesliga trophies and had lost the last five encounters with Borussia, the last of which had been a bloody 5-2 thrashing. But the men from Munich would end up winning the 2012 Super Cup and march towards their historic treble.

Right now Jürgen Klopp would love today's win against Guardiola to have the same effect on Borussia. He has cleared the first hurdle and the scene has been set for the intense rivalry that should dominate the season.

Guardiola has worked hard in his first month as Bayern coach but he now understands the full extent of what he still has to do if he wishes to dominate in Europe. He also discovers that in Germany coaches attend post-match press conferences together. The German is glowing, absolutely radiant. The Catalan is stunned. He misunderstands a question from a local journalist and struggles to give a clear assessment of the match. At times he rambles and seems to have his head elsewhere, perhaps on the Signal Iduna Park bench, as if he would dearly love to wind back the clock to 8.30pm and the start of the match so that they can play it all over again. He hasn't been particularly smart during the 90 minutes and his starting line-up was surprising for the absence of Lahm in the centre of the pitch. Why had he done away with the *Lahm formula* which had been so successful in previous games?

Throughout the joint press conference Guardiola seems to be brooding on this. He has been slow. It's as if his sabbatical year in New York has reduced the speed of his reactions. This is only the second final he has lost as a coach. The first was the 2011 Copa del Rey against Real Madrid, but he has been sluggish today, a bit like the stiflingly hot weather in Dortmund.

He is numb and appears distracted throughout the press conference, during which he mistakenly answers a question not meant for him. But he accepts the defeat graciously and warmly congratulates Klopp: 'Borussia deserved to win.'

He must be wondering if Klopp's team is his new Numancia[1], despite the huge differences between the Spanish minnows and these German giants – the initial blunder that marks the start of a glorious campaign.

For the club, it is nothing more than an insignificant slip-up – the Super Cup is considered unimportant in Germany. However, the coach feels deeply wounded. He hates losing.

His family have been in Dortmund since midday and will go back to Munich with him for a few days. His three children are wearing white shirts with red stripes. Pep wipes off his sweat and picks up his youngest daughter, Valentina, whilst explaining a few of the game's tactics to his middle son, Màrius.

By chance he sits down beside his friend Estiarte as the red bus pulls out of Westfalen Stadion. The two sit together, just as they did five years ago, returning from Barça's defeat by Numancia.

They are moving on from this moment of defeat. Three little kids in red-and-white shirts wave goodbye. The journey has begun again – as steep and as treacherous as ever.

---

[1] Numancia is a small Spanish team which defeated Barça in Guardiola's first league match as coach in August 2008.

PART TWO

THE FIRST TROPHY

'Chess, that game of logic par excellence,
consists of luck, luck and more luck.'
SAVIELLY TARTAKOWER, GRAND MASTER

15

'MAYBE IT WAS A MISTAKE.'

Munich, July 29, 2013

NEUER AND RIBÉRY train as normal with the rest of the group – a little surprisingly. Just 40 hours after the German Super Cup they are both fit again. Inevitably, questions are being asked about such a speedy recovery. If they were unable to play on Saturday night, how on earth can they have recovered in time for midday on Monday? Had Bayern erred too much on the side of caution in not using them against Borussia?

Neuer had had a little problem in his abductor muscle and Ribéry had a leg knock. The doctors had advised that their injuries were sufficiently serious for them not even to consider travelling to Dortmund, yet here they both are, rested and fit and training under the Munich downpour. It's the first thing Guardiola asks himself. At Barcelona the coach was used to exploring all the options to ensure that a player made it into the team, right up until the last moment. Whenever Barça players suffered injuries like those which kept Neuer and Ribéry out against Dortmund, they would travel with the team and undergo a last-minute medical examination just before the game. In Munich, things are done differently and the coach is not sure he approves. Perhaps, he thinks, if Neuer and Ribéry had come with them to Dortmund they might have examined them mid-afternoon to see if they were fit to play. Perhaps they would have been match fit and the final would have turned out differently. Perhaps.

'Damn that Barça match, damn it. Never again will I agree to a friendly three days before a final. Never again.'

Guardiola is still brooding on the game against his former club and its consequences. His technical assistants have reviewed the Super Cup final and think much the same as they did when they were watching it live: a series of individual errors had led to the team's downfall. The coach's decision not to protect Thiago with Lahm's support is seen as another possible contributory factor. 'Maybe it was a mistake,' admits one of the technical team. Today's training session is open to the public and hundreds of fans, huddled under their umbrellas, crowd into Säbener Strasse. An almost religious silence descends as they, too, listen to the coach's instructions.

It's a downpour. The players had hoped for a break in the weather after days of asphyxiating heat, but not like this. It's bucketing down when Mario Götze trots out on to the training pitch. The medics have given him the all-clear but, seeing the deluge, the player hangs back for a while, which gives me the opportunity to chat to him about the immense passion of his old club, Dortmund. 'It's absolutely brutal playing there. The Südkurve is the biggest stand in the world and when you're on the pitch it towers over you like a mountain.'

In a few months he'll come face to face with that mountain again.

Götze has the ball at his feet for the first time in many months. He makes several fast, intense sprints and seems to have completely recovered from the muscle tear he suffered exactly 90 days ago. Although the original injury was not particularly serious, he aggravated it by returning too early in an attempt to make the Champions League final. But there is light at the end of the tunnel now and Guardiola tells him that he wants him back with the group by next Friday.

Thiago doesn't train today. He took a bad kick to his ankle in Dortmund, but the real problem goes deeper: he is in a state of total collapse. His is the classic story of the sportsman who gives 200% for an important fixture and then immediately suffers a major physical setback. Thiago arrived in Germany highly motivated and, in the Barça and Dortmund games, forced his body to give more than he was really fit for. Now he needs a couple of days' rest. He has tried to reach for the stars and it has left him exhausted, with big black circles under his eyes and pain all over his body. He needs a break.

There will be no more signings this season, even if the press keep talking about the Polish player Robert Lewandowski. The Borussia Dortmund centre-forward is a prodigious talent and Bayern could get him immediately, but they have decided to wait another year. If Götze's signing hadn't caused such an uproar then Lewandowski would probably be training here in Säbener Strasse already, perhaps instead of Mario Mandžukić, a first-class finisher from close-in, who is unlikely to have a long career at Munich ahead of him. But from what the technical team have said there is no doubt that the club is impressed by Lewandowski, by the way he moves and controls the ball and works with his team-mates.

The club's plans are clear. There will be no more signings and two players are about to be transferred. Emre Can will move to Bayer Leverkusen on August 2 and Luiz Gustavo to Wolfsburg on the 16th of the same month – both driven by financial imperatives. Højbjerg will train with the first team but play with the B side. Kirchhoff stays for the time being, but there are plans to let him go on loan at Christmas. By now, Pep is convinced that he shouldn't use Thomas Müller as a midfielder.

Wrapped up in his raincoat, Manel Estiarte stands in the rain with Pep's son Màrius, who is watching everything his dad does with avid attention. Estiarte outlines Guardiola's objectives for his first season at Bayern. 'The main aim is to win the Bundesliga and we'll be focusing all our energies on that. The second objective is that the team learns how to play the kind of football Pep is looking for and makes progress in that direction. He wants to see them greatly improved by the end of the season. He's already taken Barça B (Barcelona's second team, whom Pep trained in 2007-8) through that process. The team was dreadful at the start, but he transformed them and they were absolutely unstoppable for the last month and a half of the championship. That's what we'd like to do here, make the team so much more than they are at the moment. And we'll also be laying the foundations for Pep's second year when he wants to see them consistently playing his style of football.'

The objective is set then. It's the Bundesliga title.

16

'WHAT DO YOU KNOW ABOUT ATHLETICISM?'

Munich, July 29, 2013

THE DAY-AND-A-HALF long master class in defence has begun. This is only the first of many the coach will lead during the season. It starts with Pep giving a yellow bib to Javi Martínez and sending him to work with the defenders. If the Spanish midfielder hasn't already read it in the papers, he now knows that the boss wants him in central defence. The rain is torrential. The four defenders, all wearing yellow bibs, are Rafinha, Javi Martínez, Dante and Alaba. Guardiola is in the middle of them, explaining the moves he wants them to make. The players Pep wants to attack are Lahm, Boateng, Van Buyten and Kirchhoff. It is significant that Lahm, the captain, isn't in the first-choice back four. It seems the coach is already thinking of him principally as a midfielder.

For 40 minutes Pep dedicates himself wholly to explaining how and where he wants the back four to mark and how to move as a group, what the full-back does when he's being attacked by a winger, where the nearest central defender should be in that situation, where the other central defender must be, what the other full-back is looking for, when the central defender needs to come out to press an opponent, up to what point he offers cover to his central defensive partner and where the *pivote* positions himself with regard to the back four. These are all pre-determined, minutely configured movements – perfectly choreographed with the aim of closing all the gaps which can be exploited to open up a defence.

Dante is in his element, but Javi is struggling. This rainy afternoon is significant for two reasons. Without anything having been openly said, it is obvious that this is a first step towards him returning to the position of central defender, and he also knows that he will have to undo almost everything he learned at Athletic Bilbao under coach Marcelo Bielsa, who also occasionally used him as a central defender but who always asked for man marking. At Bayern, Pep wants zonal marking and it is proving to be a bit of a psychological barrier for the man from Navarra, who will be starting from zero all over again. In almost every move, Javi ends up where he shouldn't be, starts a run when he shouldn't and distances himself from Dante when he should be playing close to him. It's a hellish afternoon for him and he is constantly being corrected. The group has to go over and over the same choreography, with the coach apparently trusting in their infinite patience.

Kirchhoff attacks wide down the line, Lahm tries to reach the byeline, Alaba defends with aggression, Dante covers the Austrian full-back, Javi loses concentration and Pep stops the whole action, corrects Martínez and it's, 'Once more from the top, lads...'. They have worked for 45 minutes in the thunder and lightning at the Munich stadium and still the exercises continue, unabated.

For Javi it's an ordeal – and not just because of the new playing concepts. He has come back from the holidays in very poor shape and yesterday left the training ground vomiting from fatigue. Today he needs to concentrate, hard. Pep covers the last third of the pitch with marks so that every defender knows how and where he should be moving. From afar, the training drill reminds you of the choreography of ballet. Dancers require perfect timing and balance to lift each other and these defenders need precisely the same degree of timing, movement and co-ordination to provide the mutual cover which Pep demands, particularly when one player moves out to challenge his opponent, after which that defender will resume his original position. The idea is that at no time will any of the four break the precise distance between each other that the coach wants them to maintain. In reality, it has very little to do with ballet.

Despite their exhaustion after such a prolonged period of concentration and effort, the players ask Pep's permission to go for a quick hill run at the end of the session. The coach laughs. 'What do you know about athleticism? What purpose do these long runs have other than to hurt your back?' He chuckles again and continues: 'Now they'll come back thinking that they've trained really hard because they've had a 15-minute run, but it's just the placebo effect. They think that when they're doing these positioning and conservation exercises that they're not really working.'

The coach is joking, but it is a subject he takes very seriously. The training sessions he runs are conditioned by his playing principles and always, always have a technical-tactical element. The training Pep has devised is not confined to physical development and there will be no sprints, stamina runs, nor sessions with weights. Such ideas will only be introduced if needed to fine-tune the recuperation of an injured player. Lorenzo Buenaventura, who is working alongside Pep, explains: 'Initially they were a bit taken aback that we weren't asking for 1000-metre sprints, even though Bayern were already the least traditional of the German teams. They were already working with the ball and had got used to the rhythm of weekly matches where there isn't much time for a lot of physical training. You can only really do short, sharp quality work.

'There's not a huge difference between what we do and other training methods in terms of intensity and volume of work. I'd say we might be doing 10 or 15 minutes less out on the pitch, at the most, particularly if you count the injury prevention work we do in the gym. We value quality over quantity and prefer to do more high-quality exercises together than spend time doing long stints of physical training. They've noticed not just that, but also the high percentage of ball work we do. In fact we don't do anything without the ball, just some warm ups and warm downs, or individual work with a player if he needs something specific.'

The defenders all come back, drenched in sweat after a good 15-minute run. They look very pleased with themselves. Guardiola slaps a few backs and gives the younger players a clout on the head. He goes into the dressing room, still joking and winks at them. 'Placebo effect!'

The master class in defence has only just begun.

17

'JAVI, LOOK AT DANTE, LOOK AT DANTE, THE LINE, THE LINE!'

Munich, July 30, 2013

THE NEXT MORNING, now under a blazing sun, we get to watch the first practical application of the choreography. There are three teams of six players plus a wildcard, the Bayern B goalkeeper Leo Zingerle, who is fantastic on the ball and is always called in to help the attacking team.

As expected, Javi Martínez and Dante team up on the red side. The group that scores a goal is immediately replaced by the next group and the game mustn't stop for a second, which means that everyone has to pay attention. The game, which lasts for 45 long minutes, represents yet more torture for Javi. Just 25 minutes in and he's already crippled. The exercise, which they refer to as 'double area', stops only if no one scores. In this instance, after four minutes, Hermann Gerland blows the whistle and everyone freezes. It is intense work done at high speed and demands great concentration. It is also all too easy for fatigue and confusion to set in.

Pep is cracking the whip. Although we are used to Guardiola issuing instructions in German, this morning in Säbener Strasse, he yells almost all his orders in Spanish: 'Javi, jump!

'Javi, look at Dante, look at Dante!

'Javi, no, don't go towards the forward!

'Javi, open, open, more, more!'

There is no rest for Javi. Even Dante starts shouting to help him out. Meanwhile, Ribéry and Robben do their own thing. Bish, bash, bosh, they put in one goal after another, but no one's interested in the score. Everyone's watching the master class in defence that Martínez is receiving.

Thiago Alcántara, who is stuck doing gym work and sprinting until he gets the all-clear from the medics for his knee, is one of those watching the game attentively. Guardiola says to him: 'He's almost got it. As soon as he's mastered it completely, we'll have another first-class centre-back.'

But the lesson doesn't stop here. Just before 7o'clock this Tuesday evening, the second training session kicks off with another defensive exercise. There are seven players in attack against five defending: Rafinha, Javi, Dante and Alaba, plus a midfielder, who on this occasion is Kirchhoff. The seven attack with everything they have and their five team-mates defend to the death.

'Javi, go for the forward!

'Not now, Javi, not now!

'Javi, look at Dante, look at Dante, the line, the line!'

The player's mental reset button has been set. His unofficial initiation into playing as a Bayern central defender has taken 24 hours and three training sessions. He has had to rid his mind of any lingering memory of man-to-man marking. This is a new role he's learning to play and he does so with wholehearted humility.

When the second session of the day finishes, Pep and Javi stay on the pitch. The coach explains to him, one by one, all the channels the back four need to protect and how he wants those spaces closed down. Javi Martínez asks him about the old battles fought by Barcelona and Athletic Bilbao. He wants to know the secrets of those two cup finals, when Pep thrashed the Basque team. Guardiola describes in detail everything he did to gain the advantage: how Javier Mascherano drove forward with the ball to achieve numerical superiority in the middle of the pitch; how Messi dropped deep, far from the penalty box and left a huge space in the centre-forward position; how he taught the rest of the Barcelona team to take advantage of that space and the midfield superiority in order to pull Athletic around and to catch them by surprise. Today it is Javi's turn to scratch his head whilst he relives the bad memories. He now understands precisely how Pep did it.

Three little blonde kids run and jump on the training pitch. They are Arjen Robben's three sons, Luka, Lynn and Kai, all regulars at Säbener Strasse. So blonde their hair is almost white, the boys pound balls at their dad, who has stepped in front of goal for the occasion. Twenty metres away, Toni Kroos, about to become a father for the first time, hammers ball after ball at Starke. Serving him up the cross balls from the corner spot is Manuel Neuer, who will cross or shoot at goal every single day of training as if he were just another of Bayern's attackers. Kroos has a powerful shot that he practises diligently every afternoon. Eventually, however, Pep needs to tell him to stop. He points to his quadriceps and tells him enough is enough. He can't afford any more risks. Müller is hobbling about with a calf injury, Thiago is still nursing the ankle injury he sustained during the Super Cup final and Götze's recovery has got him fit enough only for sprinting so far. As if all that isn't enough, at this precise moment Schweinsteiger is just finishing his twelfth 70-metre sprint under the supervision of Lorenzo Buenaventura, who gives him a 20-second recuperation break in between each sprint. The vice-captain has to be whipped into shape. He is far from fighting fit after his ankle operation, can barely turn and has to do everything in a straight line to avoid putting too much weight on his foot. For the next 20 minutes, three members of the Holzapfel family tend and repair the pitch. Mr Holzapfel and his twin daughters run the family business *Der Hummelmann* which has been taking care of the grass here every day for years. Meanwhile, Kroos and Neuer put the balls away, Robben goes on playing with his children and Guardiola sits down on a folding chair outside the door to the Säbener dressing room and takes a breather. The coach then begins a detailed explanation of his three fundamental principles: the defensive line, the 15-pass build-up, and how to cope with the 'free man'.

18

'IT'S NOT POSSESSION THAT MATTERS, BUT THE INTENTION BEHIND IT.'

Munich, July 30, 2013

DURING HIS BRILLIANT 2012-2013 treble-winning season, Jupp Heynckes kept his defensive line 36.1 metres from Manuel Neuer's goal line. Or at least this is the average distance from goal of his four defenders, most often Lahm, Boateng, Dante and Alaba. In his first month of competition, and with almost the same four men, Pep's Bayern advances no less than seven metres higher up the pitch, according to an article written by Christoph Gschossmann on the German league's official website, bundesliga.de. In fact, Pep's defenders will work, on average, 43.5 metres from Neuer and Bayern will be, by a long way, the Bundesliga team that defends the farthest away from goal: Wolfsburg are 41.2 metres out and Borussia Dortmund 39.4 metres.

This is no mere accident, but the result of Guardiola's tireless work to accomplish one of his main tactical aims: to have his defenders playing close to the centre circle line and, if possible, moving into the opposition's half for as long as they can. He wants his players to close the opposition down in their own area. The aim is to be tightly packed, bar the wingers, and able to press the opposition, thus cutting off counter attacks.

It won't be quite so easy to put these ideas into practice when the league season starts – at least not without taking risks and making mistakes, but there are still 10 days before the Bundesliga kicks off; no one yet knows how complex and slow the implementation of this strategy will be.

I am sitting with Guardiola outside the door to the Munich dressing room and Bayern's coach is explaining three fundamental concepts: the defensive line; the 15-pass build-up, and coping with the free man.

THE DEFENSIVE LINE

The position of the ball determines where the defensive line is. The defender who is closest to the ball is the one who sets the line, irrespective of whether it's the full-back or the centre-half. If it's the full-back, the nearest central defender needs to watch his back, the second centre-back needs to cover his partner and he, in turn will be covered by the furthest away full-back. In the latter case the danger is minimised because the ball is far away. Guardiola explains: 'The four need to move constantly like links in a chain to prevent the channels becoming too wide or long. They must prevent it being easy for an attacker or the ball to get through those channels. When one centre-half attacks the ball, that's the precise moment the other centre-back must slot into that vacated space and the *pivote* must drop in to cover him. The movements must be automatic, like the tightening and unfolding of a folding screen, or the folds in an accordion – instant and always linked.'

THE 15-PASS BUILD-UP

Possession is only a means to an end. It's a tool, not an objective or an end goal. Or, as Pep puts it: 'If there isn't a sequence of 15 passes first, it's impossible to carry out the transition between attack and defence. Impossible. But it's not possession or one-touch passing that matters, but the intention behind it. The percentage of possession a team has or the number of passes that the group or an individual makes is irrelevant in itself. What's crucial is the reason they are doing these things, what they're aiming to achieve and what the team plans to do when they have the ball. That's what matters!

'Having the ball is important if you are going for 15 consecutive passes in the middle of the field in order to maintain your shape, whilst at the same time upsetting the opposition's organisation. How do you disorganise them? With fast, tight, focused passing as part of this 15-move sequence. You need most of your men working as a unit, although some of them will need to maintain a bit of distance from each other in order to stretch out the rival team. And whilst you make those 15 moves and organise yourselves, your opponents are chasing you all over the park, trying to get the ball from you. In the process, without realising it, they'll have lost all organisation.

'If you lose the ball, if they get it off you, then the player who takes it will probably be alone and surrounded by your players, who will then get it back easily or, at the very least, ensure that rival team can't manoeuvre quickly. It's these 15 passes that prevent your rival from making any kind of co-ordinated transition.'

MANAGING THE FREE MAN

In football there are basically two propositions: one based on ball possession and the other on managing space on the pitch. 'If you want to win by dominating the ball you have to cover each other and look out for free men, what's called the *Palomero* in basketball. The guy who hangs around by your hoop waiting to take a pass and score easily,' says Pep.

He sees four specific ways to defend against such a threat: don't lose the ball in key midfield areas where it's easiest for the opposition to mount a dangerous counter; use 15 passes to make sure that your team is well positioned and close together at the point where a move might break down, so that it's easier to press and win the ball back swiftly; put high, effective pressure on the first opponent (the free man) who receives the ball after your possession breaks down – anticipate who the free man will be and react more quickly than him. In all of this the central defender, and his vigilance, is vital.

Guardiola: 'For a team which wants to dominate the ball and be the game's protagonist, managing the free or open opponent is the principal defensive objective.'

The evening is drawing to a close at Bayern's training ground. Robben's children have gone home for dinner and the rest of the players are getting ready to leave. Guardiola has explained the three pillars of his defensive philosophy. We could go on all night, but Estiarte arrives to save Guardiola – from himself. In the event Estiarte can't resist the temptation to address the question of whether Pep is a defensive coach or not: 'I don't think so, more a very complete coach. He works a lot on both his defensive and offensive strategy. He believes that the key is to bring his most talented players towards the centre of the pitch, so that his team can dominate from there.'

It's getting dark now, but Pep comes back from the dressing room. He has just remembered that he left one important question hanging: How and where did he learn these defensive concepts? Was it in Italy, during his time as a player there? 'No way, I didn't pick these things up in Italy. You learn by watching and thinking. I have always been very interested in defence, because it takes practice and a lot of hard work. Attack is more based on innate talent, defence is about the work that you put into it. That's why I spend so much time on defensive organisation and movements. You'll see how throughout the year, every few weeks, we'll go over these defensive concepts again. The team that stops doing this is lost. But if you're asking me where I developed my creative approach to defensive strategy, the secret's very simple: I have always made a point of observing and reflecting on the things I see.'

19

'I DON'T HAVE ANY MIDFIELDERS.'

Munich, July 31, 2013

PEP GUARDIOLA ARRIVES at 8am and Manuel Pellegrini at nine. It is match day and Bayern's training ground quickly fills with footballers. Today the Audi Cup, Munich's traditional summer tournament, begins and Manchester City and Bayern are training in the morning as preparation for the semi-finals in the evening. The English team has drawn AC Milan; the Bavarian side will play Sao Paulo from Brazil, so at the moment they aren't paying each other too much attention. On training pitch No.3, City are practising corners and free-kicks and Manuel Pellegrini is correcting his players' work. On training pitch No.1, Guardiola pays no attention to him because he is engrossed in a long conversation with Jérôme Boateng.

He is enthused by what he has discovered: Boateng is totally self-taught. The young German defender has been explaining that no one has ever shown him how to defend. In fact, Boateng confesses that he did not even know that the defensive line could be organised. He thought that every player defended instinctively. Guardiola is enchanted with Boateng's wide-eyed innocence on this point and realises that he has a pearl on his hands. This is someone with an enormous amount of potential as well as a clear willingness to learn. He is a player Pep can polish and the coach's intuition tells him that, if the central defender maintains his current level of dedication, then he could take a significant step forward over the next few months.

Pep therefore spends a few minutes every day going over the fundamental principles of defensive organisation with him. Until the end of the season, Guardiola and Boateng will go over the set moves many times. This training process will continue for the next 10 months, through all the defender's ups and downs, because the coach is convinced that this is a player of real potential. Whenever he finds a footballer like this, Guardiola reacts with single-minded determination. He believes this kind of daily input impacts hugely on the quality of a player's performance and always uses Éric Abidal as an example. At Barcelona, the French defender went through a comprehensive technical-tactical transformation at the age of 30. No longer a player distinguished for his physical strength alone, he grew into the complete footballer, a defender with exquisite technique and an impressive understanding of the game.

Lorenzo Buenaventura explains why this kind of progression is possible: 'There are aspects of your game you can improve at any age and one of them is basic technique. Paco Seirul.lo and I have talked about this a lot. When players come to Barça for the first time, they often struggle to adapt to that way of working. I remember David Villa's early training sessions. He's a quick, high-octane kind of guy, who already knew eight or nine players from the Spain team, yet he still battled to understand the dynamics of that particular group. There's no doubt that players over 30 can still improve their technique and tactical sense. This is also true for the physical side of things. You may think that improvement is impossible, but the body is like a sponge and here at Bayern it's happening all the time. English and German football is all about doing long runs, but if you focus on a very different working style, like ours, with the ball, you can achieve significant physical improvements – most of all in terms of the collective dynamic. If you change the kind of movements they're making and add strength and ball work you can make immense improvements.'

Guardiola is committed to his work with Boateng. He believes that the player has the potential to become a great defender and he will not give up as long as the player shows the same level of dedication. And that's the thing. When a player says enough is enough, when his determination to improve falters, when he stops believing in his own ability to progress or abandons the idea altogether, then the coach throws in the towel too. It's over. If the player is not willing to put all his energy into the task then Guardiola certainly won't insist. He reckons that as grown-up sportsmen, surrounded by advisors, analysts, and people who manage their careers, it is up to them to decide if they want to make progress or not.

What is happening with Thomas Müller is different. The coach feels that the Bavarian forward could easily take on the position of midfielder. Although lacking the technical ability of Kroos or Thiago, he is fast, aggressive, mobile, elusive and completely tenacious in his pressing of opponents. Despite all this, whenever he has included him as a midfielder, Müller's performance has been disappointing. It is not about a lack of will or effort; Müller is a conscientious team member who is ready to try anything. As Gab Ruiz, a technical analyst for the Spanish channel Digital Plus, puts it: 'Müller is the paradigm of the Bavarian player: ordered, serious, persistent, self-sacrificing. He obeys orders. He is prepared to work his fingers to the bone to comply with what is being asked of him.'

Yet Müller is not capable of achieving the level Pep demands of him in the centre of the pitch. He abandons his position when he should be maintaining it or he stays still just when he should be moving. It is not about obeying or disobeying orders, but about his difficulty in understanding what the team needs in every instance, an essential characteristic for a midfielder. Pep will push for a few weeks more, but will finally accept that it is not possible to turn this forward into a midfielder.

When Manchester City withdraw to the showers, the Bayern players, whose game starts two hours after the English team's, start the *rondos*, which by now have become a symbol of their training work. The *rondo* was a core part of Barcelona's identity under Johan Cruyff and there is no team in the world that does it better.

The Bayern players first tried the *rondos* on June 26, during their first training session with Guardiola, and in the last five weeks there has been a notable improvement in their performance, as Buenaventura explains: 'There has been an enormous change in every aspect of their game in this first month, not just in the *rondos*. Any drill you have to carry out in a reduced space when there are two or three different objectives and all the team is involved is tough to learn. But there has been a huge improvement in the *rondos*, the positional work and in working with the ball.'

Nevertheless, Bayern's best *rondos* are still those in which Guardiola himself participates, explaining and demonstrating as he goes. As the months go by, however, the differences in quality will gradually disappear and the Munich players will make unprecedented progress in this area. By the spring of 2014, Bayern's *rondos* will be a thing of beauty and will also have become a core part of their identity.

The morning training session is restricted to the *rondos*. Only Thiago does some extra work. Just as Schweinsteiger did yesterday, he does nine sets of 70-metre runs with 20 seconds' recuperation time in between each set. When he's finished, he does seven 40-metre sprints. He is still limping and although he insists that he would like to play in the afternoon's game, his performance in the running exercises Buenaventura has set him makes this impossible. Thiago will be in the stands today.

Guardiola scratches his head: 'I don't have any midfielders. Only Kroos is fit. Schweinsteiger still can't turn, Müller is no good in that position, Thiago is half lame. Just as well we brought him! Now it is up to Lahm to play in the middle.'

Pep is referring to the impression people have got that this is a Bayern of midfielders. He likes this idea, only at the moment he doesn't have any midfielders with which to put it into action. Injuries have decimated his team, and it is going to get even worse in the coming weeks when most of his players fall victim to injury or aggravate their current problems. Pep will not be able to carry out a training session with his full squad fit and well until February 5, 2014.

The medical team at Bayern is very efficient, but Pep is still not used to their way of working. For example, there are no doctors at the Säbener Strasse training sessions. If something happens, the physiotherapists see to the players. If it's serious, they have to be moved to Doctor Hans-Wilhelm Müller Wohlfhart's private clinic in the centre of the city. The doctor has a worldwide reputation and has spent more than 30 years at Bayern. Despite this, Guardiola is used to having a medic present at training sessions and this issue will keep cropping up throughout the season. The coach announced yesterday at a press conference that Mario Götze came through a set of sprints with no problems and would join the team in two days' time. However, this morning Guardiola has been informed that it will be best to wait one more week. Pep is disconcerted by all of this. He has not yet assimilated what happened in the German Super Cup, where he was prevented from using Neuer or Ribéry, who then recovered full fitness 40 hours later.

Injuries will continue to dog him for the rest of the season.

20

'WE'RE TRYING TO DO THIS RIGHT, NOT JUST WIN TITLES.'

Munich, August 1, 2013

MANCHESTER CITY SCORED five goals in the first 35 minutes of the game. They were astounding, an attacking, goalscoring machine. Then, within the next six minutes, they conceded three goals to Milan. The defensive weakness of Manuel Pellegrini's team was surprising. It was 5-3 at half-time and this would be the final score of the first semi-final of the Audi Cup. City's elimination of Milan had revealed their strengths and weaknesses, both of which would continue to be obvious throughout the season: powerful finishing and an inadequate defence. A team with personality.

In the second semi-final, Bayern fielded more or less their best available team. Of course, Neuer and Ribéry were showing no trace of their injuries. Pizarro started as a forward, a choice which hinted at Guardiola's dissatisfaction with Mandžukić's current form, and Javi Martínez, fresh from the master class in defending, started as a central defender. It was not a brilliant match for Bayern, although they completely dominated Sao Paulo, whom they beat 2-0 after having generated plenty of opportunities. Bayern's attacking prowess meant that the veteran Brazilian goalkeeper, Rogério Ceni, had to save 12 shots on goal, making him the star performer of the match. Already there were signs of Bayern's poor finishing, an unfamiliar weakness for them and something which would become an issue over the coming months.

Javi Martínez and Dante spent the game watching each other as they worked to protect the defensive line, continuously talking and exchanging advice. Javi seemed unsure of himself, but Dante was full of praise for his team-mate: 'Javi is a marvellous player and is very intelligent. If we get paired up in the future, I'll be more than happy to have him with me in defence.'

The tournament final, on Thursday, August 1, saw Guardiola and Pellegrini go head-to-head for the ninth time. In their eight previous meetings, the Chilean coach had managed only one draw (3-3, in the Camp Nou when he was coaching Villarreal). The Catalan had accumulated seven victories. Despite the balance being so much in his favour, Pep respects and values the Manchester City coach: 'I know Pellegrini well and he is a great coach. He has fantastic players.'

Although perhaps something of a cliché, his words are genuine and Guardiola has already marked City down as one of his great rivals in the battle for the Champions League.

He was asked about Mandžukić's reaction after scoring against Sao Paulo. The Croatian forward, who replaced Pizarro after the break, made a defiant gesture towards the bench: 'Mandžukić is a great penalty-box player, a great finisher. I didn't notice any reaction after the goal.'

The coach's relationship with Mandžukić has been tense for a couple of weeks. The Croatian forward's skills were highly prized by his team-mates, particularly his willingness to fight, press and throw himself 100% into a game. This kind of aggression can have its down sides, though, and whenever there was tension or any kind of a skirmish during training, Mandžukić was usually at the centre of it. Guardiola and his coaching staff had doubts about the Croatian, although certainly not for his playing style. They admired his finishing and all the work that he did for the team in the box, but they worried about his constant raging against the world and his reluctance to learn a new style of play.

Robert Lewandowski, Borussia Dortmund's centre-forward, seems a definite target for Bayern for the following season, and this does nothing to alleviate the sense of impermanence that surrounds Mandžukić. The conflict has little in common with Thomas Müller's situation. Müller, whose attitude is perfect, just needs to adapt to being a forward rather than a midfielder. In Mandžukić's case, his performance on the pitch is superb and it is his attitude that is the problem.

In Munich, word has got out that Bayern are going to play like Barça. There are three reasons for this: Thiago's signing, the 4-3-3 formation and the use of the false No.9 position. In fact, Guardiola has no intention of turning Bayern into another Barça, given that the players in the respective teams are so different. And he just laughs at the talk of formations: 'Those schematics are nothing more than telephone numbers. It certainly isn't the most important thing, it isn't meaningful. I like the type of player who's comfortable on the ball and who'll dominate the centre of the pitch. I'm very surprised by the high level of tactical ability these players possess as well as the amount they have learned during the short time we've been working together.'

In the morning training session on August 1, Arjen Robben gives us a preview of what will happen that evening during the final: 'My legs are really heavy …'

Bayern play superbly for half an hour and then collapse. While Manchester City have made nine changes to the previous day's line-up, Bayern make two: Thiago comes in for Rafinha and Müller for Pizarro. Javi Martínez plays as a central defender again; Thiago and Kroos as attacking midfielders and Mandžukić stays on the bench. It's probably true that if Guardiola had been able to use Mario Götze, he would have fielded his ideal line-up.

For 35 minutes, they are the Bayern that Pep has been dreaming of. They play calmly out from the back, draw the opposition in, over-run them all over the pitch and plant themselves on the edge of the City penalty area – all stemming from superiority of numbers in midfield. From there Robben and Ribéry cause panic, both running wide and cutting inside to help the attacking midfielders. The first half an hour is just a festival of football – and of chances. Bayern have nine shots in 30 minutes but once again lack the killer touch. Right now it's a small detail but the following weeks will see it become a chronic problem. Guardiola is so pleased that he barely makes a couple of shouted adjustments to Javi Martínez – telling him to be more aggressive in how he brings the ball out and to push higher, towards the centre circle. Pep wants him to be bold in breaking through the opponents' lines when he has the ball.

In general, Pep takes an interventionist approach from his position on the bench and the German fans and press will continue to be rather shocked by the sight, until they get used to the Catalan's mannerisms. He waves his arms about so much because he is passionate about football. He's obsessed. Whenever he starts talking about the game he is perfectly capable of losing all sense of time and hours can pass without him noticing. He could be discussing something as prosaic as the movement of a full-back when he is attacking an opposition winger and, as long as nothing interrupts him, could spend an age analysing these movements. And he doesn't do it at a leisurely pace. He jumps to his feet and starts to move his arms to demonstrate the positions of the players, fingers held up to indicate every new position they have to cover, waving arms about behind him to indicate space left vacant on the pitch. In the end, he'll have explained the 40 movements required to produce this one action and he'll have taken only a minute to do it.

It happens every day in training. He moves, gesticulates, waves his arms, points out hypothetical lines and uses his hands and arms to demonstrate possible moves his players or their opponents might make. Bayern's footballers are used to this code of signals and gestures. They already know that if he wants a player to do something, Guardiola calls him over and enthusiastically runs through his whole repertoire of vigorous gestures. He puts his arms round him, grabs him by his shoulders to modify his position or dances round him, giving him instructions about a specific action. To congratulate someone on a good play, he will probably give him a slap on the back or a kick up his behind, something which Robben discovered early on.

Having been a player himself, he knows that the players can't hear him when they are out on the pitch, which is why he likes to use sign language. He'll use his arms, putting them behind his back to indicate the areas which need covering or the defensive line which he wants held. In general he'll spend about 70% of the game gesticulating as he issues his instructions.

In the first 30 minutes of the match against City, Pep is silent and still. He likes what he sees, except the lack of cutting edge in front of goal, and has nothing to add.

After 35 minutes, Bayern's legs start to give way, just as Robben had hinted at. City turn up the heat and everything changes. Pellegrini's men start to pressurise Javi and Dante and create a string of opportunities until Alvaro Negredo gets the equaliser for the English team on the hour. Guardiola has already changed his three midfielders and now he is using Kirchhoff, Lahm and Shaqiri in the middle. It's an unusual, surprising trio, who demonstrate that the 'Bayern of midfielders' is yet to be born.

The Munich team rally and in the end win the final 2-1 playing completely differently from the first half. Their football bears no resemblance to what Guardiola wants. They go for lots of long, diagonal balls to the wings, crosses into the box and headed chances on goal. For the first time Pep doesn't seem terribly bothered by his players employing a different style from his own. He undoubtedly prefers the way they have played in the first half, but he is also starting to feel comfortable with this other style. He seems pleased at the end of the match: 'I am happy with my players. They have all worked very hard, and people like Schweinsteiger, Dante and Javi Martínez, who only had a week's preparation time, have done well. The season will be very long and we can certainly improve. I am surprised by the team. I didn't expect them to be so good at so many things. The German game is very different from the football at Barcelona and we have to refine things and build understanding between players.'

He is asked again about Mandžukić, who came on an hour into the game and scored the winning goal. Because it's a friendly, Pep has made seven changes: 'It's very important to have a forward who is strong and tall at the front. He has a fantastic attitude and the team needs him. He was hugely important to the victory.'

Many months later, when it is already evident that the forward will not be staying for the following season, I ask Pep about him: 'Look, I'd go to war with Mandžukić because he supports the team like no one else when he plays. He presses constantly and works till he drops. But when he isn't playing, well…'

They also ask him about Javi Martínez's performance. Today the Spaniard has been chosen by Pep for the starting pairing at the back with Dante, ahead of Boateng. 'I'm very pleased with him. Yesterday he played very well and today it has been harder because City are a great team. Javi has only had five training sessions and isn't in great shape, but with a bit more practice he'll find more co-ordination with Dante.'

Gaurdiola's comments as he leaves the Allianz Arena show that he is concerned with much more than winning: 'What makes a coach great is what the players say about him at the end. If I can convince these players to play this way and manage to help them grow and get even better, I will be very happy. That will be my greatest source of satisfaction. We are going to try to do this thing right, not just win titles.'

In the vast Munich stadium, Manuel Pellegrini is waiting for us in the changing rooms: 'I have no doubt that Pep is going to impose his style on Bayern. It's a style they're going to like because it involves a lot of possession and it's good football. In the first half an hour, this Bayern reminded me of Barcelona in the way they touched the ball and dominated the centre pitch. They had a lot of possession in that period, although they didn't manage to convert many chances. There is no question that the ball belonged to Bayern tonight and we need to accept that we didn't do too well. We lost the ball very quickly. They got it back too easily. And, as we all know, getting the ball back quickly and easily is one of the main features of Guardiola's teams.'

Neither of the two men anticipated that they would be facing each other again in less than two months' time, in no less a competition than the Champions League.

21

'BRING THE BALL OUT WELL AND YOU WILL PLAY WELL.'

Munich, August 9, 2013

'WINNING THE BUNDESLIGA. That's the main objective. Winning the Bundesliga,' Estiarte reminds me as the league season starts.

Pep has a new office inside the Allianz Arena. The players' dressing room is a spacious rectangle with a grey floor and scarlet lockers for kit and boots. There's a basic wooden bench and each player has his photo on his locker. Ribéry changes beside Robben, Shaqiri next to Schweinsteiger, Neuer beside Starke and Javi Martínez alongside Dante. The shower cubicles, decorated with plain white tiles, are at one end and the physios' massage tables at the other. Beyond them is the place Jupp Heynckes used to work, up to a few months ago, seated behind a translucent screen.

Instead Pep has asked for a small office separate from the dressing room and the club has provided him with one, a dozen metres away. It's a spartan box with a red carpet, a little grey couch and a black desk. A small television and a whiteboard adorn the walls, which are otherwise totally bare. Before every match, water will be left in an ice bucket for him and there will be a bottle of white wine waiting after the match. There's no paperwork on the desk, nor is there a computer. Pep keeps everything on his laptop. The room is small and austere, very much like his office at the Camp Nou. He has always preferred his work space to be separate from the players because he considers the dressing room their territory. In fact he only ever goes into the dressing room during the half-time break, when he makes a brief analysis of what has happened and explains what he wants in the rest of the match. You will never see him in there at any other time. Not before or after the game. As a player he was never happy when the boss invaded his space in the dressing room and since becoming a coach has held true to that principle.

Guardiola also likes some peace and calm before a match and appreciates being cut off from the boisterous atmosphere in the dressing room. He prefers to maintain a bit of distance whilst the physios bandage up ankles and Lorenzo Buenaventura leads the warm-up, always short and intense. Never longer than 20 minutes, it follows a strict sequence of exercises. Minutes before kick-off, Pep comes out of his office, goes down a short white corridor lined with enormous photographs of current players (Alaba and Thiago are first in line), goes down the 22 stairs in the long tunnel and finally climbs the last 15 steps to the bench.

His first Bundesliga has started.

The first game of the German league always takes place in the reigning champion's ground. Today, Bayern's opponents are Borussia Mönchengladbach. This has been chosen by the German Football League as the most attractive fixture for the first match of the new season. Jupp Heynckes was a legendary player for Borussia Mönchengladbach, and they were also Bayern's opponents for his last match as coach. Now that Pep has taken over, the Bundesliga has decided to make a symbolic gesture by having the two sides meet for his league debut.

Guardiola is immaculately dressed in a grey suit. The checked shirt he has worn for his last few matches has been left at home today – an indication that his wife, Cristina, must already be installed in Munich. Over the months, we'll share a few jokes on this very subject. Pep's famous sartorial elegance is mainly down to his wife, heiress to the family-owned clothing boutique Serra Claret.

In planning the line-up that will kick off Bayern's league campaign, Guardiola has had to bear in mind a couple of factors. Firstly, that Javi Martínez has started to experience discomfort on the left of his groin and probably should not start the game today. His second consideration is the fact that Thiago has had to manage his own pre-season training regime. The player arrived at Bayern with the minimum of physical preparation and then pushed himself too hard for the German Super Cup. Lorenzo Buenaventura has suggested that the midfielder spend three weeks in August getting fit and as a result he is not even part of the squad today. Left with too few midfielders once again, Guardiola has reluctantly turned to Müller. Bayern's line-up as the Bundesliga kicks off is: Neuer; Lahm, Boateng, Dante, Alaba; Schweinsteiger, Müller, Kroos; Robben, Mandžukić and Ribéry. Bayern make up for the absence of Müller's attacking power by placing the captain, Lahm, high up the pitch. The team is using a 3-3-3-1 formation, with Lahm, Schweinsteiger and Kroos in the centre of the pitch.

The men from Munich make a confident start and within 15 minutes are leading 2-0. Robben gets the first goal, a deft touch on a Ribéry 'allez oop'. The second goal is Mandžukić's. Robben takes a free-kick from the touchline, eight Mönchengladbach players defend three Bayern players in the box.

This symbolizes another of Pep's idea. Arrive in the penalty box, don't crowd it. With his team in flying form Pep gets a surprise. There isn't a Bundesliga rival who is not excellent on the counter-attack. With half an hour gone, Neuer saves a powerful Max Kruse shot and then Dante knocks in an own-goal off a Juan Arango cross. The first goal against Bayern goes past Neuer from a team-mate. The result isn't really in jeopardy, but Guardiola's defence still leaves the coach less than content – particularly Alaba. Every time he is attacked he drops back and allows the opposition to get into the Bayern half without the least resistance, instead of pressing to rob possession. He is doing exactly the opposite of what Guardiola has asked for during the last seven weeks: cut off counter-attacks at the source so that the opposition don't make it into Neuer's area. One of his best defenders seems to have forgotten everything he's learned and it will take weeks for him to correct his mistakes. Alaba then converts a penalty for another goal. By then it's playground football with both teams streaming up and down the pitch.

Pep keeps scratching his head. He asked for control and intelligence, nous until reaching the middle of the pitch and then direct, speedy attacking.

Bayern are not controlling the game or the ball and instead are running helter-skelter up and down the park. It is enough to beat Mönchengladbach comfortably, but it leaves the coach with a bitter taste in his mouth. This is not what he expected from his men.

Bayern win two penalties. The nominated taker, Müller, takes the first. Ter Stegan guesses which way he is going to shoot and saves. But the Spanish defender Álvaro Domínguez, who gave away the first penalty by using his right arm, now uses his other arm to divert the ball and this time Alaba scores from the spot, inaugurating an era during which penalties will be a much-talked about subject at Bayern.

Guardiola, though not terribly happy, has won his debut Bundesliga match, just as he won his first cup game a few days ago, 5-0 at BSV Rehden in Osnabrück. He will also take a victory from the friendly against Hungarian champions, Györi ETO next Sunday, when Mario Götze will make his first brief appearance of the season. After that the internationals in his squad will be called up to play the traditional mid-August friendlies. Pep will spend those days working with the youngsters in the second team and reflecting on how to improve the dynamics of the first team.

His second Bundesliga match is not much of an improvement. Bayern beat Eintracht in Frankfurt with a majestic volley from Mandžukić, the 39th consecutive game in which they have scored. Although they have beaten the club record of 27 games without losing (which dates back to the 1985-86 season) they continue to allow the opposition to easily move the ball into attacking positions without the high, aggressive pressing which Guardiola is looking for.

This time the coach tries Shaqiri in midfield with Schweinsteiger and Kroos, but it's no better in terms of controlling the possession or the match. While Bayern batter their opponent's goal, brilliantly defended by Kevin Trapp, they give away cheap counter-attacks and look fragile defensively.

The coach is not at all happy, despite the scores. Bayern have not yet managed to achieve a consistent, steady rhythm of play. Guardiola seeks this control as it leaves less to chance. He likes his men to be running exactly where he has planned so that the whole team are completely secure about what is happening and risk is reduced to a minimum. This is the reason he insists on concepts like playing out from the back, and pressing a counter-attack instantly.

Playing out from the back is not about passing the ball for its own sake, it is to advance the lines of the team. Right now Bayern are almost always passing the ball without advancing, the ball's movement drawing out a U shape: from Lahm to Boateng to Dante to Alaba, sometimes with Schweinsteiger back amongst them, five of them passing the ball to each other without advancing the team or pushing the opposition back. For Guardiola, playing out from the back implies aggression – crossing the opponents' lines without fear of the big space Bayern's back four are leaving behind them. For Guardiola this is essential. He learned it from Johan Cruyff. 'If you bring the ball out well initially,' the Dutchman would say, 'then you'll play well. If you don't do that then there's no chance of playing well.'

Cruyff always believed that equilibrium in team play resided in control of the ball. Lose the ball less and there will be equilibrium in your play. For Pep it's a precept. His team must drive forward from the back – as one, without fear – to try to breach the opponents' lines of attack and midfield without losing possession.

Guardiola is asking a lot. In fact, he wants it all.

He leaves Frankfurt frustrated and feeling that he still has a long way to go. The players give the impression that they understand what their coach wants but are not managing to implement his instructions consistently. If they play it out from the back, perhaps they won't be capable of pressing high up and avoiding the counter.

They start concentrating on holding on to the ball, but then lose their aggression. Guardiola keeps scratching his head, which is what he does when he is worried. As they're travelling back to Säbener

Strasse, a member of the technical team reminds him of what they were talking about 10 days ago.

'Winning the Bundesliga. That's the season's objective. Winning the Bundesliga.'

22

'I LOATHE ALL THAT PASSING – THAT *TIQUITACA.*'

Munich, August 24, 2013

PEP TUCKS INTO a a starter of pureed potatoes, with obvious pleasure. He looks like he hasn't eaten anything since last night and, when I ask, he nods. He can't eat a thing on matchdays.

It's Saturday night and it's pouring. We are having dinner with his first group of visitors: some friends from New York and others from Barcelona. They've all been to the Allianz Arena to watch Bayern beat Nürnberg in a bad-tempered Munich derby. It was a strange match, generating ambivalent feelings. A match in which Götze made his debut and Thiago was badly injured. He just phoned to ask us to wait for him before we eat, but then 12 minutes later calls back to tell us he won't make it. His foot is too painful for him to come out and he's going to stay in the hotel. He'll undergo an ankle operation within a matter of hours.

Bayern were dreadful in the first half. It's as if the players want to please Pep by making sure they pass the ball, one of the group remarks, which immediately sets the coach off on one of his long explanations. 'I loathe all that passing for the sake of it, all that *tiquitaca*. It's so much rubbish and has no purpose. You have to pass the ball with a clear intention, with the aim of making it into the opposition's goal. It's not about passing for the sake of it.'

Pep's three kids and the children from New York are all hungry, but they have to make do with the pureed potatoes. Their father has told them that they must wait for their Barcelona friends to arrive. This is the first visit he's received, apart from family members, since he arrived in Munich two months ago. This strikes me as pretty surprising and emphasises the apparent indifference towards Guardiola now felt by a Barcelona that once idiolised him. This situation won't change much throughout the season, either in terms of Pep's friends and acquaintances or the Spanish and Catalan press who are not sufficiently interested to send journalists to Munich to find out first-hand what the coach is doing.

Pep spends much of the dinner sharing his thoughts and feelings. He talks about the similarities and differences between Barça and Bayern, enjoying the opportunity to express the worries he was struggling with two months ago. The Nürnberg match has been the perfect culture medium for him: dreadful at the start and explosive at the end. Everyone at the table wants to know what he said to his players at half-time to make them completely change the quality of their game. 'Not very much. Just four words: What *are* you DOING!?'

He told them to loosen up and let themselves go and reminded them that not once in his two months in charge had he asked them to play like Barça. He insisted that he had never asked them to play like that just to please him, and pointed out that the people they needed to please were the 71,000 fans who fill the Allianz week in, week out. All Pep asked his players to do was lose any self-consciousness and be themselves.

'I just want them to start off moving forward together for a few metres so that, if we lose the ball, the opposition can't take advantage of our lack of unity. Every team in Germany is capable of mounting a counter-attack before you've had the chance to even breathe and if we lose our unity it gives them a chance to break through and make chances.

'The only thing I want is that if Dante hits a long, diagonal ball to Robben, he doesn't attempt it from in or around our own penalty box, but from a position around the centre of the field, once we've played up there. If Robben then loses the ball we are all up there relatively close to him and we can win it right back without a problem. But if Dante launches the ball too soon and Robben loses it then we are all straggled out and – pam! pam! – the opposition will certainly hit us with an effective counter-attack.'

As he talks, Pep throws his arms about just as he does when he's on the bench. It feels like he might at any minute demand that we all get up and take our positions on the imaginary football pitch, here in the restaurant. He grabs his American friend by the arm and says, 'Bastian's [Schweinsteiger] DNA is pure Bayern. You can see his body demanding that he keep running up and down the pitch. I love that.'

'But in that case,' interrupts one of his Barcelona pals 'how do you get the nous and patience in the play you want, with that very same German DNA?'

Guardiola replies: 'Once they've moved as a unit to the middle of the field, that's when I want them to be more Bayern than ever. I want them to dig into that DNA, let themselves go, run, liberate themselves. That's where they excel. They like running, they love it. And I love to see them doing it. Let them run. Let them open up the wing play and cross into the box. Not necessarily to hit the goal every time on the volley – that's hard to achieve – but so that we can take advantage of rebounds off the keeper, of the second ball – that is where we create most danger. If we play like that jointly then the rebounds will fall to us and the extra danger we create is that the defenders are wrong footed and on the turn while we are running on to the chance. That's what I've told them to do. That's what I want.'

The coach believes that it would be absurd and unworkable to try to recreate Barça's playing model here. He places a high value on Johan Cruyff's historic role in the formation of Barcelona, as well as recognising those visionary coaches throughout the Catalan club's history who helped bring youngsters up through the ranks and into the first team. The valiant individuals who took time and trouble with the kids in the youth teams. There's immense pride here. 'I'm a Barça man and always will be.'

This doesn't mean, however, that he'll ever be back training Barcelona. In fact, if I were a betting man, I'd say that his future is going to be Bayern and then England. Who knows? He may end up in eight-to-ten years taking a curtain call by coaching a national team. He isn't planning a very long career and the family agreement seems to be just that: a limited but intense career span. Barça doesn't seem likely to figure in this hypothetical 10-year plan, but one can never say never.

It's also difficult to envisage Pep doing anything other than coaching. This is what he loves. When anyone suggests other roles in football, like sports director or president, he shows no interest, as if his coach's brain can't even imagine doing those jobs. He is also unimpressed by talk of the *entorno*, the people, the press and the powerbrokers around FC Barcelona. 'Forget them. The way it's been set up at Barça you have two options: either you're a powerbroker or you're not. I was forced to choose, against my will.'

Before turning his thoughts to Bayern once again, Pep wants to share one last memory from his Barça days. He's thinking of the dramatic 2012 Champions League semi-final against Chelsea, during which Barcelona had 46 shots on Petr Cech's goal (23 in the away leg and another 23 at home) but were still knocked out. Chelsea went on to the final in the Allianz Arena against Bayern, whom they beat in a penalty shoot-out.

'I made a mistake that day. I've gone over it a thousand times in my mind. I told the players to cross the ball into the area but I didn't get across to them that I wasn't looking for them to score on the volley, but to win the second ball or the rebound and – pam! – score that way. I didn't manage to get them to understand the exact instructions. I reckon that if I'd got that across properly we'd have won and we'd have been in the final.'

This brings him back to Bayern and the second ball. 'I need to help the players free themselves so that they can run and show everyone what they are capable of. I need to adapt to them, not the reverse. I don't want them doing something just for the sake, as some people claim, of pleasing me. What I want is players who are happy and confident in their game.'

The second half of the Nürnberg match was a good example of what Guardiola wants for Bayern. They were like a whirlwind. It was a tempest during which it was possible to see the first traces of what

Pep's trying to teach them. His defenders take up position around the centre circle and, from then, the brakes are off: Bayern play flat out. They hit the Nürnberg penalty box 32 times in 45 minutes. A Bavarian avalanche. Now *that* is the language of Bayern.

It is no accident that the proud, triumphant Bavarians have turned to Pep. They're looking for a football identity, a brand, a direction, a powerful language which will mark them out. Hoeness, Rummenigge and Sammer knew exactly what they wanted from this third phase. They weren't just looking to add an extra diamond to the crown: they wanted to re-draw from a clean sheet. They were not looking for the Barça Pep, but the Bayern Pep, a man still in the process of evolving. Make no mistake, we are witnessing two parallel processes here. Whilst Guardiola works to reform Bayern in this so-called third phase, he is also creating his own identity, free from the Barça straitjacket. 'All I want to do is share my game philosophy with the players so that they can reduce risk to a minimum and achieve their potential.'

Guardiola has linguini with truffles. He doesn't eat anything during the day so he tends to have a lavish meal in the evening. Even the prospect of playing a friendly leaves him tense and robs him of his appetite. He manages only to drink water, bottle after bottle. So he really makes up for it in the evening. He's already put away a whole bowl of pureed potatoes, a tomato and mozzarella salad, half a dozen *rostbratwurst* with sauerkraut – the legendary Nürnberg sausage – and the linguini with truffles. Now he's ready to attack a juicy sirloin steak. None of this stops him talking nineteen to the dozen, however.

When Guardiola was appointed at Barça in 2008, he took on a disillusioned, foundering team which was still capable of producing excellent football. Barça teams have spent 25 years following the guiding light of Cruyff, from the youngsters right through every category. They all follow the same ideas. Identical methods are used for training sessions. In other words, they play the same way. On average, a *cantera* player who makes it into the first team will have spent between 12 and 15 years playing the same kind of game, which amounts to a minimum of 6000 hours. And he'll go on to add another 4000 hours. Not only will they have taught him the language of Barça but they will have turned his natural talent into a specific football personality. He will be fluent in the Barça language. The player will play a brand of football that has been developed and designed, planned and controlled. After so many years of systematic repetition it becomes an automatic response which causes difficulties if the player leaves Barça for another team. What Barça does is special and personal to them, whether or not they win or lose. So it was in the dark years and in the glory days of Team Pep, when they won everything. Football language exists independently of victories, although it is those victories which give it influence.

Bayern has had tremendous success, but the team has never developed its own language. The success is inherited from a long tradition, from the likes of Beckenbauer and Gerd Müller. Gary Lineker's famous quote nails it: 'In football you play 11 against 11 and then the Germans win.'

These were amazing victories: three consecutive European Cups in the 1970s; 22 league titles before Guardiola's arrival; Heynckes' sublime treble. The club has made history and is one of the foundation stones of world football. But what is its football identity? An insatiable desire to win is an advantage, but it is a character trait rather than a hallmark of identity and the two things are very different.

Two of the most important players in Bayern's history, Uli Hoeness and Kalle Rummenigge, decided that the time had come to create the language of Bayern. That's why they approached Guardiola. They didn't say: teach us to play like Barça. They said: we want to go on winning, but we want to do it with a distinctive style, so that people will say, *that's* how Bayern play.

Pep is clear about everything. Not the little details but certainly the broad ideas. He gets up from the table with little Maria half asleep in his arms and keeps talking, now a little agitated. He is obviously thinking about how much he has to do.

'I need to talk to Müller tomorrow morning, first thing. I want to ask him why the hell he doesn't always play like he did today. I need to talk to Ribéry. He's always telling me that he prefers giving an assist to actually scoring himself but today he really revelled in his goal against Nürnberg. I need to make him see that scoring should be a priority.'

He goes out into the street, still talking. 'I have to fit Götze and Thiago into our game. It's going to be tough and I don't know how to go about it yet. But it's got to be done. Götze and Thiago are key.'

It's stopped raining now and out on the pavement in Maximilien Strasse he walks with his sleeping daughter in his arms whilst he talks about diagonal passes, crosses and footballers being given freedom to run and run.

23

'LAHM ... THE GUY IS FUCKING EXCEPTIONAL!'

Munich, August 25, 2013

HAVING RISEN EARLY after a late night, Pep is up and reading nutritionist Mona Nemmer's latest report by 8am. And he is not pleased. Only four of the 14 men who played yesterday against Nürnberg chose to stay for dinner at the Allianz Arena's players' restaurant. For Guardiola, this is a priority issue. His players' nutritional intake after the intense physical exertion of a game is a crucial part of their physiological recovery. Scientific studies show that the requisite nutrients must be consumed within an hour of the match finishing in what is known as the 'metabolic window'. Other studies allow for two hours and some research suggests that you can wait even longer. In any case, it is certainly true that plenty of carbohydrates and a certain amount of protein are essential for good recovery and injury prevention, particularly when the players are facing a match every three days.

Guardiola, Lorenzo Buenaventura and, of course, Nemmer, have explained all this to the squad several times already and Pep is annoyed. He cannot understand why professional footballers would choose to ignore something that could make such a massive difference to their continued wellbeing in the course of such a long season.

The players' lounge is on the second floor of the Allianz Arena. It is a large restaurant which seats 200 and entrance is by invitation only. To reach it you have to go through the sponsors' restaurant, a gigantic area which runs the whole length of the stadium's main stand. The sponsors' guests congregate there and are offered a snack before the match, followed by dinner afterwards. Each sponsor has tables reserved for their own invited guests, who are treated to Bayern's first-class catering service amid all the noise and fun of what is usually a highly-entertaining evening.

The door to the players' lounge is tucked away, half hidden in a corner of the restaurant, discretely guarded by doormen who make sure that no one gets in without an invitation. Each player and member of the coaching staff is given two tickets to the game, plus two invitations to the players' lounge, given that the Allianz Arena is sold out for the whole season. In stark contrast to the sponsors' area, the players' restaurant is a haven of peace and exudes a sense of deep calm, broken only by the sound of small children clamouring for autographs or photographs with their favourite footballers, a practice which is, theoretically, against the rules.

Once showered, the players leave the dressing room, go through the mixed zone where the press ask them about the game, then walk down a corridor and take the lift up to the restaurant. There, family and friends will be waiting for them. There's a simple buffet laid out: two kinds of soup, two Italian pasta dishes, parmesan cheese, rice, salad, tomato; some meat, fish, fruit and, usually, small portions of *Apfelstrudel*.

Some players aren't particularly hungry after a game, because of fatigue or nervous tension. Others prefer to eat a little cheese and wait a few hours before going out to a Munich restaurant with their partners. Whatever the reason, yesterday only four of them ate at the stadium, whilst the rest waited until later. This angers Pep, who believes that it is vital for anyone playing at the elite level to pay attention to the most minute of details.

Guardiola usually dines in the players' lounge, except on rare occasions like last night, when he had a date with friends, or the evening of the *Clásico* between Barça and Real Madrid, when he said a quick goodbye to his team and hurried home to watch the game on television. In general, the coach and his family are in the private restaurant two hours after the match, eating with the rest of the squad and their friends.

This is when you'll see Guardiola at his most spontaneous and chatty. No longer the serious, focused coach who supervises the last training session before a game or the introverted, tense guy waiting for the game to start. First, there's a television interview to get out of the way, and then he spends some time with the opposition coach as they wait for the joint press conference. In Barcelona he used to invite the visiting coach for a glass of wine in his office, but in Munich he contents himself with a chat in the corridor outside the press room. Aware that different timetabling arrangements in Germany mean that the visitors can get home the same day, he doesn't want to risk the other coach missing his plane.

After the joint press conference, Pep has a chat in his office with Hoeness, Rummenigge and Jan-Christian Dreesen, the club's financial director. All of them love deconstructing the tactical details of the game. These are usually long conversations and there will be days when, an hour after the final whistle, Pep and Uli will still be chatting about the way they have played. To round off the evening, Guardiola goes up to the players' restaurant to eat with Cristina and their three children, although he will stop to chat at the tables of the players and their friends, taking a bite of something each time. Here, a little cheese; there, a few chips. This is when he is at his analytical best, when he is happy to sum up in a few precise words the things his team have done well or badly: 'Bah, that Lahm is a scandal! He is super-intelligent, understands the game brilliantly, knows when to come inside or to stay wide. The guy is fucking exceptional,' he says.

They have just finished their first 'normal' week. There has been no midweek game and the double training sessions have finished. In fact, this will have been one of the few weeks, between July and Christmas, when the players haven't had a game in midweek, be it with Bayern or on international duty. Out of the 22 weeks that make up the first part of the season, only two will have a clear midweek. In Germany the term *Englische Woche* (English Week) is used to define the practice of having two games per week. So 20 of the 22 weeks will have been English Weeks.

The decrease in training sessions has also made a big difference. Until now, the coaching staff have been arriving at Säbener Strasse at 8am and staying until 9pm. This timetable has been necessary to cover the double training sessions every day, but this week they have left their hotel and moved home with their families. Pep's children have started school. Now the staff start at 9am and work until 4pm. Pep's life has regained a bit of normality and he gives the impression of being at cruising speed.

Guardiola spent last Monday visiting Dachau, the Nazi concentration camp near Munich. He and Cristina had doubts about whether the children should come with them on such an emotional visit to what is, after all, a memorial to human cruelty. In the end the whole family plus Manel Estiarte made the trip. As they had feared, that night the children slept poorly and had nightmares. Despite this, their parents considered it an important learning experience for them.

Pep used the week profitably given that it was his last chance of extended free time before Christmas. He went to an art gallery, played golf and starred in an advert for the beer company which sponsors Bayern, dressed in *lederhosen* (Bavarian breeches and braces). He also took the chance to stroll around Munich, commenting, 'It's a bit surprising to be able to walk about the city and go into restaurants without people coming up to talk to me. The people here are extraordinary. They treat you with real respect and leave you in peace'.

When asked about appearing in the advert dressed as a Bavarian, Pep laughs and says that Cristina liked how he looked in *lederhosen*. He goes on to outline his policy on promotional events: 'I don't have any problem with all that because what is important for the club is also important for me. At Barça I didn't do much of this kind of thing but I am not here to compare clubs. Each has its culture and its way of doing things. It doesn't matter what has happened in the past. What is important is the present. I have to adapt to Bayern, and Bayern has to accept my work on the pitch and behind the scenes. We will be focusing on what the club and the team needs.'

Pep is getting used to the way they do things at Bayern. It's all quite different to what happened at Barcelona. Bayern's official club newspaper headlines an article with: '*Optimaler Start, aber…*' (Optimum Start, but…), and the coach begins to understand that self-criticism forms part of the club's culture and has to be accepted as an intrinsic part of the Bavarian character.

The derby against Nürnberg left him with mixed feelings – that sense of disappointment in the first half, and the pleasure at his team's domination in the second half. 'We have worked well this week. When we attack it is important to defend as well, and when we defend it is important to know how to attack. Football is attacking and defending. It is about attacking a lot and conceding very few opportunities. Against Eintracht in Frankfurt we were even better, although we conceded a few chances at the end. We have spoken about it a lot with the players during the week and it shows.'

The Bavarian derby produced some interesting statistics. The 2-0 victory, with goals from Ribéry and Robben, who seem to be competing for the prize of fittest player, was their 28th consecutive game in the league without a loss and they achieved 81% possession, a record for the Bundesliga. Pep didn't seem too bothered about statistics at yesterday's dinner, however. The developing narrative around penalties turned another page, too, with the opposition keeper, Raphael Schäfer, saving David Alaba's spot-kick after half an hour.

Whilst the rain falls this Sunday morning in Munich, Guardiola takes notes about nutrition as he prepares for what he is going to say to his players in a short while. He struggled to sleep last night, as is almost always the case after games, and has been ruminating on his players' weaknesses. They have improved, certainly, but they still aren't capable of cutting off counter-attacks at the beginning of that move. It's bugging him. They are also sterile at the start of the game, whenever they start that inconsequential *tiquitaca*, passing without getting free of their rival, without breaking the lines as they know they should … and are quite capable of doing. He has to go through all of this with them this morning.

And one last thing. He's going to have to think about how he fits Götze and Thiago into this model of play. Although Thiago is going to be out for a long time to come.

24

'PAM! PAM! *THAT'S* OUR STYLE OF PLAY!'

Munich, August 25, 2014

HE DIDN'T EXPECT to receive two pieces of bad news on Sunday morning. It's raining and whilst hundreds of fans gather in silence around the pitches in Säbener Strasse, huddled together under umbrellas, Guardiola is meeting with his squad in a room on the floor above the dressing room. It's a huge space, laid out like a cinema and they usually have their pre-match talks here. Today it's more of a post-match talk, with two themes: food and football. Pep makes a start: 'I've already explained on two occasions the importance of having dinner within an hour of finishing a game. Mona has also made this point but yesterday we noticed that almost none of you followed those instructions. Only four of you had dinner at the right time. I understand that you would all prefer to leave the stadium and go out with your partners to your favourite restaurants, but if we are playing every three days then this is the only way to recuperate physiologically. When we're playing away from the Allianz there's no problem – it's shower, bus and a plate of pasta. But when we're here in the Allianz I need you to do what I'm asking. It's absolutely essential and I won't ask again. You must eat within an hour of the match and since you are all professionals playing at the highest level I trust that you'll do it from now on.'

He takes less than four minutes to cover this first topic and uses the next five to talk about their game. 'Secondly. Let yourselves go, let yourselves go. Be yourselves a bit more. I'm only asking that you all drive forward in a unified way at the beginning, playing the ball out from the back, but once you are high up the pitch, past the halfway line in fact, hit the diagonal ball to the winger so that he can cross to the striker and then, lads, everyone hunting the rebound and the second ball.

'Be yourselves. That's what you're best at, so do it. You need to dig into your own DNA and run when you think you need to, just as long as you've crossed the centre of the pitch. And another thing…

'I hate *tiquitaca*. I hate it. *Tiquitaca* means passing the ball for the sake of it, with no clear intention. And it's pointless. Don't believe what people say. Barça didn't do *tiquitaca*! It's completely made up! Don't believe a word of it! In all team sports, the secret is to overload one side of the pitch so that the opponent must tilt its own defence to cope. You overload on one side and draw them in so that they leave the other side weak. And when we've done all that, we attack and score from the other side. That's why you have to pass the ball, but only if you're doing it with a clear intention. It's only to overload the opponent, to draw them in and then to hit them with the sucker punch. That's what our game needs to be. Nothing to do with *tiquitaca*.'

Just in case they hadn't already got it, he has reassured them that they don't have to be the FC Barcelona of Munich and, just to drive this idea home, the substitutes' training session, which is particularly intense and demanding, is based around opening up the wings, crosses to the box and arriving for the cross in two distinct waves. The first to attack the cross and try to score, the second to snaffle up the rebound and score from that. Pep roars: 'Pam! Pam! *That's* our style of play.'

It's raining hard and someone points out that summer must be over. The comment causes Toni Tapalovic, the goalkeeping coach, to start teasing Pep: 'Just you wait for the winter – we'll be training outside in minus-10 degrees and half a metre of snow. Then we'll go directly from the pitch to the sauna without taking our boots off.'

Javi Martínez's parents are visiting and have their own meteorological wisdom to impart: 'In Munich it's like the Bilbao drizzle, but here it's snow rather than rain. You're not really noticing it but it keeps falling until eventually you have half a metre of snow.'

Guardiola and Thomas Müller are arguing out on the pitch. The coach has asked him straight out why he doesn't always play the way he did yesterday, with that level of intense pressing. As we stand listening in the quiet of the morning, the player replies that it's because he wants freedom of movement and feels that he plays better when he doesn't have any particular responsibilities. The coach tells him, gesticulating all the while, that if every player in the team demanded a similar level of freedom, it would be a disaster. The argument will be settled sooner rather than later.

Perhaps because of his experience working with players with strong characters like Samuel Eto'o and Zlatan Ibrahimovic at Barcelona, Pep is always direct with his players, but also happy to engage in dialogue. He has always believed that every player is different and needs to be treated as such and is already applying this credo in Munich. Having discovered that Schweinsteiger is obsessed with football and loves to talk endlessly about tactics, Pep jumps in with both feet. One day we watched them chatting about a particular move for 30 minutes after training. On the way to the dressing room they were still talking and then 20 minutes later, when they emerged from their shower to get the bus to go to the team hotel for the game, they were still going strong, both of them waving their hands about as if they were in the middle of a Champions League final.

He can give Philipp Lahm as many instructions as he likes and the captain takes it all in without a problem. On the other hand, when it comes to Franck Ribéry, a drip-feed approach is required. This is a street player, a self-taught footballer who works on his instincts. Trying to teach him even just two tactical concepts at the same time can completely block him when he goes out to play. Ribéry still plays the same way he did as a kid on the streets of Boulogne-sur-Mer. He gets the ball and immediately goes on the attack.

He has to be vigilant where Mandžukić is concerned. In less than two months he has changed from a receptive team member to being defiant and negative and then, recently, back to a great team player again. At the moment he is giving 100% and is the one who pushes the whole group and accepts everything positively. His attitude is excellent. However, we have yet to see what will happen if Götze takes his place.

If Mandžukić can accept the fact that he will be a substitute from time to time and that in the difficult days of rain and cold, he will be an almost certain starter, everything will go swimmingly for him and he will be a key member of the team. It will all be different next season when the 'other guy' comes (in August 2013 nobody in Säbener Strasse is allowed to talk about signing Robert Lewandowski, Borussia Dortmund's centre-forward).

The trick is working out how to interact with each individual. Whilst his players are constantly learning and incorporating new concepts into their game, their boss is also learning and improving the way he communicates with each of them. He's tough on one guy and soft on the next. He might give long, tactical explanations to a kid in the youth set-up and then respond brusquely to a key member of the first team. He's always looking for the right code to unlock the talents of each player and take them to the next level.

There's some bad news. Thiago Alcántara's right ankle is seriously injured and he has to be operated on tomorrow in Stuttgart, with two-and-a-half months of recovery time required. He's going to have to wave goodbye to half the season. It's a devastating blow. *Thiago oder nichts*.

And there's other, equally bad news. Javi Martínez can hardly walk. He has intense pain deep inside his groin muscles, not unlike a hernia, and he can't even kick the ball with his left leg. What worries him most, though, over and above the pain, is the fact that the doctors can offer no immediate solution to the problem.

By now Pep is constantly scratching his head, which tells us he is deeply worried. He's lost Thiago, Javi's lame and Schweinsteiger has taken his foot off the pedal. It's a bad state to be in, particularly because they'll be facing José Mourinho's Chelsea this week in the European Super Cup final, a match in which Bayern will be looking for revenge, in a big way.

But first they have another appointment. In two days' time, on Tuesday, they have to play a league game in Freiburg, the southernmost city in Germany, on the border with France. There are a few changes planned and five or six of the usual starting line-up will be on the bench. Pep wants to save them for the Super Cup.

After training Pep meets up in one of the training ground's dining rooms with the friends he ate with last night. He talks to them about the family atmosphere at Bayern. 'People told me before I arrived but you have to experience it to believe it. It's absolutely true. We're like one big family here.'

He goes on to talk about his bosses. He feels very close to Hoeness, whom he adores, and talks about Rummenigge's professionalism, something which Pep finds unusual in football. He is also profoundly grateful to Sammer for all the support he gives him. Guardiola feels very much at home here in Munich.

When someone mentions the upcoming Super Cup and his reunion with Mourinho, he dismisses the topic quickly: 'I know Jose far too well already.'

But his head is already elsewhere, in Freiburg. He's still considering all his options. Is it wise to field so many players who are normally substitutes on Tuesday and leave five or six of his usual starters out? In the next 48 hours he'll go over and over his plans, a thousand times. As always.

25

'BAYERN WERE LIKE SOMETHING OUT OF A MOVIE TODAY.'

Freiburg im Breisgau, August 26, 2013

PIERRE-EMILE HØJBJERG leaves Guardiola's office in tears. The young Dane had asked for an appointment with his boss two hours ago, but this is the first time Pep could see him, because of a press conference. Højbjerg gets straight to the point and with a tremor in his voice tells Pep what has happened: his dad has been diagnosed with pancreatic cancer and the family is devastated. Hs older brother is stuck on a boat somewhere, and will take two weeks to get home. Young Højbjerg is going to have to step up and support his family right now. Neither the coach nor the player can hold back the tears and they embrace as the emotion overcomes them. They sob uncontrollably for a few minutes. The player is just 17, he's been at Munich only for a year and suddenly his whole world has collapsed. As for Pep, his deep sadness for Højbjerg has brought back the painful memories of Éric Abidal and Tito Vilanova, who both suffered similar illnesses. Training will start half an hour late today.

At midday, before hearing the dreadful news, Pep was in a crucial press conference. It had turned into one of the longest of the season and focused almost entirely on tactics. Speaking about Thiago's operation, Pep said: 'We've lost a hugely important player, someone who could make a huge difference to us.' Anxious to temper people's enthusiasm about the team's Bundesliga record-breaking 81% possession, he insisted: 'We are looking to maintain unity and avoid being hurt on the counter-attack.'

The coach also had praise for the German league. 'It's been such a great surprise. The stadia are phenomenal, we have easy access to the referees and the atmosphere is sensational, despite the rivalries that exist.'

Guardiola takes the opportunity to enthuse about both Mario Mandžukić – 'He's a hugely important player to us, a fighter who has a strong character and is very honest' – and David Alaba, whom he says 'is as good as a young Abidal. He's going to be great. In fact, he's already great'.

He also ensures that he points out the progress his men have made in terms of preventing opposition counter-attacks. 'My players have understood it perfectly and we only conceded one counter-attack on Saturday.'

Pep then spends five minutes detailing how he wants his team to play. He presents the journalists with a concise summary of the concepts he talked about on Saturday night over his dinner with friends and on Sunday morning with the squad. The conference is taking place in Säbener Strasse's small press centre, which is an annex attached to the Bayern staff canteen. This has been a public declaration of intent.

By 4pm the players are on the training pitch kicking balls about whilst they wait for the session to start. Neither Pep not Højbjerg is there but they come out 20 minutes later just after Lorenzo Buenaventura has started the warm-up. Pep will be very serious throughout this session. He can't help but think about his friend and assistant at Barcelona, Vilanova and Abidal, who was close to signing for Bayern at the end of June. Pep had wanted him when Barcelona let the player go, but Hoeness and Rummenigge were concerned about why the Catalan club hadn't wanted to renew his contract. Pep was convinced that Abidal would have reinforced the team as a full-back and central defender, mentored Alaba in his quest for perfection and served as an example of forbearance and excellence in the dressing room. He didn't hesitate when the Monaco manager Claudio Ranieri got in touch for some advice. 'Sign him up. You won't regret it!' By October Ranieri had made a follow-up call to thank him. Abidal was already a regular starter at Monaco.

In training this Monday Pep trains obsessively on how to bring the ball out from the back. 'Freiburg will press high and close us down and it's a warning we've to freshen up our movements, our ideas,' he explains.

He'll do this every four or five games. He puts the keeper, the back four and the midfield on the pitch and walks them through the kind of movements he wants them to make automatic. He repeats this over and again so that they take it in fully. At Barcelona not two weeks went by without him doing exactly this. Here at Bayern it will be almost the same. Every 15 days, in detail, as if they were preparing for an exam.

Elsewhere on the pitch seven players have taken it upon themselves to practise taking penalties. Alaba, the first-choice taker, isn't with them. He's doing defensive work with Pep. Last Saturday Alaba missed a penalty against Nürnberg with the score at 0-0. When asked about it in the press conference Pep gave his backing to the Austrian full-back. 'He's good at it, as are Müller, Kroos and Schweinsteiger. Alaba will continue to take penalties.' In fact, Guardiola hadn't even bothered to appoint an official penalty taker. It's the kind of thing he usually leaves to the players to sort out. That's why they've decided to organise this practice session, in case the European Super Cup ends up with penalties.

Bayern have not forgotten what happened in May 2012, when Roberto di Matteo's Chelsea lifted the Champions League trophy in the Allianz Arena after winning the penalty shoot-out 4-3. That night the Munich team took the first penalty and Lahm, Mario Gómez and Neuer all scored. Ivica Olic and Bastian Schweinsteiger then missed and the memory still haunts the Bavarian team. Today, seven of them are working hard to perfect their technique.

Tom Starke is in goal since Neuer has joined Alaba to work on defensive organisation with Pep. One after the other they shoot at goal: Müller, Kroos, Robben, Shaqiri, Pizarro, Schweinsteiger and Götze. Ribéry, who never practises penalties or direct free-kicks, isn't part of the group. Neither is Mandžukić. The ball keeps hitting its target. Each player takes six penalties and all 42 shots end up in the net. Schweinsteiger jokes: 'Okay, okay, well done lads. A perfect score. But just remember, we're not under pressure now. Let's just see how we all do when there's some real pressure!'

Javi Martínez hasn't even come with them to Freiburg. His groin pain has become so bad that the doctors have agreed with the player and his coach that immediate surgery is necessary. What with Thiago's operation and now this, things are getting complicated. Pep is left with no midfielders.

Freiburg in Breisgau is a charming town with cobbled alleyways and paved streets which can be lethal for the unsuspecting traveller dragging luggage on wheels. The little alleys are so narrow that you almost have to turn sideways to get down them and they boast an open system of gutters called the *bächle*, which was once used as an irrigation system. Freiburg Cathedral's bell tower is 116 metres tall and houses 19 bells, all of which are rung throughout the day at a quarter past the hour, half past, on the hour and so on. It is a fitting tribute to the musical traditions of this former French town, once part of the Habsburg Empire, and the resulting din reaches its glorious apotheosis in a crescendo of noise between 6 and 7am. It catches me unawares and, rather dismayed, I realise too late why a set of earplugs had been left on my bedside table last night.

Close to the Dreisarn River, half hidden by the lush vegetation of the town which sits at the edge of Germany's Black Forest, the Mage Solar stadium is small but passionate, a seething cauldron stuffed to the brim with 24,000 fans. They are waiting for Bayern.

Guardiola, true to his word, has left six of his main starters on the bench: Lahm, Alaba, Boateng, Ribéry, Robben and Mandžukić are all sitting beside Starke. Freiburg press very high, just as Pep anticipated, and try to provoke Bayern into messing up as they bring the ball out from the back.

Bayern dominate the game, with Shaqiri scoring first. They are vastly superior to Freiburg and have 17 chances on the opposition's goal, which is well defended by the formidable Oliver Baumann.

Guardiola's strategy seems to be working well until the 80th minute, when everything goes wrong. Firstly Schweinsteiger sprains his ankle and then Freiburg equalise on the counter-attack. Two bad knocks. Once again, with only three days to go before a final, a key member of the team has been injured. They lose two vital points which, at this stage of the season and given Borussia Dortmund's relentless start, feels like a blow.

Guardiola seems a bit down when he talks to the press. The two points they've lost have hurt him but he is happy with the game his team has played. 'We weren't passive out there and controlled and defended effectively. We played well and I don't have any comment or criticism of my men. These things happen in football. You just have to deal with it.'

The local team's coach, Christian Streich, offers his own opinion at the door of the dressing room: 'I'll tell you something. Bayern were like something out of a movie today. A movie. And I'll tell you something else. They are far and away the favourite to win the Bundesliga this year. No doubt about it. They may have lost two points, but they played fabulous football. They played with us the way *they* wanted to, playing out terrifically from the back. If we had to play 10 games against this Bayern side, and look at the number of players who weren't playing today, we'd draw one and lose the other nine. They are a winning machine and my players are absolutely destroyed, exhausted. This is going to be an amazing campaign for Bayern. What Guardiola does is exceptional. All that he has achieved at only 42. It's tremendous.'

However, Streich's words of praise do nothing to calm Guardiola. He's just encountered his German Numancia – the team that beat him as he began his first league campaign with Barça. He gets on the bus and sees Schweinsteiger. It definitely looks like the player won't be fit for the Super Cup. Pep has no midfielders.

'We'll be going to Prague to compete to the maximum. We have three days to rest and that will do us. I have only one plan for the Chelsea game: play well, control the counter-attacks and attack,

attack, attack,' explains the coach, standing at the front of the bus.

Then, he has a discussion with Sammer. It's 9pm and the pair have just decided to make an urgent call to Munich.

'Doctor, you'll have to delay Javi Martínez's operation. We'll need him in Prague.'

26

'LADS, I DON'T KNOW HOW TO TAKE PENALTIES. I'VE NEVER TAKEN ONE IN MY LIFE. BUT HERE'S THE BEST PENALTY TAKER IN THE WORLD.'

Prague, August 30, 2013

IT'S A FEVERISH, tense, agonising final. Bayern equalise 51 seconds after the official 120 minutes have been played. Swedish referee Jonas Eriksson has added one minute for stoppages, and there are nine seconds to go before Guardiola's team loses its second final in a month when a player who only three days ago was booked in for surgery, scores for Bayern. Once again, they're going head-to-head with Chelsea in a penalty shoot-out, and everyone's thoughts turn to the Allianz Arena, one year ago. That day the English team beat Bayern in the Champions League final, in a penalty shoot-out. This could be payback time but, given the option, Guardiola wouldn't have wished for penalties. In the last four weeks the men from Munich have scored only three of the five penalties they have taken.

On the way back from Freiburg, Guardiola realises that Schweinsteiger will miss the European Super Cup. His ankle is terribly swollen and they're going to have to postpone Javi Martínez's groin surgery. Thiago had surgery yesterday and the combination of injuries and the fact that Mario Götze has had very little training means that Pep will be forced to put Thomas Müller in the centre of the field as an attacking midfielder again. Given the results of this experiment so far, he had promised himself never to repeat this strategy, but there is nobody else he can use. He decides that Toni Kroos will be the organising midfielder, with captain Lahm on hand to protect him as a No.8. Pep draws up his final line-up with great reluctance. Having Kroos as *pivote* is a real problem, particularly against Mourinho, the expert in making his teams get in behind a *pivote* via speedy counter-attacks.

Bayern's line-up tonight reads like this: Neuer; Rafinha, Boateng, Dante, Alaba; Kroos, Lahm, Müller; Robben, Mandžukić and Ribéry.

This final will be the 16th time Guardiola and Mourinho have met and the balance of victories up till now is in Pep's favour. He has won seven of the games against Mourinho's three, with five draws. They know each other inside out. When Guardiola was captain at Barça, Mourinho was assistant coach. They shared a dressing room, training sessions, confidences and knowledge. Years later they would fight it out in unforgettable tactical battles. There are no secrets between these two men. Mourinho knows that Pep wants his team to get the ball and come out attacking. Guardiola knows that Mourinho will start with his team in banks of defence, just waiting to pounce on a lost or loose ball and inflict deadly damage.

In this latest tussle between a team that likes to dominate the ball and one that wants to control the space, Chelsea come out on top. All it takes is a threat in the shape of Fernando Torres for Kroos to lose his position. Then Eden Hazard gets away from Rafinha and Bayern's defensive organisation crumbles. Chelsea attack aggressively and score the first goal whilst the Munich defenders look on passively.

Thirty minutes into the match something happens that will affect Bayern's entire season. Kroos continues to suffer every time Chelsea play the ball behind him, because turning quickly and then defending isn't his greatest attribute. Assistant coach Domènec Torrent turns to Pep and says: 'Why don't we try Lahm as *pivote*?'

Guardiola hesitates for the time it takes him to take a sip of water, then he leaps to his feet and, almost running on to the pitch, shouts at Kroos: 'Toni! You, No.8. You, No.8 and Philipp, No.6!'

This moment, switching the two, marks the start of Philipp Lahm's metamorphosis into a midfielder.

Lahm started playing for Bayern aged 11, having come from FT Gern and, during his time in the youth categories, trained under Hermann Gerland, who was assistant coach under Jupp Heynckes and stayed on to work for Guardiola. He had used Lahm in a variety of positions: from right-back to winger and even occasionally in midfield, when he was coached by Roman Grill, who is now his agent. When Ottmar Hitzfeld promoted Lahm into the first team at 19, the full-back positions were filled by the likes of Willy Sagnol and Bixente Lizarazu, so Gerland took it upon himself to persuade Felix Magath, then Stuttgart's coach, to take Lahm on loan. Once there, he shone at left-back. Ten years later, Guardiola started to use him as a midfielder and now, in the middle of the European Super Cup final, whilst losing, puts him into the intricate position of *pivote* – the linchpin of the team.

Months later, towards the end of November, Guardiola will recall this moment: 'It was Domè's (Torrent) suggestion that made all the difference. If we win something this season, that will be the reason. I'm completely serious. If we win anything this season it will be thanks to that decision to move Lahm. All the other pieces fell into place the minute we put him in central midfield.'

Very slowly Bayern begin to dominate. Pep not only puts Lahm in midfield, but moves Rafinha higher up the pitch, and the team starts to attack using a 3-3-1-3 formation. Rafinha helps tighten things up in midfield, aiding Lahm, which frees Kroos to play creatively and Müller to play off the strikers. After half-time Ribéry scores with a fierce shot – a chance created by Kroos's excellent build-up work.

A euphoric Ribéry runs straight to his coach to celebrate. Guardiola grabs him by the neck and the two bump heads. Ribéry raises his left fist as if dedicating his second goal in six days to his boss. Having been voted the best European player of 2013, he was in Monaco last night and unable to train with the team. Pep insisted that he be there to receive his much-merited award. He has set himself the task of trying to convince Ribéry that he has huge potential as a goal-scorer and the player is responding magnificently.

After the equaliser Bayern control the rhythm of the game. Guardiola decides that a few more adjustments might just win them the game. The day before, he and Javi Martínez had decided that the player should get an anti-inflammatory injection so that he would be fit to play. Now, 10 minutes after the break, Pep takes Rafinha off and brings on Martínez in an attempt to stretch the game – more attacking depth. He hopes Javi can change things by getting up and down the middle. At first Bayern suffer because, with Lahm giving over the *pivote* position to Javi, the German must do a double-shift at right-back and on the right of midfield. And the manager makes another change – Götze for Müller. But Chelsea go up a gear, making three good chances. Neuer needs to excel and Chelsea hit the bar. Kroos and Ribéry both have scoring chances but what scars the closing moments is Ramires' violent foul on Götze, which sees him sent off with five minutes of normal time left.

Götze is left with a serious ankle injury and will end up in plaster next week.

In the break before extra time Guardiola tells his players he wants aggression, particularly when they are defending. He doesn't want Chelsea getting another goal and wants to see his men maintaining the pressure.

The total opposite happens. Ninety seconds into extra time David Luiz frees the fabulous Hazard, who is wide on the left. He runs at the penalty area, easily passing Lahm and then Boateng, who barely tries to tackle, meekly allowing him past. He shoots and Neuer fumbles badly. With 10 men, Mourinho's team is back in front and now the clock is in their favour.

The Bayern supporters react with greater speed than the players themselves and their impassioned chanting echoes around the stadium. They are losing with just a few minutes to go but the fans of the European champions are holding out for the equaliser. The Munich support unfurl their flags, roar their lungs out and spur their players on to an epic comeback. Inspired by the fervour and excitement in the stands, Guardiola's men produce an avalanche of shots on Petr Čech's goal. By now Kroos is back at *pivote*, Lahm is running the whole of the right touchline. Javi Martínez is alternating between second striker and centre-forward. Time and again Bayern make scoring chances, time and again they are thwarted by the formidable Czech goalkeeper. Shaqiri, Mandžukić, and Javi all fail to score. Shaqiri misses for a second time, as do Götze and Ribéry and then, at the end of 120 minutes of play, Mandžukić too fails to hit the mark. Bayern have had 38 shots, have taken 19 corners and hit three times as many accurate passes as Chelsea but, with 60 seconds left, they are losing the final.

German teams have a reputation for fighting until the last second. They will only accept defeat once they're in the shower. And in this final Pep's men more than live up to this reputation. With nine seconds left Alaba crosses, Mandžukić lays it off, the ball bounces off Dante and drops to the left leg of the injured Javi Martínez – who scores. The combined efforts of an Austrian, a Croat, a Brazilian and a Spaniard have the German supporters leaping to their feet in an explosion of joy that thunders across the Prague night.

Mourinho turns to Guardiola's bench and clasps his hands in a gesture that says, 'pure, dumb luck!' And he's right. There are four principal protagonists in football: the ball, space, time and luck. Of these, Chelsea have certainly been the master of space today, but Pep's team have had the ball, the right timing and now, at last, Lady Luck has intervened on their behalf. Of course, there's still the penalty shoot-out…

In the middle of all the euphoria Pep steps up to the plate, emotional but icily calm. He calls his people together in one big huddle. Everyone is there: doctors, physios, assistant coaches, players, substitutes and even the injured men, like Schweinsteiger. This is Pep at his brilliant best. The guy who rises to the big occasions and dazzles his men. Just as everyone is expecting him to mobilise his players with a call to arms of epic proportions, Pep tells them a simple story. Relaxed and smiling, he pays no heed to the thousands of frenzied supporters around them. Apparently unaffected by the tension, he issues no battle cry, opting instead for an anecdote. About water polo.

'Lads, I don't know how to take penalties myself. I've never taken one in my life. But here's the best penalty taker in the whole world.' And he points to a figure half hidden, right at the back of the huddle.

'I'm talking about Manel [Estiarte]. He was the best water polo player in the world. He took penalties better than anyone. Hundreds of them. Water polo is like football. Only four out of every five penalty kicks hit the target, but Manel put them all away! He is the world expert on penalties.'

Pep hasn't just managed to get the player's attention. He has completely changed the expressions on their faces. They had been waiting for war cries and motivational oratory, an adrenalin boost. What they receive, standing here in the midst of the clamouring, heaving mass of humanity that rocks the stadium, is a simple tale. Van Buyten and Starke stand just behind Pep in their tracksuits, hugging each other; Doctor Müller-Wohlfhart is beside them. Kroos, Lahm and Ribéry are right at the front. Alaba is leaning his elbow on Müller, also wearing a tracksuit, like Robben. Then there's a second circle: Javi Martínez, Shaqiri, Dante, Boateng and Mandžukić; the assistant coaches, Domènec Torrent and Hermann Gerland; Kirchhoff, the substitute; physio Gianni Bianchi; fitness coaches Lorenzo Buenaventura and Andreas Kornmayer; Götze; Claudio Pizarro; Rafinha and Contento. Matthias Sammer and Bastian Schweinsteiger are slightly separated from the main group and Manuel Neuer isn't here. He's off getting Toni Tapalovic's advice about the Chelsea penalty takers. Estiarte, too, has stepped back a few metres.

The players are smiling. Silent but relaxed. They're enjoying the tone of this team talk. 'I've learned two things from Manel and his penalties, so listen up. These are the only two things you need to do now. Firstly, make up your mind immediately as to where you're going to put the ball and stick with that decision. I'll say it again. Decide now, and don't change your mind no matter what happens. Secondly, keep telling yourselves that you're going to score. Repeat it a thousand times and don't stop until after you've taken the penalty. Don't worry and don't change your minds.'

'What a team talk. Incredible!' Matthias Sammer says later.

But Pep hasn't finished. He gives them his advice and then says: 'Lads, there's no list. You can choose whether or not to take one. You choose. You're all going to score anyway, so you decide who's taking them. Who's up for it?'

Alaba is the first to step forward, Kroos lifts his left hand next, followed quickly by Lahm. Pep gives his captain one of his little taps on the cheek. Next, Ribéry adds his name to the list and the coach slaps him encouragingly on the chest. It's Shaqiri's turn after that and he's rewarded with a 'Bravo, Shaq!' The players have come up with the list themselves, but what about the order they'll take them in?

'You sort that out. Take them in any order you want. Whatever you're comfortable with. It doesn't matter anyway, because they're all going in.'

They decide to take them in the same order they volunteered. The referee indicates that it's time and they all turn away. Pep grabs Ribéry and Lahm, stopping the whole group in their tracks.

'Just one last thing. Don't forget. You've decided where you're putting the ball. Go and do it. And from now until you shoot keep telling yourself, 'It's going in'. With every step you take, say it, 'goal, goal, goal…"

Of the seven players who had practised on Monday scoring 42 out of 42, only Kroos and Shaqiri are penalty takers today. Müller and Robben have both been substituted. Pizarro started on the substitutes' bench and of course Schweinsteiger is injured. Of the players who had not taken part in the practice session, Alaba, Lahm and Ribéry have been happy to volunteer. All five score. Neuer saves Chelsea's fifth penalty, taken by Romelu Lukaku, and Bayern have won the title that has so far eluded them. Pep has his first trophy with Bayern and his third European Super Cup.

Voted man of the match, Franck Ribéry dedicates the honour to his boss. 'I know how much this means to him, his first title. I also know about his old rivalry with Mourinho.'

The Portuguese coach has left the pitch without congratulating Guardiola, in stark contrast to the obvious warmth between the two teams.

An hour later, in a corner of the press room in Prague's Eden Stadion,

Guardiola and Estiarte chat to a couple of Catalan journalists, Isaac Lluch, of *Ara* and Ramon Besa of *El País*. Pep is absolutely radiant. His eyes are shining with happiness, but above all there is a sense of enormous relief.

'The team needed this win. If we hadn't won, I don't know how we would have moved forward.'

PART THREE

2013: A PRODIGIOUS YEAR

'The most dangerous man is the man who is afraid.'
LUDWIG BÖRNE

27

'RIGHT NOW I'M NOT THE BEST IN THE WORLD.'

Munich, September 5, 2013

GUARDIOLA'S ACHILLES' HEEL is his anxiety. He carries with him a deep fear of coming under attack, which was probably born during his playing career. He was physically fragile and lacked athleticism – rather on the puny side. Working alone to cover an enormous section of the pitch, he was an easy and exposed target for the opposition. If they tackled Pep and succeeded in neutralising him, the whole structure of Barça's game would collapse. He carried this fear throughout his whole playing career, but was also smart enough to develop the ideal antidote. Pep found that he could cope with his fear by playing with a touch of audacity.

Pep has developed enormous courage precisely because of this fear. During his time as Barcelona coach he explained a hundred times that he preferred to face teams who play tight around their goal area, who create a kind of bunker. 'In those games the ball tends to stay far from my goal and that feels much less threatening.' In other words, those teams scare him less.

He compensates for his anxiety with a level of audacity that can sometimes become excessive. He has developed the antibodies to deal with his fear and now, as a coach, has a capacity for extraordinary courage and single-minded determination. He doesn't like being attacked, so he goes on the attack first. It's his way of correcting this weakness. As we've already seen in the German and European Super Cups, such boldness can at times tip over into recklessness. Putting Thomas Müller in midfield is a case in point.

On the other hand, one of Guardiola's main virtues is his prescience, a counterbalance for all the fear he experiences. Let's look, for example, at what he said on May 28, 2011, at the end of the Champions League final at Wembley in which Barcelona beat Manchester United 3-1. That day his players had given one of their greatest exhibitions of *Team Pep* football. In the midst of all the euphoria following this extraordinary victory his mind turned to the rumours circulating about him having only one year left at Barcelona (in fact this turned out to be true). Alex Ferguson had just advised him publicly not to leave the Catalan club because, he argued, he would never have it so good anywhere else. It was then that Guardiola showed his strong, intuitive side. 'I don't know what will happen if I go to another club. I'll have to look at the kind of players they have and perhaps will struggle to find the players of the same calibre as Barça's. It will definitely be a big test but I believe that you have to keep looking for personal challenges. There will come a time when it will be good for me to go to another club and try to play as well as possible with a different set of players. Any coach depends on his players and the way they play. It will be a big challenge.'

Two years later his predictions came true. Why had he really left Barça? Because the number of problems had finally outstripped the level of his enthusiasm. President Rosell's cold indifference, combined with the fact that both Pep and his players were worn out, weighed more heavily than his desire to keep on winning.

Why did he sign for Bayern? Hoeness and Rummenigge inspired in him a confidence that he found irresistible. But the overwhelming reason was his desire to play good football with a different type of player.

After the final of the European Super Cup in Prague on August 30, Guardiola was asked if he felt like the best coach in the world. 'Perhaps I did for a while at Barça, but that's no longer the case. Right now I'm not the best in the world. Maybe that's what I need to do – get back to showing people what I'm really capable of. Particularly my players.'

For the time being those players are happy with his leadership and seem to trust him. Ribéry's reaction after his goal in Prague and the collective boost of confidence delivered by his talk before the penalties provide more than enough evidence of that. Captain Lahm uses the verb *lernen* (to learn) a lot. He employs it almost every time he speaks, giving the very definite impression that he, too, feels that the team is currently on a learning curve as they try to master the new language. Ribéry explains it like this: 'Pep is completely different to Heynckes, but we are really happy with him.'

'The players are my principal concern,' Guardiola says time and time again. Naturally demonstrative, he likes to give his players little slaps on the cheeks and smacks or kicks up the behind. It's just the way he is and, although it can come as a bit of a surprise initially, his players tend to get used to it eventually. When he's worried he scratches his head and if he has an idea to convey, throws his arms about like a lunatic. Body language is one more part of this new way of communicating. And both players and coach are going to have to get used to each other.

By the start of September Pep is already comfortably installed in the centre of Munich and is enjoying the city. 'I'm really happy. Munich is a beautiful city and the club is hugely supportive.'

So what does he do in his 12-hour working day? About 50% of his time is spent analysing his opponents in depth, a task which usually takes him two-and-a-half days. He also spends a lot of time supervising training and planning the next session with Buenaventura, Torrent and Gerland. Finally, he spends one or two hours a day having one-to-one chats with players. Sometimes he'll show them some kind of instructive video, at others they'll have a coffee or lunch together and chat about personal things. The players are the important ones, the key to success and Pep has learned that he must devote time to them. What else does he get up to in Säbener Strasse? He studies, he analyses, he thinks and deconstructs other teams' moves, and some of the moves that were popular in the distant past. He reinvents, watches, reflects, communicates and convinces.

Just a few hours after winning the European Super Cup in the dramatic penalty shoot-out in Prague, most of his players abandoned Säbener Strasse for international duty. They had almost no time to celebrate and, with Javi Martínez in hospital for his operation, Pep found himself almost completely alone in the sports ground. Mario Götze's ankle had been put in plaster and he would spend the next few weeks on the injury list with Martínez, Thiago and Schweinsteiger. Together they would make a powerful and creative midfield, but Pep will have to put this particular dream on hold until well into the autumn.

What he would really love to do is manage the youth programme – train young players, oversee their development, teach them the fundamentals and get everything he can out of them. Perhaps he'll do it one day, although it certainly won't happen any time soon. He has three years in Munich and, if he doesn't extend his contract, possibly a stint in England. Perhaps after that he'll decide to abandon the world of the elite and start working with youngsters.

One day in the Camp Nou, towards the end of 2010, Pep instructed two of his youth players – Gerard Deulofeu and Rafa Alcántara, Thiago's brother – to join the senior players' training session for the first time. He told me all about it: 'I *loved* working with them. It's much easier to train youngsters than it is older players. Much easier. You feel like you're really coaching. With older guys you have to watch and review what you say, how you say it, you have to take into account the result of your last match. You stand there watching the expressions on their faces and making sure you're using exactly the right words. With the kids, you just take them by the scruff of the neck and bring all the talent out, just like squeezing an orange. I get so much more out of it – and it's a lot more fun.'

These first few days in September are the best he's had here so far. He's only got four players to train (Starke, Rafinha, Contento and Kirchhoff), and he puts them to work with the B team, which itself has a new coach. Matthias Sammer has appointed Dutchman Eric ten Hag and for two weeks the two coaches work together to ensure that Bayern II begin to apply the same criteria to their game as the first team. The work they do now is about to yield great results. Bayern II will have a wonderful season and win the league. They will finish as the team which has scored most goals, whilst conceding the fewest. Nevertheless, they miss promotion to the Third Division because of an away goal conceded in the last second of the decisive play-off match.

Guardiola is keeping an eye on the Bayern youth academy. Some of his big stars have come through the youth sections at Säbener Strasse, guys like Müller, Lahm, Schweinsteiger and Alaba. However, so far this generation of youth players is showing no sign of being exceptional. Hermann Gerland, *Tiger* Gerland, who took over the club's youth teams in 1990 and has a sixth sense for spotting young talent, is not optimistic about the short-term potential, although there are some notable exceptions, such as Højbjerg and Julian Green. Pep has grown enormously fond of Gerland. 'He's giving me so much help. So much! He takes me through every club and every player in the Bundesliga. He's very loyal to Bayern and I'm delighted that the club suggested he work with me. I trust him and his advice completely. And I really admire the mutual respect that exists between him and the players.'

As well as working with the youngsters and running the training sessions with Gerland, Pep gets to spend some time with some of the legends of world football. People like Gerd Müller, who works with Ten Hag with Bayern II, and Mehmet Scholl, whose son, Lucas, plays for the under-19 team. But these pleasant encounters are few and far between and he can't allow himself to get distracted. He's worried about medical care at the club. There are specific concerns such as Götze and Schweinsteiger's slow recoveries, although he understands that this is because their injuries are so serious. Then there are other issues, such as what happened in Dortmund when Neuer and Ribéry were training as if nothing had happened within 40 hours of the match they missed. At the time, Pep suggested amending the protocol. If the original injury isn't serious he would like the players to travel with the team so that the decision can be made at the last minute. There is also the matter of the club's arrangement with Doctor Müller-Wohlfahrt, widely recognised as the expert in his field. Many of the world's top sportsmen and women have been treated in the 'MW' clinic, attracted by the doctor's extraordinary diagnostic powers. He is capable of diagnosing most injuries just by placing his hands on the affected area and also specialises in the use of homeopathic remedies, which he uses in injections. Sprinter Usain Bolt, marathon runner Paula Radcliffe and golfer José María Olazábal, amongst others, swear that the medic's 'healing hands' have cured painful muscular and joint-related injuries. Michael Jordan, Cristiano Ronaldo, Andy Murray, Boris Becker and even Luciano Pavarotti and Bono have all passed through Müller-Wohlfahrt's hands.

Guardiola, however, would like a doctor present at training. At the moment the physios deal with anything that happens. Müller-Wohlfahrt insists that hanging about the training ground all day would be a huge waste of time for him or one of his assistants and points out that it is unlikely to cause injured players too much distress if they have to come to his clinic on Diener Strasse. He works in the centre of Munich in a building in the old quarter that was home to Emperor Luis of Bavaria in the 13th century. The doctor sees a huge number of patients every day, although if a Bayern player needs a diagnosis he will always get immediate attention. In the clinic, though – not at the training ground. This is one issue that will run and run and the season will end without any kind of satisfactory resolution.

28

'HOENESS IS THE HEART AND SOUL OF THIS CLUB – HE'S VITAL TO ME.'

Munich, September 13, 2013

'IT'S A BIT like a recipe,' Pep says. 'League titles are won in the last eight games, but they are lost in the first eight.' Experience has taught him the importance of not losing the league in the first two months of the championship. Sure, you can drop a few points, but not too many. Two or three points behind, four at the most is all any team can afford at the end of the first eight games. That way you still have room for manoeuvre. Then, when it comes down to hand-to-hand combat, you will still be in a position to win, to show what your team is made of. You can't fall at this final hurdle either, of course. This is the moment your men have to strain every nerve and sinew for victory. At least that's the theory.

We are still very much at the start of the campaign. With four Bundesliga games under their belts, Bayern are in second place, two points behind their great rival, Borussia Dortmund. It's as far behind as Guardiola's team can afford to be but, quite apart from the two-point difference, there are problems on the horizon. One more slip-up like Freiburg and…

Vollgas is the word Uli Hoeness used to express what he expected from Bayern from September onwards. Full steam ahead. And Guardiola was happy to pick up the gauntlet. 'The president has told us it's full steam ahead from now on and he's absolutely right. We are now entering one of the most exciting moments of the year, with the start of the league, the Champions League and the DFB-Pokal. And we are ready for the challenge.'

Although in private Pep is tense and worried about the two-point disadvantage, he is always calm when he deals with the media. 'I'm not stressed by the difference in points. I knew from the moment I signed for Bayern that I would be under a lot of pressure. We have only played four games and now isn't the crucial time. That will come in May. Let's see how we're doing then. I'm completely confident that we'll be in a strong position after the winter break. I have a good feeling about it. We're going to have a great season and we'll be in a strong position to fight for titles by April or May.'

Pep really enjoys working with Hoeness. He's obsessed with football and as such could not have chosen a better club than Bayern, where he regularly spends time with some of the great legends of football. He lunches with Hoeness, the two of them competing to see who can consume the most *rostbratwurst* sausages. He has coffee with Rummenigge every day, chats to Paul Breitner at least once a week on the training ground, reads *Kaiser* Beckenbauer's latest views, walks on the same patch of grass as *Torpedo* Müller, *der Bomber der Nation*, and shares the team's ups and downs with Matthias Sammer. This is a dream come true for football-mad Pep.

Hoeness and Rummenigge are in trouble. The former because of an accusation of tax evasion which, within months, will land him in prison and the latter because he has failed to declare some luxury watches which were gifted to him in Qatar. He is facing a heavy fine. Despite all the evidence (Hoeness turned himself in to the German revenue), Guardiola is not about to start criticising them. These are the two men responsible for his appointment. He therefore takes great care about what he says. 'Hoeness is the heart and soul of this club and is vital to me. When you listen to him speak about Bayern you realise how gravely important the subject is to him – it's everything.'

I want to pause here and look for a moment at the Bayern management model, which has been analysed by experts all over Europe precisely because it is so successful. This is a debt-free club which has developed multiple sources of income. They have attracted committed and loyal sponsors, as well as more than 230,000 members who fill the stadium to capacity every week. With an annual income of more than €430million, they have also reported a profit every year for the last 20 years. In 2013 the club sold more than a million shirts and their coffers remain extremely healthy. A sense of deep pride underpins everything the management do, deservedly so given the long list of European clubs who are technically on the verge of bankruptcy. In general, people attribute their success to the fact that the club is managed by two ex-players but, in my opinion, this is nonsense. Bayern are successful because Hoeness and Rummenigge have been great managers, not because they are former players.

When he was forced to retire with knee problems in 1979 Hoeness, who was only 27, was appointed Bayern's commercial director. He has now been involved in the management of the club for 35 years, is familiar with every department and knows every aspect of the club's life, inside out. For three-and-a-half decades he has steered the club in the right direction, strengthening the business and building it into a huge but sustainable concern which has pursued sporting excellence whilst retaining the sense of being one big family. Rummenigge brings a modern, global vision of sport as well as a management style which combines individual accountability with collective responsibility.

Vollgas, Hoeness said. The coach has commissioned a statistical analysis of Bayern's attacking performance during the first five weeks of competition. He is not happy with his forwards' results. The evidence is conclusive. In the seven games they played before the international break, Pep's men took 162 shots at goal, an average of 23 per game, and they scored 16 goals, resulting in a conversion ratio of 10%. Unfortunately, it's getting worse. Bayern are improving the way they deal with counter-attacks, but their efficacy up front is deteriorating with every game. In the last couple of matches they have managed only a conversion rate of 5%.

It's Friday, September 13, 30 minutes before training starts and Pep is showing these stats to his men, recently returned from their respective national teams. He doesn't bother asking them to be more accurate in front of goal because that would be pointless. They're not missing deliberately. But he wants them to know the facts and insists again on the importance of cutting off counter-attacks at the source.

Bayern play Hannover 96 the following day in the Allianz Arena and already the storm clouds are gathering.

29

'WE ARE ALL HIDING BEHIND THE COACH.'

Munich, September 15, 2013

PEP WAS PLEASANTLY surprised by the reaction of Uli Hoeness and Kalle Rummenigge the day after the European Super Cup match in Prague. Bayern's top executives had immediately sprung to his defence. 'Mourinho's comments are completely out of order ... but then perhaps it was a different match he was watching.'

The Chelsea coach had said: 'Every time I play Pep I end up with 10 men. It must be some sort of UEFA rule.' What Mourinho forgot to say that day in Prague was that Ramires' tackle on Mario Götze had torn the ligaments of the German player's ankle. It was Ramires' second yellow card and he was sent off, but in truth, the severity of the tackle should have resulted in a straight red.

Pep was taken aback because he was so unused to getting this level of support from his bosses. During his time at Barça he had had to deal with numerous unwarranted and serious attacks on the team and the whole institution, and his was often the sole voice raised in their defence. In April 2011 Barcelona and Real Madrid had a run of four derbies in 18 days. These *Clásicos* were marred by excessive levels of hostility and a few Madrid players played with an aggression bordering on violence, whilst more than one Barça player indulged in diving and other unsportsmanlike conduct.

After the Copa del Rey final, which Madrid won with a Cristiano Ronaldo goal, the Barcelona coach congratulated the opposition, adding that his own team had been very close to victory themselves. The referee had, rightly, disallowed a goal by Pedro for offside. Guardiola said later: 'A two-centimetre decision from a linesman who must have had a very good view ruled out Pedro's goal.'

On April 26, 2011, Pep and his players were having lunch in the private restaurant of the Eurostars Madrid Tower Hotel. The television was showing Mourinho's press conference ahead of the Champions League semi-final they would be playing the next day. Pep had his back to the screen and wasn't paying attention when one of his assistants suggested he turn around and listen.

'We have started a new cycle. Up until now there was a very small group of coaches who didn't talk about referees and a very large group, in which I am included, who criticise referees. Now, with Pep's comments, we have started a new era with a third group, featuring only one person, a man who criticises the referee when he makes good decisions. This is completely new to me.'

Pep's players were also listening by this stage and were furious at Mourinho's words and his mocking tone. It was the last straw for Guardiola. 'The time has come!'

A few months earlier, Pep had said to his closest colleagues: 'I know Mourinho only too well and he's trying to provoke me into a reaction, but it won't work. I'm not going to react. I'm not going to answer back. Only when I think the time is right.'

Mourinho was relentless and had often managed to wind Pep up. The Catalan had, however, maintained a dignified silence so far. Now his moment had come.

At 8pm on the day before the match, the players left the training session at the Bernabéu stadium, sensing that Pep was about to respond in kind to Mourinho. Word had got out and even senior management had heard that Pep was preparing a strongly-worded statement. Leaving the dressing room, one of the players closest to Guardiola wished him luck with the press conference, as did sports director Andoni Zubizarreta, who surprised him by saying, 'We don't answer back, eh, Pep? We don't answer back. We like a low profile. A low profile'.

Once again Pep was left feeling that the club had hung him out to dry and he decided to ignore management's advice and go ahead anyway. This time he responded with unprecedented fury. 'Señor Mourinho has permitted himself the luxury of calling me Pep, so I will call him Jose. Tomorrow at 8.45pm we face each other on the pitch. He has won the battle off the pitch. He's bested me in that arena the entire season and no doubt will continue to do so. If he wants his own personal Champions League trophy away from the pitch, let him take it home and enjoy it. In this room [the Bernabéu press room] Mourinho is the fucking chief, the fucking boss. He knows all about this and I don't want to compete with him in here. I'd just like to remind him that I worked with him for four years [at Barcelona]. He knows me and I know him. If he prefers to value the views of the journalist friends who take their information in a drip feed from Florentino Pérez more than the relationship we had for four years then that's his choice. I congratulated Real Madrid for winning the Cup. The offside call was a matter of centimetres. The referee was extremely smart and on the ball. I try to learn from Jose on the pitch when we play him or when I watch his team on television, but I prefer to learn as little as possible from him off the pitch.'

Pep's response that evening had inflamed an already tense situation. When he arrived at the team hotel, his men were waiting to give him a standing ovation. They were delighted with his response, which they considered long overdue. These were players who, although used to receiving their fair share of praise and adulation, had also been accused of a range of transgressions including doping, dirty tricks, play acting and exerting undue influence over referees – and all of this whilst the club's management pursued their apathetic policy of maintaining a low profile. The senior executives were not interested in defending them, but now Guardiola had stepped in. And he'd done it in the right place at exactly the right time.

In Munich, people are used to plain speaking. Men like Beckenbauer and Hoeness have never held back from criticising the coach or one of their players. What in Spain would be considered outright war in Bavaria is seen as a frank exchange of views. Nobody was surprised, for example, when the Allianz Arena's Master of Ceremonies, Stephan

Lehmann, asked Paul Breitner about a penalty they had been given. The ex-player told him: 'That wasn't a penalty. They gifted it to us.' The conversation took place on the pitch at half-time in the Bayern-Nürnberg derby on August 24 and nobody felt that Breitner's blunt honesty had been inappropriate.

Guardiola has had to get used to this new culture and midway through September 2013 finds himself caught up in 'Hurricane Sammer'.

Bayern are up against Hannover 96 and the match goes in much the same direction as the one against Nuremberg three weeks before: a slow, dull, monotonous first half followed by an impassioned wake-up call by Guardiola at half-time and then a fast, furious second half which again ends with a 2-0 win.

The coach isn't happy with his men's performance but he's also not particularly surprised.

He has always had concerns about the first game after an international call-up. For almost two weeks the players train differently and have to adapt their playing style to the national team. Their return to the club is usually a bit chaotic. 'After eight or nine days with their national teams the players' rhythm has completely changed. But we are ready to play the Champions League,' says Pep after the match. He has chosen his words carefully, not wanting to betray his true feelings.

Perhaps for the first time since coming to Bayern, he is depressed and angry. It isn't about the disconcerting sight of Thomas Müller being forced to play in midfield again because of all the injuries. In fact, playing a striker in midfield is actually beginning to show the player up.

It seems the players still do not fully understand him and he is not managing to make the team function well enough. Matthias Sammer is quick to intervene. Quietly but forcefully he makes his opinion clear: 'We must forget the titles we've won – we are lethargic out there, unemotional. We're just going through the motions and should be moving out of our comfort zone. Why am I saying this?

Because the coach shouldn't have to intervene to wake the players up every time they play. We are all hiding behind the coach.'

Despite all predictions to the contrary, Guardiola and Sammer have developed a strong, mutually-supportive relationship. They have immediately sensed how important they could be for each other and are determined to work together to take the club forward. Sammer also has the intuition of a former player whose talent made him a team leader. He has been quick to spot the team's laid-back approach to games and that is why he has decided to drop this bomb without warning Pep. The coach is taken aback by the sports director's directness but is nonetheless quite pleased and is quick to defend Sammer in the storm that blows up in the aftermath of his declaration.

As usually happens in Munich, Sammer's words elicit a response. This time it is president Hoeness who speaks up in German newspaper *Bild*: 'Apparently we should be apologising for only winning 2-0. Maybe we've actually lost four or five games. They must be laughing themselves silly at Dortmund.'

Kicker magazine adds: 'We understand that Matthias wanted to make things better, but if it ain't broke, don't fix it.'

Next Rummenigge enters the fray: 'This is great for the press but it is not what either the team or the coach needed.'

Beckenbauer and Lotthar Matthäus also have their own opinions on the matter. As do the players. Toni Kroos and Manuel Neuer accept the criticisms publicly, agreeing that they did indeed play badly against Hannover and describing Sammer's comments as a much needed wake-up call. Captain Philipp Lahm, on the other hand, appeals for criticisms like these to be aired privately in the dressing room rather than in public.

Two days later, the day before their first Champions League match, Guardiola speaks about the controversy. 'This is about cultural differences and I have come to realise that in Germany this type of reaction is normal and I have to adapt. If the same thing happened in Spain – *bam!* – we'd have a huge problem on our hands, but it's completely normal here and I wasn't at all surprised by Sammer's comments. He's like me, very emotional.'

This doesn't prevent Hoeness and Rummenigge calling Sammer to a tense face-to-face meeting. But the sports director has always gone out of his way to support Guardiola, and the coach returns the favour, saying firmly: 'Matthias is one of us.'

It's Sunday, September 15, 18 hours after the Hannover game, and Pep is still down but doing his best to hide it from the players at the morning training session. He has an intense, serious chat with them, waving his hands aggressively, surprising many of them by declaring: 'I want to hold one of you up as an example to the rest. Mario Mandžukić. He and I didn't have the best of starts and knew immediately that we were never going to be mates. But I can tell you that there is no one better than him. Nobody that tries harder, who comes to the ground more fired-up. This is a player who gives everything out there. That's why he's the best. He's the one who sacrifices most for the team and in all my years as a coach I have never had a forward like him. Nobody has been better for the reasons I've just given you. In this team there's Mario and 10 others.'

He little imagines that his low mood will result in one of the best ideas he has ever had.

30

'GENTLEMEN, THIS IS *TIQUITACA* AND IT IS SHIT.'

Munich, September 15, 2013

'MARIA! MÀRIUS! COME quickly!'

Pep's two oldest children stop playing and run to the corner of the house where their father works. This is Guardiola's second hideaway. The other one is his main office at Säbener Strasse. This one is a tiny room at the end of the hall in his flat in the centre of Munich. Just a few metres square, it contains a table, a chair and a laptop.

Today Pep is very down. Yesterday's match has really discouraged him. His results are good enough. Bayern have won the European Super Cup and are second in the league, lying only two points behind Borussia Dortmund. Pep's men have lost just one game in a month and a half, the German Super Cup, but he is still dissatisfied. Like any coach he needs to get the right results but for Pep it is the way his team plays that matters.

He felt like this during yesterday's match against Hannover 96, despite the fact that he'd managed to give his troops a rousing speech at half-time and introduce several tactical changes that helped them win the match. He also pretended to be perfectly happy with the result and the team's performance in the press conference later, but in reality he was deeply disappointed. Distracted during the post-match dinner in the players' lounge, Pep was concerned that he was failing to get his ideas through to the players. He was failing to help them give of their best.

He leaves immediately after morning training instead of staying to chat to his assistants as usual. After a quick lunch he shuts himself up in his hideaway, telling his wife: 'Sorry Cristina, I've got work to do.'

Cristina has been with him long enough not to need explanations. When he is like this – depressed, silent and brooding – it's because he blames himself for something. He isn't about to blame the Bayern players for their weak performances. He holds himself responsible for not managing to bring out their potential, for not finding the right words or exercises, for not putting them in the correct positions or providing the launch pad they need to express themselves. Pep is the son and grandson of a *paleta*, as it's called in Catalan. His father, Valentín, is a bricklayer in Santpedor, near Manresa, in central Catalonia. He taught his son to stand on his own two feet and take responsibility for his actions without blaming others.

Pep might be one of the most respected coaches in the world, in charge of one of the world's biggest clubs, but he is still a bricklayer's son and he takes responsibility for his own actions.

He spends six hours watching videos of Saturday's game and taking notes. He draws diagrams in his notebook, erases them and then starts to rethink his ideas. A bricklayer is a humble kind of builder. Pep goes over and over his problem all evening and then, at last, he sees the answer. He shouts: 'Maria! Màrius! Come quickly! I've got it!'

This is not the exultant 'Eureka!' of an inventor but the relieved shout of a student who feels he's ready for his exam, the satisfied cry of someone who has found the solution to the problem but knows that he still has to run it past his teachers.

Maria and Màrius are his teachers. Pep always tells them every detail of his matches and his kids love it. They are both fanatically interested in tactics and, what's more, never hold back if they think he is wrong. But tonight he gets the thumbs up. Full marks.

By 8am the following day the coach is already ensconced in his Säbener Strasse office with Manel Estiarte. The table is covered with paperwork and they're watching the Hannover match on the computer. There are loads of tactical formations drawn up on the whiteboards. Estiarte recalls that morning with a smile. 'That was one of Pep's 10 best moments. And this guy has had lots of wonderful moments. It was amazing.'

Guardiola is as high as a kite. Saturday's pessimism ('I'm not getting it right with the team') has turned into Monday's euphoria ('We've got it, we've got it!'). He explains his ideas, starting slowly at first and then speeding up to such an extent that he loses his guest in a confusion of gestures and details.

This is what he is suggesting, more or less: 'We keep Lahm in the midfield. That's not up for discussion. On either side of him, backing him up, Boateng and Dante, so that Lahm can make aggressive runs to break up the opposition. Bastian [Schweinsteiger] and Kroos in front as attacking midfielders and then we delineate the movements. Rafinha and Alaba are no longer full-backs at that point – they join the midfield. In principle they occupy space slightly infield, although they can move to help Robben and Ribéry on the touchlines if it's the right thing to do. When we are in possession we play vertically, building from the superiority in midfield which the addition of Rafinha and Alba has given us. If we lose the ball then we've all the right players located close to each other high up in the centre of the pitch: it'll be easy to win the ball back.' The formation looks like 3-4-2-1. In the line of three there are Dante, Boateng and Lahm. This is where the play begins again. Right now Lahm, the captain, is Bayern's best organising midfielder – the best at bringing the ball out. He knows how to open up the opponents' attacking line and find gaps; he knows precisely what to do in each instant. He plays with daring and opponents don't get the ball off him. The two full-backs are to join up with the two creative midfielders to make a cluster of four attacking players, but also the first line of defence to put the brakes on an opposition counter-attack should Bayern lose the ball. Because of his training, Alaba won't find it difficult to take up this role and thus Rafinha is the key component: if the Brazilian can function well in this plan then the idea will work. The line of two are Robben and Ribéry – with liberty to make runs inside or outside. If either of them moves inside, their full-back must take up the wide space to complement the movement. Then, up top, the single striker. Mandžukić – but in due course Müller, especially once any idea that he can play in midfield is put to bed.

The team talk on Monday 16th, the day before their Champions League debut, focuses solely on this 3-4-2-1. The players are called to Säbener Strasse's video room, which is laid out like a cinema, but Guardiola gets them on their feet and tells them to go outside to the terrace. He points to training pitch No.1, where there are four lines newly painted to delineate the central area of the pitch, like a giant extension of the Bayern penalty area. Later in the book we'll talk in greater detail about these lines.

'The only important thing about our game is what happens in those four lines,' Pep tells his men. 'Nothing else matters.'

They go back inside and Pep shows his players the video analysis of their U movement on the pitch. The images show that again and again they re-start the play from the back in a manner which is predictable and sterile, an innocuous movement of the ball from side to side. From Ribéry to Alaba, to Dante, on to Boateng, to Rafinha and then, finally, to Robben. The whole shape of the ball movement draws out a capital U. Sometimes Neuer is involved in that passing movement too, even Lahm at *pivote*. It is a horizontal trajectory which takes the team nowhere. The opponent can defend almost effortlessly because Bayern players simply don't try to break their lines.

'Gentlemen, this is *tiquitaca* and it is shit. We're not interested in this type of possession. It's totally meaningless. It's about passing for the sake of it. We need our central midfielder and our defenders to move out with an offensive mentality and break the opposition lines in order to push the whole team high up. The U needs to go.'

The 3-4-2-1 is now installed, flexible and intelligent, with the positioning of the two full-backs in line with the two attacking midfielders. These false attacking midfielders (the full-backs) are without doubt the biggest tactical advance of his first season at Bayern. The all-out war against *tiquitaca* – shuffling the ball about in meaningless possession – is also established.

CSKA Moscow will be the first victim of the new strategy the next night. It has been 511 days since Pep last heard the Champions League music and his first match back is a joy. Not only do Bayern beat the Moscow team 3-0 but they are playing fluid, aggressive football. They go on the offensive; the U and their sterile passing are things of the past. Lahm is in midfield again; Rafinha and Alaba do well in their new roles; Müller enjoys playing as second striker behind Mandžukić and Schweinsteiger has a few minutes game time to test out Kroos' position. What's more, their second goal comes from a move they had practised the previous day at training: from a wide free-kick Ribéry and Robben pretend to fall out over who will take it, almost bumping into each other as they both approach the ball but then suddenly the Dutchman whips it in to Mandžukić, who heads home unmarked. Even though he looks offside, the Russian defence has been bamboozled into dozing off.

Domènec Torrent and Hermann Gerland embrace Pep enthusiastically. His strategic ideas have worked. It is gratifying for the technical team to see their tactics converted into a goal and for Guardiola it is the first time in a match this year that he has felt that the team is moving in the right direction. Nobody has needed a half-time lecture to change the dynamic and his wingers have understood exactly what he wants. For the first time in six years the Champions League starts with the reigning champions winning their first match (the last time was when AC Milan beat Benfica 2-1 in 2007; all successive champions have drawn their first match.)

Months later writer Ronald Reng, author of *A Life Too Short* about the tragically premature death of goalkeeper Robert Enke, would tell me: 'They played brilliantly and were passing with such speed and fluidity that they made CSKA look like a Third Division team. They reminded me of Barça in 2009, but with Bayern's typical speed on the counter-attack and their ability to close down spaces when they lost the ball. That game was our first sighting of a team the likes of which we had never seen before in Germany.'

The whole playing philosophy is reinforced after the visit to Gelsenkirchen, and a cauldron of a stadium, to face Schalke 04. With the ball, Bayern are clearly playing 3-4-2-1 and when they lose it they defend in a 4-3-3. The team plays with much more fluidity. The forward three players are given freedom and they slash through Schalke both down the middle and out wide. Robben plays predominantly down the right wing and that allows Rafinha to move inside and do damage there. Down the left Ribéry and Alaba incessantly switch positions, one inside, one out.

When he looks back at this time Guardiola has good reason to smile. A week earlier he had been depressed, unable to find the right ingredients to make his team excel; now, seven days later, he has three wins under his belt, with the scores getting increasingly better (2-0 against Hannover; 3-0 against CSKA and 4-0 against Schalke). More importantly, they are well on the way to developing the balance their game requires. The idea of using full-backs as midfielders is bearing fruit. Everything has fallen into place.

Two hours earlier and a considerable distance away, Borussia Dortmund drew in Nuremberg. So, after the sixth league game of the season, the two great rivals are neck-and-neck with 16 points. The league is won or lost in those first eight games.

31

THE TREASURE MAP

Munich, September 18, 2013

GUARDIOLA HAS THE treasure map stored in his head. It's a secret map containing riddles and mysteries, a devious puzzle – dots which will be joined up as and when the mysteries which arise along the route are resolved. Contained in this map are all the questions and most of the answers. Some Pep will solve in public, others on the pitch. There are a few which are just in stasis for the time being, waiting for the right moment.

This might all seem trivial, but it assumes great importance in the life of the Catalan coach. It means that he knows that during the length of a particular career cycle (be that four months, a season or the entirety of a contract at a club) he will have to confront a series of decisions and tactical alterations – they are inevitable and related inherently to his personal football philosophy. For example, his first year at Barcelona had very little in common with his third. Here we are talking about tactical organisation, individual player movements within the team framework, or how the team interacted collectively.

Pep traces out a tactical business plan for each such cycle. It is kept inside his head, there is no written evidence. Take the formidable Bayern which he inherits from Heynckcs. Guardiola knows that there's only so much new software he can introduce into the existing hardware of this ultra-dominant team. If he overdoses on new ideas then he will probably overload, or collapse the whole system and surely some individual components. Thus he prepares by establishing a plan of how to roll out his ideas – a goal-related strategy which sets objectives to be achieved within a given time period. They are not milestones which are easy to explain in words, nor will they necessarily be pertinent if extrapolated for other teams, players or coaches. They are relevant to his personal way of understanding football. It's not even that he aims for his players to understand every single thing. He is well aware there are some players who have a high capacity for complex explanations, and others whose understanding will be more limited. He will have clear defining lines between those who will be given short, contained, partial information bytes and those who have the ability to see the big picture.

Pep will use quite different language from one category of players to another. That's not new to him. In fact, one of the great conflicts within sport is what type of language and communication coaches should use when they are trying to get technical messages across to their players. Sometimes the communication is sophisticated, sometimes very basic.

What's utterly vital is getting the means of communication, the content, the amount and the precise timing of every such conversation just right. Without that, a coach can't develop his tactical ideas adequately with his players. Guardiola faces a challenge in this respect. He is very agile and talented at drawing this personal treasure map, his business plan. He has terrific foresight in terms of knowing how much he can expect from a four-month cycle or a season and thus which innovations he'll need to store up for the next cycle, whenever that may be.

Going over his four years with Barça he will recall every single evolution he tried to roll out and also those which he would have applied if he had stayed with the Catalan club. Ask him about Bayern and he is more reserved; he'll explain only the short-term upgrades he intends to enforce. He'll clam up if you ask about the following season – even though he knows full well what he wants to try to achieve then, too.

Despite all this clarity of ideology it is very hard to transmit it successfully to his players. It's not so much a problem of the language, nor of finding the right football terminology. It is a problem of excess software. Sometimes he has so many things to say, he wants to reach such infinite detail that some players just can't follow it all. In such cases he can take time to realise that the player in question simply needs much less information, and in simpler form, too.

Let's take Franck Ribéry as an example. You could compare him to a 100m runner in terms of his characteristic comprehension and behavior. If you make the message sophisticated for Ribéry you are only complicating the progress of the desired evolution. Guardiola took months to find just the right way to pick and choose his words when explaining things to the player. From the first training session he asked the winger to move inside and play false 9. Pep is convinced that Ribéry can be doubly dangerous if he'll do the things he does on the wing, but around the edge of the box instead. There's no chalk line to limit you on one side and, logically, you have more space in which to search for openings and run at players. Pep is a firm believer that the Frenchman could make a big difference to the team down the middle, but Ribéry isn't particularly quick at picking up on the type of movements the coach is explaining. They are too sophisticated, too complex to assimilate quickly and Pep decides to put the whole thing off until an opportune moment arises, possibly months in the future.

The opposite example is Lahm, for whom you can make the message just as complex as you wish. Pep and he have dedicated many hours to such conversations. Not a training session goes by when they don't spend at least 15 minutes at the end talking about specific player movements or individual actions. That's when Pep steps back and gets into one of his favourite rituals – indicating where every individual player should be at any given moment with a symphony of gestures, his arms waving around. Who has got to cover whom; where should the *pivote* be; how should the central defender make a choice to attack the ball; how does the full-back on the side which is overloaded with opposition react. It demands great concentration just to recall what the original objective of the conversation was.

Every time I was present for one of these chats and Pep hypothesised these complex collective movements, I ended up lost. It's not easy following his vision. But Lahm always got it.

'When a club like Bayern calls you have to respond.' Guardiola prepares to greet a press pack of 247 journalists – the biggest number ever to attend such an event at the club – at his official announcement as Bayern Munich head coach. *Getty Images*

'Any team that has won four titles doesn't need much of an overhaul.' The images of Bayern's treble-winning players loom large over Guardiola in the home changing room at the Allianz Arena. *Getty Images*

Despite insisting that his squad did not need many new personnel, Guardiola's technical revolution meant a sharp learning curve for his players, who would have to adapt their traditional German style to a more possession-based approach. *Getty Images*

Guardiola surprised his new players by conversing with them in passable German during training sessions. 'Our language on the pitch is all about giving instructions,' he said. *Getty Images*

'I know how much this means to him, his first title. I also know about his old rivalry with Mourinho.' Franck Ribéry celebrates with Guardiola after his second-half strike against Jose Mourinho's Chelsea in the UEFA Super Cup in August 2013. The Frenchman dedicated his man-of-the-match award to his new boss. *Getty Images*

'Have you seen how well Lahm anticipates the next pass? How he turns and protects the ball? He can play on the wing or in the middle of the field.' Guardiola's conversion of Bayern captain Philipp Lahm from right-back to midfield linchpin was one of the foundations of their success *Getty Images*

Teenage midfielder Pierre-Emile Højbjerg was quickly identified by Guardiola as a prodigious talent and would go on to feature in the DFB-Pokal final in May after a traumatic season in which he lost his father. 'He's shown me how important it is to play without fear. Just to get on with playing whether you're up against Xabi Alonso or a complete amateur,' said Højbjerg. *Getty Images*

Guardiola quickly revolutionised Bayern's training methods, introducing tactical and positional work at the expense of hard running. The Catalan would frequently tease his players over their insistence on running. 'What purpose do these long runs have other than to hurt your back?' he would laugh. *Getty Images*

Pep stretches after a training session while chatting with the author. 'Pep is very fussy about his appearance,' writes Perarnau.

Guardiola chats with the author in his office. The Bayern boss gave Perarnau unprecedented access to the club throughout the 2013-14 season on the proviso that he did not write about what he saw until the campaign had ended.

Lorenzo Buenaventura (left), Bayern's head fitness coach, explains the team's physical preparation strategy to the author. 'He is trying to introduce new concepts to football and he likes to see it evolving year by year,' says Buenaventura of Guardiola.

'I'm trying to implement something that flies in the face of the culture here.' Pep explains the details of his game plan, the player positions, sequences and movements to his coaches before training.

Guardiola and his wife, Cristina, embrace Oktoberfest in Munich by dressing in traditional German costume. 'I don't have any problem with all that because what is important for the club is also important for me,' says Guardiola. 'At Barça I didn't do much of this kind of thing… each has its culture and its way of doing things.'

Guardiola's relationship with Arjen Robben would prove pivotal to his revolution at Bayern. 'I love this style of football because it reminds me a bit of the traditional Dutch game, the football Van Gaal used to play,' said Robben. *Getty Images*

Bastian Schweinsteiger scores in the 1-1 draw during Bayern's last 16 second-leg match against Arsenal in March 2014. 'With a 2-0 lead from the away game, it made no sense to take risks,' reflected Guardiola, who watched his side claim their place in the Champions League quarter-finals. *Getty Images*

Pep issues instructions to Franck Ribéry, Javi Martínez and Philipp Lahm during Bayern's Bundesliga match against Werder Bremen on April 2014. 'I want them to dig into that DNA, let themselves go, run, liberate themselves,' insists Guardiola. *Getty Images*

Manchester United's goalkeeper, David de Gea, is unable to save Arjen Robben's strike during the Champions League quarter-final second leg at the Allianz Arena. It was a tough evening for the home side who fell behind to Patrice Evra's strike and struggled to break United down, before emerging 3-1 winners on the night. 'What else did you expect? They're a brilliant team,' insisted Guardiola. *Getty Images*

Guardiola faced his old El Clásico nemesis Real Madrid in the 2014 Champions League semi-final. It would prove to be an unhappy reunion for the Catalan, who lost the first leg 1-0 and then changed tactics for the second leg at the behest of his players, only to go down 4-0. 'I got it totally wrong,' he admitted. *Getty Images*

Sergio Ramos scores Real Madrid's second goal during the Champions League semi-final second leg. Astonishingly, after a season of defensive solidity, Bayern conceded three of Madrid's four goals from set plays. *Getty Images*

A dejected Philipp Lahm looks on as Real Madrid's players celebrate their progression to the Champions League final. Guardiola's decision to move Lahm from his influential berth in midfield to right-back proved a serious tactical error against the Spaniards. *Getty Images*

Bayern secured the Bundesliga title with a record seven games still to play. It fulfilled Guardiola's stated ambition to put domestic superiority ahead of everything else in his first season, but also disrupted his team's momentum in the Champions League. *Getty Images*

Jérôme Boateng showers his manager with beer as they celebrate the Bundesliga title. 'I loved every minute of that shower because of what it symbolised: we are the champions. No mean feat!' said Guardiola. *Getty Images*

Pep holds aloft the Bundesliga trophy after Bayerns's home win over VfB Stuttgart. 'I particularly appreciate all the effort made by players … it has not been easy to come back from a treble-winning season and stay mentally or physically at peak,' said Guardiola. *Getty Images*

Seven days after lifting the Bundesliga, Arjen Robben celebrates scoring against Borussia Dortmund during the DFB Pokal final at Berlin's Olympiastadion. The 2-0 victory after extra-time is a tactical triumph for Guardiola, who employed a more conservative approach after learning lessons from the Champions League loss to Real Madrid. *Getty Images*

Guardiola is flung into the night sky in Berlin after victory in Berlin, mimicking the same celebration during his spell at Barcelona. *Getty Images*

'Ich liebe euch. Ich bin ein Münchener [I love you. I'm a Munich man now]'. Cradling the DFB-Pokal, Guardiola joins his team on the Munich town hall balcony at Marienplatz before addressing the fans. *Getty Images*

Bayern became the second team to follow a treble-winning season with a double, the other being PSV Eindhoven in 1987/8 and 1988/9. *Getty Images*

'We've won a lot and everyone is delighted because winning titles buys you the time you need to start building the future.' Season 2014-15 will bring a host of new challenges for Guardiola, both domestically and in Europe. *Getty Images*

32

'LAHM? HE'S AS FOOTBALL-INTELLIGENT AS INIESTA.'

Munich, September 25, 2013

THE CONCEPT OF using full-backs as midfielders, forming a line of four in the middle with the two attacking midfielders, had already been used frequently at Barcelona, albeit with variations. Pep had even started to talk about the idea at the end of some of the early training sessions with Bayern in Trentino, when he had only just arrived. He even hinted at it in a press conference: 'No question, Alaba could also play as a midfielder.' In reality he wasn't really thinking of Alaba in the middle of the pitch – rather as a full-back who would be pushed up to join the line of the existing midfielders. How did the idea arise? Well, it had been there in Pep's playing manual, just waiting for the right moment to have the dust shaken off.

Let's look at how Pep rolled the idea out to his squad. First he analysed the problem. Bayern were circulating the ball back and forwards in a passive U shape between the two wings, Ribéry and Robben, using the two centre-halves and both full-backs. Thus he rescued an idea which he had not been able to use during his four seasons at the Camp Nou. 'Every year at Barça,' he told me, 'we'd achieve new ways to evolve from what we'd already established, and the team was improving, but from the World Club Cup final onwards [they beat Neymar's Santos 4-0] it really wasn't easy to find a way forward with the same players. We had managed to play better than ever before and to find a way to move forward wasn't simple.'

One of the ideas he was developing in this era concerned the left-back (not the right, as Dani Alves is not exactly the model of tactical rigour).

'The tactical evolution which I'd envisaged at that time with Barça consisted of using the left-back to step forward and play as a second *pivote*. We already knew that the full-backs could move up as high as the *pivote* while he was bringing the ball out from the back, but without overlapping him until he'd already played the ball forward. The idea was to then leave the left-back paired with the *pivote* so that, if necessary, we could defend with a *doble pivote* system in midfield – even though the team didn't line up that way.'

He explained all this to us in pre-season. 'It's an idea I'm going to save up, perhaps use it in the future.'

Sunday, September 15, beaten and down in the dumps, but in solution-seeking mode, Guardiola reached for the idea and adapted it. Erasing some of the existing delineations, he reached the idea of a formation which seemed ideal: it wouldn't be the left-back who teamed up with the central midfielder but, instead, both full-backs, who would advance sufficiently to be in a line of four with the two attacking midfielders – a line which would be higher up the pitch than the *pivote*. Things suddenly clicked.

Ten days later they faced Hannover 96 once again, but this time in a one-off cup game. 'I prefer using this system in Germany, not Spain [where the Copa del Rey is played largely over two-legged ties], because every cup game is a final here. It's much higher risk but much more attractive like this. And it's positive for the players because 11 straight months of competition is a barbarity and we need to place emphasis on the quality of the matches we ask them to play, rather than augment the quantity of them.'

Mirko Slomko was Hannover coach at that time (by Christmas he would be out, replaced by Tayfun Korkut) and had previously commented that any German team could inflict the perfect counter-attack in less than 11 seconds. Pep disagreed. 'I think it's even quicker than Mirko says. This league is remarkable in terms of counter-attacks. In Spain there are great sides which hit you with good counters but I've never seen anywhere to equal the Bundesliga for the number of teams who can hit you with so many effective, massively quick counter-attacks.'

Bayern beat Hannover 4-1, notwithstanding a continuing irregularity in their play. They went ahead quickly and played with real aggression to ensure there was no chance of a counter-attack. But once they reached 2-0 they relaxed and conceded a number of dangerous chances from which the visitors might have scored.

Bayern had dozed off again and Pep was angry. The second half saw the usual reaction and they confirmed their passage to the quarter-finals with two more goals. 'In the first half we committed a novice error,' he explained. 'All the attacking passes we made were inside, instead of playing them wide. If you play the ball inside and Hannover nick the ball from you then – pam! – they've got a well-organised counter-attack on a plate. In the second half we corrected that.'

It was almost 100 days since Pep arrived at Bayern and the coach was willing to weigh things up. 'I'm happy. My German isn't great yet but my players give me loads of help with it. I still haven't learned to express myself that well, and get through to them easily, but they have a brilliant attitude towards training. I see all the details in my players which convince me that we are capable of playing really well. Those are the moments which make me really happy.'

In the corridor outside the Allianz Arena dressing room we talk to Rafinha, the Brazilian full-back who, with Lahm's move to central midfield, has become first choice at the back. He's constantly got a joke on the go and he refers to himself as a *canterano* (academy product) knowing that Pep just loves to play *canteranos* in his teams. Rafinha says: 'Pep explains himself pretty well in German and when he hits difficulties both Pizarro and I are there for him to translate from Spanish into German.'

One of the technical team comments: 'Rafinha is just about the most important member of the team right now. If he got injured we'd have to really conjure up a solution.'

That's how it is. Rafinha allows Lahm to play as organising midfielder, something which has been vital to the team's performance.

Rafinha's full of beans. 'How do you think I'm going to be with Pep? Enjoying life, that's how! Last year there were 11 players who got 50-plus games each, with the rest playing 15 or maybe 20 at best. Now things are much more shared around and it's logical that if you are playing more you're happier. It was time for change. Jupp was terrific and he got us playing well, but our opponents really got to know us and how we like to do things. Now we play a bit differently and that's a good thing. For the full-backs it's a big deal because we have permission to insert ourselves into an attacking move wherever it seems best to do. We can move inside, go outside, and we are allowed almost constant licence to attack.'

Guardiola is delighted with how Lahm is doing as Bayern's organising midfielder. 'He's played incredibly well in that position. I know that when all our players are fit Philipp could return to full-back but perhaps he'll remain as our *pivote*. He's a fabulous player.'

A few days later, during a training session behind closed doors, he'll add a few more details about his captain. 'Lahm is incredibly intelligent. He takes all the information in immediately. He's very quick, mentally, and he reads the game well in advance of things actually happening. He's as football-intelligent as Iniesta.'

Another player who constantly talks to Pep is Bastian Schweinsteiger. 'Pep's really clever, which makes training with him very interesting and enriching,' said Schweinsteiger. 'The language? Well, German is a very tough language for foreigners to learn, so when Pep began his time here by speaking in our language it was to his great merit. In a face-to-face conversation he communicates perfectly. Maybe when he's instructing a group it's a little tougher for him to manage it perfectly – it's not quite as clear as face-to-face.'

Pep has changed a great deal in the three months he's been in Munich. He has already given an interview to the club magazine. In the future he will do the same for Bayern's television station. He will attend, and enjoy, the famous Oktoberfest, he will be the star of an advert to promote the beer which sponsors Bayern (and he'll do it in *lederhosen*). In general he'll seem much more relaxed than at Barcelona, partly because the people around this club help that atmosphere a bit more than at the Camp Nou, but partly, also, because of his own personal evolution.

The objective over the next couple of weeks is that the team copes with Oktoberfest without difficulties. It's a time in the calendar which, traditionally, can hinder Bayern and their new coach wants to make sure that they get through it without messing up. He wants to remain competitive in the league, not giving an inch to Dortmund and to be ultra-firm in the Champions League. Right now they are progressing in the cup despite the midfield absences of Javi Martínez, Mario Götze and Thiago. Domènec Torrent, the assistant coach, makes it clear: 'Götze is fantastic. Pep's full of enthusiasm for him because he's technically excellent, he's agile and, above all, he's got the calm intelligence that we require. When he and Thiago play together they'll be absolutely formidable.'

33

'FOR 80 MINUTES WE PLAYED PERFECT FOOTBALL – THE BEST FOOTBALL I'VE SEEN IN MY LIFE.'

Manchester, October 2, 2013

A GRAND TOTAL of 94 consecutive passes across three minutes and 27 seconds was emblematic of the 'taking of Manchester' – a night when Bayern conquered the Etihad Stadium and Pep Guardiola was finally able to smile in satisfaction. Inevitably, Bayern's play in this 3-1 win at the home of Manchester City drew to mind that of Barça on that remarkable night in 2010 when they hammered Mourinho's Real Madrid 5-0 at the Camp Nou.

Those 94 passes marked a special moment in European football. The reigning champions were in an intimidating and formidable football stadium, City had bought notable reinforcements during the close season and their coach was the excellent Manuel Pellegrini – unbeaten at home until that point.

Everything went right for Bayern for 80 sweet minutes. They were almost perfect – it was the game in which Pep proved to himself that he could get a team to play with the agility and quality of Barcelona without actually having those *Azulgrana* players. All along, everyone, including Guardiola, had strenuously attempted to be clear that this wasn't supposed to be Barça 2.0.

Arjen Robben summed up the feelings of the dressing room: 'We have produced 80 fantastic minutes but we aren't Barcelona MkII. I understand the comparisons but we don't have players like Xavi or Messi and we are, basically, different. We just want to dominate games by dominating possession.'

Before speaking to the media, Guardiola is in the dressing room and takes time to phone a friend: 'Calm, and feet on the ground kiddo, but

... what an exhibition! What an *exhibition*!'

It is one of his all-time great moments as a coach. Bayern applied all the key things which Guardiola has been demanding: constantly looking to break into the penalty box, using possession aggressively, playing with constant fluidity and mobility.

The game will live with Guardiola forever because it is the first time 'his' Bayern has played in the manner he had imagined. Naturally, in front of the media he plays things down. 'We have lots to improve.'

The last 10 minutes were totally dominated by City who, with the introduction of Álvaro Negredo, turned around their timid game. They beat Neuer once, hit the bar and left the Bayern defence, from which Boateng was removed by a late red card, floundering.

Bayern had arrived in Manchester suffering from a certain anxiety. Their penultimate match, in the Bundesliga against Wolfsburg in Munich, had been complicated. Bayern won 1-0 but it was probably the trickiest day of the first three months of the season. Apart from a few minutes in the second half, when the team found its tempo and flooded forward in attack, Bayern were flat. Wolfsburg defended extraordinarily well and Pep couldn't find a way to break them down. His players shot at goal only 11 times. With such a test on the horizon, it did not inspire confidence.

For the game in Manchester, Müller is chosen ahead of Mandžukić as the central striker. Lahm is already the chosen central midfielder, the man around whom the team's play revolves. Schweinsteiger has materialised into the role of attacking midfielder and plays with much more fluidity than he did as the *pivote*. Partly that is because he's still not fully recovered from his ankle problems. There's a slight limp. That type of constant pain undermines a player, decreases his absolute confidence on the ball. If he's the attacking midfielder he can afford to be more expansive in his play, to be more creative and to take more risks. He's got less to fear should he lose the ball. The pieces are falling into place for Guardiola.

The Bayern goals come from their three forward players. Ribéry repeats his jink into space and fierce shot which squared the score against Chelsea in the Super Cup. Müller is terrific in losing Gael

Clichy, who is over-run, in order to hit the second, after which Bayern string together a succession of passes over 40 seconds which leaves their rival in tatters. After Kroos robs the ball back in the centre circle, Robben zig-zags around so much that he leaves Matija Nastasic sea-sick and scores with a right-foot shot.

Pellegrini's side has just whipped Manchester United 4-1, but for a while it's like Bayern are making them dance. The shielding players, the formidable Yaya Touré and Fernandinho, are tied up by Ribéry, Müller, Robben and Schweinsteiger over and over again. Along with Kroos, they give a recital in how to control possession, so disorientating the home players that the Spanish TV commentator, Gaby Ruiz, a specialist in German football, says: 'For the City players, what we are seeing is a little embarrassing. In fact, City are hauling up the white flag of surrender.'

Then, in the 65th minute, Bayern lay on a gigantic *rondo* – a succession of passes which astonishes the world of football for its precision, speed and duration. During nearly three-and-a-half minutes, Bayern put together 94 passes involving all 10 outfield players. The team pass the ball for more than 200 seconds during which time the Etihad Stadium goes silent and the City players pretty much surrender. During this succession of passes the ball bounces off the English defenders twice, it is deflected by Clichy once and Jesús Navas wins it back once, but manages to keep it in City's possession for only seven seconds before Lahm robs it back with a brilliant tackle. All in all it's so spectacular that that very night various YouTube users put all 3 minutes 27 seconds up on the internet – sometimes with accelerated motion and accompanied by the theme tune from The Benny Hill Show. The giant *rondo* sums up what Pep has been asking his players to learn how to do. The stats tell the story: Toni Kroos passes the ball 18 times in this one action, then Robben (14), Schweinsteiger (13), Ribéry (12), Rafinha (11) and Lahm (10). The defenders and centre-forward have been involved slightly less – Boateng (7 passes), Alaba (6), Müller (2), Dante (1). If the performances of the midfielders have been memorable (Kroos and Schweinsteiger both boast 95% pass accuracy), the exhibition laid on by Müller leaves Pep speechless. Even more than fulfilling the essence of the false 9, he has given a fluid forward display, flitting in and out of all the attacking positions and popping up where he is least expected.

Müller's performance is the microcosm of a triumph where the team has shown all of its variety: mixing the long and short games, moving possession at high speed, pressing very aggressively high up the pitch, winning the ball high up, winning the majority of tackles they attempt and completing almost all their passes. They pretty much kidnap the ball – and always in order to do damage to City. In fact it's an exhibition which blends the midfield play Pep has been demanding with an attack in the style of Heynckes' Bayern.

And the display unleashes a stream of praise. Michael Owen talks about his amazement at 'this great exhibition'. Franco Baresi, the former Milan and Italy captain, talks about 'a great level of super-positive football with everyone participating, and which is great fun to watch'. Rio Ferdinand says: 'It was hard to imagine the Bayern which won the treble improving but Pep is achieving just that.'

The then Bayern president, Uli Hoeness, glows: 'For 80 minutes we played perfect football – the best football I've seen in my life.'

During the post-match dinner which Bayern always lays on for players, coaches, sponsors and media, whether they win or lose, Kalle Rummenigge sums it all up in just a few words: 'A fiesta for the eyes.'

The applause of the City fans, who months later will see their team crowned Premier League champions, is the greatest compliment for a Bayern team which, despite that praise, has shown some deficiencies. They shoot on goal 20 times but continue to show this strange lack of clinical edge. They relax again, and once more show a lack of defensive organisation when they do so. During those last 10 minutes City are all over them and deserve more than just the goal which Negredo scores.

Despite these evident defects, Guardiola is exultant. He has 101 days under his belt at Bayern and they have been celebrated with a formidable exhibition. He is reminded that on the last two occasions

Bayern have won the Champions League (2001 and 2013) they have gone to England and beaten Premier League opponents. Perhaps this is a positive omen. Pep doesn't take much notice of the suggestion. 'The Bundesliga – the objective remains the Bundesliga,' he reiterates. The same phrase has been on his lips for the last month now: 'We have to get through the Oktoberfest without tripping up.'

It might appear a modest goal but he still thinks it's tough to get through September without Javi Martínez, Götze and Thiago, and with Schweinsteiger far from his best.

'We can win games via the defenders and the strikers but if you don't have midfielders then you just can't play well. I want us to survive these weeks and let's see whether we can get the injured guys back,' he argues. Then he returns to one of his basic precepts of football. 'I love midfielders, I'd love to have thousands of them in my team. Thankfully I have Lahm who, even though he may be the best full-back in the world, can play anywhere – he could be our striker if we asked him. In midfield he's just prodigious.'

From this point, Bayern begin to play the football their new coach wants. 'For everything to come off for us, the players need to run their legs off but to use the ball like they did when they were kids,' Pep explains. His players are bubbling with excitement.

Ribéry: 'They are little details but really important. Pep has boosted my confidence.'

Schweinsteiger: 'He's got incredible ideas.'

Robben: 'His arrival has been refreshing, a great stimulus. I'm 29 but under Pep I'm learning tactical concepts I'd never heard of before.'

Right now we can't be absolutely certain if the Etihad is the turning point of Bayern's entire season, but it is unquestionable that October 2, 2013 will forever be a red letter day for Guardiola. When they land back in Munich the coach reads a quote from Lothar Matthäus in a newspaper: '*Tiquitaca* has reached Bavaria.'

Pep throws it in the bin.

34

'IF ANYONE WOULD PREFER ME NOT TO MAKE THE DECISIONS, NO PROBLEM. YOU DECIDE WHO'S GOING TO PLAY.'

Munich, October 18, 2013

PEP'S TACTICAL TALK delays the start of training by half an hour. He usually gives three per match. The day before he tells his players how their opponents will attack. Then, on the morning of the match, he describes their offensive and defensive strategy and that evening, in the team hotel, he runs over his tactical plan for Bayern's attack.

It's Friday and his men have been scattered by international call-ups for 12 days. He wants to rally the troops and shake them out of relaxed mode. Players tend to come back from these training breaks in different states of mind. Those who have won with their national side will be feeling pretty high, whilst those on the losing side will be suffering. In any case, everyone's happy to be back together again and there is a good deal of joking around. The Säbener Strasse dressing room is jumping. Pep, however, wants concentration and serious focus. He's looking for the same level of intensity they produced in Manchester and Leverkusen.

Thirteen days previously they left Leverkusen with a 1-1 draw, the same result as the Freiburg game at the end of August. This time however, Bayern had put on a prodigious display of football, just like in Manchester, and Dortmund's defeat by Borussia Mönchengladbach propelled Guardiola's team to the top of the Bundesliga table for the first time in the championship. Week eight and Bayern were right on track.

Bayern had taken the euphoria from Europe-wide recognition for the manner of their victory in the Etihad Stadium to Leverkusen, and celebrated another festival of football three days later. This time they didn't win despite the overwhelming domination of their third-placed rivals. With the ball at their feet for 80% of the game, Bayern completed 90% of their passes accurately and had 27 shots at the redoubtable Bernd Leno's goal, 18 of which hit the target. But Pep's men managed to score just one goal, for a conversion rate of only 3.7%. Leverkusen produced a terrific series of blocks and saves and needed only three shots on target to score.

It has been two weeks since the midfield trio of Lahm, Kroos and Schweinsteiger were so impressive in Manchester and Leverkusen, and Guardiola wants everyone back on track. The international break was a parenthesis which he now wants closed as quickly as possible. His talk goes on for 35 minutes, twice as long as usual. The coach explains how tomorrow's opponents, Mainz 05, play, describes how he wants to deal with them and finishes up with some instructions about the importance of maintaining solidarity.

'We must all show respect to each other. I know that you all want to play but that just isn't possible and I have to choose the players I think are the most suitable. It doesn't mean that those of you who don't get a game and end up sitting on the bench are less able. It just means I haven't picked you this time. But if you run off to the press or your agents saying that you should have played, you will be showing a lack of respect – not for me, but for the guy who did get a game, your team-mate. If anyone would prefer me not to make the decisions, no problem. Be my guest. You get together and decide who's going to play and who's not.'

Clearly the aim of this unexpected and rather startling onslaught is not to incite a management takeover but to puncture some of the rather over-inflated egos which have returned from the fortnight's break. Pep wants to reactivate his men's all-for-one mentality. He wants to stop them slipping back into their comfort zone.

Today the giant screens have come out for the first time. Pep demanded them on his first day, back in June. He wanted to cover up training pitch No.1 so that the press and scouts from other clubs could not spy on them. We know only too well that the coach prefers to work quietly, in privacy, away from prying eyes. Aware that a nearby hill offers a bird's-eye view of Säbener Strasse, he asked that the club go a step further than just shutting the gates. He wanted one training pitch completely shielded from public view. After an unacceptable delay of four months (due to the initial difficulty in finding materials which would do the job effectively), today, at last, a thick grey screen, blocking off the whole pitch, is installed. The sun is blazing in the Munich sky and just as he finishes his talk, Pep and his assistants comment that the screen probably isn't sufficiently opaque to hide the training session completely. Anyone with their wits about them will still be able to see everything from the nearby mountain.

'Mountain? How do you say 'mountain' in German again? I can't remember.' Heinz Jünger, Säbener Strasse's head of security, who is always helpful and interested, intervenes to remind him that *berg* is the word Pep is looking for.

Bastian Schweinsteiger is the first player out onto the pitch. He is startled by the screen. Punching the air with both arms and shouting something unintelligible (or at least something we prefer to ignore) about the press, he indicates a distant point and says that someone is bound to turn up there and get a good shot, despite the screen's arrival. As it turns out the vice-captain is spot-on. A little later Markus Hörwick, the super-efficient communications director, rushes up to close a tiny crack through which a newspaper photographer is trying to grab an exclusive.

Pep is very quiet. He's thinking about tomorrow's game against Mainz. The training sessions immediately prior to a match are special for him. He will already have spent the previous evening shut up in his office going over his rival's strengths and weaknesses. He'll know what he needs to do to win. But he dislikes the international breaks because his players come back a little dazed. He wants to reinvigorate the team so that it starts to feel that their triumphant performances against Manchester City and Bayer Leverkusen took place only a couple of days ago, instead of the actual two weeks.

In the last few days he has asked for up-to-date stats on the team's finishing, which continues to disappoint. It's not something you can teach in training and in any case, high goal-scoring phases are just that: phases. However, greater focus and concentration will help a lot. He uses this afternoon's talk to praise his men for their excellent defending and points out that the team allowed Leverkusen only three meagre chances. He then goes on to remind them that of their 18 shots on target, they managed only one goal.

'Focus, gentlemen. If we are concentrating all the time we will get it right more often.'

Except for Thiago, who's in the gym working on his ankle and Shaqiri, who is out for six months with a muscle tear, Guardiola has his whole team back, although Javi Martínez has not joined them today. He is working at the foot of the nearby mountain with Thomas Wilhelmi, the fitness coach responsible for player recuperation. Javi will work for 80 minutes today, trying to recover his much-depleted fitness levels after a groin operation, dental surgery and a difficult start to the season. Lorenzo Buenaventura will lead the rest of the squad in an intense and demanding training session, carried out in the shadow of the grey screen installed by the club.

The evening goes very well. The ball flies across the grass in a possession drill; nine minutes continuously until they stop for the obligatory drinks break. The main course will be an 11-against-10 mini-match using the whole pitch and done at maximum intensity, followed by another game in a smaller part of the pitch. Philipp Lahm is, of course, in midfield.

Lahm has been the great discovery of European football this autumn, which is pretty amazing considering that this is a 30-year-old who has spent his whole career as a full-back. The coach's decision to move him into midfield and the captain's response on the pitch have created an unexpected revolution. Despite the fact that he has told the club magazine that Lahm will go back to being a full-back once the injured players are fit, Pep is very pleased with the outcome so far. 'If we achieve something this season, it will be because of that decision,' he repeats.

I ask Philipp Lahm's agent, Roman Grill, what he thought when Pep told Lahm to move into the midfield. 'To be honest, I thought: "Finally! A coach who can see the natural place for Philipp."

'Up until now German football has focused more on the physical aspects rather than the technical side of things. Coaches here have missed a lot of opportunities. I had been thinking for ages that Philipp would be perfect in that position.'

Roman Grill played for Bayern II as a *pivote* and coached at youth level. 'Obviously I have the advantage of having coached Philipp when he was a kid. I used him in the midfield then. His strongest qualities are his football intelligence and his ability to read a game tactically. That's why he should be in the centre. Philipp contributes a lot to the defensive organisation but also to the fluidity of the game. As a full-back he had this ability to spot his team-mate and make exactly the right pass which, in turn, helped the whole group. And in the midfield he has even more opportunity to use that skill.'

Today, just before the Bundesliga resumes, Guardiola is saying very little but doing a lot of thinking. His players have spent 10 days working with their national sides across the globe and it really bothers him. He's had some good news, however. Joachim Löw's decision to give Mario Götze 45 minutes for Germany has had a huge impact on Bayern's big signing, who is not yet 100% fit. Guardiola is also delighted that Löw chose to put Lahm in the midfield during the last 15 minutes of the Sweden game. Most coaches wouldn't have done it, but Löw has opted to be guided by the empirical evidence rather than his own ego. Apparently untroubled by people in the world of football suggesting that his decision was a weak attempt to copy Guardiola, the coach has put the interests of his team first.

Some nice words have also come Pep's way today from Barcelona, where Gerard Piqué has been talking to *So Foot* magazine. 'Guardiola is the best coach I have ever had. The guy used to work 24 hours a day.'

Pep, as human as the rest of us, is tickled pink by the compliment and marks the moment with one of his favourite sayings: 'These are the kinds of things that make sense of this job.'

By the afternoon, however, he is totally focused on Mainz and is much quieter, much more serious than usual. Until, that is, he opens his mouth – and lets rip. Completely silent during the 11-against-10 match, he then starts to shout at the top of his voice when they move to a smaller area of the pitch. He corrects positions and shouts for greater intensity as he spurs his men on. Guardiola really lets go. He whips his men up, demanding more and more. It's as if he's dealing with novice players who have never won anything, who have it all to do. He's squeezing everything out of them, extracting their juice like so many oranges. This is another time when the collective flow underpins every move. Robben flies like a man possessed, Ribéry runs non-stop, Götze's obviously loving every minute and Lahm and Kroos work together effortlessly without having to look at each other. On this warm October evening this is a Bayern possessed by some fantastical force until, that is, Ribéry falls to his knees, a victim of an accidental kick from Kirchhoff. He'll be out tomorrow. There's no doubt about it.

Despite this, Guardiola allows himself the first smile of the evening as he walks to the shower. He is more than happy to join in the teasing about *tiquitaca*, the term used to describe any playing style that involves more than three consecutive passes.

'I hate *tiquitaca*. I always will,' he says. 'I want nothing more to do with *tiquitaca*. *Tiquitaca* is a load of shit, a made-up term. It means passing the ball for the sake of passing, with no real aim and no aggression – nothing, nothing. I will not allow my brilliant players to fall for all that rubbish.'

35

'I'M NOT SAYING MY WAY IS BETTER. IT'S JUST MY WAY.'

Munich, October 20, 2013

THERE ARE FOUR white lines painted on the grass. Pep's four lines. They divide training pitch No.1 into five lanes, all more or less the same width. The two external lanes or corridors are formed by continuing the white line from the exterior (vertical) line of the penalty box all the way upfield to connect with the exterior line of the opposite penalty area. This leaves a big square of space between the horizontal edges of each penalty box. The two further white lines painted on the grass run from box to box, thus making the five vertical lanes of roughly similar width.

Despite the fact that it's almost the end of October, we are sweating under a fierce Mediterranean sun. Training finished an hour ago and anyone who played in the win against Mainz 05 stuck to a simple warm-up, some *rondos* followed by a few short joint-mobility exercises to assist in post-match recuperation. This lasted all of 20 minutes for Arjen Robben, but he has also completed his own daily workout in the gym. Thirty minutes before and after training the Dutch player warms up on the exercise bike, does some stretching and injury-prevention work. He finishes off with some abdominal and other specific muscle-building exercises, followed by some proprioceptive and isometric muscle-concentration work. Robben follows this routine every day without fail. It's an essential part of maintaining the powerful musculo-articular physique which makes him so explosive. He takes the same high-speed approach to his food, too, cutting up his steak at maximum velocity, just as if he were dribbling past an opponent and then chomping it down with similar haste. This need for speed is one of his virtues but it's also a weakness. He has, on occasion, injured himself by attempting some tricky move at this same explosive speed, so preventative work is vital.

The rest of yesterday's team are content just to do the standard post-match training: warm up, *rondos*, some loosening off and that's it until Tuesday. The team is showing signs of tiredness. They've had a lot of 'English weeks' (a game every three days) plus the international break, which inevitably leaves them in a bit of a mess. Players like Lahm are absolutely done-in by the constant demands made of them, although the damage is more mental than physical. However, there is no time to rest. In three days' time they play Viktoria Plzen in the Champions League and face Hertha in the Bundesliga three days after that. These matches are an important part of maintaining their momentum.

'They need a break,' says Pep. 'But right now I can't give them one. After the Hertha match we've a whole week before the next game and I'm going to give them two or three days of complete rest. I might give Lahm as many as four days. They need to go home and disconnect.'

Out on the Säbener Strasse pitch the men who were not in the line-up against Mainz or had just a few minutes that day play a game in two areas. Lorenzo Buenaventura has just sent Rafinha off to have his shower. 'I want to play but Lorenzo won't let me,' smiles the Brazilian as he walks through the dressing room. 'You're much too important Rafa!' the physical trainer tells him.

Götze, Kirchhoff, Alaba, Pizarro, Starke, Van Buyten and some of the youth-team players are playing. Javi Martínez has joined them as the wild card. 'Finally, I'm feeling good. I've no more pain in my groin and it makes such a difference.'

Pep is slowly putting his team back together, although it seems absurd to say that considering Shaqiri's muscle tear (six weeks out), the deep cut Dante took to his ankle against Mainz (two weeks out) and Ribéry's ankle injury. As well as Thiago's problems, of course.

The normal rules apply to the training match. Maximum intensity and aggression whilst the public, given access today for the Sunday session, look on in respectful silence. No matter how many times you witness it, the sight of 1000 fans, many of them children, sitting in absolute silence is actually quite unnerving for those of us with a Latin temperament, more used to shouting and cheering from the stands. However, the German supporters are happy to watch quietly for 90 minutes, no matter what happens on the pitch. All you can hear are Guardiola's instructions, the sound of Hermann Gerland's whistle as one exercise ends and the next starts, and the shouts of the players looking for a goal. These are the only sounds.

The fans get noisy only when Tiger Gerland blows his whistle to indicate the end of the session. Then the air is filled with frenzied shouts as the supporters clamour for their idols' autographs. This is another house rule: look after the public. No matter how tired the players are, they'll head over to the youngest supporters. It makes the fans' day and it's no surprise that quite a few of the players take a full 30 minutes to get to the showers. Today it will be Alaba and Javi Martínez's turn to share a little stardust with the hundreds of kids there. They then give everyone a thrill by jumping aboard the kitman's buggy (normally used to transport water bottles and isotonic drinks) and racing it up and down the pitch.

At midday Dante comes out of the medical room using crutches to keep one foot off the ground. Thiago has just completed another recuperation session and is obviously delighted to be working on the eliptical trainer. He also does some running on the Alter-G, an anti-gravity treadmill, which will help him regain mobility in his injured ankle. Thiago loves it. 'This machine is a real luxury. You start very gently, it's like you're running in lower gravity and the machine is calibrated so that it counters your body weight and you don't do damage to the ankle.'

Thiago is furious about the wasted months and all the missed opportunities. The team has reached cruising speed and he is still not yet on board. 'I'll be back soon. Real soon,' he insists, although we know that he has another long month ahead of him.

Javi Martínez, on the other hand, does see light at the end of his particular tunnel and next Saturday he's likely to get his first minutes in a league game. Pep's face lights up when he talks about first getting Javi back and then Götze, Schweinsteiger and Thiago: 'It has been a very tough start and there have been times when I've thought that we couldn't move forward because the whole structure in the middle of the pitch had broken down.'

Toni Kroos is the only true midfield player who has made it through from the start of the year. For one reason or another, Javi, Thiago, Schweinsteiger and Götze, over and above the positions Pep had in mind for each of them, have not been able to contribute much during these three-and-half months and he has had to patch up his midfield time and again. It looks like the dark times are at an end – just as problems start to appear in defence.

With Dante injured and Boateng banned, Bayern will have to play their next Champions League game, against Viktoria Plzen, with the veteran Van Buyten and Diego Contento partnered at the back. There is nothing else for it. Javi won't be fit in time and Kirchhoff has already shown time and again that defensive power is not his forte. Contento will be the other centre-half.

It has been such a lovely Sunday that we are treated to one of those moments when Guardiola relaxes enough to break with the etiquette of a working day and open up a bit. It all starts with Matthias Sammer, who turns up full of cheeky grins and starts a bit of leg pulling: 'Do me a favour. Go on YouTube and type in 'Guardiola goals'. You'll never guess what comes back! 404 not found!'

The joke's on Pep, but he roars with laughter as the sports director guffaws his way through a 10-minute anecdote about the coach's woeful goal-scoring record (in almost 400 matches with Barça, he managed 13 goals).

'Zero. A complete blank. Zero. Just look on YouTube and you'll see it keeps giving you an error message.'

Pep responds by addressing him as *Torpedo* Sammer, an allusion to *der Bomber der Nation*, Gerd Müller. This leads to general hilarity amongst the entire technical team and Pep relaxes and starts to talk.

'These guys are beasts. Their acceleration is super human. They all have this German talent for the sensational comeback. It's the spirit of Beckenbauer and the rest. I feel like I can achieve anything with these men. You could be in a Champions League semi-final two goals behind and these players would do it. It doesn't matter what it is, they can do it. They have such a special spirit.'

I ask if he had to give his men a bit of a tongue lashing yesterday at half-time when Mainz 05 were winning 1-0. After the break, goals from Robben, Müller (two) and Mandžukić turned the game around, so that Bayern came away with a win which put them at the top of the league by a single point. It is assistant coach Domènec Torrent who answers.

'Never. When things are going badly we'd never give them a hard time. We only do that when things are going well because that's when it can be useful. In the difficult moments all we do is change positions and adjust details. We'd never start telling them off. If the game's going badly you only earn credibility by correcting what they're doing rather than shouting about it.'

Pep is pleased with yesterday's comeback. Instead of shouting the odds, all he did was change part of the tactical framework, putting them in a 4-2-1-3, with Mario Götze in the No.10 position behind Mandžukić. This simple alteration played havoc with super-organised Mainz, coached by the excellent Thomas Tuchel, currently one of the most promising German coaches. 'The time we really struggled was against Wolfsburg. They were defending like champions and I really worried that we wouldn't get a win that day,' adds Pep. He then goes on to point out the strengths and weaknesses of his team. 'We've managed to staunch the blood-letting caused by counter-attacks. German teams are capable of executing a successful counter-attack in three seconds flat. We started out badly because Alaba wasn't moving forward to press his winger. He was moving back too quickly and gifting them too much space. But he managed to correct it very quickly.'

In contrast, bringing the ball out, avoiding the dull U-movement of the ball remains a work in progress. 'We aren't aggressive in how we do it. If the opponent holds off, you have to go after him, to create division in their lines.'

To make a notable difference in this Pep opts to have Lahm drop back in between the two centre-halves in order to gain the powerful, daring playing out from the back which is modelled on that of the Argentinian coach Ricardo La Volpe.

'Playing out with three men from the back is very useful because it conditions the response of your rival. Even if they press you, it'll be with the centre-forward and second striker, obliging them to move into a 4-4-2 shape and you can therefore over-run them by achieving superiority.'

Pep's vision of the game means that he looks for superiority in every area of the pitch. But he explains that tactical ideas are tools for the team to use, not the reverse.

'That's always the case. The players are the important people and you have to adapt the tactics to them. Look at my last year with Barça. We changed everything and started using a 3-4-3 system so that we could accommodate Cesc Fàbregas. And that was one hell of an era, with Messi and Cesc playing like a double No.10, with all the repertoire of skills they bring, hunting around the opposition penalty box whenever they smelled blood,' he explains.

Pep is also delighted with Arjen Robben's performance every time he puts the Dutchman on the left side of the attack. 'Maybe it's a coincidence but every time you put him on the left he scores a goal.' He's now thinking about using Robben in all areas of the attack.

Matthias Sammer has to leave, but before he does he grabs my arm and says quietly: 'It's not just that he's a genius, which he is. It's not just that he's a born winner, which he is. It's that, above all else, Pep is a great guy with a big heart. He's a lovely person.'

With Sammer gone the language of choice now switches to Catalan. There's Pep, Domènec Torrent and Cadiz-born Lorenzo Buenaventura, who understands Catalan perfectly. Manel Estiarte,

Carles Planchart and Miquel Soler (*Nanu* Soler holds the record for having played in the most Spanish first division teams: Espanyol, Barcelona, Atlético de Madrid, Sevilla, Real Madrid, Zaragoza and Mallorca – seven in total) are all still here, too.

'Pep, do you remember what I told you about crossing to the front post?' asks Soler.

'Yes, of course, we've been working on it. A cross from the side which fizzes in towards the near post is like a half-scored goal. If the striker running in to it doesn't score then there's a good chance the defender will put it in his own net. It's why you always need to try to clear a front-post cross before it reaches the front post. I said that to Contento today: "Always clear it before it reaches the goalmouth."'

After the diatribe he gets back to a perennial preoccupation – counter-attacks. 'They are very good, these German teams. When they leave free players high up the pitch they're excellent. I'm going to have to talk with Svetislav Pesic [Bayern's basketball coach] so he can explain to me why in basketball it's not feasible to defend with 4 v 5 and leave a free guy up the court. This fascinates me.'

Guardiola has kicked off his football boots but stands on the grass chatting as though this were an extended part of training. He gesticulates, jumps about and acts out the moves he refers to. 'I worry about giving my players too many tactical concepts. It just struck me one day. They were starting to collapse under the weight of it all, so I decided to be a bit more selective about what I share.'

He then contradicts himself as he leads us over to the four white lines on Pitch No.1 and launches into a formidable monologue, which lasts 20 long minutes and is impossible to reproduce here. He details exactly what each of his men do, going through the squad player by player. He moves across the pitch, through each of the demarcated lanes, crossing the dividing lines as he delivers his master class. He's a whirlwind of movement and gestures and much of what he says is just too difficult to follow without losing the thread of his whole explanation.

'We work in these five corridors and the fundamental thing is that the winger and the full-back from the same side of the team can't ever be in the same corridor. Depending on what position the central defender takes up, the full-back and the winger on his side must position themselves in one or other of the available lanes. The ideal is that if the centre-half is moving open, the full-back should be in the next door lane, inside, and the winger in the wide lane, outside, so that the ball can be passed directly to him. If you achieve a wide pass directly to the winger you've vaulted the whole of the enemy midfield, and if the ball is lost then the full-back is inside and can close down space immediately.

'It's trying to force the opposition's plans to change via your own actions. Our full-back comes inside, dragging their winger with him. If the winger doesn't follow him, you've got a free man. If it's their attacking midfielder who goes to cover him then our tracking midfielder isn't marked now, and so it goes.'

Pep breaks down one by one every step each player needs to take. Not just his own, but especially those required in relation to what a team-mate does. 'When we attack via a build-up from the back, the winger hangs wide and our centre-forward must do that, too, to drag his centre-half with him. That space down the middle is created so that our attacking midfielder or full-back can take advantage. If our full-back starts wide, the striker also copies that move, in which case it's our winger (operating down the channel or corridor inside the furthest wide one) who attacks the opened-up space.'

These lanes are the instruments with which the orchestra will co-ordinate their movements but the overall aim, as always, is to disorganise their opponents. 'We have to shake up our rivals' organisational structure. Always. That's our objective.'

In order to do this, Pep wants to establish superiority in the central area. 'I want a lot of players inside, in fact that's where most of them should be. Most coaches want the opposite. They want most of their men on the outside. I'm not saying my way is better. It's just my way.'

Having presented his impassioned master class, Pep is now starving. 'Ok, after all that talking I'm going to go and get my family and find us a nice terrace to have lunch.'

The coach's family have adapted brilliantly to Munich and the three kids are happy. If they struggled a bit with English in New York, their current fluency means they are now all top of their respective classes.

As he leaves the sports ground on his way to Wettersteinplatz metro stop, Miquel Soler wonders: 'Will Pep be able to keep this up for more than three years? I really doubt it. The guy uses up so much energy. He lives everything at 1000 miles an hour. I think the same thing will happen here as happened in Barça. He'll be exhausted after three or four years and he'll have to take another break. Then he'll be off to England and more of the same. He just can't keep this momentum up.'

36

'DIEGO! I LOVE YOU!'

Munich, October 24, 2013

'IT'S ABOUT COMPETING well even when you're not in great shape,' Lorenzo Buenaventura tells us.

Bayern aren't in great shape as we approach the end of October. There are two reasons for this: injuries and new concepts. But they *are* winning matches.

Sometimes the final score speaks of complete domination, such as the 5-0 win against Viktoria Plzen in the Champions League, or the 3-0 win against Augsburg in the Bundesliga. At other times (3-2 at Hertha and a 2-1 win away to Hoffenheim) Bayern struggle through the first half as if trying to digest a heavy meal. Pep accepts there is a problem. 'We tend to play well in the second half of matches in the Allianz Arena but the first half is always much tougher.'

His players are assimilating the new concepts well but putting them into practice is another matter entirely, and the high rate of injuries is slowing down this process even further. If it is not Ribéry it's Dante; when Shaqiri is fit, suddenly Kroos or Robben develop a problem. The team is in constant flux and it's impossible to achieve any kind of stability.

Pep might get two vital players like Götze and Javi Martínez back in the fold, but he then has to part with a crucial team member like Bastian Schweinsteiger, whose performance has dipped because of the unbearable pain in his ankle. He needs an operation.

Guardiola continues to find imaginative solutions. They play in the Champions League with Diego Contento in central defence. It's an experiment – against Viktoria Plzen they used four full-backs: Rafinha, Contento, Alaba and Lahm.

The coach is not complaining. He knows that coping with unforeseen events and problematic situations is all part of the job. He's pleased with his players although not entirely satisfied.

'My objective is to get the best out of these men. I don't like the way we play in the first half. It's the only thing that really worries me. I want people enjoying it from the first minute, not the 46th. We have to play better. Much, much better.'

Improving their game will remain an obsession for the rest of the season. The league table paints a more positive picture than Pep. Bayern are top, one point ahead of Borussia Dortmund, and have only one point less than this time last year, when Heynckes' men were basking in the praise being heaped upon them, but Manel Estiarte dismisses any attempt to draw comparisons. 'It's not about that. There's no point in making comparisons. We just have to get on with the job.'

If anyone ever feels tempted to relax a little, even for a second, Estiarte is always there to remind him that there are no guarantees and that success only comes from hard work, day in day out. Manel's is the voice of moderation. He's the one who gives them a boost in the difficult times and who pierces the moments of euphoria with reminders that they have everything still to fight for. If this team doesn't triumph in the end, it certainly won't be for lack of effort. Even Gennaro Gattuso, the former AC Milan player who was a formidable midfielder in his day, is pretty taken aback by what he sees at Säbener Strasse: 'Do they always train this hard? They're like machines.'

Pep doesn't let up, even in training sessions. The morning after thrashing Viktoria Plzen 5-0, he's out on the grass going through his routine of gestures, instructions and orders, all delivered at maximum volume.

Everyone knows what to expect at work. The day immediately after a match the starting players do some *rondos* (in which Neuer and Müller count the touches and compete mercilessly) followed by joint mobility and recuperation exercises. Meanwhile, anyone who was a substitute is nose to the grindstone, toiling away as if every chance in the box, every cross, every shot might determine his place in the first team. In fact, that's exactly what's happening. In Pep's eyes it's not star quality or status that gets you a game. Every man has to earn his spot by sweating it out every day on the pitch. Even in a training session for second-choice players, he's here, in the middle of the action, shouting, yelling, pushing them on.

By the end of October the team has already completed 107 training sessions and there has been a resulting shift in terms of the players' grasp of Pep's concepts. They're starting to understand his football language, although they are still not consistently repeating the level of performance they showed in Manchester.

Fitness coach Lorenzo Buenaventura confirms that they are assimilating the new concepts well. 'Pep deals with new concepts by introducing them from the warm-up, the simplest passing exercises onwards. Today he'll share a few details and then give them some more tomorrow. The day after that he'll talk about how to choose what angle the body is at to receive a pass, then, next time, how to take the ball on the move, followed by how to practise passing off your weaker foot. Little by little the players start to understand and assimilate and very soon it's coming easily and they're putting it all together at speed.'

They reached peak performance in Manchester and have suffered a dip in the subsequent weeks. Guardiola agrees with Buenaventura but resists any attempt to draw definitive conclusions. 'We're only at the end of October. There's a long way to go yet!'

We watch today's training session. Buenaventura talks us through it. 'We never start off with the same warm-up. What do I mean by never? I mean that we have the next exercise planned and that dictates the kind of warm-up we do. Normally we start with some joint mobility exercises, then some injury prevention and after that, how to find space. That usually lasts between six and 10 minutes depending on the next exercise. At other times we prefer to start off with joint mobility work and a game of some sort. Or the focus might be on injury prevention, which we work on in the gym twice a week, usually after matches. We always do it post-match – a mix of mobility, stretching, balance and strength. Then when it's one-on-one, each player works on mobility, but in relation to what the last type of injury problem he's had, or whether he is lacking balance or strength or whatever.'

After that they do the *rondos*, an absolute imperative for Guardiola. There won't be a single session this year when they miss them out. 'Once the warm-up is finished the *rondos* are next. Apart from once per week – either the day before a game or the morning training session before a game – when we are a bit less demanding. The *rondos* normally put emphasis on one aspect or another: one day on who should play in the middle of the circle, then on how to win the ball back, another on how to support the man with the ball, or on how to find the third-man movement.'

Some days we make it more fun and we'll have seven-against-two or eight-against-two, but usually we do small *rondos* of four-against-one or, most often, five-against-two or six-against-two.' The *rondo* is the cornerstone of Pep's football philosophy and that's why he dedicates 20 minutes a day to it.

Next there is circuit work. Today this is high intensity strength-resistance conditioning. Buenaventura has designed an attacking exercise, emphasising strength, which meets Pep's demands. 'He has asked me to ensure that the drill ends up with the wide man centring for a shot and that there are movements within the drill which attack space and divide the opposition defence lines. He gives me general instructions and then I organise all the drill movements accordingly. I'm looking for strength conditioning in tackling and running, reaction strength [jumping] and elasticity of strength [repeated jumps]. All of it is designed to emphasise how the coach wants the team to attack in terms of movements. Normally it's two or three drills with the ball and a few others just focusing on strength alone.

'I'll make them do strength-strength-strength-anticipation; or strength-strength-strength-pass; strength-strength-strength-one-two and shot. Then I make their return to set up for the next drill a part of the process. I'll ask them to show intensity then too, not to relax, and they get very short amounts of time to recuperate. The aim is that they complete three in a row – doing one every 30-40 seconds. That's how you hit the level of work required. Maximum intensity at all times. Today every player has completed a circuit which has ended with them shooting at goal a total of 18 times. It's always a balance of physical/tactical/technical.'

The session has two further goals. The first is positional play, another fundamental in Pep's manual. There are two teams within a rectangle of 20 x 12 metres – each team has seven men, but there are four players who act as wild cards (any of them can link with the team which has the ball and occasionally he'll augment this to five of them). The idea is that a team tries to pass the ball as often as possible without being intercepted by the other side. Whoever has the ball tries to open up the pitch, even given the restrictive dimensions. The other team presses at maximum intensity and intelligence. Each player needs to know how to show for the ball, what first touch to give, where to move to, how best to circulate it rapidly – although usually with one touch.

It's a drill which demands total concentration, technical excellence, vision in the pass and domination of the entire repertoire of football skills in every single movement. Sometimes Pep will ask players like Thiago, Kroos, Schweinsteiger and Lahm to use two touches, while everyone else is obliged to play one-touch. That makes the exercise still more complex. Today Pep has ordered three of these drills – five minutes each with two minutes of recuperation between them. While the exercise is going on there is not a second's relaxation and Pep constantly corrects them as they do it. Without question we are watching the most valuable of all the drills, one which requires prodigious choreography given the diminished space in which they're working.

There are no smiles, jokes, relaxation, ribbing – instead a constant and obsessive search for the right movement, the correct space, individual and team. And then there are what Pep christens the *tac-tac* moments. It's the sound to which Säbener Strasse constantly echoes when the ball moves not only cleanly but at lightning speed, back and forwards in the space of split seconds between two phenomenal players like Lahm and Thiago, or Kroos and Thiago. Two passes within split seconds of each other, but again and again and again.

It's now time for the last activity of the session. The forwards are released and, as always, they spend 20 minutes bombarding Neuer and Starke's goal. Müller, Mandžukić and Kroos always take part, Pizarro also often joins in but today, Robben, who almost never practices shots on goal, has also joined the group.

The coach has also planned an activity for the defenders. It's all about controlling counter-attacks. Rafinha, Van Buyten, Contento and Alaba line up. Javi Martínez, Højbjerg and four youth-team players attack, putting passes between the centre-half and his full-back, looking for the winger to be able to reach the pass and cross. The idea is to force the central defender to cover the front post of the goal. For 30 minutes Pep shouts instructions until it's obvious the defenders have won. Pep is ecstatic with Diego Contento. 'Bravo Diego! I love you!' he says in English and trots off to practise corners with his forwards. Kroos, Ribéry and Robben will be here for another 20 minutes, practising throw-ins while adding in some of the details which Pep has asked for. 'If you do these things before taking the throw, you'll begin to make the opposing defence drop their guard and their concentration. Even if it's only for a tenth of a second it can make the difference between them covering or losing the guy they are supposed to be marking.'

37

'PUT THE GOOD PLAYERS IN THE MIDFIELD. THAT'S MY IDEA AND I'M GOING TO STICK WITH IT.'

Dortmund, November 23, 2013

GÖTZE AND THIAGO are warming up in a hallway in Westfalen Stadion (aka Signal Iduna Park). The second half of a decisive league game has just started and the score is nil-nil. It's freezing outside and it's a very different experience from that evening last summer when Borussia won the German Super Cup in suffocating, Mediterranean temperatures. Guardiola initially hoped not to have to subject Mario Götze to the fury of Signal Iduna Park's 'Sudkürve', the single most frenzied football stand in the world, where 25,000 chanting fans leap about for the full 90 minutes. Now that he's a Bayern player, Götze is not well received at his former club, but Guardiola needs him out there. It's time to go on the attack.

Dortmund have come to the game four points behind (they lost last week in Wolfsburg) and with a long injury list which has left them with the following line-up: Weidenfeller; Grosskreutz, Friedrich, Sokratis, Durm; Bender, Sahin; Blaszczykowski, Mkhitaryan, Reus; Lewandowski.

Bayern also have a few problems and several players missing, the most crucial being Ribéry. Mandžukić also has problems. He twisted his ankle during last night's final training exercise and the club doctor has had to do give him a pain-killing injection. However, he won't last more than 50 minutes. Guardiola's strategy for the first half is to take control by wearing Dortmund down. His line-up is: Neuer; Rafinha, Boateng, Dante, Alaba; Lahm, Kroos, Javi Martínez; Müller, Mandžukić, Robben.

This is the first time Guardiola has used Javi Martínez as an attacking midfielder. He puts him high up the pitch in an attempt to short-circuit

Nuri Sahin, the instigator of most of Borussia's counter-attacks. Most of the first half has only two facets. Dortmund try to force Bayern to play out from the back via only Rafinha and Alaba, the outside corridors of Pep's divided pitch, and Bayern try to use Martínez to prevent Dortmund springing counter-attacks via Nuri Sahin. 'If you give him space to run, you're dead,' Pep told him yesterday.

The teams are pretty evenly matched in the first half, although the home side is slightly more dangerous and Lewandowski has two good shots on target, matched by two from Mandžukić.

Bayern get stagnated, even wide. They are obliged to use the width because of the network of pressing coverage Dortmund mount across the entire midfield. On the other hand, Dortmund can't produce their usual greased-lightning fluidity in counter-attacks. It's a stalemate.

Pep still has a thorn in his side from the Super Cup defeat. He also has a dream. A dream he prefers not to share, even with his friends and allies. But Xavier Sala i Martín, a close and trusted friend, is willing to tell me: 'Pep wants to prove to himself that he is capable of playing like Barça, without the players that he had there. I'm not talking in terms of playing style. It's more about his ability to dominate matches, to be the superior team, the one with total authority over the game. He wants to show that he can build another, equally dominant team.'

He's already achieved this in the big games. In Manchester, against City, Bayern were by far the dominant side. And it's just about to happen again. In Dortmund. Bayern are in a strong position at half-time. With the score 0-0, Pep's team could emerge from this battleground with their four-point lead intact, but the coach wants more. He tells Götze and Thiago to start warming up.

Lorenzo Buenaventura supervises the two players plus Van Buyten as they go through their warm-up exercises in a long corridor inside the stadium. Van Buyten has to stoop as he works because the ceiling is so low. He is almost two metres tall. The coach wants the two little guys on the pitch even though they are not yet fully fit. Thiago hasn't played a single minute since he was injured at the end of August, but Pep knows he can buy his team the time they need to deactivate

Dortmund and propel Bayern forward. The little guys are going to win the match for him.

After 56 minutes Götze comes on for Mandžukić and Signal Iduna Park greets their former player with jeers and boos. Pep is using Götze as a false No.9 for the first time, instead of an attacking midfielder or No.10. It's as if he reserves this move for the big games, like he did in 2009 with Messi against Real Madrid. Guardiola makes his move at a crucial moment. He also starts to make radical changes to Bayern's midfield. Up until now Pep has always ensured that the midfield is crowded with his men, but during the first half he's been particularly cautious and conservative. Rafinha and Alaba have stayed wide, protecting their wings, instead of edging inside to help Lahm at *pivote*. Given that Javi Martínez is pitted right up against Sahin, Lahm has really only two passing options when bringing the ball out: to the two full-backs, wide, or to Kroos. It is a total contradiction of Pep's rule in the previous months that Lahm, when playing out from the back, must have numerous passing options at all times.

Guardiola reflects on his strategy at half-time and decides to make some changes. The conservative approach is not suiting his men. He comes up with the following conclusions: Götze and Thiago start warming up; Javi Martínez moves to *pivote*, Lahm plays as an attacking midfielder. The full-backs both now have permission to come off the touchline and help in the middle of midfield.

Domènec Torrent turns to us and winks: 'We could have settled for 0-0, but at half-time Pep told them to go out and win. That's when he brought out the big guns.'

With Götze playing in the midst of all the fury coming from the Dortmund stands, Bayern make a major shift and move to a six-man midfield: Rafinha, Alaba, Martínez at *pivote*, Lahm and Kroos, and Götze at false 9. Suddenly the game has changed colour. All we're seeing is red.

Bayern are suddenly free of the asphyxiation in midfield, the passing game cranks up and the wide men, Müller and Robben, get the ball over and over again, whilst Götze is making the game a living nightmare for Dortmund's centre-halves, Sokratis and Friedrich, who can't decide whether to go after him or stay in the defensive zone. These are the same horrors Real Madrid's Metzelder and Cannavaro endured a few years back when Messi unveiled his new role.

Guardiola smells blood and decides to up the ante. He wants Thiago to shake things up a bit. Pep is tense, but it's the kind of tension he experiences on the big occasions. He talks at a hundred miles an hour, giving non-stop instructions. He doesn't want Thiago taking any risks and tells him: 'Thiago, Thiago, for God's sake, don't lose the ball. Don't lose it! Control, control, lots of control. Don't take any risks. Not even one risky pass. Control, control. Look for your team-mate and make the easy pass. It doesn't matter if you don't get many touches, we just need the game to keep flowing but, above all, *don't lose it*. For God's sake don't take any risks Thiago!'

Thiago is about to go on and, standing here in front of the bench, he appears oblivious to the uproar in the stadium. He emits a sense of detached calm which amazes his coach and says with a smile: 'Don't worry, *míster*, don't worry. You don't need to worry about me. I know what I'm doing.' And he runs out to play.

It has been exactly three months since he injured himself against Nuremberg and he hasn't played a minute since August 24. But it doesn't matter. He runs on to the pitch and immediately takes over. Javi Martínez moves to centre-half, Lahm to *pivote* and Thiago takes up the attacking, creative responsibility in front of him. Bayern return to the same form they achieved in Manchester a month before. Just two minutes after Thiago has come on, this domination results in a goal from Götze. For the first time since 2009 (under Van Gaal), Bayern are winning away at their biggest rivals.

Rarely has Pep managed an ongoing match with quite the level of prescience he shows now. He notices that Klopp has changed his tactics in the hope of getting the equaliser. Marco Reus almost does it, and forces Neuer into a tremendous, lunging save. Guardiola responds by reorganising his men for the fourth time. Van Buyten comes on for Rafinha, Javi Martínez goes back to *pivote* and Lahm is now right-back. Bayern are going all-out to destroy Dortmund, but this time they're using their rival's weapon of choice: the counter-attack. Thiago spots Robben in space and breaks all the Dortmund defensive lines with a fabulous diagonal pass. Robben tucks it away. Two minutes later, Martínez surges forward down the middle, feeds Robben, Lahm overlaps and his pass lets Müller make it 3-0.

It's a glorious victory for Bayern, whose victory leaves Dortmund seven points behind, a gap which will be impossible to close. But what they take away from the game above all else is renewed confidence in their own ability. The players now believe that their performance in Manchester was no one-off, but the result of all the organisational work they've been doing. And the coach's idea to put his best men in the midfield has been vindicated. It's a winning formula.

This is a Bayern in constant flux, capable of adapting and changing throughout a match. The two outstanding examples of this are Lahm and Javi Martínez. The captain has begun at *pivote*, moved to attacking midfield and ended up at right-back. Within 90 minutes, the Spaniard has been in attacking midfield, *pivote*, centre-half and then back again to offensive midfield.

The next day, back in Munich, Pep is still talking about Dortmund's counter-attacking: 'They're like a steamroller, unstoppable. There are other teams who counter-attack brilliantly, like Madrid for example, but Dortmund are unique. I've never seen anything like it. They are completely focused for 90 minutes, waiting for you to mess up a pass so that they can set their sprinters on you. I must take some time to really study this and see if there's any way to stop them. They're just so good.'

Pep has received lots of praise for the way he altered the course of the match from the bench by changing players and positions. 'Praise doesn't matter. The important people are the players. These are super-talented guys who are up for anything. They are all working to improve and make progress.'

Their triumph in Dortmund has strengthened his convictions. 'Put the good players in the midfield. That's my idea and I'm going to stick with it. Get the good players inside, hold on to the ball and be aggressive. It's vital not to keep rethinking it. This is definitely the line to follow.'

The dream Xavier Sala i Martín described to us has been realised once again in Dortmund. Pep's Bayern have shown superiority and domination on the pitch, just as they did in Manchester and Leverkusen. These are Pep's most private aspirations. Guardiola wants to build another team whose domination of the game will act as a bulwark against the vagaries of fate. But he wants to do it with a different kind of player. He's clear that he doesn't want Bayern's game to mimic the way Barça played while he was in charge. However, he does want Bayern to dominate with the same authority. 'Götze and Thiago,' he says. 'That's how we have to play. Not like in the first half. We'll certainly score if we bombard the box, but we won't be dominating the game. The way we dominate is by putting the best players inside and leaving the two wingers really wide on the touchlines. In the middle we'll have Thiago, Toni, Lahm, Götze, Alaba … and if we lose, it won't matter. I'll go home happy just the same knowing that I did what I believe is right.'

38

'THE WHOLE CLUB HAS TOLD ME THAT FRANCK WANTS TO TALK TO ME. I WANT TO TALK TO HIM, TOO.'

Munich, December 2, 2013

PHILIPP LAHM SUFFERED his first ever muscle injury on November 27 in Moscow with the temperature at five degrees below zero on a slippery, snow-covered pitch. The 12-hour journey had been a nightmare. Flight delays plus a monumental Moscow traffic jam had combined to make Bayern so late arriving at their hotel that they had not been able to train the day before the Champions League match against CSKA. Instead, Lorenzo Buenaventura had to improvise a stretching and joint mobility session on the carpet in one of the hotel's lounges.

Pep's team put on an efficient, workmanlike performance although understandably, given the conditions, there was no trace of star quality on display. The resulting 3-1 victory, their fifth win in five games, was a record and, added to five wins under Heynckes, meant that Bayern had won 10 consecutive Champions League matches.

However, the match took its toll on Lahm, leaving him with the first non-impact muscle injury of his career – at the age of 30. It wasn't a particularly serious injury and cost him only a couple of weeks, but it was a new and uncomfortable experience for the captain, who took a while to accept it. Although Lahm was given the all-clear from the medics relatively quickly, the player himself would not feel fully fit until well into December. It was one more problem for Guardiola, who had not yet been able to use all his first-choice midfielders in the same team. Now he was losing his key man, the one who draws in and then divides the opposition, the cornerstone around which he had built his team. If Pep had to choose a dream team from all the players he had managed at

Barcelona and Bayern then, without doubt, Philipp Lahm would be on that list. 'If we win anything this season it will because of what we did with Lahm. Putting him in the midfield meant that all the pieces fell into place.'

They left Moscow in the early hours of the morning and, despite being given a rest day on Thursday, looked exhausted at Friday's training session. Pep broke with tradition and told them to take it easy. 'I've done hundreds of journeys in my life, all over the world, but that was the toughest yet. My worst journey ever,' said Thiago.

Carles Planchart, who is in charge of the team's analysts, agreed: 'I'm completely destroyed. My body, everything – imagine how the players are feeling.'

Despite their exhaustion, a small group of players topped the training session off with a series of 60-metre sprints. Guardiola laughed. 'Look at them. What a bunch! I give them an easy time because they're on their knees and then they decide to go for a run. And they've dragged Thiago into it. Thiago!'

Manel Estiarte was also amused. 'Leave them to it. They need to sort their heads out. They need it mentally and anything that's good for you mentally must be good for your legs.'

Later, Thiago explained why it had been important for him to join his team-mates in their impromptu running session. 'I came here to become German, to toughen up and become more resilient.'

The coach is pleased with his signing. 'Thiago has a huge heart. He may not yet be fully fit but he just gobbles up the pitch. Javi, too. He's not in perfect shape because he couldn't do a proper pre-season, but he's managing everything I ask him to do.'

The tiredness was still evident the following day when Bayern played Eintracht Braunschweig, winning 2-0. The players were clearly enjoying being back with their families after a few days away and that evening the Allianz Arena's players' restaurant looked more like a crèche, given the number of kids who had come along to spend time with their dads. Even Guardiola's parents had decided to join the family in Munich for a few days. Their son ate with them but continued to talk football, this time focusing on goals conceded. 'You see, we've played 14 games and we've only conceded seven goals. It's brilliant. Just seven. That makes one goal every two games. That's what I like best about what we're doing.'

By 10 o'clock on Sunday morning he was already planning the DFB-Pokal match against Augsburg the following Wednesday. 'It's absolutely vital. If we get through this round and beat Bremen on Saturday in the league, by Christmas we'll be in much better shape than I could have hoped for. We'll still be alive in all three competitions. I just want to get to the start of the winter break still seven points ahead. Dortmund and Leverkusen are playing on Saturday, so let's hope Leverkusen win. Hoeness reckons a draw would be better but, for my money, Dortmund are the more dangerous of the two.'

Bayern have managed to retain the league title only once in the last 10 years, in season 2005-06. Pep wants to change this and is determined to bring success and consistency to the club. For the first time this season he voiced his intentions – up until now it has been his assistants who have talked about this. 'The objective this year is to win the Bundesliga. It's a much tougher league here than people think. For example, yesterday Braunschweig didn't even open up when they were losing 2-0. Their striker spent more time marking our attacking midfielder than trying to score. He never stopped running. Often it's easier against the big sides because they don't park the bus, or at least do so less, and they play with pride. They try to demonstrate their power and potential. The centre-forward for a big club doesn't try to kill the game like this.'

This took the conversation on to Real Madrid: 'Madrid are playing brilliantly. They have three terrific players at the front and Xabi Alonso is there to support them. But if you play them you know that Cristiano Ronaldo won't go deep to defend and that gives you options. He'll try to stay high up and be ready to get behind your back when the ball is played through.'

Inevitably we got on to the Champions League: 'Forget about it, forget about it. We need to think about the Bundesliga. Nobody's won the Champions League twice in a row.' He zipped up his anorak and said: 'I'm going down to the pitch. I want to visualise tomorrow's exercises.'

Since it was a rest day, only the injured players were working. Lorenzo Buenaventura and Domènec Torrent were on pitch No.1, putting out the cones and the markings for the next day's tactical exercises. Everyone knows it inside out, having done it so many times already, but Guardiola had one of his brainwaves, one of his special intuitions. 'I had an idea last night and I want to go down to the pitch to visualise the exercise. I want to see it clearly in my head and work out the best way to do it on Tuesday. If it goes well I may go with three at the back and one of the full-backs high up – but I need to see if we can do it well first.'

And so he dedicated an hour of his day off to running up and down the pitch, the one with the four painted lines, working out if he could convey his ideas well enough so that his men would understand how to play three at the back and still bring the ball out effectively, the way he imagined. As he worked with Torrent and Buenaventura, two of Pep's basic characteristics were in evidence: intuition and hard work. The most imaginative tactical ideas cannot be implemented effectively unless you practise them repeatedly on the pitch.

On December 1, Pep was in the second phase of a five-stage process. Stage one – the idea – had come to him the day before and he was now at stage two – double checking how to implement it. The following day he would practise it with the players and by Wednesday morning would have decided whether to use it in the game, depending on what had happened in training. All being well we would then see the culmination of the process – stage five – on the pitch in Augsburg.

'Augsburg is a final,' he said.

It's midday on December 2, a bright, freezing Munich Monday and Pep is showing all the signs of a high-pressure week.

'Augsburg is a final,' he repeats. 'We'll play without a safety net, full-on for the 90 minutes. But if we win we'll be in the quarter-finals and then those guys [the players] will see that the final is within their grasp, only two matches away and that's when they'll be unstoppable.'

Ribéry has trained as if his life depended on it – 90 minutes under the guidance of Thomas Wilhelmi, the recuperation coach who has programmed a session of short, explosive exercises to be repeated over and over. His face is showing his exhaustion after such a heavy session but he's delighted with his fitness levels. 'I want a word with Pep,' Ribéry tells Estiarte. 'And I think that he wants to talk to me, too.'

Ribéry is still out of breath and he chokes out the words as he puffs and pants. He has hardly taken a break in the whole 90 minutes – sprints followed by jumping exercises, quick turns and drills which push him up against a marker who will liberally use elbows in the Frenchman's ribs to see whether he's fully fit or not.

'I'm fine, Manel, I'm fine. I can play. I must talk to Pep and I know he wants to talk to me,' he says again. 'Don't worry Franck,' Estiarte responds, 'I'll tell Pep and he'll have a word when he gets back from the other training pitch.'

Bayern had beaten Dortmund without Ribéry, something which would have been considered Mission Impossible at the start of the season. Then they'd had a good win in Moscow. Robben and Götze are both playing well and Ribéry doesn't want to miss any more games: 'Tell him I want to talk to him. I'm fine Manel. I'm good to go.'

Augsburg is a final and Thiago has also come down to Säbener Strasse. After three months out, he has played three games in a week and by Sunday he couldn't move. He's come down to do a bit of stretching, some Pilates moves and a few recovery exercises. He wants to be on top form for Wednesday. 'Augsburg is a final,' he says. 'Everything in the 90 minutes, a one-off opportunity – it's a final for us.'

At this rate, Guardiola will have nothing to do in terms of motivating his men. They all understand the importance of the game. Fredi Binder, the head physio, approaches Estiarte.

'Manel, Ribéry wants to talk to Pep.'

'I know, I know,' Estiarte says again.

'He's in great shape and has no problems at all,' says Binder. 'The only pain he's felt is when we gave him a muscle-relaxing injection a couple of days ago. Wilhelmi really hammered him in the ribs and he's in perfect shape. Remember – he wants to talk to Pep.'

Pep arrives to review the layout of the pitch for tomorrow and Estiarte tells him about Ribéry: 'I know Manel, I know. The whole club has told me that Franck wants to talk to me. I want to talk to him, too. I want to see how he is. I'd be delighted to have him playing against Augsburg. The only thing is that Franck is not the kind of guy you can put on the bench. He needs to start. I need to see him and decide then. Augsburg is a final, Manel, a final. It's almost a final.'

39

'EXCELLENCE IS LIKE A BUBBLE. YOU CAN LOOK FOR IT, BUT IT ONLY APPEARS FROM TIME TO TIME.'

Munich, December 5, 2013

RIBÉRY RETURNED TO the team for the Augsburg game, but Pep was to lose Robben that same day. The Dutch player has been in sublime form and in the third minute of the match scored his 13th goal of the season, thereby equalling his total for all of season 2012/13. He has also matched his total assists for last season, with 10.

Robben's career at Bayern, as well as at Chelsea and Real Madrid, had been marred by repeated injuries. His most productive season was 2009-10, his first in Munich, when he managed 37 games, with 23 goals and eight assists. Now, at the beginning of December, he has 20 games, 13 goals and 10 assists and looks set for an outstanding season. And all of this at the age of 30.

Then, 15 minutes into the match, a hard tackle by goalkeeper Marwin Hitz cuts short 2013 for Robben, leaving him with a badly damaged knee joint. He would not be back until January 24. 'It's a huge loss,' said Guardiola. 'He was playing exceptionally well.'

Injury prevention has become a central part of Robben's regime. The bad experiences down the years have taught him to look after himself and he has introduced a daily regime of a 30-minute personal exercise plan focusing on strength, balance and core work to protect his back muscles as well as his abductors and hamstrings. This is followed by a post-training 30-minute routine of joint mobility work and stretching. This preventative work is the key to achieving and maintaining consistent fitness levels for the player.

The DFB-Pokal match in Augsburg was just as intense as Guardiola had predicted, although he decided against employing the tactic of bringing the ball out from the back using three men, given that the practice drills the previous day hadn't gone that well. Assuming that this rival would press aggressively and high, he opted for Thiago in the *pivote* role, thereby prioritising Bayern's ability to circulate the ball fluidly.

In the space of only five months, Pep had used six organising midfielders: Lahm, Schweinsteiger, Kroos, Javi Martínez, Thiago and Kirchhoff, which gives you some idea of the impact injuries had had on the team.

In the team talk in the hotel Pep asked his defenders and midfielders to aggressively attack Augsburg's first line of pressure. He wanted them to avoid shifting the ball from side to side, the dreaded U shape, and instructed them to use possession daringly. In the event, his men were not able to comply fully with his instructions, although Robben's goal gifted them an early advantage. Whilst the opposition pressed relentlessly, Ribéry managed a full 30 minutes and Müller lived up to everyone's expectations by delivering a *Müller*: one of those scruffy kinds of goals, almost an accident, which only he seems capable of producing. On this occasion, the goal seemed to come off some part of his back.

Guardiola was still dissatisfied. 'We're not playing well, not at all. We're getting good results and I'm happy with the players, but we're not playing as well as we should be. I need all my men back and then we need to start improving. I want to understand exactly what this team requires in order to realise their potential because so far we haven't played brilliantly.'

At the moment Paul Breitner is more optimistic than anyone else. 'I actually expected the players to take far longer to understand Guardiola's ideas – far, far longer. But they're taking it all in, no problem. Okay, at the moment we're not playing as brilliantly as we did a few weeks ago in Manchester and Leverkusen, but you don't succeed in the German league or the Champions League by playing brilliantly. Victory comes through hard work. And this team personifies both qualities: they play brilliant football and they know what hard work means. Look at yesterday's game in Augsburg and the one in Moscow or any of our matches over the last few weeks. Hard graft, that's the thing that matters, much more than brilliance. If you have a team of artisans who know how to work hard and who understand that you'll have moments of superb football and other times when it's just a matter of slogging away, well that's the perfect combination. That's what makes the difference. That is what defines the character of a team and this Bayern, under this coach, has enormous character. There's no doubt in my mind that we are going to do great things in the next three, four, five years.'

As always after a game, Guardiola is totally fired up. On the one hand what he's seen in the last match has generated a wave of new ideas which are surging around in his head. On the other hand he needs to start dissecting his next opponent and working out the best way to attack, defend and win the game.

'It's costing a lot for our *pivote* to break through the offensive pressing line if the rival strings five guys across the middle of the pitch. That's why I put Thiago at *pivote* for half an hour, even though it's not his main speciality. As a player he's brave and daring in his thinking – even if this means he can be caught losing possession. Now I'm going to spend time talking things through with Javi, working out how to break through this opposition line of five men in the middle of the pitch via inside channels, but also about how to give the impression of overloading one side of our move forward, only to then switch to the other, now under-defended wing. If you can do that, you disrupt the rival and make them turn and run back. Then you've achieved your objective. What's more, I'll tell you this: instead of the defenders moving the ball about in that damned U shape, I'd much rather they tried a long, diagonal pass because if the ball is lost like that it's much easier to win it back.'

Guardiola is well aware that he is demanding a lot from whoever is in the midfield. 'I know, I know, there are very few players in the world with the ability to break the line of pressing with an inside pass. Busquets, Xabi Alonso, Lahm – look what Lahm did for our first goal in Dortmund. He was superb. He fooled his marker, dragged him out of position and broke their pressing line by sending the ball to the opposite side of the pitch. Højbjerg is also very good at it, but obviously he's still very young. And I'll tell you something else: I was good at it, too. Why do you think I lasted so long at Barça? It wasn't for my speed, or my muscle power, or my headers, or my goals, obviously.' And he bursts out laughing.

Pep has been reading Barcelona defender Gerard Piqué's comments that there are more and more teams who want to play open, possession-based football. 'I hope Piqué's right. That's exactly what I want to see. Let the others all play out from the back, because then we can rob the ball off them! But, I'm afraid, the norm is that they close ranks at the back with four defenders and two defensive midfielders and look to release their four quick guys on the counter. They lob the ball over the top of Thiago or Kroos and, if we aren't in position, we're lost. That's why we can't launch the ball and look to go up and support it, because that will leave Thiago and Kroos running up and down the pitch the whole time. We need to go step by step, all of us in unison. Lose the ball and – pam! – we win it back quickly because our positional play has us all tightly linked.'

Pep has exactly two days to prepare for the Werder Bremen match, less time than he really needs. Usually he likes to have two-and-a-half days to analyse his opponents. He watches their games and works out how to attack them. He then prepares his three team talks. Given that they generally have two matches a week, Pep has time to plan only for the next game, although his assistants always provide him with a basic summary of their last encounter, which the coach studies into the small hours of the night.

Before immersing himself in his plan for Werder Bremen, he'll spend some time with Javi Martínez at the end of morning training, going over the problems with the U and the need for more boldness. He'll also take time out to have that tactical talk with Ribéry, postponed a few months ago when he realised that he needed to go a bit more slowly with the Frenchman. Today the pair sit down and study footage of a false No.9. Pep wants to convince the player that he can play in this zone, not necessarily permanently but certainly for a few minutes every game. He needs him to understand that he can do exactly the same as he does on the wing, only with no exterior line to restrict him. In the middle he'll be able to move with total freedom.

Pep is determined about this. He has no intention of changing Ribéry, forcing him to move from the wing to the centre of the pitch, but he does want him to develop the ability to move to the centre for short bursts. He is convinced that it will be a useful extension to the Frenchman's repertoire as well as a qualitative leap forward for the whole team.

I suggest to Guardiola that this would be one more step in his quest for constant improvement, the pursuit of excellence, but he laughs. 'Excellence! And what exactly is excellence? Excellence is like a bubble. You can look for it as much as you like, but it only appears from time to time. Okay, you have to be ready, you have to be in the right place when it does come along.'

40

'MISTAKES COME WHEN YOU RELAX.'

Munich, December 14, 2013

IN THE NORTH of Germany, Hurricane Xaver was whipping up winds of 90 miles per hour and the resulting downpour was close to bringing the Werder Bremen match to a halt. In the Weserstadion, Franck Ribéry dropped in and out of the central attacking position, as per the instructions he received two days previously, and with shattering results. The Frenchman played superbly and was a lethal part of Bremen's worst-ever home defeat – 7-0.

Bayern played with five midfielders (Rafinha, Kroos, Thiago, Götze and Alaba), with the three forwards taking on very different roles: Müller played wide, like a winger, but with licence to make constant diagonal runs infield; Mandžukić started centrally but repeatedly drifted wide left, leaving the centre-forward position wide open; and Ribéry dropped in to combine with the midfielders, effectively performing like a false 9. This constant movement, change of position and combination play demolished their opponents and drew this comment from Pep Guardiola: 'This is the first time we've played a great match using my definition of positional play.

'I'd like to thank my players for what they have done. It's an honour to be their coach.'

The then president Uli Hoeness was quick to highlight one of the coach's main qualities: 'This is incredible. Whoever's playing, they play well, but Pep always wants to correct something.'

It was a thrilling experience and for Pep, there were two particularly spectacular moments in the match. The opening goal came from Ribéry's cross to the front post. Alaba and Mandžukić powered towards the cross like hungry wolves as Werder defender Lukimya put the ball in his own net. It reminded Pep of Miguel Soler's phrase: 'A hard, low cross towards the front post is like a goal half scored.'

The second stand-out moment for Guardiola was the sixth goal, created by Ribéry. The Frenchman started it by taking a corner and ended up tucking the goal away himself. This apparently impossible sequence of events was in fact a set-piece Bayern had practised repeatedly in training. Ribéry passed it hard and low to Pizarro, who held it up just about on the vertical edge of the six-yard box. Alaba had been outside the box but sprinted in, beyond Pizarro and the Chilean flicked the ball back to him. Alaba was now on the touchline and immediately cut it back to Ribéry, who had run in unmarked from the corner spot, to score. An exceptional goal, created in seven seconds and scored by the guy who began it at the corner flag.

Bayern were euphoric and the technical team was particularly satisfied, having just seen the results of their strategic planning, the hours of analysis and experimentation they had put in.

The match marked Guardiola's 200th win in 274 official games across his time with Barcelona and Bayern. As Bayern coach he had now also beaten a Bundesliga record, having avoided defeat in his first 15 matches (a record he would continue to extend). And there was more good news awaiting Pep: Bayer Leverkusen had won 1-0 at Dortmund, which meant that Jürgen Klopp's side were now trailing the champions by 10 points. Bayern were on cloud nine.

It was left to Manuel Pellegrini to bring them crashing back down to earth.

Guardiola gets irritated by errors made on the pitch, but he is willing to forgive them. Although he is less permissive in private than he might appear in public, he accepts that mistakes do happen. He was a player himself and remembers the many times he messed up in his playing days. However, he is infuriated if he believes a player is moving down a gear because he thinks it's already in the bag. Guardiola holds dear the belief that you have to earn everything in sport with daily effort and concentration. No wonder his passion is excited by footballers like Mascherano and Iniesta at Barcelona or Lahm and Neuer at Bayern. None of them drops their concentration in any game.

One evening, dining at the Allianz Arena, Pep joined us to watch an unusual video which I had filmed from the main stand of the stadium. It focused exclusively on Neuer as Bayern incessantly attacked, over and again, at the other end of the pitch.

In the film you could only see Neuer, with brief appearances from Dante and Boateng, because Bayern were exercising almost total control of the game. The opposition were pinned back in their own area, but Neuer followed every single move as if he were involved in them, even though the action was 60 metres or more away. Not once did he lose focus as he moved around his area, and outside it, in unison with his team – constantly trying to preview where the play might result in a gap in the Bayern structure, which might need him to intervene. Guardiola was knocked out by it. 'Manuel is unique, just unique.'

As if still propelled by the Bremen hurricane, Bayern hit the ground running against Manchester City in the Allianz. Ribéry was at false 9 again, Mandžukić had been allowed to drop wide as regularly as he wanted and Müller was pegged to the right wing. Behind them Thiago, Kroos and Götze stroked the ball about at high tempo, joined by Lahm at right-back. With 11 minutes gone Müller and Götze had made it 2-0 and another demolition was on the cards. Bayern were en route to six straight Champions League wins in the group stage, something no reigning champion had managed since the competition replaced the old European Cup in 1992/3.

Then it happened. Bayern started to rest on their laurels. The chances had been flooding in and their domination had been overwhelming. Pep's players were taking victory for granted.

'Mistakes come when you relax, if you lose focus when you pass the ball, or receive it, or press for it. It's when you think everything's done,' Pep explained later.

Boateng watched the ball go into the box without intervening;

Dante bundled James Milner over in the box when the Englishman had already let the ball get away from him. And finally, at the hour mark, Boateng topped a grim night by failing to clear an easy ball in the box. These three errors allowed City three goals past Neuer, who until then hadn't let one in for five consecutive matches.

In fact, since joining Bayern, Neuer had never conceded three goals in the same game.

Pep responded by taking a large gulp of water from his bottle and turning to Torrent and Gerland, seated beside him, who reminded him that if City scored one more then they, not Bayern, would top the group. This was significant in that it would mean losing the advantage of playing away first in the next round. Bayern would also have to face a group winner, probably one of the great European clubs. Pep paused momentarily then, with 10 minutes left, called Müller over to the touchline to give him very firm instructions. 'Kill the game Thomas, get them to kill it off like this – they mustn't score again.'

From the moment City scored their third, Bayern had looked groggy, incapable of recovering their normal level of play. Pep decided to protect Bayern's position in the group.

The big surprise wasn't that Bayern closed the game down but that City didn't accelerate. Nobody in the English club – not the coach, not his technical staff, nor their sports director – realised that a fourth goal would make them group winners. After the match, they admitted as much (as a result of the final standings, City would draw Barcelona in the last 16 and lose 4-1 over two legs).

Bayern's Catalan coach was offended more by the manner of the defeat, by the fact that his players relaxed. Matthias Sammer, who two months previously had rocked the club with his demands that the players abandon their comfort zone, was still more irritated than Pep. But neither of them acknowledged this in public.

Both men know that the big rows usually come after a victory. After a defeat – calm. Publicly Pep commented: 'Congratulations to City for their great win. Now and again you lose a game. I want to congratulate my players for winning the group and hope that they now realise how difficult it can be playing in Europe. Of course they have the right to have an off day every now and again. We've got more work to do.'

Nor, over the next few days, would Pep talk to them about the defeat, leaving his players to reflect on what had happened and why. Having observed the way they absorb new tactical concepts he had concluded that, sometimes, less is more. Better, also, to teach the lessons from this defeat at exactly the right moment.

Four days later, on December 14, Bayern play their last match of the year at the Allianz. Hamburg are sent home with a 3-1 defeat in a game which, once more, stands out for the connection between Thiago and Götze, which has gone from strength to strength. Dortmund draw at Hoffenheim and Leverkusen lose at home to Eintracht Frankfurt, meaning that Bayern now head to Marrakech with a seven-point advantage at the top of the table – ahead of Bayer Leverkusen and 12 ahead of Dortmund. It is a decisive distance unimaginable to Pep only two months previously.

Bayern will go to Marrakech in search of one more trophy: the Club World Cup. En route to the airport, Guardiola sums up the year. Bayern have played 33 Bundesliga matches in 2013, winning 30, drawing three for a historic record of 93 points. Heynckes managed 17 of them, drawing once, Pep the rest, 14 wins and two draws. The new man's first 16 games are unbeaten for 44 points with 42 goals for and only eight against.

The Hamburg win means Bayern are 41 games unbeaten in the league (35 wins and six draws) and that's it for home games until 2014. There's a sense of invincibility in the air. Naturally, Pep is not of that mind.

'We've a lot to improve – a *lot*.'

41

'HERE WE ARE AGAIN. ANOTHER FINAL.'

Marrakech, December 21, 2013

WHAT SURPRISED GUARDIOLA most was the festive atmosphere in the streets of Marrakech. 'People had come from miles around. It reminded me of Barcelona the day we won the Champions League. There were thousands and thousands of people out and it was a real struggle getting to the hotel.'

Pep had attended the semi-final between Raja Casablanca and Atlético Mineiro with a few members of his technical team. They were all surprised by the score. The Moroccan team defeated Ronaldinho and company with two breathtaking counter-attacks of Bundesliga quality.

Hoping to avoid the triumphant crowds who were certain to flood the streets, Pep and his party left early, six minutes before the end. Just in time, as it turned out, because thousands of fans were already pouring into the centre of Marrakech to celebrate their victory. Raja had made it to the final of the Club World Cup and were about to go up against the mighty Bayern, who, the day before, in Agadir, had scored all three of their goals against Marcello Lippi's Guangzhou Evergrande in an explosive seven-minute period.

In the bus en route from Agadir to Marrakech, Manel Estiarte didn't have a lot to say except: 'Here we are again. Another final.' It would be Guardiola's 15th final and his eighth in international competition. He had been defeated in only two: by Jose Mourinho's Real Madrid in extra-time of the 2011 Copa del Rey and by Jürgen Klopp's Borussia Dortmund in the 2013 German Super Cup. His record suggested that, as long as his team made it to a final, there was a far better than even chance they'd win.

And so it proves. They dance rings round Raja and after 20 minutes they lead 2-0 through goals from Dante and Thiago. Pep's men look so comfortable out on the pitch and change position so frequently that, at times, their game evokes Barcelona's performance against Santos in the same competition in 2011. That day the Brazilian side's coach swore that Guardiola had played with a 3-7-0. Without going quite that far, the German champions have certainly varied their formation, switching seamlessly at times from a 3-1-6-0 to a 3-2-5-0, given that Müller has once again performed fluidly, certainly not occupying the traditional centre-forward position. Pep has asked them to play three at the back and bring the ball out with courage and panache – the system he practised at the beginning of the month but didn't use at Augsburg.

Lorenzo Buenaventura tells us more about Pep's approach: 'Sometimes Pep will spend 10 minutes of the team talk explaining exactly what they have to do. Then, once he's given them this in-depth tutorial, he'll say, "Okay lads, forget everything I've just said and do this instead..."' [Buenaventura cracks up laughing here]. 'He teaches the lesson but only he knows when it's the right time to actually apply it.'

Having won the Intercontinental Cup in 1976 and 2001, Bayern's win in Marrakech represents their third world title and gives Guardiola, champion in 2009, 2011 and 2013, his 16th trophy from the 22 he has contested as a coach. He won 14 out of a possible 19 with Barcelona, two out of three so far with Bayern, plus (let's not forget), the Third Division title with Barça B. Pep has lifted the World Club Cup with two different clubs (until now only Carlos Bianchi held this honour). What's more, he has also won all of the international finals he has contested: two Champions Leagues, three European Super Cups and three World Club Cups.

2013 has indeed been a prodigious year for Bayern. Under Jupp Heynckes they had won the three most-coveted trophies: the Bundesliga, the DFB-Pokal and the Champions League. Guardiola has now added the European Super Cup and the World Club Cup. Only their defeat in Dortmund has prevented them from achieving a clean sweep. The Munich club is now firmly established as the dominant power in football, although high expectations will bring unprecedented levels of pressure in 2014.

Pep celebrates his victory with close friends, among them the economist Xavier Sala i Martín, and the filmmaker David Trueba, who used Pep's dad, Valentí Guardiola, in his film *Living is Easy with Eyes Closed*, which triumphed at the annual Spanish cinema awards. They all travel to Barcelona in a private jet.

Pep has now entered a new phase and anything that he wins in 2014 will be completely unrelated to Heynckes' success. All Bayern's trophies from now on will be the fruit of Pep's own work.

If for the rest of Bayern, the year had been one of unimaginable success (with five trophies and only three defeats in 12 months), for Pep there was still room for improvement. There had been a lack of consistency in his six months in charge, notwithstanding the sublime moments. The team had also suffered an epidemic of injury problems which had prevented him from fully implementing his ideas. In other words, despite his outstanding results so far (just two defeats in 29 matches) Pep is still not satisfied. As he travels home, already relaxing into holiday mode, he is straightforward about his ambitions. 'We have to play better. Much, much better.'

PART FOUR

THE LEAGUE IN MARCH

*'People are very open-minded about new things
– as long as they're exactly like the old ones.'*
CHARLES KETTERING

42

'IN SIX MONTHS HERE PEP HAS TRIED MORE THINGS THAN IN FOUR YEARS AT BARÇA.'

Doha, January 12, 2014

'PEP'S CHANGING BAYERN and Germany's changing Pep.'

Lorenzo Buenaventura isn't referring to the couple of kilos which Pep has put on over the Christmas holidays. As he is introducing his DNA to Bayern, he is also going through a metamorphosis. Physically he appears to be just the same guy who landed in Munich last June, but life in Germany has had a powerful influence on his character.

Pep feels free and happy in Germany. He gets a huge amount of affection and support from the club which, in the case of the president, Hoeness, has developed into a firm friendship. Such a contrast from the sour relations over two years with the former Barcelona president Sandro Rosell.

The way Bayern support him is remarkable. Pep is less in charge than he was at Barcelona. Here he's just the coach, but instead of making him feel uncomfortable, this 'lesser' role has been a liberation. His friend, Xavier Sala i Martín, puts it like this: 'The burnout factor for Pep in Munich is less than at Barcelona because there he had to step into roles which shouldn't really have been his, due to the lack of leadership there. There were moments when he seemed almost to be the president of Catalunya, the coach of FC Barcelona and the club spokesman. He had to fight accusations of doping, battle Mourinho and deal with UEFA. His work in Munich is much more normal.'

Pep loves his players' immediate pre-disposition to hard work, the care with which Markus Hörwick prepares the press conferences, the minute detail to which team delegate Kathleen Krüger dedicates herself, the affability with which Hermann Gerland is teaching him about the variety of characteristics the Bundesliga exhibits, the outright passion of Matthias Sammer...

Germany is moulding Pep, who now seems more open, more serene, more disposed to new initiatives with every passing day. He's not just conceding interviews to the club magazine and television station, but happily lends himself to some of Bayern's publicity drives. He knows that the business of transfer policy is taken care of in the offices of Rummenigge and Hoeness and he's just fine with that. 'Here I'm the coach, full stop, which is very different from Barça. I coach the players, I try to drive the team towards the best results and I've got Sammer's support, which is very important. He's the key.'

His kids are learning German swiftly, they never miss a Bayern home match, even the night games, and have made good friends at school. Cristina, Pep's wife, is still running her clothes shop and has probably visited every art gallery in the city. The Guardiola family feels the same peace of mind here as Pep does. As Sala i Martín explains: 'They're all happy in Munich. There's no homesickness at all. Pep's kids are the most important factor for him. He's obsessed with the importance of them studying abroad and learning lots of languages. He always insists that the best thing he can do for them is give them a good education and lots of language learning.'

German football is in his blood now. While he is trying to correct small but important details in his team, he is soaking up the influence of a very different kind of football – quicker, more aggressive and full of lightning-fast counter-attacks. Whatever tactical deficiencies exist in German football, they are compensated for with aggression, teamwork and effort. So, as he alters Bayern, the Bundesliga alters him.

'He's full of re-invention – in six months here Pep has tried more things than in four years at Barça,' says Domenèc Torrent, who still shares the bench with him, having begun together at Barça B back in 2007.

In terms of tactics, there have been six areas of big development during the first six months.

1: THE DEFENSIVE LINE

Pep has moved it forward from a starting point of 45 metres in front of the keeper. If Bayern are fully on the attack high up the pitch then he wants the two centre-halves to take up positions 56 metres ahead of Neuer – in the opposition half.

2: PLAYING AND MOVING FORWARD FROM THE BACK, IN TOTAL UNISON

The team has got this: it's a journey they must take together. How they play out from the back is of absolute importance to how things then develop in the attacking phase.

3: ORDER IN THE PLAY

The passing sequences need to balance the team's positioning. If properly effected, from beginning to end it means their attack will be ordered and if the ball is lost it can be won back quickly, with little wasted effort.

4: SUPERIORITY IN MIDFIELD

This is the essence of Pep's playing philosophy. He always wants his team to have midfield superiority, whether numerical or positional. Achieving this guarantees his team will dominate the game.

5: FALSE ATTACKING MIDFIELDERS

This is the big tactical innovation within Pep's first season. Given the powerful wing play of Robben and Ribéry and also the need to immediately cut off the counter-attacks of opponents high up the pitch, Pep has decided to position his full-backs almost as old-fashioned inside-forwards, right alongside the other attacking midfielders, high up the pitch.

6: PLAYING WITHOUT THE FALSE 9

From being the absolute key figure at Barcelona, the false 9 is now just one more potential tactic for Bayern. It will be used sporadically, depending on the specific needs of a particular match or phase within a game.

From what he has learned from German football, Pep most values five things:

1: COUNTER-ATTACKS

He has sometimes branded it the Bundesliga-counter, based on the efficacy and speed of the counters he has had to plan for. The efficacy, particularly, has fascinated him. And he's loved it when Bayern have been capable of employing it themselves. Nevertheless, one of the great tasks of his season has been working out how to counter the counter.

2: AERIAL PLAY – OFFENSIVE AND DEFENSIVE STRATEGIES

The physical qualities of the players in German football make aerial tactics essential, both from set plays and open play. His Barça team was full of little guys, but Bayern have height and this has meant a new coaching approach to the strategy of the aerial ball.

3: AGGRESSIVE PRESSING

Against the power of the Bundesliga counter-attack, it's vital to have a high, effective and aggressive pressing game – particularly if Bayern lose the ball high up the pitch. It was a tactic at Barcelona, but in Munich the coach has needed to augment the collective aggression and intensity of this action.

4: DOUBLE *PIVOTE*

Although he's been the flag bearer for using just one organisational midfielder throughout his coaching career, Pep has accepted the need to renounce this commandment on occasion, if it will bring an improvement in his team's midfield play. He will often ignore the single-*pivote* concept in the latter part of this season.

5: WIDTH

At Barça, the ball was played wide with pretty much the sole intention of distracting and confusing the opposition so that it could then be slotted back into the inside-forward positions in and around the box, in search of the breakthrough pass or a shot on goal. At Bayern, with the two full-backs often pushed up, it becomes essential for the wingers to maintain width.

So what's on Pep's menu as 2014 begins? Just what you'd imagine – a combination of his old ideas and the innovations he has picked up in Germany.

Torrent explains: 'He'll maintain the essence of his philosophy: moving the ball as a device to keep the team's positional play organised and strategically as far as about three-quarters of the way upfield; keeping a very high defensive line and always looking to achieve an extra man in midfield – however that's achieved. But you can't any longer expect a fixed tactical system from him, nor a fixed starting XI. These will both change from match to match. And the analysis of our rivals will become increasingly more crucial.'

The January training camp in Doha will be a turning point. The players have been through their learning period. They have been acquiring knowledge and are flying in the Bundesliga. With two more trophies in the bag (the European Super Cup and the Club World Cup) confidence in Guardiola is at a peak. He is no longer the charismatic and legendary coach at Barcelona who had the advantage of already having done it all there as a player. Now he is his own coach – the guy who leads all the training sessions, rain or shine or snow, with the kids, the substitutes or the first team. Unlike at Barcelona, he's not automatically a reverential figure. In this environment he is flesh and blood – the boss who has got a smile, a joke, a kick up the backside, a growl of anger, a row – and bundles of technical and tactical ideas. Pep hasn't simply won his first couple of trophies with his new club, he has won over the majority of his players.

In Doha the hard work starts all over again. The training camp comes after two full weeks off. The rest was badly needed. Leg muscles have relaxed and the players have cleared their minds after what has been a prodigious but utterly exhausting year. Guardiola comes back from the Christmas break carrying two extra kilos. His technical staff watch him do all the same running as the players, doing the sit-ups and turning down pasta for plates of salad instead. Pep is very fussy about his appearance.

In Doha, they prepare for round two. This is a crucial moment in the battle for the title and the winter break has been a real blessing.

'This break is fantastic for everyone, physically and mentally,' Lorenzo Buenaventura points out. 'You only have to talk to the medics and the physios. In England they do the opposite. They have games every two days during the Christmas break and any doctor will tell you how hard that is on the body. By the middle of January the players are all struggling badly. After the intense programme of matches Bayern has played in 2013, two weeks of holiday, plus three of pre-season training, are an absolute blessing.'

The technical staff programme the work similarly to the pre-season in Trentino last July, but there is an important difference: this isn't the same team any more. These guys have put in hundreds of hours of work and assimilated new concepts. Pep has installed a new kind of software in them and, after some early gremlins, his men have adapted to his ideas. They now speak a different football language.

TZ online puts out a video of training in Doha and it's a surprise to anyone who has not had the good fortune to see Pep's Bayern sessions in person. It whizzes round the world and gives a taste of what daily life is like working under Pep – the intensity he puts into ensuring that his players implement the correct moves and reactions, every second of the session. Each session is as intense and focused as this. Eighty minutes of maximum effort, every time, in search of the correct moves – moves which will mean a qualitative improvement in the players and the team as a whole.

I quiz Manel Estiarte about this change in Guardiola, something which the fans and the German journalists probably aren't even aware of, but which is apparent to anyone who knew him at Barcelona.

'There's no fuss, fanfare or luxury here at Bayern but there's absolutely everything a professional needs to do his work well. Fundamentally, it's full of good professionals. And there's an enormous respect for work ethic. Yesterday I said to Pep, "we're in precisely the right place at exactly the right time. It may or may not be the club where we win the most trophies, but I struggle to imagine anywhere else right now with such ideal conditions. The players individually and collectively are determined to progress and improve. They are hungry to learn and just as hungry to win. It means that right now, thanks to the union of the club and the squad, this is an unparalleled environment for us. Perhaps in a few seasons it won't be, but right now it definitely is".

'All of that has had an effect on Pep and changed him.'

The prodigious calendar year of 2013 has finished and it is time to put all the clocks back to zero. Football's revolving wheel is about to start turning again. The Bayern which leaves its winter camp in Doha is one in full gallop in search of more trophies and it will shortly swallow up the Bundesliga.

43

'I'M GOING TO HAVE TO MAKE SOME RADICAL CHANGES.'

Stuttgart, January 29, 2014

'THERE ARE DAYS when you play badly and nothing works for you. You think, "what the hell am I doing out here?" But then you give an assist and score the goal of your life.'

Bayern pretty much win the league on this cold January evening when, despite having a poor game, Thiago Alcántara scores a colossal goal in the final minutes.

Bayern's game has been boring, clunky and chaotic and the home team's excellent performance has certainly warranted a better result. They've done everything right. With a compact and solid defence, they have conceded very little and when Bayern do break through the double defensive line, their keeper, Ulreich, who has had an exceptional game, is there to frustrate them. Stuttgart attack with precision and intelligence, ruthlessly taking advantage of any lapse in Bayern's positional play and causing the defence genuine, if infrequent, problems. And when Bayern finally do find their rhythm, Stuttgart disrupt it by slowing down restarts and throw-ins.

The home side's coach, Thomas Schneider, who will be out of a job in six weeks, has shown himself to be a first-class tactician. Bayern have looked lost, as if they are no longer thinking clearly. Perhaps losing this match, which has been postponed from December, would be no big deal. They do, after all, have a 14-point lead over Borussia Dortmund.

For the first time this season Guardiola has repeated his line-up of the Friday before, when they produced a sizzling 2-0 victory in Mönchengladbach's Borussia Park in the first league match after the winter break. How on earth could a group of players who played such aggressive, penetrating, brilliant football just five days before have dipped so dramatically?

'It was like we couldn't give any more. We were blocked mentally after Friday's match against Gladbach, which had been really tough,' Thiago explains as he bounces out of the Mercedes Benz Arena dressing room in Stuttgart, obviously on cloud nine. 'These things happen in football. Sometimes you just collapse and can't do any more. The minutes tick by and you're praying for it to end because you can see no way forward. But in the end, we found one.'

This time the solution has come from the bench. There were three reasons for Pep's decision to turn out the same line-up: Firstly, it's his preferred option, with Lahm at *pivote*, Kroos and Thiago slightly advanced of him and Götze, Müller and Shaqiri constantly swapping positions in attack; secondly, Ribéry, Robben, Schweinsteiger and Javi Martínez were out through injury or other problems and, thirdly, because Mandžukić was being punished for his apathetic attitude to training. Pep was not willing to start the striker unless he was prepared to put in some effort to earn his place.

In Stuttgart however, nothing has gone the way the coach had hoped. Bayern have bossed possession, moving the ball around just outside the penalty area at will with Thiago and Götze easily getting between the two Stuttgart lines of midfield and defence. However, the final passes have been poor and the shooting still less effective. As has happened before in other games, Bayern's overwhelming domination has not translated into a serious threat and, as the minutes pass, the opposition's counter-attacks begin to make an impact. Stuttgart take the lead at the 30-minute mark and Bayern's game continues to deteriorate.

At half-time Pep decides to change tactics and Mandžukić, Pizarro and Contento start to warm up in the first minute of the second half.

Pep radically transforms the game. He's tried it before without success, but in Stuttgart his alterations do the trick.

Guardiola has always taken an interventionist approach to what is happening on the pitch, but now he has one undoubted advantage, lacking in his Barcelona days: he has different players who are capable of completely altering the way they are playing.

'We're going nowhere, Domè,' he tells Torrent the minute they get into the dressing room. 'I'm going to have to make some radical changes because we can't win like this.'

His team are so stuck that Pep breaks his own rules by making two changes within the first minutes of the second half, putting Mandžukić and Pizarro on for Shaqiri and Kroos. He goes further. He uses a double *pivote* composed of Thiago and Lahm, he puts Pizarro in the No.10 position and tells him to spread the play wide to either wing. It's now a 4-2-3-1 shape and the defenders are told to get the ball as quickly as possible to Thiago and Lahm. Either of them feeds Pizarro and the Peruvian, at the top of his game, keeps on opening up the play to Müller and Götze wide, then pushes up quickly to support Mandžukić in the striker role.

Pep's changes represent a radical shift away from his usual game plan. In fact, you could say that they are the antithesis of his normal playing style. In November, in Dortmund, he put all his emphasis on the most agile, technical players flooding the middle of the pitch, especially Thiago and Götze, in order to win 3-0. You could call that the most 'Guardiola' of tactics. But in Stuttgart, he demands that the ball goes wide to the wingers and they cross in to Mandžukić.

It is possible to conclude that Pep has betrayed his own principles, but when asked this very question after the game, his response is blunt. 'What the fuck are you talking about, mate? We needed to win the game…'

The pieces take a few minutes to fall into place, but it quickly becomes clear that Stuttgart are going to struggle to hold back this reformed Bayern, even if players like Götze and Thiago are clearly exhausted. Just like Guardiola said months ago, when a fightback is needed, Bayern are capable of anything. They have started to push up into Ulreich's area and are looking dangerous. They equalise with 15 minutes to go, Pizarro getting it after Thiago's free-kick. Pep makes a third change which could prove decisive. Contento comes on for the flagging Götze and Alaba is now a left winger. They continue to slog away despite a series of terrific counter-attacks which put Neuer under real pressure.

Pep tells his men to execute a manoeuvre which, although fairly straightforward, could be difficult for them to even recall in the heat of battle. He wants them to remember how to overload the play down one wing, suddenly switch to the other open wing and then cross into the middle. It was the same message he applied to great effect in the epic European Super Cup final against Chelsea. Overload the left with bodies, switch suddenly to the right and then get the cross into the box. In the 93rd minute this is how they score.

Alaba, Contento, Thiago and Pizarro all combine down the left before Lahm instantly switches to Rafinha, who has appeared down the right. The Brazilian wing-back crosses accurately and Thiago produces a brilliant overhead kick – the volley which seals the game and practically the league title, too.

The Bavarian team's euphoria brings to mind a certain night in Prague when Javi Martínez equalised in the last second of extra-time against Chelsea, as well as the Dortmund match when Bayern routed their great rival. This is the goal which will earn them the Meisterchale, the silver shield given to the league champions.

'Did it come off your shin?' the player is asked in the dressing room.

'No, no. I used my whole boot. It was a dream goal, just a clean volley.'

'*Thiago oder nichts.*' Thiago or nobody.

It was Thiago's first goal in the Bundesliga, and it kept the team on their record-breaking run: 43 consecutive league matches undefeated; 28 away games with at least one goal scored; and the first club to win 16 out of their first 18 games – records which they would continue to smash over the next few months, during which Bayern would add 10 more consecutive victories to effectively win the title by the end of March, earlier than anyone else in history.

Guardiola was delighted with their comeback in Stuttgart, but hid his emotions behind one of his blank, Egyptian-mummy expressions.

He had joined in the ecstatic celebrations in the dressing room but now, on his way to the press room, he put the win out of his mind and started reflecting on other pending issues: we have to get Ribéry, Robben and Javi back immediately; I have to persuade Mandžukić to keep working full-out even if he's not getting 90 minutes every game; I need to ensure that contract negotiations don't distract Kroos (the player is demanding an increase in salary); I need to make sure that the team doesn't relax now that they think that the league is in the bag (despite a 17-point lead) and most importantly I need to work out how to deal with Arsene Wenger's Arsenal. The Champions League is just around the corner and the whole of Europe's eyes are on Munich.

As he leaves the dressing room, Lorenzo Buenaventura explains why he backed Pep's decision to change the dynamic of the game: 'We were completely bogged down. It was completely the reverse of what happened in Mönchengladbach. Pep managed to change the game for two reasons: because he now has a host of new ideas, learned from watching his players and opponents here, and because he has a group of players with the skill to adjust the way they are playing. And there's a third factor, this guy's no inflexible ideologue. He's smart enough to have studied, analysed and adapted to the Bundesliga, still without abandoning the basic concepts which define his playing style.'

But Pep isn't listening. His thoughts have turned to their upcoming games.

'Loren, we need to rotate the team. From now on we need to choose very carefully.'

'Pep, let's make sure that we don't make the same mistake so many have done before us,' adds Domènec Torrent. 'We can't risk running the players into the ground just for the sake of breaking a few records.'

He had had his five minutes of celebration in the dressing room and now he is looking to the future once again.

44

'I LOOK AT THE FOOTAGE OF OUR OPPONENTS AND THEN TRY TO WORK OUT HOW TO DEMOLISH THEM.'

Munich, January 31, 2014

PEP YELLS: 'MY feet are like ice! It's bloody freezing here!'

Stuttgart and that epic last-minute victory is behind them. Thiago has been lapping up all the praise and the front-page coverage, but it's time to get back to the usual routine. There's a new opponent to face and Pep needs to analyse them and prepare the tools with which he will try to win.

As a rule, Guardiola gives three team talks before each match, each of them about 15 minutes long. He uses images to clarify his points, usually video footage that doesn't last more than seven minutes. The three talks follow the same pattern.

The day before the match Pep dissects their opponent's attacking play. Using video footage he points out where their adversary is likely to be most dangerous, drawing attention to the way key players work. The coach then gives his men specific instructions about the defensive moves Bayern should make to stop the other team. His men then implement these instructions in the training session that follows.

He gives his second talk just before the training session on the morning of the match. It consists of a detailed explanation of how they use defensive and attacking throw-ins and free-kicks. Assistant coach Torrent has studied the last 50 corner kicks the rival has taken and explains anything significant that they regularly try. Torrent will remind the substitutes of the positions they need to be in for set-plays, just before they enter the match. After this talk the team does some light training during which they run through the attacking and defensive moves they have just covered. Pep still won't have decided on his line-up so everyone has to take part in all the moves. If it's an away match they don't do this. Instead, they review video footage of them practising those free-kicks in Säbener Strasse.

Pep delivers his third and final talk two hours before the match in the team hotel (he prefers not to do it in the dressing room). You could call it a motivational talk, but it will also include a technical review of Bayern's attacking tactics. This is also the moment the coach tells his men which of them are in the starting XI.

The players know exactly what to expect by now. This talk will focus solely on how to attack. Precisely how they'll use the first corner kick or wide free-kick they win will also be specified by the coach.

Usually, although not always, Pep will also use the talk as a motivational tool. For example, in the return leg of the Champions League quarter-final against Manchester United in early April, Pep dropped this third talk. On that occasion he had already named the team the day before, they had practised their attacking moves and he felt there was nothing else to add. In contrast, the team arrived at Mönchengladbach's Borussia Park with just minutes to spare for the first match of 2014 on January 24 because Pep's talk had delayed them. He wanted to leave his men in no doubt as to why they had been resoundingly thrashed six days before in a friendly in Salzburg: they hadn't bothered to run and their game had lacked intensity.

'I can take us so far,' he told them. 'I can analyse our opponents and use my tactical know-how to place you in the best positions. So, for example, today David [Alaba], I don't want you going too far up the pitch because Stuttgart's right wing [Martin Harnik] could do us some damage. But from here on in lads, it's down to you. If you choose not to play with intensity, if you decide you're not going to run your legs off out there, well, we won't win the match.'

Pep plans his three talks only after a detailed analysis of the opposition and his own team. These talks also reveal his talent for innovation. Xavier Sala i Martín, who is an economics professor at Columbia University, puts it like this: 'For me, Pep is a great innovator. He wins matches by analysing his opponent's weak point and then attacking it. But, more than that, he introduces constant innovations so that even if his opponents catch on and correct their own errors, Guardiola has already altered his strategy. He is always one step ahead and manages to stick to his own game philosophy of superiority in the middle of the field whilst at the same time adapting Bayern's game to the characteristics of their current opponent.'

In October 2012 in New York he had chatted with Garry Kasparov about how to attack the adversary in chess and other sports, and Kasparov had told him: 'You wouldn't attack in the same way from a mountain top as you would from wide open countryside.'

He had also dined in New York at the end of 2012 with Ferran Adrià, the gastronomic genius who was about to close his restaurant *El Bulli*. The chef told him: 'Pep, you're more than a coach, you're a great innovator.'

The coach had responded: 'Look Ferran, all I do is look at the footage of our opponents and then try to work out how to demolish them (in actual fact he used a rather more prosaic and somewhat obscene term). All I do is study my arsenal of weapons and pick the ones I need for each occasion.'

In the opinion of Sala i Martín, Guardiola's natural talent for innovation is a perfect fit with the German spirit of enterprise.

'I don't know what the German footballing public would say but I do know many of the people in charge of government and business in this country and they are all innovators and perfectionists. They live to do things right and avoid mistakes. They're always looking for perfection. It doesn't matter whether you're talking about BMW, Siemens or Audi. They value innovative ideas and are always looking for the perfect product, which tallies exactly with Pep's working style which is all about constant evolution and innovation. And adaptation. Just look at what's happened here. Pep hasn't tried to make Bayern play like Barça. Instead, he has adapted to the country and the players. Having said that, of course, there is no relationship between the way the team is playing now and what they were doing on July 1, 2013.'

In order to fully understand how this analysis of Bayern and their opponents is generated, we need to talk to Carles Planchart, who is in charge of Guardiola's team of analysts and who has worked with the coach since 2007, when he took over at Barça B. Planchart explains the different stages he and his team go through: 'There are basically two parts to this job: the analysis of your own team and that of your opponent. And they are two entirely different tasks. You're working in a club that has a game every three days, so you just don't have time to correct all their mistakes on the pitch. You therefore need to use other methods to communicate the corrections which are impossible to get through to them during a game. If you happen to have a whole week of training sessions then, of course, you can plan a series of exercises to correct the errors. For example, if the defensive line is too high or too deep, or if there's too much space between the team lines, or there's a problem dealing with crosses, or if we are defending badly at the front post. Otherwise, the most efficient method is to show them visual images, because that gets the idea across very quickly.'

At the end of every match the analysts agree their conclusions about the play they've been watching. They'll comment on collective and individual action as well as the strategic and tactical side of things. Pep will then work one-to-one with specific players during the week, or decide to save the information for a more appropriate time. Usually, however, strategic and individual adjustments have to be made immediately and these will then inform the analysis of the next game.

This season Planchart's team has added another dimension. They now analyse each player's moves as well as looking at the tactical plays. By the end of the match they have a detailed account of all the specific moves each of the Bayern players has made and can judge whether or not they have made the right decisions. They have opened a file on each player in which all his plays are noted in detail. After the match they organise these into categories of play. For example, there will be a list of aerial challenges, headers, dribbles and so on. They can then show each man specific images which help him as an individual or in the context of his position in the team line, or with a view to tactical priorities. All of the footage is filmed with a wide angle, so that they can judge the player and his work in terms of the tactical work of the team, not just how he does individually and technically.

'Pep always like to see the whole match and we load it on to his computer as soon as the match is over,' continues Planchart. 'He might then look at the whole game or watch the particular moves we've categorised, either player by player, or by type of move, or under different tactical headings. He'll also find my notes there, both details from the match and specific things we've agreed to watch out for. As well as getting the match broken down like this, Pep likes to review the match himself and he produces his own analysis.'

The other part of this analytical process consists of breaking the rival down, a vital stage in the process of choosing Bayern's own approach to the game. The German league records every Bundesliga and 2.Bundesliga (second division) match in panoramic format and then makes the footage available to clubs first thing every Monday morning. The Champions League has no equivalent service and it is hugely difficult to tape the matches – so much so that clubs have been known to indulge in trickery such as using a small, hand-held camera to record from the stands, or wearing glasses fitted with a recording device.

It is absolutely vital to record matches in situ in panoramic format so that the action can be studied from a tactical point of view. 'In Germany, scouting is considered a part of the job and not some form of espionage. The clubs themselves even pass footage to each other. It's normal practice here,' Planchart explains.

It is also vital to analyse the opponent in order to select the right playing system, the players you'll need and even the training exercises they'll do in the run-up to the match. 'In Barcelona, whenever we played a Champions League final we would analyse our opponent's last 12 matches, and for ordinary games we'd watch an average of five or six. We have to take account of the time of year and the type of team our opponents are facing in each game. It makes a difference whether they are taking the initiative or waiting for a chance to counter-attack, if they have a similar playing style to ourselves, etc. If your opponents are going up against teams that are similar to us, that's fantastic. If not, it's much less meaningful.'

After analysing the five or six games, Planchart prepares a report for Pep, organised according to concepts and the related moves. It will be a visual presentation, which is much easier to understand, and which will offer three examples of each concept in action. If Pep finds this helpful, he'll then base his own work around the information presented.

'Normally as soon as the match is over or first thing the next morning, I give him the report on our next opponent. I work two weeks ahead, but he just concentrates on the next game. Sometimes I'll give him some of the Champions League information a bit earlier and then, if he has a week without a Wednesday fixture, he can have a look at it a bit earlier than usual. But usually he just works from game to game and only once a match is over can he think about the next one.'

Guardiola has a look at the report first. It covers around 50 or 60 different moves and allows him to get a general idea of how to prepare his next game. Sometimes it even gives him a clear idea of the line-up he'll need. He can then start to plan the training activities with Torrent and Buenaventura, bearing in mind specific aspects of the game. In the next few days, he'll do a detailed analysis of their opponents, looking at matches, or parts of matches and drawing his own conclusions. He makes lots of notes and decides on the key ideas he needs to transmit to his men. Sometimes he combines these with concepts developed from previous matches, either because he wants to revisit a particular move or tactical idea or for motivational purposes.

During the match, Planchart and his team also send images of specific moves to the bench where Domènec Torrent receives them on his iPad: 'Carles sends things he's noticed himself or specific moves we've asked for to my iPad – corner kicks, a type of counter-attack … we ask for it in image form so that Pep can see it almost simultaneously.'

The analysts in the stands have their camera connected to Torrent's iPad, to the computer in Pep's office and to the computer in the dressing room, which is connected to a screen on the wall. In real time, Planchart selects and sends those moves he thinks are relevant and saves others for later. Then, five minutes before half-time, he nips down to Pep's office and files the entire footage of the first half. Obviously they don't have the same network of connections away from home and Planchart has to take his own computer down to the dressing room.

He usually picks three or four concepts to cover at half-time and will use two or three three-second videos to demonstrate what he means about each one. In total, there will be rapid shots of roughly 10 specific moves. 'What are we doing at half-time? That'll be Pep's first question. He comes into his office and asks, "what are you seeing up there?" Because you get a completely different view of the action from up above and you spot different things. He always listens attentively when I make my report. In fact Pep is always listening, always analysing. He'll discuss with Torrent how to correct faults or how to change the game. He then makes a note of the few concepts he wants to correct and goes off to the players' dressing room. With about five or six minutes to go, he'll call the relevant players over, show them the images and tell them what he wants to change. And then off he goes, back to the bench.'

As Pep said to Ferran Adrià, innovation can sometimes be the most prosaic of processes.

'All I do is look at footage of our opponents and then try to work out how to demolish them.'

45

'PERFECT FOOTBALL IS DAMN DIFFICULT TO ACHIEVE.'

Munich, February 15, 2014

IN EARLY FEBRUARY Mario Götze scores the Allianz Arena's first goal of 2014. It's been seven weeks since Bayern played on home turf and in that short time plenty of things have changed. It's not just that Pep seems different, it's that his team is functioning differently – quicker, more electric, as if propelled by a new energy despite the never-ending injury list. Thiago has transformed into the emblem of this devastating Bayern.

'He just needed a great goal like the one he scored in Stuttgart,' Pep explains. 'It has helped the fans understand what enormous quality he has. Thiago won't ever be a prolific scorer but a great footballer? Yes. Just look at what he did back in Dortmund. Three months without a match and he takes over the whole game.'

Thiago's increased influence stems from reasons beyond the psychological effect of that terrific goal. It's tactical, too. Guardiola has abandoned the single *pivote* and the false 9. Circumstances have dictated. In various games he has had to use a centre-forward and a second striker just off him, which has meant a little bit more protection down the middle of the pitch. This had its roots in the month of October: every time he put Götze on as a second striker behind Mandžukić he had to alter the positioning of the midfielders and use them in a double *pivote* formation. Then in January, during the epic fightback in the Mercedes Benz Arena in Stuttgart, he needed to do the same thing, with Thiago and Lahm as double *pivote*, so that Pizarro could play off Mandžukić.

Such was the improvement in the team's dynamic that the coach chose to modify his traditional philosophy. 'When he is in this position

Thiago is in constant contact with the ball, he's taking one or two touches and he generates fluidity and continuity in our play. Lahm is there to support him, especially in the fluidity of moving the ball. Philipp is terrific and he'll help make Thiago still better than he is now.'

Torrent puts it like this: 'The use of the double *pivote* was born out of the disappearance of our false 9. When we have to use a second central striker, linking between him and midfield, we have to close up behind them using two organising midfielders in the middle. The *pivotes* also feel much more secure playing with just one attacking midfielder than with two.'

There has been a lot of team rotation, as many as seven starters changing from one match to another, despite which the football in the Allianz has been spectacular since the turn of the year. Götze and Thiago are flying and Lahm is comfortable at *pivote*. From February 2 the *Schickeria*, the stand where Bayern's ultras congregate, echoes to cries of: 'Champions in March!' and Bayern do indeed blast their way through the next few weeks. From that day until March 8, Bayern win eight out of eight games with an overwhelming goal difference, scoring 33 and conceding just twice. In the Allianz they beat Eintracht Frankfurt 5-0, Freiburg 4-0, and Schalke 5-1. Away from home they defeat Nuremberg 2-0, Hannover 4-0 and Wolfsburg 6-1. In the DFB-Pokal they eliminate Hamburg 5-0 and in the Champions League they take the Emirates Stadium, beating Arsenal 2-0. Bayern have become a demolition machine. Torrent reckons it stems from the winter break. 'The training camp in Qatar marked an extraordinary change in us. Perhaps because after the holidays the players were refreshed and they'd had time not just to learn but to fully assimilate all that we'd been teaching them. Qatar was like a catalyst. Everything clicked and we became more than the sum of our parts. The team shot forwards because the players fully understood what was happening and why.'

Guardiola seems slightly less satisfied than his assistant. 'Perfect football is damn difficult to achieve. Heynckes' Bayern managed it last season, but I still require some time to really learn the Bundesliga and it will also be a while before my players are playing at their absolute maximum.'

Right now those players seem driven by a bottomless energy. The team is unmoved by the fact that Kroos is sent to the bench as a punishment for having reacted badly to being substituted. The collective energy overrides any individual dip. Even when the players go from one side of the stadium to another to acknowledge their fans after yet another win, yet another record, they *run*. They show that they can play direct, vertical football against Frankfurt or use long, continuous ball-possession against Hamburg in the DFB-Pokal, when they own the ball for 84% of the first half. It's unheard of in Germany but it doesn't necessarily impress Pep.

'It's normal enough when the opposition parks the bus like that. That all changes if your opponent happens to be aggressive and wants to contest the ball – how much ball you have isn't of supreme importance. What's really important is that the ball needs to be far away from our goal – that's what makes me happy.'

Contrary to what many think, Guardiola is not interested in owning the ball for the majority of the match, nor in pure statistics. What is eternally and crucially important for him is the idea of running – something which will only gain in importance in the coming months.

'We enjoy our work when we play well and we run and run and run. In order to enjoy our best play, we need to run a lot.'

The other great factor in the month of February is the flood of consecutive games. 'Right now we're constantly playing every three days and we can't allow anything to distract us and affect our focus,' Pep insists. 'The next game is always the most important and that means we can only think of that and not about the Champions League or anything else. We must concentrate only on the next step forward. Always serious, always focused. Every single victory needs to be constructed from zero because the most difficult thing isn't to win but to continue winning once you've hit winning form and the whole world just supposes that you'll keep on winning. We have to wipe everything else out of our minds, including last year's treble, and our wins this season. We have to work every single day as if we'd won nothing – as if we're starting from zero.'

At the end of this unstoppable February, perhaps the most emblematic moment actually comes on March 1, when the visitors, Schalke, don't even manage to cross the halfway line until the 29th minute and Neuer doesn't touch the ball until four minutes before half-time. It's just one more indication of Bayern's devastating dominance. Pep, nevertheless, wants nothing to do with such a flood of remarkable statistics, nor with the records his team is accumulating. 'A sportsman always needs to centre himself totally on today, in the very moment if possible. Who knows what tomorrow will bring?'

Run ceaselessly and focus on the here and now: the two fundamental principles which will underpin Bayern's performances in February, when they continue to triumph despite having already won everything. Principles which will then be forgotten in early April, when the title is won and the team hits its only dip of the season – and it's a big one.

Before this happens, Bayern will continue to hammer their rivals with the same regularity as they recover and then lose players. Schweinsteiger and Martínez are back but Shaqiri is injured once more and Ribéry needs surgery. On Wednesday, February 6, Pep has all his squad (except long-term absentee Badstuber) fit for the first time. It lasts one measly day. By Thursday, Ribéry undergoes his back operation. Thanks to injuries, thanks to tactical alterations and because of the dreadful burden of matches, the coach can't talk about the starting XI. Instead, he operates with a main group of 15 or 16 interchangeable players – amongst whom guys like Pizarro continue to perform well when called upon. This is a Bayern which mutates smoothly from one tactical schematic to another and which changes formation constantly and easily depending on the demands of their coach and the characteristic of their rivals.

I reminded Christian Streich, Freiburg coach, about a chat we'd had six months previously at his Mage Solar Stadium. Back then he'd predicted how impressive Pep's Bayern were going to be. 'Yes, I remember saying that to you. I told you that Bayern were going to be a brutal rival and that's what they've become. If you try to play defensively, they'll just unpick you with passes. Press them high and they can rip you apart. They have so many strings to their bow and are just overpowering. Six months ago they weren't playing like this, but during that time, under Pep's tutelage, they've done it. Bayern are a machine.'

Pep continues to alter his line-up depending on the next opponent, or injuries and the need to rest players, but these practical decisions also reflect Guardiola's immutable belief that constant evolution is a fundamental imperative. Evolution as a way of being – a necessity, a duty. Pep states it bluntly: 'The character of a team is the character of its coach.'

46

'HE'S SO INTENSE THAT HE'LL EXHAUST US.'

Munich, February 16, 2014

DEFINING PEP – THAT'S a tough challenge. There isn't a single adjective which will wholly sum up the complexities of a personality like his. Sometimes he seems like he's made out of steel, sometimes out of butter. All the same it is tempting to seek out some definitive word. Like 'obsessive'.

'If being obsessive means being passionate and detailed in your preparation,' says his friend Sala i Martín, 'then Pep is obsessive. But in my opinion that kind of obsession isn't a negative thing if you're obsessed about something you love and you're trying to achieve to a perfect degree. Pep's obsessive in the same way a great musician or a great artist is obsessed. It's just that his key, his palate is football.'

The professor of economics talks to us about what he sees as in-depth preparation. 'During his sabbatical year in New York he'd sometimes attend my classes on innovation and economics at Columbia University and he was extremely interested in individual communication – far more so than group communication. He'd already figured out that this was no longer an era to show his players a 'Gladiator' video [as he did before the Rome Champions League final of 2009] or use Cruyff's turn of phrase from the 1992 European Cup final ['Go out and enjoy yourselves']. Pep was much more interested in personalised communication – finding other ways of getting feelings and beliefs across to his players. He wanted to understand Twitter and social networking with a view to possibly using some of those concepts and rules while communicating within the dressing room or on the training pitch. Because he knew he should be doing that. So in the US he dedicated himself to working out how to harness the power of modern technology to communicate with players. He spent a year working it out. It became an obsession even when he didn't yet have a team to apply all this to. In the heart of Manhattan life he was consumed by how all this was going to help him change and improve his work, long before he had some to do.'

Sala i Martín evokes another ingredient which is essential to understand Guardiola: passion. 'Kasparov told him clearly: Pep, you can't play without passion.'

Buenaventura, too, believes that passion is fundamental to victory in football. 'If you talk to Diego Simeone he'll tell you something which pretty much stands out: "I'm the footballer who got the most out of the least resources. You know why? Because I have passion! How the hell was I going to get 100 games for Argentina? As a player I was a bit of a lump, but everything I achieved was down to my passion."'

Pep isn't out to intellectualise football, or his ideas and concepts. He doesn't use complicated vocabulary. He's an ordinary guy and uses simple words. This is the son of a bricklayer who has never forgotten his roots.

'The players will end up drained by Pep,' Thiago once predicted. 'He's so intense that he'll exhaust us. He's an even better psychologist than he is a tactician.'

Thiago really knows him. He's taken his rows and he's earned his demonstrations of affection – his warnings and his praise. 'Pep will never be satisfied. He doesn't enjoy himself. He'll never enjoy football because he is always looking for what has gone wrong in order to correct it. Pep is never happy because he's a perfectionist.'

47

'THEY LIKE THE IDEA OF TELLING THEIR FRIENDS: I PLAY FOR PEP GUARDIOLA.'

Munich, February 17, 2014

THE TEAM IS more than prepared for the great challenges of the season. They're on top form and they're hungry. The league title is within reach. With two weeks to go before the end of February, Bayern are 16 points ahead of Bayer Leverkusen and 17 above Borussia Dortmund. Guardiola jokes: 'If we don't win the league, I'll resign.'

Given that the team are on such a high, it seems a good time to chat to a few experts and I start with Alexis Menuge, the German correspondent for the French paper *L'Équipe* and author of *Franck*, Franck Ribéry's biography. 'Bayern are stronger now than they were at the end of 2013. I think that's down to the fact that the players understand more about what Pep wants. The Qatar training camp was very intense and they trained well. But apart from all the hard work I think that tactics have had a role to play here. For the last few weeks Pep has allowed his men to play with a 4-2-3-1 more frequently. That's how they played under Heynckes and I think his players feel more comfortable as a result.'

Next I interview Roman Grill, Philipp Lahm's agent and a man who understands football tactics inside out. Grill has strong opinions. 'The team's improvement is mostly down to Pep Guardiola's ability to teach effectively and in my opinion he's the first Bayern Munich coach Philipp's worked under who teaches his players something new every day. He has had a very positive influence on them and, given his record with Barça, has the kind of authority that inspires the players to learn.'

As well as working so closely with Lahm, Roman Grill played for Bayern II and also coached the youth team. There's no doubt in his mind as to the reason for the team's improvement. 'This team needed someone like Pep. And I really can't see any other coach doing what he has done here. Last year Bayern already had the best squad in their entire history, whether it was created by sheer good luck or by first-class planning on the part of the management, but there were some very dodgy tactical decisions made under Jupp Heynckes. Heynckes used his charisma and authority as a respected, experienced coach to manage his men, but the players were coming up with the tactical solutions themselves on the pitch and it just couldn't have gone on for another year, particularly after they won everything. They needed the stimulus of a coach with ideas, a coach who has a plan which he implements on a daily basis. There's no other coach in the world who could have given them this – only Guardiola. The team has gone through an amazing process of evolution and I have never seen a Bayern team play with this level of intensity. The match against City in Manchester was a fantastic spectacle, extraordinary. Pep always knows exactly what he wants. He's a man who wants to help his players, work with them, not against them but he is also clear about what he wants, what his objectives are.'

The day after this chat I catch up with Daniel Rathjen, a *Eurosport Germany* reporter, who has followed Bayern's season closely. 'Winter was an important turning point for Pep and for Bayern. He came here in the summer with his philosophy and his new ideas but it was still Heynckes' team. You could see it in the players, in the bosses and even in Pep himself. You could see it in the way they played and it was an enormous challenge to turn this around. It was always going to take time. I think that Marrakech was the catalyst, after they won the Club World Cup. Back then Pep thanked Heynckes again saying, 'Danke, Jupp, for giving us the chance to win this title'. But it was a watershed moment. It was the last title won by the 'old' team. In Qatar, after the winter break, Pep's reign really began. Players like Robben, Schweinsteiger, Lahm and Ribéry understood that they could continue to win trophies and it was then much easier for Pep to reap the rewards of the seeds he had sown. The weeks prior to

February were spent getting to know each other, establishing routines and recovering from the plague of injuries that had hit them. And all the while Bayern still managed to achieve overwhelming domination of the league. Their second stage of evolution really started from January onwards, when they began to function as a solid group.'

I also speak to the renowned author Ronald Reng, who has written several books, the most famous of which is *Robert Enke: A Life too Short*. Ronald lived in Barcelona for several years and witnessed Guardiola's Barça at first hand. He is, therefore, well placed to make comparisons with Bayern. 'The Bayern players have surprised me much more than Pep himself. I already knew Pep from Barça and was aware of his talent for innovation and his tactical ideas. But the humility with which the players have been prepared to learn has surprised me. In some cases this has meant a radical transformation, almost as if they've moved to a foreign country. In any case, there are huge differences between Bayern's game and Barça's. There is the occasional game, usually at home, that you can see some similarities, but they are very rare. Bayern have this ability to hit you hard from a standing start. Barça don't have anything like that. It's the capacity to create something out of nothing.'

Perhaps the most interesting part of the process for Reng has been the fact that winning the treble in 2013 didn't dissipate their hunger in any way. 'First, it's important to say that the prospective change of coach had an impact on the team even during their treble campaign. By January the players knew that Pep was going to be appointed and that affected them psychologically. Consciously or subconsciously many of them started to give Heynckes more support because he was the guy who was leaving. It was even easier for Jupp to manage a team of men who had so much affection for him. Players like Robben and Ribéry, who were a key part of the title wins, were no longer focusing on themselves and their own egos. They were thinking of their coach, who was leaving. So in essence the 'Pep effect' actually started before he even got here. And right now they're playing at a much higher level. Their results are outstanding, but so is the way they are playing: the type of game they're playing now is much more difficult than what they did last year. More passing, more definition, more complex tactics – it's actually quite a curious phenomenon that rarely happens in football. These players had won everything but they still liked the idea of being able to tell their friends, 'I play for Pep Guardiola'. That's not what usually happens, I can tell you. In fact players are usually very critical of their coaches, only too ready to find fault. Here the opposite happened. There was a huge amount of curiosity about Pep and they were also surprised by the kind of training sessions he introduced. In truth, Pep's arrival was the biggest stimulus this team could have had. The greatest discovery of this season has been that veterans playing at this elite level are still capable of changing, and in such a short space of time.'

February will be Bayern's month of consolidation. January's good impressions not only translate into victories and a devastating gap at the top of the Bundesliga, but also allow them to shift their focus to the Champions League, something that Guardiola had wanted to avoid until they were guaranteed the league title. But it is unavoidable and the players are now very conscious of it. They fly through training sessions. They have had a taste of victory in the Champions League and have no intention of letting the ultimate European prize slip through their fingers.

Watching a positional play training exercise is like watching a recital of ball control by Thiago, who manages to open up space every time he controls a pass. This is the traditional drill which is practised in a rectangle of 20 x 12 metres where it is 7 v 7 plus five players who always switch to assist the team with the ball. Only the chosen few – Thiago, Lahm, Schweini and Kroos – are allowed two touches on the ball. Everyone else gets only one. Pep ceaselessly corrects. It doesn't matter if it's Kroos, Robben, Schweinsteiger.

'Tac, tac, tac, pass, look, move the other way, keep the ball, take up the right position.'

The team radiates a sense of security. It seems that Bayern, for the first time since Pep took over, has reached that intangible state where they feel completely shielded against the whims and caprices of bad luck. Pep has provided them with a safety net that gives them a deep sense of security and the belief that they can achieve anything. Memories of the good times in Barcelona flood back, the days when the Catalan team felt wrapped up in an aura of invincibility.

At the end of the last training session before they meet Arsenal in London in the last 16 of the Champions League, I ask Thiago Alcántara about this sensation.

'You're absolutely right,' says Thiago. 'I was thinking about it last night and that's exactly what I'm feeling: a sense of security. The team feels secure and capable of just about anything. I had the same feeling last summer in the Under-21 Euros. The Spain team believed that we would win and that the only team capable of beating us was ourselves. And we won.'

There was one person left to talk to about what Bayern was going through. Someone who never takes the pressure off, who never relaxes. Matthias Sammer, the club's sports director. 'We're in good form. We're strong, fast, focused and hungry. We want to win. But we need to do more. We are Bayern. We have to give our utmost in every training session and in every match. That's the only way to achieve excellence, to reach that elite level only reserved for the few true greats. This is a historic opportunity. We are Bayern and we need to make the most of this opportunity. We mustn't stop now.'

48

'JUST AS WELL WE HAD MANU. WITHOUT THAT HAND I DON'T KNOW WHERE WE'D BE.'

London, February 19, 2014

IT'S 5PM IN London and the players have just had something to eat under the palm trees of the Landmark Hotel's Winter Garden, a stone's throw from Regent's Park. Pep is waiting for them in one of the hotel's meeting rooms. He's about to deliver the pre-match talk for the Arsenal-Bayern match, the away leg of the Champions League last 16. There's been a major change in the line-up. Javi Martínez will be the solo *pivote*, Lahm returns to right-back and Rafinha is benched. After announcing the team, the coach explains his plan for the game against Arsène Wenger's side: 'Lads, we all have experience of this kind of game. We've all played in Champions League knockout rounds and you know what they're like and what they mean. You know how intense they are. Intense, complicated, aggressive and dangerous. I'm going to give you some very precise instructions.'

Pep stops for a moment. It's a theatrical pause. 'This is what I want: for the first 10 or 12 minutes I want you to kill the game, and shatter Arsenal's confidence in the process. They'll come out all guns blazing, ready to attack. I want you kill the game dead. Keep passing the ball. For once, I want you to do exactly what I hate most, the thing I've told you is total shit. *Tiquitaca*. I apologise, but today I want you to do precisely that, just for a while. Pass the ball aimlessly. Pass it for the sake of it. You'll be bored and you'll feel like it's a pointless exercise, but it does have a purpose. We want to keep the ball and bore the pants off Arsenal, keep them from taking the ball off us. They'll soon see that all their aggression is pointless because they won't come in striking distance of the ball.

'You won't need me to tell you when to move on. After 10 minutes, when you can see that they're running out of gas, they're getting bored and losing heart, when you see that they're not chasing the ball as aggressively, gentlemen, that's when I want you to start the real game. That's when we stop the *tiquitaca* and start to play our football. That's when we go for the jugular.'

In the event, his men do everything but follow his instructions and the start of the match bears no resemblance to Guardiola's instructions. Within the first 10 minutes Bayern lose possession six times, hoof long balls into the Arsenal half and gift them possession. But hadn't they agreed to hijack the ball? Why were they giving it away?

For the first 10 minutes, which feel like a lifetime to Guardiola, Arsenal toss Bayern about like a rag doll. Happily for Bayern, Manuel Neuer – once again – plays a blinder. Not only does he save a Mesut Özil penalty and several other shots, but he works to calm his team-mates, yelling at them to follow the coach's instructions. Neuer saves them and soothes them at the same time but it's a nervous 10 minutes for Guardiola, who is struggling to understand how players of this calibre are booting long balls instead of protecting the possession as he has demanded. Nor is his decision to put Javi Martínez in the fulcrum of the team working: the Spaniard adds muscle in the centre of the camp, but loses control. Why have the team completely failed to follow his instructions?

'Because it's football,' Pep explains the next day, now much calmer. 'Because we're men, not robots. Because we want to get it right but sometimes we don't know how, we just mess up. Because training is relaxed and a game is very tense. Because our opponents are also talented despite the fact that people often criticise the other team. Because that's football, my friend.'

Those moments when his team lost control seemed like an eternity to the coach. In the post-match press conference he talks about '20 minutes of hell' although the next day, having looked at the video, he realises that it had lasted just seven minutes, not 20.

'Yes, but it felt like an eternity. If it hadn't been for Manu ... fuck, you can't afford to give away even five minutes in the Champions League!'

After Neuer saved the penalty, Bayern took control of the match and the ball. Thiago came into his own and the team began to make chances. A long, high ball from Kroos to Robben caused Wojciech Szczęsny to foul the Dutchman and the goalkeeper was immediately sent off. Alaba hit the post and by half-time it was 0-0 despite the 17 crosses Bayern had launched into the Arsenal box.

Everything changed in the second half. One substitution was enough: Rafinha for Boateng, Martínez to centre-half, Lahm to *pivote* and Thiago left wing. The change was devastating. Lahm dominated the ball and Arsenal, one man down, saw all hope snuffed out.

Kroos, more than anyone, had an outstanding second half – 152 passes with 97% accuracy, and swept in a Lahm pass for the crucial opening goal, before Müller headed a second late on. If anyone still had doubts about the player, his majestic performance in this game marked him out as a world star. Guardiola had drawn on previously-learned lessons. Against 10 men while with Barça he had used too many strikers against banked defences, with nine men defending their area. He made sure not to repeat the error here in the Emirates Stadium.

Opting to populate midfield high up the pitch, he used the trick of drawing defenders to one side of the field then suddenly switching play to the other touchline. Kroos got it perfectly and spent the rest of the night sending Arsenal scurrying from one side to the other to the extent that Arsenal managed only just over 20% possession and a mere 30 passes in the second half, compared to Bayern's 550 (their 95% accuracy was a Champions League record).

Lahm's ability to predict the next move, Kroos' exhibition of first-class football and Pizarro's rapid understanding of exactly what was required all played a decisive role in Bayern's 2-0 victory, just as Pep's reading of the situation, based on previous bitter experience against 10-man teams who parked the bus, had intended. Bayern left England with another Champions League win, a very good omen, but nobody could persuade Pep to relax after the shock of those early minutes.

'It seemed to last an eternity. Just as well we had Manu. Without that hand I don't know where we'd be in the Champions League right now.'

49

'LAHM BRINGS THIS TEAM TO LIFE.'

Munich, March 8, 2014

THE LEAGUE IS already effectively won. The only question is where and when. Bayern are 20 points ahead of Borussia Dortmund and even a breathtaking performance from Wolfsburg in their match against the Munich team fails to halt the champions, who have been amassing goals and victories in equal measure. Everyone's in a very good mood.

In the Friday training session, the day before the Wolfsburg match, the assistant coach, Tiger Gerland, disallowed a goal for being offside in the 'double area' training game. Such is the level of competitiveness that several players, amongst them Ribéry, rounded on Gerland. Although it was all good humoured, there was a serious side to their complaints. These guys don't like to lose, even in training. The dissent lasted all of 60 seconds, until Ribéry produced an outstanding goal, which he then followed with triumphant celebrations and a laughing, affectionate, two-fingered salute in Gerland's direction. The joke, however, was not to end here. Guardiola himself decided to join in the fun and surprise his men. Saying nothing, he finished training and flew with the team to Wolfsburg. After dinner he gave his obligatory tactical talk, including a video, which, to the players' amazement, was immediately followed by footage of the disallowed goal from training. And not just that. Carles Planchart had edited in several replays, showing where the nominal offside line would have been, so that it was now clear that the goal had in fact been completely legal! As all hell broke loose, half the team jumped to Gerland's defence and the other half shouted abuse. That night when they went to bed, everyone was still chuckling at the joke.

On Saturday, Bayern beat Wolfsburg 6-1 in a match which is actually much tougher than the score suggests. Pep's choice for the starting line-up serves to highlight the difficulties he has had this season because, for the first time since October 26, 2013, both Robben and Ribéry are starters. It has been 19 weeks, 133 days and 22 matches since the last time (against Hertha Berlín in Munich) – statistics which go some way to convey the sheer volume of injuries the squad has suffered.

The problems caused by the injury toll have been dealt with by, amongst other measures, the fluidity of their game in midfield, with their best performances coming when Lahm, Kroos and Thiago play together. Thiago's presence has freed up Toni Kroos, who seems less self-conscious and more willing to take risks. Kroos is already carving out a place for himself in the pecking order, something which Mario Götze has yet to achieve, perhaps because of his natural timidity. Pep has repeatedly urged him to stamp his personality on the team. But, of course, head and shoulders above them all stands Philipp Lahm. 'Philipp is a machine,' says Pep. 'He gets the ball and he does whatever he wants with it. He takes it wherever he wants it to go and always in the right direction.'

Sitting beside Pep at the post-match dinner, which is when he offers his most detailed and extended analysis, Manel Estiarte puts it like this: 'He doesn't lose the ball. He turns and drives the team. He's an astonishing player. Lahm brings this team to life.'

It's impossible to fully understand Bayern's triumphant league campaign without taking account of Lahm's role in the position of *pivote*. His place in the club's history was secured once and for all on August 30, 2013, in Prague. A day that is still fresh in Pep's memory. 'If we win anything this season it will be down to what I did with Lahm.' And there is a footnote to the player's story. In the Nürnberg derby in February, Lahm gets a goal, his first league goal in 95 matches (the last time he scored was three years before, in February 2011).

What Lahm has achieved this season is all the more impressive because it has been so difficult for a player who is not, in theory, a specialist in midfield. Nobody knows this better than his agent, Roman Grill. 'Philipp obviously brings a great deal to the defensive organisation, but also the fluidity of the team's play. Even as a dedicated full-back he already had this gift of seeing a team-mate and giving the ball to him in just the right way at just the right time and it was a huge boon then. When he plays as an organising midfielder, this gift of his stands out even more. Across the board Javi Martínez is the strongest aerially, Schweinsteiger's positional sense is very good, but if you add every facet together then Philipp is probably the most complete in this *pivote* role.'

Grill also agrees that the trio of Lahm, Kroos and Thiago has brought greater fluidity to Bayern's game: 'Watching Bayern play, it seems to me that they perform better when those three very technically gifted players are in the midfield. The team is much better at holding on to the ball, not losing it. It has meant a quantum leap in the quality of Bayern's performance: an inverted triangle with just the one organising midfielder at its base.'

All the same, and despite the top performances when this trio are in harness, Pep wants to add refinements in the middle of the pitch. Some are tactical, such as placing the two full-backs high up, tight to the attacking midfielders. Grill is impressed by that. 'Pep's idea of putting the full-backs high and inside, to flank the creative midfielders in a line of four stands out. It has been both intelligent and strategic. But it has also been the product of how he understands his own players. It has been done with one aim and it's very clear what he's going for. He wants control in the middle of the pitch and for that he needs superiority either in ball possession or the number of players there. He can therefore only attack down the wings, with one man on each touchline. For that he's got Robben and Ribéry and that's enough. Pep has had to be clear and smart in his understanding of his players. Does he try to exert influence on Robben and Ribéry and alter their basic game? That's a very complicated process and he's put the two full-backs inside because he has understood that the two wide front men weren't going to be willing to give him what he wants. His tactic has ended up not only giving Bayern superiority in the middle of the pitch, thanks to Rafinha and Alaba, but also allowing the two creative midfielders in that line of four, usually Thiago or Götze, to push up in a higher attacking position, meaning that he's got superiority in the middle and more players attacking the danger zone around the opposition penalty box. It's a winning, intelligent, aggressive tactic which I must applaud.'

As well as Pep's distinctive tactical refinements, the club also has its own approach to personal matters and prides itself on taking care of its own, ensuring that no one is abandoned in their hour of need. They see themselves as one big family and that applies whether they're dealing with long-term injury, as in the case of Holger Badstuber, whose recovery would save them having to sign a new player, or even legal troubles.

Bayern had welcomed the Brazilian Breno Borges back after the player served a year-long prison sentence for burning his own house down. On his return, Borges was appointed as a member of the technical staff in charge of the youth team.

Schweinsteiger's fitness has also caused the club difficulties, albeit on a different scale. After undergoing two ankle operations in just five months (June and November) his season has been a nightmare. In October the club had the chance to sign one of the best midfielders in the world for next season. It would have been an excellent deal, considering the technical and tactical abilities of the player in question as well as the financial terms, but the club turned it down, opting instead to continue to give their full support to Schweinsteiger.

In February, when Lahm, Kroos and Thiago were performing brilliantly, Pep decided to modify the team's structure. Why? There was only one reason: he wanted to retain a role for Schweinsteiger. It's a real dilemma for the coach but regardless of the short-term damage it might do to the team's overall performance, he wants Schweini back. For Roman Grill, this decision is a serious threat to the team's fluidity: 'We've not yet seen everything Philipp, Thiago, Kroos or Götze can do in the midfield and I've been a bit disappointed that Pep has changed the set-up in his last two or three games. He's moved Lahm back to right-back [in order to fit Schweinsteiger in] and it's a pity because I think that it would be helpful to give these guys a lot more experience. They're all adapting to something new – not only Lahm, but also Toni Kroos, who brings a lot of savvy and calm to the creative play, but who can still lose concentration from time to time during matches. It would have been great if they could have continued with this system and I'm disappointed that Pep seems to have changed it.'

Grill is right. Putting Lahm, Kroos and Thiago together works better and gives Bayern increased fluidity and greater consistency. On the other hand, Guardiola's decision is understandable. He doesn't want to lose a player of Schweinsteiger's calibre, no matter how difficult his season has been. Achieving a compromise between the two options is like squaring a circle: impossible. But that's what the coach is paid for: to take these kinds of decisions, even if he doesn't always get it right.

50

'I'VE GONE FOR CONTROL. CONTROL AND MORE CONTROL.'

Munich, March 11, 2014

HE HASN'T YET decided on his starting line-up for tonight. With just nine hours to go before the return leg against Arsenal in the last 16 of the Champions League Pep is still locked away in his Säbener Strasse hideaway, ruminating on whether to put Schweinsteiger or Lahm in the centre of midfield. Kroos has a slight cold but the expression on his face makes it clear that he is not willing to miss this match, no matter what. Pep still has doubts. He goes over and over the team in his head.

'I'm not happy until I decide who's playing. It's not just about how to attack, but who are the best men to do it. It's one thing to have a clear idea of how we're going to approach the match but it's quite another to choose the best players to do it. That's the key decision.'

It's noon in Munich and the team have done their morning training and listened to the second-last team talk. This is the one that strips down their opponent's strategy, followed by a quick run through on how to attack and defend corners and wide free-kicks. But Pep is still thinking about his line-up. He has a couple of problems: Kroos, who has a cold, and, despite his protestations to the contrary, Schweinsteiger is still not 100%.

Pep has doubts. His technical assistants advise him to go with the players who have got the team this far in the Champions League, the guys who have taken them through the tough times and their epidemic of injuries, many of them a hangover from a punishing 2012/13 season. One of the assistants has a coffee with me outside the dressing room and tells me: 'My advice would be to reward the guys who have got us this far. This is like a final. It would be a real success to get through to the quarter-finals and sticking to the same guys when everyone's fit would serve to increase competition for places. If we get knocked out tonight, then it's going to make the last few weeks of the season very long indeed.'

That would mean Rafinha at right-back, with Lahm and Kroos together in a two-man defensive midfield. But Pep is in two minds. Yesterday, he was on the point of agreeing with his assistants. It was mid-afternoon and for a moment it looked like he was sure: 'One option would be to play the guys who have got us this far – the guys who had to play more because of all the injuries.'

It's strange how he changes his mind from one day to the next. Yesterday he was absolutely clear. This match represented a key milestone in their season. The result would either mean giving up on one of their major objectives or embarking on their final push.

'Tomorrow's game is important because, given that we've already won the league, if we go out, the rest of the season is going to drag. We must get to the quarter-finals and then really go for it.'

But who should play? Overnight Pep had had a change of heart. He decided not to take any risks. The quarter-finals were within reach. All they had to do was control the match, close it down, do what they didn't manage to do in the Emirates Stadium in the first few minutes. That's how they'd do it. If they succeeded in controlling the match for 90 minutes, only four games would stand between them and another European final.

Pep's not sure which is the better strategy: attack or control. He almost always goes on the attack but today he's not so sure. So much so that by noon he's still undecided. Deep down he likes having his back against the wall, when he doesn't have enough players and has to play a Champions League final with an improvised back four because of suspension or injury, like he did in 2009 and 2011. In that kind of situation his talent for invention comes to the fore. But this is a new experience for him – he has his whole squad to pick from. It's a good problem to have, what they call in Munich a Luxusproblem. And his players are professionals. They'll understand. Or not.

He had had lunch with Toni Kroos the previous week and told him that he wanted him to become one of the group leaders over the next few seasons. He avoided any mention of the financial negotiations between the player and the club, nor did he make any wild promises about a guaranteed place as a starter. This is something he couldn't promise any player. He did, however, leave Kroos in no doubt as to his coach's high regard for him. Years before, at Barcelona, he had done exactly the same thing with Yayá Touré. He told Kroos that he wanted him beside him and offered to help him become an even better player. However, today Kroos won't be starting. He's got a cold and Pep also wants to cement Schweinsteiger's place in the group. He wants everyone in peak fitness for April and May.

Badstuber apart, everyone is fit. This is a first – he's had to wait until March 10 to have all his men available. Even the guys who have taken a few kicks have no problems in training. The pain has gone. The players are wearing their Champions League kit and that fact alone has a curative effect. Nobody is willing to miss their date with Arsenal.

At training the day before the match there are no clues as to the starting line-up. Pep still hasn't decided whether they're going out to get goals or erring on the side of safety and settling for ball domination. The session doesn't focus on either of these approaches. Instead they rehearse how to defend the way that Arsenal begin their attacks from the keeper. They go over the co-ordinated movement the back line must make when the ball is being put long from the Arsenal keeper.

'We know that [Lukasz] Fabianski almost always sends the ball to his right,' Planchart reminds them. 'If it reaches [Olivier] Giroud it's so that he can chest it down and hold it up. If he puts it to [Bacary] Sagna it's to make our full-back push up towards him and Sagna will try to head the ball onwards and into the space behind our full-back.'

And on Monday evening they go over and over the way to defend against these Arsenal goal-kicks, with Neuer in the role of Fabianski. For 20 minutes, Dante and Schweinsteiger are busy marking Pizarro, who acts as Giroud, and Alaba tries to perfect the way to close down Sagna, whose role is taken by Rafinha.

Next, Pep explains in detail how Mikel Arteta tries to draw in the opposing *pivote* in order to create a space in the middle of midfield into which Mesut Özil will try to appear. Pep walks through Arteta's movements whilst emphasising to his players, who are spread out in front of him: 'Özil is the dangerous one – he's the one we really need to keep the closest eye on. Arteta draws you in, Özil pops up in that zone with [Santi] Cazorla and [Alex Oxlade-] Chamberlain around him and that's the way that they achieve superiority in a key area. We can't afford that to happen.'

They test out the way to defend against this Arteta-Özil movement. The idea is that Robben and Ribéry squeeze infield and that Martínez, in his central-defensive role, pushes into the empty space which Arteta has created. In turn, Rafinha's task will be to fill the space which the Spaniard has had to leave open in the middle of the back four.

They go through a series of different actions, moving constantly. Pep keeps shouting out the names of Arsenal players – Arteta, Özil, Cazorla, Mertesacker – and these echo round Säbener Strasse whilst the Bayern players push themselves to a degree unheard of for a training session the day before a game. In fairness, they don't go on for long. Just 20 minutes. It's the rhythm and speed they're working at that is so unusual. Something is changing. The players perform brilliantly and there is a growing sense of pride and total security so that it seems absolutely impossible for them not to win. Everyone is sweating at the end. Pep explains the thinking behind his approach. 'You play at the rhythm you train at. In the match it's down to each player to do the right thing tactically but the team's rhythm depends on the training they've done. If you train badly, you play badly. If you work like a beast in training, you play the same way. And these guys, they train like beasts.'

Guardiola chooses control over aggression and picks Schweinsteiger instead of Kroos. By the time the bus is leaving the training ground for the Dolce Hotel, where they will spend the intervening six hours, the coach is relieved to have made his decision. He's feeling very positive. 'Control. I've gone for control. Control and more control.'

Robben has an outstanding game. He runs, defends and attacks with precision. As a player who can be inconsistent – capable of alternating superb football with major dips in performance – he is showing a new-found maturity. He is now a 30-something but has perfected the ability to head up the attacking, suffocating triangle of pressure Bayern put on opponents who are trying to play the ball. Later Pep will celebrate this exhibition of fine football by giving the Dutchman a warm hug.

In the 54th minute, Schweinsteiger breaks from the middle of the pitch and Cazorla doesn't track him. The German hits the edge of the box in time to connect with a cross from Ribéry, from which he opens the scoring. Two minutes later Arsenal equalise through Lukas Podolski but that's that for the game. Bayern certainly don't play brilliantly but, overall, they have had total control of the tie, which has been in their hands pretty much for 173 of the 180 minutes. Only in the initial minutes of the first leg, up until the point Neuer saved Özil's penalty, have they wavered.

It all ends with a similar theme, with Fabianski saving Müller's penalty to deny the Bavarians two wins.

Pep is euphoric. Some commentators will suggest that Bayern have given a mediocre performance, but the coach is happier than ever. 'I wanted control and that's what my men gave me. Okay, our finishing was off, but we ran the game and that's what I wanted. I know that in Munich people like us to attack and run up and down the pitch but this match needed the opposite of that. With a 2-0 lead from the away game, it made no sense to take risks. Okay, we weren't particularly fluid in the centre of the pitch but we played the game we needed to play.'

By 10 the next morning he has already reviewed the match and expresses the same mix of satisfaction with the win and self-criticism for the mistakes that were made. 'We did commit an error, which was to allow Lahm and Robben to work in the same channel on one side and Alaba and Ribéry on the other [in reference to the lined marking of lanes on the training pitch which Pep wants the players to make the structure of their positional play]. This duplication of positions took away our option of creating superiority. It is so, so important that the full-back and the winger don't operate in the same channel. If the winger is open and wide then the full-back must be inside in the next channel and vice versa.'

He is, as always, coming up with new solutions. 'The full-backs must position themselves as if they were attacking midfielders so that Götze can float and appear where he chooses to. But the full-backs need to be inside. And when their winger comes inside they must switch and move wide to the touchline and Götze will provide our superiority. But if the winger and the full-back play in the same channel, the full-back will be behind the winger and it all converts back into one-v-one – and we don't achieve superiority of numbers in the midfield. This must be corrected.'

And so, on this glorious morning with Säbener Strasse overflowing with a sense of sheer joy, Pep makes one more decision: Ribéry and Götze are slightly off form and need a 'mini pre-season' training plan. Over the next three weeks, Lorenzo Buenaventura will give them special attention so that they are fully fit for the quarter-finals on April 1. The Champions League is now the absolute priority.

51

'ULI IS OUR HEART. IT'S HARD TO IMAGINE BAYERN WITHOUT HIM.'

Munich, March 14, 2014

YESTERDAY WE WERE scheduled to fly to Basel together to watch a Europa League game between FC Basel and Red Bull Salzburg. Pep is very taken with Roger Schmidt, the Salzburg coach who, by April, will be hired by Bayer Leverkusen to take charge of their first team for season 2014/15. Guardiola has been studying Red Bull Salzburg for a while now. When they and Bayern met in a friendly back in January the Austrians won 3-0. What Pep witnessed was sufficient to convince him that Schmidt is a top-quality coach. It's for that reason that he has decided to watch this guy and his team in person. However, the evening before the trip it becomes clear that he will not be able to go, after all.

It is announced that there will be a judicial ruling on Uli Hoeness' case by midday on Thursday. On Wednesday Bayern Munich is the heart of a great empire. But then, in an instant...

Three-and-a-half-years in jail. Earth shattering. But perhaps not a surprise given that it had emerged during his trial for tax evasion that Hoeness had defrauded the German taxman of millions. Nevertheless, the decision came as a terrible blow for everyone around Bayern. While his crime was unconnected to the club, Hoeness wasn't simply Bayern's president and a brilliant former player. He was the club's very soul. You could say Hoeness was the club.

Since 1977 he had been in charge of Bayern's commercial development and had become the great constructor of the modern Bayern, making it a hugely successful, even model institution. Of course, the sentence meant his resignation as president. In a statement issued by Bayern he took full responsibility for his actions, publicly accepted the judgment and offered his resignation.

Pep was the first senior figure at Bayern to speak publicly following the announcement of the prison sentence. Midday Friday, in the press conference prior to playing Leverkusen, he said: 'Uli is our heart. The minute you join the club it's clear why everyone at Bayern adores him. I've never seen a club director so loved. It's hard to imagine Bayern without him.'

That Pep spoke up was not an insignificant detail and could be interpreted in a number of different ways. One might see it as an indication of the club's total faith in him as spokesman and therefore something he could be justifiably proud of. On the other hand, perhaps senior management had opted on this occasion to stay in the background and use him as a shield. This idea worried him a little, given the way in which he had been treated at Barcelona. In any case, being the first to speak certainly didn't mean half measures and Pep made no attempt to hide the emotion of the moment: 'Uli has earned our total respect. My work with him since arriving has gone incredibly well. He is my friend and will continue to be so. I hope that, in the future, he will return to support and help us as he has done up till now. My nine months here have shown me how important Uli is to this club. He is the most important man at Bayern and within the organisation everyone loves and values him. Uli is everything at Bayern: the No.1. Uli is the club.'

Pep's words reflected his depth of feeling for Hoeness. They had eaten together every week, sharing their visions for football, and had developed a friendship based on mutual respect. Without him Pep would feel a little orphaned within Bayern, despite the fact that Rummenigge would try very hard in the following months to fill the vacuum which the departing president had left.

Rummenigge himself explained the situation to the players through a short address in the lecture hall at Säbener Strasse. It was an institutional message, designed to safeguard club and team stability, but Rummenigge's delivery was intensely emotional. His face was haggard, his voice faint and by the third word it was clear that he would not control the tears. The squad and staff were tremendously moved as their chief executive forced himself to complete his speech through his sobs.

The upheaval was so tough for Bayern that just about any scenario looked feasible: from total support for Guardiola to a complete breakdown in relations. Pep felt that Hoeness was the club's father figure. It was he who had offered him the contract, he who had taken the firm decision to go after Pep. How would the dice fall without him?

Going forward, Pep would be more isolated. Would this have an effect on how long he would stay in Munich? His colleagues in the technical team thought so, even though it was far too soon to say so with absolute certainty. In Pep's mind, if Hoeness asked him to wait, to stay with Bayern until he got out of prison, he would say yes. It's something which, a few days later, the Catalan would touch on.

'I want to go on for two or three years, giving my best to this club, because my dream is to start over again working with Uli when he returns. Without him none of this would have been possible for me.' During the game against Bayer Leverkusen Pep felt the German's absence. Normally, three board members – Hoeness, Rummenigge and Jan-Christian Dreesen, the financial director – would come down to the coach's office after every match. There they would chat for a few minutes and then Rummenigge and Dreesen would go off to the dressing room to touch base with the players, but Hoeness would always stay with Pep to share opinions about the game. In the early days, Hoeness tried to boost Pep's spirits when he was still trying to make the team his own.

Now, even though the match had been a stroll, ending in a 2-1 win over Leverkusen, Guardiola missed his friend. Bayern were on a 50-game unbeaten streak (25 each for Heynckes and Guardiola) and their last league defeat was back in October 2012. Pep had beaten his own record of consecutive wins, 17 for Bayern and 16 with Barça. Dortmund had lost to Borussia Mönchengladbach and with players like Robben, Mandžukić, Kroos and company exiting to a standing ovation, the league title was pretty much sewn up.

After the opposing fans had done battle in song, in the 75th minute the Bayern supporters began to voice their support for the former president: 'Uli Hoeness, *du bist der beste Mann!*' Uli Hoeness, you are the greatest. Their songs talked of nostalgia. There were banners bearing his name dotted all over the stadium, all hand-written by fans who, setting aside moral judgements and their own private views of Hoeness' tax evasion, simply wanted to say goodbye to the man who had led their club in both the good and the bad times.

52

'PICKING A LINE-UP IS LIKE SITTING IN FRONT OF YOUR CHESS PIECES.'

Munich, March 15, 2014

RIBÉRY WASN'T GOING to play against Bayer Leverkusen. It wouldn't be a good idea, given his fitness levels. What with his disgust at failing to win the Balon d'Or, a muscle injury and an operation to relieve a trapped nerve in his back, Franck's 2014 had been a dead loss so far. Pep, who was beginning to despair, decided that a mini pre-season training programme would be good for the Frenchman and mentioned it to him just before the Leverkusen match. Two weeks of hard work to get back to full fitness.

Claudio Pizarro had been injured after a kick to his hip in the final training session before the match and Ribéry had to take his place. Before kick-off Pep called him to his office and told the player that he needed him to get back to his 2013 fitness levels, when his dribbling skills were unsurpassable.

However, over the next six weeks Ribéry would continue to have problems and his distress at his own failure to recover his best form would quickly become a mental block. Pep was concerned, although he took care to hide this in public, as did the rest of the team, who did what they could to support their team-mate's recuperation. It is impossible for any sportsman to be permanently on top form, but Ribéry found himself with these problems at the most decisive point of the season.

After beating Leverkusen, the league title was just about Bayern's. They would win it 10 days later in Berlin after establishing a 25-point lead over Borussia Dortmund with seven matches to go. It would be only the second time since 2000 that Bayern would retain the league title – a detail Rummenigge, Hoeness and Pep had often talked about.

The club had had seven different coaches in 10 years and after every success they would trip up. In private the Bayern management team had suggested to their coach that the most likely impact of the 2013 treble would be a total wash-out season.

Of course it hadn't turned out that way, largely due to the fact that the players were enthused and stimulated by Guardiola's arrival. Each player had his own reasons for this but, unusually for all-conquering champions, they had approached the season as if starting from scratch. They were now into the final sprint with three titles won (the European Super Cup, the World Club Cup and the Bundesliga) and two more on the horizon.

After the Bayer Leverkusen game I had dinner with Pep and assistant coach Domènec Torrent and I listed all the league records they had already broken. Pep hadn't known about their 50 games unbeaten, nor that he had equalled Heynckes' record of 25 matches without a defeat, nor any of the other stats. But Torrent was as dogmatic as ever. 'Listen Pep, let's not worry about beating records. We need to forget about being record breakers and get on with the job in hand, the Champions League. It doesn't matter if we start losing games and letting in goals from now on. Let's leave the records till next season.'

'You're quite right,' Guardiola replied. 'We should win the league as quickly as possible and focus on the DFB-Pokal and the Champions League.'

The conversation then turned to the players and the importance of getting men like Ribéry, Götze and Schweinsteiger back on form.

As the evening wore on the coach's conversation turned to his favourite subject: how he wants his team to play.

'It's clear. The team needs to play with more width. Two wingers pegged to their touchlines, a striker in the area, not necessarily to volley or head on goal, but to snap up the second ball. Then four players also waiting for the second ball or the rebound: two high up wing-backs, plus two attacking midfielders, or a creative midfielder plus the *pivote* – all to take advantage of the ball either being cut back, breaking off a defender or the keeper. Those guys queuing up on the edge of the box is how we cut off the counter-attack early, too.'

He then added one key objective: 'Next season we need to play better.'

I decided to put him on the spot. 'And how will you play better with the same players?'

Pep looked distracted and didn't answer, preferring to change the topic by throwing out a question so intriguing that for a moment I was lost for words: 'If we were playing the Champions League final tomorrow, who would you pick?'

This was a chance to suggest a line-up to the coach of Bayern and his assistant and I could not pass it up. So, fired up by an almost irrational lack of self-consciousness, I answered:

'No problem at all. I'd pick the 11 players who are on peak form at the moment and I'd play them in a 4-2-1-3.'

I then named my team, although, looking back, I can't believe I even attempted it. Pep listened in silence, saying nothing, but it took Domènec Torrent less than two seconds to jump in.

'And if we were up against Cristiano and Bale's Madrid, you wouldn't play Boateng, who is our fastest centre-half? And if it was against Barça, would you seriously consider taking on Messi without Bastian? And you'd play Chelsea with a traditional centre-forward but without Götze and Müller?'

Ouch! There were just too many variables to consider. That was the night I learned that sometimes it's better to keep your mouth shut. Pep hadn't commented on my line-up but Torrent's questions made it crystal clear that having all the information is not enough. It also struck me that looking in from outside requires none of the meticulous attention to detail that the decision-makers have to apply. The men the rest of us are so ready to criticise.

I also realised that Guardiola's eternal doubts are not part of his character, nor a sign of a lack of decisiveness or nerve. No, his doubts come from his determination to calibrate all the possibilities. My thoughts automatically turned to the chess player who analyses all the possible variables before making his move and I decided to share this with him. 'The process of picking a line-up is a bit like sitting in front of your chess pieces.'

'You've no idea how similar the two things are,' said Pep. 'You didn't read the interview Leontxo García did with Magnus Carlsen [the world chess champion] in El País by any chance? There was one thing Carlsen said that I loved. He said that it doesn't matter if he has to make some sacrifices at the start of the game because he knows that he is at his strongest in the latter stages. It really got me thinking and I must learn how I can apply it to football.'

53

'I LOVE YOU PEP.
YOU ARE IN MY HEART, MAN.'

Berlin, March 25, 2014

DURING THE DRESSING-ROOM celebrations in Berlin, Ribéry split Manel Estiarte's lip.

With seven games still to play Bayern had won the Bundesliga title. They had faithfully applied and even exceeded the objectives set out by Pep's recipe for winning a league: don't lose it in the first eight matches and then nail it in the last eight. After today's game, they were 25 points ahead of Borussia Dortmund with only 21 still up for grabs. They had beaten his formula by seven days.

This was the seventh consecutive time that Bayern had clinched the title away from home and they had done so with style. They were two up within 12 minutes and looked unstoppable. Pep altered the plans for the game which had been constructed over the previous few days and asked the two wing-backs to play wide, not inside. It was based on his understanding that Hertha would man-mark; if he put Rafinha and Alaba wide whilst attacking it would oblige Hertha to defend with six guys in a defensive line in order to cover the two wing-backs, the wingers, the striker and an attacking midfielder. That would mean that the middle of the pitch would be open territory for Bayern. As planned, Müller, Götze, Robben, Kroos and Schweinsteiger took total control of the midfield and at half-time, with the title pretty much in the bag, several players commented to Pep that things had gone precisely as he predicted they would.

The entire squad attended the game in Berlin's Olympiastadion, although Badstuber and Contento, who were still injured, travelled on the day of the match with Javi Martínez, who had momentarily lost his memory three days before, during the Mainz tie, after taking a kick to his head.

Bayern won 3-1, and in doing so became the first team to win the Bundesliga in March, and had won the league title earlier in the season than any other team in the history of any of the great European football championships. After 27 games they had accumulated 25 wins and two draws, with 79 goals scored and only 13 conceded. Their record-breaking league campaign had produced an average of almost three goals per game (2.92) as well as an unprecedented defensive record (0.48 goals per match conceded).

The dressing-room celebrations ended up with everyone in the swimming pool. Earlier in the evening Hermann Gerland, normally a serious man of few words, told Guardiola: 'Pep, you are a genius.'

By midnight, Estiarte was sporting a couple of stitches in his lip after Ribéry elbowed him accidentally as the team dragged him into the swimming pool. The team then moved on to the official party, where the festivities really took off. In actual fact, the club had had nothing to do with this part of the evening, which had been masterminded by Schweinsteiger, the squad's self-appointed party planner. Just eight days previously Schweini had thrown a fancy-dress party for his team-mates and their partners and tonight he was playing host in Berlin's Kitty Cheng Bar, in the Mitte district.

At 2am, Pep Guardiola stepped on to the dance floor, a novel spectacle for even his closest friends, who were more used to seeing him sitting surrounded by friends and colleagues chatting about a million and one things, most of them related to football. In Marrakech after winning the Club World Cup, for example, he had celebrated by having a quiet chat with his mates Sala i Martín and David Trueba. In fairness, almost nobody had been interested in dancing that night – just Cristina, Pep's wife and Maria, his eldest daughter, as well as Cristina's mum and Sala i Martín's wife. Eventually Dante and Rafinha, the fun-loving Brazilians had, rather shyly, joined the throng.

But in Berlin things were to take a very different turn. David Alaba took charge of the music, acting both as DJ and lead vocalist. The sheer exuberance of his players proved so infectious that for the first time in his coaching life Guardiola decided to get up and dance with them. Just for tonight he was one of the lads, having a few drinks and really letting his hair down. Sometime during the night, Ribéry grabbed him round the neck and announced: 'I love you Pep. You are in my heart, man. I'm just a street kid but you will always be in my heart. Never in my life did I think I could learn as much as I have this year.'

The festivities continued well into the early hours, with Pep calling it a night just before 5am whilst several of his players made it all the way through to breakfast time. On the flight home to Munich everyone was showing the effects, and the captains repeatedly begged Pep to cancel the following day's training so that they could sleep it off. In the end, the coach gave in. Their brilliant league campaign and ultimate triumph had earned them a rest.

I was keen to observe the team in their first training session after this triumph. The day after a great victory can be hugely illuminating. Would they be complacent after winning? Would they see this victory as a catalyst for future triumphs or the end of a chapter?

In the event the players were still in high spirits, particularly Schweinsteiger, who turned up at training wearing the face mask belonging to local ski champion Felix Neureuther. However, the hilarity ceased the second Pep appeared and started the warm-up. His players instantly switched into work mode as he divided them into three groups of seven for four five-minute games of 'double area' plus nine speed drills centred on quick reactions and six drills for explosive speed.

Not once did they slow down or relax and, at one point, Pep came over to me to say, delightedly: 'Ribéry's having his best session of the year. The guy's a beast. An absolute beast.'

So I had the evidence of the first training session after a major victory and it was clear that this was a team still hungry for success. A team in which every single player was fighting hard for his place in the starting line-up. There were more momentous Champions League fixtures to contest and nobody wanted to be left on the bench. At this stage no one could have imagined the thrashing they were about to suffer at Real Madrid's hands.

With the league in the bag and the Champions League looming on the horizon, it felt like a good time to sit down with Pep.

'Our worst 10 minutes this season were in the Emirates. Manu's [Neuer] hand saved us that day,' he reflected. 'Our best? Probably the game against City in Manchester or the first 40 minutes of the Hertha match in Berlin.'

I mention all the records they have broken. 'To hell with breaking records! I just hope we can get our minds off breaking records. It really doesn't matter from now on if we win or lose, if we concede goals or not. We're thinking about the Champions League and the DFB-Pokal now. The league is done as far as we're concerned.'

With only four days before their quarter-final tie with Manchester United, Pep was clear about the size of the challenge. 'Look, even if a team appears weaker than us, they could still do us damage in the Champions League. Be in no doubt, United will put us under pressure.

'We'll need to attack with our full-backs high and wide because theirs close in tight to their centre-backs, and we'll also have to be very careful of their counter-attacks via Rooney around the edge of the box and the wide pace of Valencia and Young. They don't mind putting the ball long and I want to have our best players in the middle of the pitch in order to have and hold the ball and dominate the midfield. But, watch out – you say OLD TRAFFORD in capital letters. Mr Ferguson will be there watching and that carries a certain weight.'

Bayern were going into the quarter-final as clear favourites, but Pep was sticking to his position. 'I know all that,' he told me, 'but where is it written that Bayern are a guaranteed semi-finalist, man? The only thing I know for sure is that we have two Champions League games ahead of us and we have to win them on the pitch. That's what I'll be telling them in the pre-match talk in Manchester – we have two games to play and we have to win them if we want to play the two after that.'

As he speaks, he remembers something and scribbles a reminder in his notebook: 'I've got to speak to Boateng because the other day against Mainz he made a miracle tackle to stop the striker getting away from him, but it was almost a red-card intervention. If he had mistimed it by a second then he'd have been off. If something like that happens in the Champions League I'd rather we let the opponents score than be left with 10 men.'

I decide to take advantage of this moment of relaxed reflection to ask Guardiola for his assessment of the team's progress.

'They've come on in leaps and bounds in positional play. At the beginning they struggled with it because it's a tough thing to master and they had to start from scratch, but they've done brilliantly and are total experts now. Nowadays I never need to tell them when to press or when to hold their position.'

Although the positional play drills, like the *rondos*, are fundamental elements of Pep's work, they are nonetheless just a part of his methodology. 'There's still a lot to work on and we'll start on that next season. I have taught enough for this season and we just need to apply it in competition. Next season we'll cover more concepts. We might even lose more matches but our overall game will improve. The players will have one year of this new language behind them and they will be much more solid from the outset. We'll try out a wider variety of approaches: one day we'll play with three defenders, the next with the wingers pegged to the touchlines and we'll really circulate the ball in the middle of the pitch via the No.10 and the attacking midfielders. Overall I think we'll grow next season.'

He talks about the ball as the key to everything. 'In football, it's the ball that gives you speed, your passing. In basketball if you are dribbling the ball all the time, the defence has an easier time of it. But if instead you pass it rapidly from one player to another you create huge problems for your opponents. It's exactly the same in football: to you, back to me, *tac-tac* and you get the other guy chasing his tail, even if it doesn't seem like you're doing very much at all. That's why I'm committed to making sure that we pass the ball so often, so quickly in the opponents' half. I want my two strikers to occupy the four rival defenders. Better still, I'd like to achieve that with only one striker even though he'd have to be absolutely expert to achieve it, leaving the rest of the attacking players to move the ball, to create openings in the middle of the pitch. Pass and pass – not simply to retain the ball but to kill the opponent. Moving the ball like that gives us order and leaves the rival in disarray. Coaches like Juanma Lillo [the itinerant Spanish coach who is a mentor to Pep] and Raúl Caneda [who worked closely with Lillo in Mexico and Spain] have always said this. It may not seem like much, but rapid-fire passing not only maintains your own organisation, but it also really messes up the other team.'

However, none of this is possible if your players don't trust the system. '*Eccolo qua*! [a favourite Italian expression of Pep's – 'that's exactly it']. That's the key question. How do you seduce your players into listening to you and accepting new concepts? And I mean 'seduce' not 'motivate'. What happened at Barça was not that I failed to motivate them – they are wonderful footballers and marvellous people. No, I failed to seduce them! I had introduced a million tiny tactical innovations over the four years and the next step wasn't going to be easy. You look into your players' eyes and it's a bit like looking at a lover. Either you see passion and a willingness to be seduced or you watch as the passion ebbs away. The same thing will happen here at Bayern. After a few years I'll no longer know how to seduce my players and that will be the time to leave. It's all in the eyes. It's all about seduction.'

PART FIVE

FALLING DOWN
AND GETTING BACK UP AGAIN

*'You can't measure success
if you have never failed.'*
STEFFI GRAF

54

'IT HURTS – IT MAKES YOU FEEL LIKE YOUR SKIN IS BURNING.'

Munich, March 29, 2014

IF MARCH WAS magical for Bayern, April is a tragic month. With the league in the bag, Pep makes copious changes against Hoffenheim. Thiago needs to play because over the last two weeks he has played very little, due to a badly bruised leg. He urgently needs to recover the sharpness which made him the fulcrum of the team from January onwards. Thus, he's a starter in the Allianz because Pep wants him also to be in the line-up for the game in Manchester, against United, a few days later. But 10 minutes into the game he tears his ligaments. The referee blows for a foul and as play unwinds Thiago just relaxes his right leg in a challenge with Kevin Volland. A grave error. His leg turns 180 degrees and produces an 80% tear in the medial collateral ligament.

The previous day Pep had turned down two offers. The first was the chance to buy a very well-known central defender, but the Catalan was unconvinced of his tactical rigour and so rejected the idea. The second was the offer of a blank cheque for his salary if he'd move and take over at another European giant at the end of the season. Naturally, he said no to that, too.

This was the day he chose to close the file on a league well won. 'I'm very content to have won this title already,' he announced. 'Out of professional respect for the Bundesliga we'll keep fighting hard in every game, but on Tuesday we've a 'final' in Manchester. Yes it's only called a quarter-final but it really is a final because we've only got three more guaranteed competitive games – these two against United and the DFB-Pokal semi-final against Kaiserslautern. Setting records doesn't matter to me now, only winning these three games.'

With these words Pep hoped to close one chapter and open another – with the objective of the Bundesliga complete, he wanted total focus on winning the DFB-Pokal and the Champions League. He didn't want the minds of his players on peripheral things like setting records.

This very idea ended up provoking a substantial dropping away in his players' general performance. It was the seed for what flowered into a disastrous 'de-mob happy' atmosphere.

Hoffenheim play a high pressing game and it hurts a Bayern team full of subs: Starke, Van Buyten, Contento, Pizarro, Shaqiri. In previous weeks teams like Nuremberg, Mainz and Wolfsburg had applied identical pressure on the Bayern defenders, high up the pitch, with the idea of pinning them back as they played out from the back, but Pep's team had won all those matches. Still, winning couldn't hide the fact that some German coaches – like Markus Weinzierl of Augsburg, Mainz 05's Thomas Tuchel and Wolfsburg's Dieter Hecking – had begun to find solutions to Guardiola's strategy and were finding out that pressing high, if done well, was a very interesting antidote to Bayern's playing style.

Hoffenheim press so much that Bayern have to change their game plan and play on the counter-attack – something which is just about as shocking as the final result, a 3-3 draw. For the first and only time in this Bundesliga season, Bayern's opponents have more shots on goal – 20 against 11 from Pep's team. It's an uncomfortable experience for the home team, whose run of 19 straight wins since October comes to an end. It is the first home draw in the league for 15 long months and the first time in two years that Bayern have conceded three goals in a Bundesliga match. Thiago is injured on 21 minutes and just as Pep's plans for Manchester are thrown into disarray, the battalions of his fortress are also beginning to crack. Thiago is the crucial man. Not just for the quality of his passing but for the way in which he holds together and brings more out of all the other players in the middle of the pitch. He is a magnet. Pep admits that it is possible that Thiago's absence might make all the difference to their chances of winning the Champions League. During the players' dinner Lorenzo Buenaventura finds a Twitter picture of the moment at which Thiago's injury occurred. He comments to Arjen Robben: 'You've always got to go in fully engaged to win the ball, never relax your challenge. Take care between now and the end of the season that you don't let the same thing happen to you.'

Minutes later Thiago phones Buenaventura from the hospital with the diagnosis. 'Nearly a total rupture of the ligaments, minimum eight weeks out. Bye bye World Cup.'

The fitness coach passes the news to Javi Martínez and they head directly to Thiago's home to console him. Meanwhile there's a misunderstanding which, even at this dark hour, causes a few smiles. Thiago calls his dad, Mazinho, a World Cup winner with Brazil in 1994, and tells him the diagnosis, but Mazinho doesn't quite grasp the message and then phones Buenaventura, with whom he's great friends, and says in a tearful voice: 'Loren, I'm in pieces! Thiago's injury is really, really serious – six to eight months out!'

Mazinho had understood the injury to be cruciate ligament damage, something which would take over six months to heal. Somehow it all makes Buenaventura and Thiago laugh at the mix-up and they calm Mazinho down, explaining that it's not six months, but about six weeks. It is the only upbeat moment of a pretty dire evening. On the morning of Sunday, March 30, those players who drew 3-3 with Hoffenheim divide into two groups in training. One stays on the pitch, including Pizarro, who has slept badly. It was his first full 90 minutes of the season and he suffered bad cramps as a result. Others like Ribéry, Van Buyten, Schweinsteiger, Götze and Shaqiri get on their bikes and head round the city's cycle tracks for half an hour.

Thiago and Pep meet with Doctor Müller-Wohlfhart to talk about the correct rehab for the injury. The doctor sets Thiago's leg in a cast but the player insists that his treatment must be with his old surgeon, Ramon Cugat in Barcelona. There will be growth factor injected directly into the ligament.

'I know that it hurts when this happens because it makes you feel like your skin is burning,' Thiago says. 'But I'll just have to put up with the pain.'

On leaving the dressing room his team-mates wish him a speedy recovery. 'Don't be long Thiago, we need you,' Neuer tells him.

'It's been a real bummer,' says Thiago. 'I was completely down in the dumps last night. But I found my strength again this morning. I've been here for breakfast with the rest of the team and my attitude is: "that's one day less until I'm back." Your mental attitude makes a big difference in how quickly you recuperate from something like this and now my head is in the right place. They tell me six-to-eight weeks, but I want to make it back in five.'

Pep makes Thiago a promise that he'll make sure the team does everything to make it to the finals of the DFB-Pokal and the Champions League for him and Thiago promises that he'll try to be back and ready for both dates. Of course, it's not going to be easy for either to fulfil his promise.

55

'ALWAYS PICK THE GOOD ONES. ALWAYS.'

Munich, March 29, 2014

THIS IS GUARDIOLA at his fascinating, volcanic best – post-match Pep.

Immediately after dealing with the media he goes to the players' restaurant in the Allianz, takes a glass of champagne, spears a few cubes of parmesan cheese and spends the next half hour talking about the match.

Usually he stays on his feet or occasionally sits down at one of the tables. But, although he won't have eaten all day, he's nowhere near ready to eat yet. Once the game finishes he's voraciously hungry but he's still not in the right frame of mind to relax and eat the dish of marinated salmon he loves so much. First he needs at least 30 minutes to burn off the adrenalin accumulated not just during the match but over the previous couple of days. So he gets right down to it. He talks almost incessantly about everything that has happened during the match. Everything has stuck in his memory. 'Did you see what Rafinha did in the 18th minute? He moved two metres inside and closed off the channel where they were queuing up to attack us.'

No, I hadn't noticed any of that. Pep is blessed with an almost photographic memory which allows him to remember and analyse everything that has happened in the match. In this he resembles Rafa Nadal, a tennis star capable of recalling every shot and every point of his matches, his level of dominance or the error he or his opponent made and which moment was most significant. And all of this remains with him long after the match is over. Similarly, Guardiola remembers every move: how it developed, what happened, which players got involved and what the consequences were. On the other hand, he pays no attention to stats.

'You didn't have nearly as much possession – only 63%,' I say to him.

'Yeah, really? Wow.'

'But Starke had more touches on the ball than any one of the Hoffenheim players!'

'Wow. No way. That's really good.'

Statistics don't turn him on. What gets him passionate is the play itself and his post-match analysis of it.

'Have you seen how smart Philipp [Lahm] is? How the guy turns and protects possession and also splits the opposition?'

Or: 'I'll have to speak to Kroos because against [Manchester] United he definitely won't be able to try that move where he controls and turns to the right, because they'll anticipate, rob him and start a counter-attack.'

He calls Planchart over to the table: 'Carles, tomorrow morning get me a video of the 36th minute – the thing you mentioned to me. I want to show the centre-half how better to position himself.'

During this pretty amazing half hour, standing in his corner of the restaurant, gesturing wildly as if he's still mid-match, Pep reproduces most of the preceding game. He breaks it down and it's like he's performing an autopsy. The skeleton is stripped of every muscle and tendon. He'll analyse his players, the opposition, each phase of the game, every important move. He goes over how the goals happened – this involves him recalling exactly how the move started and developed and then tracking it right up to the point the ball actually went in.

Then his thoughts will turn to other matches. While he's still doing his replay of this match, he'll start to explain what the next one will be like, how he's going to coach the team during the week, who is going to be rested – then he'll spool back a bit, still eating chunks of cheese but with the champagne almost untouched, and he'll agree with Torrent that before the next game they'll have to practise a specific free-kick. There's a hug for Robben, who has come over to say goodbye with his three lovely blonde kids. Pep reminds the Dutchman of the sharp little movement he produced with his right foot 10 minutes before the end and tells him to 'do it more often please'.

Seconds later he's praising the work of the Red Bull Salzburg coach Roger Schmidt and breaking down the way in which the Austrian champions play. How the forwards press, how the full-backs push on and the positions the attacking midfielders take up.

All the while he's explaining this in such detail that you'd think his team is playing Salzburg tomorrow and I'm wondering why on earth he has gone off on this tangent.

But this is Pep, and two minutes later he's changed tack and is talking about the little forward chip Iniesta used to put the ball over the two centre-halves and make them turn during the Barça-Espanyol game earlier this evening.

'But when did you see that move?' I ask him.

'When I was waiting in the hall. What a marvel Andrés is. He's a genius.'

This is Pep at his most passionate, and it is a joy to be around him. This half hour of champagne and cheese is the manifestation of his passion for football but it is also a lesson in foresight and pragmatism.

One night I'm accompanied by Patricia González, the very young coach of the Azerbaijan Under-19 women's team. During the dinner Pep gazes at her and says: 'Patricia, I'll give you some advice: always pick the good ones. Always!'

The young coach then asks him a really good question. 'Pep, who are the good ones? Is it the most famous players?'

'No. The really good players are the ones who never lose the ball. Those who know how to pass it and who never lose it. They are the good ones. And that's who you must always use, even if they are lower-profile than the rest.'

56

'THE ESSENCE OF FOOTBALL IS WORKING OUT THE BEST WAY TO ATTACK YOUR OPPONENTS.'

Manchester, April 1, 2014

THIS IS THE third time this season Bayern have travelled to England on Champions League duty. In Manchester City's Etihad Stadium they put on an exhibition of football, winning 3-1, and in Arsenal's Emirates Stadium, although they had struggled for the first seven minutes, they found their rhythm and won 2-0.

Bayern also dominate at Old Trafford, but victory eludes them. Manchester United have had a difficult season but today they defend with courage and pride and hold the German team to a 1-1 draw.

Bayern have got United holed-up in their own penalty area with six men behind the ball, which leaves them almost no chance of mounting counter-attacks. In one of the few they do achieve, Danny Welbeck gets a chance to run at Boateng, who is the last man. Boateng hesitates, perhaps conscious of the instruction Guardiola has given him about red-card tackles, and Welbeck is one-on-one with Neuer. Crucially, the German comes out on top.

With Lahm in central midfield and with Kroos and Schweinsteiger either side of him, Bayern take total control of the game. But they show some recognisably bad habits: the domination of the ball translates into too few clear chances; and Bayern's capacity to finish those chances is far too low, a season-long tendency which is encouraged by the fact that so many of Bayern's opponents pack their defence and leave precious little space. Ribéry is going through a quiet spell, leaving all the emphasis on the right side and Robben. Meanwhile, Schweinsteiger is much more important for his goals (another here marks his fourth in six games) than for his midfield play, which sometimes slows down Bayern's game.

These are small indications that all is not well and overall Bayern storm through the game only conceding, somewhat surprisingly, a Nemanja Vidic header from a corner. 'Surprisingly' because up till now Bayern have lost only three goals from corner kicks all season: to Hertha striker Adrián Ramos, to Niklas Süle, Hoffenheim's defender who puts away a rebound after a Neuer mistake, and Rafinha's own-goal against Schalke. Three goals lost to corners in 45 competitive matches using one of Pep's defining football principles, the zonal marking defence. 'It makes your defence much stronger because each player just has to take care of his own zone and watch the back of the team-mate in front of him,' says the coach.

Bayern are now accustomed to facing corners either with a 4-3-2-1 or 5-3-1-1 formation, depending on the rival. Lahm will usually push out to stop the opponent taking a short corner. The first defensive zone will always be occupied by those who are best aerially – normally Martínez and Mandžukić. Next the two central defenders and finally, at the back post, Alaba, who is the best at following the ball if he has to run backwards because the corner is taken long. Of course, this approach to defending is not foolproof and has its flaws, but Pep believes in it and certainly prefers it to man marking. 'If you are man-marking, four opponents can make runs to drag your defence to the back post then they sneak someone in to score at the front post – or vice-versa. If you defend zonally this won't happen to you.'

For Guardiola, this concept extends to the team's entire playing style. 'Zonal defending is much more effective than man marking. It's so much simpler for a player to stick to his own zone. He knows he's responsible for that area and that sense of individual responsibility then becomes collective responsibility and in turn strengthens team solidarity.'

For Pep, defending well is based upon about half-a-dozen good habits which, if trained repetitively, become automatic.

'The essence of football consists of working out the best way to attack your opponent. You have to start the play, building from the back, with crystal clear understanding of how your rival likes to defend and attack.

'You have to go over and over the most important ideas. Like, for example, how to defend against a particular opponent. We spend 20 minutes on this before every important game and tell the players how the other team will attack as well as instructing them on how to find spaces and where we can do some damage. The players trust the technical team completely because we're usually absolutely correct in our predictions.'

In reality, Vidic's goal is the culmination of a series of tiny mistakes on the part of the Bayern players and one player in particular fails to stick to the zonal marking system. It's a symptom of the occasional lapses in attention creeping into Bayern's game which, within weeks, will culminate in a catastrophic encounter with Real Madrid. United, however, concede a goal nine minutes later scored by Schweinsteiger, who finishes after Rafinha's cross is knocked down for him by Mandžukić in the penalty area.

So Bayern leave Old Trafford with a result which bears little resemblance to the one which had been on offer to them. They firmly dominate the match but put away only one of the 15 chances they create. All the same, the game shows two interesting defensive innovations: for United's throw-ins Lahm becomes a third centre-half while the full-back on the opposite side tucks in very tight, so that the half of the pitch nearest the throw-in is packed with Bayern players. Secondly, when United try to organise an attack Bayern push them towards one of the touchlines to shut them in via a pressing move which consists of players in the shape of an imaginary triangle, with Robben at the tip. Pep is willing to mob United's ball carrier and leave the remainder of the pitch empty because he doesn't think there is any danger of United exploiting it.

And so, the conquerors of the Etihad and the Emirates leave Old Trafford once more unbeaten and, with the league secured, inevitably begin to envisage another treble-winning season. But can they pull off this dream, this unprecedented utopia? No team in history has achieved two treble-winning seasons. Only Celtic, Ajax, PSV Eindhoven, Manchester United, Barcelona, Inter and Bayern have succeeded in winning the league, their domestic cup and the

European Cup in the same season. And none of them have done it more than once. Neither, across two decades of competition, has any club managed to win the Champions League two years running.

Considering all this, what justification is there for anyone at Bayern dreaming of winning a second treble? I put this question to no less an expert than Jupp Heynckes, who sizes up their chances. 'Historically there have been a number of superb Bayern sides. Mythical players like Sepp Maier, Beckenbauer and Gerd Müller. And yet, even those guys didn't manage it. At the moment the club is fighting for the treble and Pep has already won the league, but it's still a very tough task, very, very tough.'

I catch up with Heynckes shortly after the Manchester game and ask him to evaluate Guardiola's first year at Bayern: 'I've known Pep since he played for Barça. He was devastating in the midfield and had a great touch and a superb vision of the game. He's also someone I admire on a personal level and I've not been surprised at all by all he has achieved. I was in Spain for a number of years and am familiar with both his and Barça's playing philosophy. I know how his teams play. We all knew the kind of changes he would make at Bayern, for example making the full-backs play inside, as he's doing. The Germans have difficulty understanding this idea [he smiles] because it leaves the two centre-halves isolated and puts the full-backs right up alongside players like Kroos. It's a move which German football has found a little shocking.

'When we were up against Barça in the Champions League semi-finals last year people asked me if I was going to contact Pep for some advice, but I didn't need to. I already knew Barça's style well and have therefore not been surprised by what Pep is doing in Munich. He understands what sets Bayern apart: the organisation, the stature of the club and the quality of its staff. He fits the Bayern model perfectly because he, too, is a person of quality.'

I ask him if he believes that Guardiola's innovations have been a step too far for German football culture. 'Everyone has his own playing philosophy, his own approach to managing a team. Pep learned his trade from Johan Cruyff, following the Ajax and La Masia models. I, on the other hand, was born in Mönchengladbach and my mentor was Hennes Weisweiler. It's probably true that my own journey has been very different from Pep's but I have to say that I've really enjoyed watching Bayern's football this year. These guys were my players last year and we won the treble, the first German club to do so in 50 years of Bundesliga history. This is a team with real character, with players who work brilliantly together and Pep is a first-class coach who established his pedigree at Barcelona. That's why I love watching this Bayern side.'

Unfortunately just about now Bayern's game starts to head into a downward spiral. There are three principal reasons for this: Thiago's absence, the squad relaxing after winning their sixth trophy in 12 months and Pep's decision to rest his regular starters. The deterioration is marked by Bayern's first league defeat of the season, which takes place in Augsburg, always difficult territory for the team. The coach leaves Lahm, Robben and Ribéry at home and puts Rafinha, Dante, Boateng, Alaba, Götze and Müller on the bench. Starke is also absent, due to a problem with torn elbow ligaments.

Bayern's unstoppable progress through the league comes to a halt. They have played 53 consecutive games unbeaten, from October 28, 2012 to April 5, 2014, with Heynckes in charge for the first 25 and Pep for the last 28. This is the first time in 66 games they have failed to score. In itself, of course, it's no big deal. It's just one defeat. But the signs of the team's decompression are there. After their phenomenal league campaign they are now entirely focused on the Champions League, but it becomes increasingly difficult for Bayern to adjust precisely and correctly between when to compete at full tilt and when not to.

57

'I'VE NEVER PLAYED LIKE THIS … NOT EVEN IN MY BOLDEST DAYS AT BARÇA.'

Munich, April 8, 2014

'NOW IT'S OVER to them. They hold their own fate in their hands. I have given them every single tactical tool I can and it's all on them now. I'm not even going to bother with a pre-match talk tomorrow. It's not necessary because they know it all already. All I'm going to do is say "hi" and give them a hug. This is their moment.'

The last training session before their game against Manchester United is over. Within 24 hours the Allianz will play host to another great European tie – the return leg of the Champions League quarter-finals against Wayne Rooney and his men. Pep has spent the last two days taking his men through his blueprint for their assault on the great English side. Currently, Guardiola's sole objective is the defence of their title as European champions and he has made good his promise to discard any thought of breaking records. Although he had discussed this many times with Domènec Torrent, I wasn't convinced that he would manage to carry this commitment through to his team's performance on the pitch. But he has done just that, despite the fact that it has meant drawing against Hoffenheim and losing in Augsburg.

Focus on the Champions League has been to the detriment of their remaining league fixtures and Pep has already received some flak for his approach. The critics claimed that choosing to field a significantly weaker Bayern side was nothing less than a betrayal of the Bundesliga. 'I completely understand how they feel,' he confessed to me a couple of days before the United tie, 'but we've won the league and right now my duty is to think about the Champions League.'

Several newspapers suggested that in taking this stance, Pep was putting Bayern's possible treble at risk, but the coach wasn't particularly bothered by the criticism. 'Critical feedback is very healthy. In fact it's vital for a great club like ours. I reckon that people think it offends me but it really doesn't. Criticism means that you have to stay alert. That's why I'm critical of myself and my players.'

Pep had left three of his key players, Lahm, Ribéry and Robben, at home for the Augsburg game on Saturday and gave the whole team a day off on Sunday. He wanted the squad fresh for their double session on Monday. He wanted to spend time going over his plans with his men and needed them as alert as possible. This would not, however, be an ordinary game plan.

Pep, Torrent, Planchart and the other analysts had examined Manchester United from every possible angle. They had produced an exhaustive analysis of their opponents which had then been perfected by the coach himself and by 9am on Monday the game plan and the line-up had been agreed. Pep used the morning and afternoon sessions to share these with his men. First they worked on the way the English team functions at both attacking and defensive dead-ball situations, watching these on video and then playing them out on the training pitch. Pep emphasised one thing again and again: at Old Trafford, United had managed only two genuinely dangerous moments – the one-on-one between Welbeck and Neuer, and the Vidic goal. Bayern's objectives had been fixed from the outset of the preparation for this game: better awareness at set-plays and conceding even fewer chances at home than in Manchester.

By Monday morning the players already had a good idea as to the line-up. Javi Martínez and Schweinsteiger were banned and Thiago was injured (the player had left for Barcelona to receive treatment for his injured knee from Doctor Cugat). What did take the players by surprise was the game plan Pep laid out for them on Tuesday, just after lunch. 'We're going to use a 2-3-3-2.'

The team were delighted. Pep then read out the team sheet. Neuer; Boateng, Dante; Lahm, Kroos, Alaba; Robben, Götze, Ribéry; Müller and Mandžukić. Not only did he give them the starting XI far ahead of normal, but had also shown them a new way of attacking this game via four separate, quite distinct, lines. Given that Bayern would probably be attacking for 75% of the match and in the opposition half, Pep wanted to populate the back line with the two centre-halves and have the two full-backs push right up next to Kroos.

He had spoken with Lahm and detailed what he needed. Although the line-up made him look like a full-back, that was not what Pep wanted from the captain. Instead, he was to play as a midfielder in the line of three with Kroos and Alaba. Moreover, given Kroos' tendency to move to the left, Lahm would need to squeeze in and occupy the middle of the line, as if he were the *pivote*. If Kroos moved left, Alaba was to push on higher, on the left touchline. Of course, if United were to get the ball in an attacking situation and Bayern were defending correctly, then both Lahm and Rafinha would need to double back and occupy normal full-back positions in a defensive line of four. In front of these three midfielders, Götze would have total liberty of movement. In the construction of attacking play he should find himself at the tip of a diamond shape linking with Alaba, Kroos and Lahm. When the ball moved high up the pitch he would be free to take on the role of another, anarchic striker. It meant that Pep had unified his most reliable passers in the middle of the pitch. Robben and Ribéry were to play on the wings. In the opposition half, they would be the sole occupants of the wide space – not Lahm or Alaba. 'Arjen and Franck: you'll have to be wing-backs in this match. You'll drop back to the middle of the pitch to pick the ball up and bring it up the wing. Tomorrow that's going to be your responsibility exclusively because the full-backs are playing as midfielders.'

Hours later Pep would confess: 'I've never played like this, with the wingers playing as full-backs. Not even in my boldest days at Barça. It's completely new for me, too, but it just seems right. And they're going to do it perfectly. I see it in Arjen and Franck's eyes. I can feel it and see it in the way they handle themselves. Müller's going to do brilliantly too. You can just see it.'

Müller is to be in the front line with Mandžukić. Two centre-forwards whose job is to get in between the United centre-backs and the full-backs. It's an idea Pep has often discussed with his backroom staff. 'Two guys occupying four defenders. Müller and Mandžukić need to tie up the entire United back four. If they manage it, think of the space that Robben and Ribéry will have to receive the ball wide.'

Rafinha, however, will lose out in the process and the Brazilian will not be in the starting line-up on a day when the Brazil national coach, Luiz Felipe Scolari, will be in attendance.

For the first time this season, Pep announces the line-up and the game plan the day before the match. They then run through the relevant moves in the training session. The starters wear green bibs and line up in a 2-3-3-2 formation, whilst Pizarro copies Rooney's likely moves and Javi Martínez and Van Buyten take on the roles of Vidic and Ferdinand. The closed session is taking place on training pitch No.1, far from prying eyes and Pep takes the time to run over what he wants one more time.

The ball needs to reach Ribéry or Robben quickly and directly, right out on the touchline, while the two strikers occupy the back four. If the wingers have only one marker then they are to go at him and try to reach the byeline. If they are double marked when the ball gets to them, they've to return it to the nearest midfielder, Lahm or Alaba, or look to hit Götze or the two strikers with a pass.

After each of Pep's repeated explanations, the players play out the scenario, at full tilt, on the training pitch. They try to pin the surrogate Manchester United back line into their penalty area. Guardiola reckons that United will come out at the Allianz with the idea of closed-ranks defending, looking to use Rooney in a successful counter-attack.

As the afternoon wears on, the players practise again and again with the coach suggesting multiple variants for each situation. One of his technical team comments: 'He's explained as much as it's possible to explain. They understand it all and now all they have to do is put it into practice.'

Some positional-play drills close the training session, although Pep bans Robben from taking part – the player had taken a kick to his leg the day before and Pep doesn't want to take any risks. Just the week before, the second-choice goalkeeper Tom Starke had been badly hurt. In addition, both Thiago and Shaqiri, who was injured in Augsburg, are absent. 'It's such a shame not to have Thiago on the bench. He's the guy to get us out of trouble when things get tricky,' says Guardiola.

The nerves are beginning to set in.

'My stomach's in knots,' Estiarte tells me. 'I can't eat anything the day before these kinds of matches. We've worked hard all year for exactly this kind of game.'

Manuel Neuer is also keen to share. 'Bring it on. Match day is always better than the day before. You spend some time at the team hotel and then you're on the bus, you get to the stadium, warm up and, before you know it, the game has started. But the day before just drags by.'

Neuer deputises for Robben in the positional-play exercises. As always on the day before a Champions League game, Lorenzo Buenaventura orders only two repetitions of five minutes in the drills – not the normal three reps. This is to avoid over-tiring the players just in case the next day's game goes to extra time. They do the exercises brilliantly and it all ends with an unexpected shout from Pep: 'That's it! If we play like this tomorrow, we're through!'

Neuer has just demonstrated his mastery of the ball at his feet and I tell Pep about the recent Twitter story that Neuer had asked to play in the midfield in light of Thiago, Schweinsteiger and Javi's absences. Pep laughs. 'It's not such a ridiculous idea, not at all. Manu is capable of anything.'

We are left alone together on the training pitch and I ask him if he is feeling the nerves as well.

'Yes of course, but not too much. If we play the 2-3-3-2 well, we'll win. We need to score from the second-ball actions. Remember what I told you in August about what I learned from the Barcelona-

Chelsea match in 2012? Well, this is the day we have to do what I didn't manage that day for Barça. Seek out the rebounds in the box and punish the second ball wherever it lands in the penalty area. They know everything they need to know and are capable of doing this. I'm not doing a pre-match talk. They know it all already. All we need is for them to go out and play with courage and do what they do best. If they do that, then we're through. This is the players' moment.'

58

'ARJEN'S A BEAST.'

Munich, April 9, 2014

IF YOU WANT to fully understand the essence of Pep Guardiola the coach, a football man through and through, it would be helpful to consider what is happening in his office at 11.15 this Wednesday night. It's just 45 minutes since Bayern have secured their place in the semi-finals of the Champions League for the fourth time in five years. It is also the fifth time in five seasons that Guardiola himself has made it to that stage. This has been an enormous achievement and everyone is euphoric: players, supporters, directors, everyone is celebrating. Guardiola most of all. He's given every one of his players a hug in the dressing room, had a chat with Uli Hoeness, who has come down to congratulate him and is just about to speak to the press. But first he does something rather bizarre for someone who has just won such an important game. In the midst of the dressing-room festivities, Pep turns to Manel Estiarte and asks him to get hold of a certain visitor.

Two minutes later Pep is shut up in his office with his guest and for 15 minutes the pair of them discuss one of Bayern's three possible opponents in the semi-finals, going over the key elements of their playing style. Before he can allow himself to fully savour this victory he wants to prepare for the next battle and if he can get some first-hand pointers, so much the better. This is the real Pep in action: a man incapable of savouring his success because he's too busy thinking about the next move.

And this has not been an easy victory despite the fact that everything happened exactly as Pep predicted. Bayern have gone out with the 2-3-3-2 formation, the full-backs next to Kroos, who tries to close down

Rooney. Bayern control the ball and the first half, shooting at goal 13 times to United's one. But United defend well. At half-time the Bayern technical analysis is just this: total domination but not enough of the free space with which to put the game to bed.

With the scoreboard at 0-0 at half-time Bayern are already on their way to the semi-finals except the minute things start looking good, Pep's players ease up the pressure. It has happened before, in the Champions League against City and in the league against Mönchengladbach and Hoffenheim. This same sense of superiority assails them against United and, with the score at 0-0, with the German side poised to go through, the players sit back and concentrate only on maintaining control. Pep keeps waving his arms about. He wants more intensity, more pressure. He tells his men to play deeper, but it takes Patrice Evra's thunderous shot past Neuer to deliver the sucker punch they need. In that instant, 56 minutes into the match, Bayern are facing elimination.

Suddenly they're wide awake. Sixty-nine seconds later Ribéry and Götze cause havoc down the left and Müller draws both United centre-halves out of position, so Mandžukić only has to beat Evra in the air to equalise.

Right at this moment Pep modifies his plan, introducing Rafinha for Götze and putting Lahm and Götze in as double *pivotes*. Within about 10 minutes Bayern, with the brakes off, have completely overwhelmed United with goals from Müller and Robben. It's so impressive that Pep turns to the fans in the Allianz to demand an ovation for his players.

It's midnight before he finally makes it to the team restaurant, where he hugs his three children and gives his wife a long, lingering kiss. He's starving, as he always is after a game. Tonight he goes for his favourite meal, marinated salmon, and as soon as he's finished his first serving he's up for another. 'Extra pepper please,' he tells the cook. Instead of his usual glass of champagne, he asks for two. 'No, bring me four glasses. Or the whole bottle.'

Post-match Pep. But tonight is special. He's through to his fifth

Champions League semi-final. Five out of five. He has never gone out before this stage. The dinner becomes a detailed match replay. He points out what they did well and the mistakes they made, the guys who played brilliantly and those that were somewhat below par.

'Arjen's a beast. A beast. Rafinha was first class, he was completely focused the second he left the bench. That's the mark of an outstanding player. And what about Kroos? Tremendous Toni. A year ago he was playing like a second striker and today he marked Rooney out of the game playing as a holding midfielder. Rooney! I'm so proud of my men.'

I remind him how difficult it was for Bayern to break down the English defence.

'Of course it was. What else did you expect? They're a brilliant team. I was pleased with our 2-3-3-2, but it was definitely rough finding spaces. We only managed it in the first half thanks to Robben and then it came much more easily in the second half.'

I also point out that Bayern had had the brakes on right up until Evra's goal. 'You're right, completely right and I don't really understand why. We've had a chat with Lahm and he can't explain it either. Sometimes things just happen and there's no real explanation.'

Pep is in full flow. He's in ideas mode, analysing the game whilst at the same time describing how they'll deal with whoever they face next. He'd prefer Atlético.

'And if you make it to the final?'

'It won't matter, as long as we make it. And I hope we do – for Thiago.'

In the early hours of the morning Pep will leave the stadium with his daughter Valentina asleep in his arms. He'll struggle to get to sleep, but will be up and working in his office by 8.30am, reviewing his plans for his next league opponents, the great Borussia Dortmund.

Training will be held on Pitch No.2 and will be a relaxed and playful affair although, as always, Pep will draw a halt to the jokes early on. This is an open session, although the men who played against United are out of sight on Pitch No.1, doing *rondo* drills. In one of them

Dante is nutmegged and is roundly teased, at high volume. It's all laughs and jokes. The high jinks get out of hand however and Pep, annoyed by all the hilarity, comes straight over and demands that the players calm down and show some respect for the supporters who have come along to Säbener Strasse. The starters then complete the session, which consists of a dozen 60-metre runs, done at a light tempo, in front of the watching public and in complete silence.

59

'I DON'T CONSIDER MYSELF A GOOD COACH.'

Munich, April 12, 2014

GUARDIOLA STARTED WITH a defeat in Dortmund, in the German Super Cup on July 27, 2013, and today, eight-and-a-half months later, his team slips up once more against the same opponents. This time it's a league game in Munich. It's fitting that it should be Jürgen Klopp to bring his great rival down to earth, although the German coach is at pains to point out that: 'Pep isn't my rival. I'm up against another 16 teams, so in reality each of us has 17 rivals, not just one.'

Klopp very kindly delays his departure from the Allianz Arena to spend some time evaluating Guardiola's style: 'He has an incredible ability for developing his teams. His style of play is very complex, really very complex. It's unique and extremely difficult to combat. He did it in Barcelona and he's doing it here in Munich.'

But the Dortmund coach sees Pep's great strength, above and beyond his style of play, as his ability to maintain his teams' competitive spirit at a consistent level. 'He does something that is very, very difficult. It's phenomenally hard to be consistently enthusiastic about and focused on your next game, particularly when you are so successful. It's struck me on several occasions this year. The most important thing that Pep has achieved, quite apart from playing brilliant football, has been to maintain this consistent, high-tempo rhythm, one game after another, going from one day to the next. That's what's so hard. But he's done it, and I don't think they're going to stop.'

Klopp is delighted. Dortmund have won 3-0 at the Allianz Arena, matching Pep's result in Dortmund at the end of November 2013. Of course it doesn't have the same significance. In Dortmund they were still battling for the league and now in Munich there is nothing left to salvage, save some pride. But for Bayern it is a blow. Just one more setback in a month full of moments of weakness.

There seems little wrong with Pep's match plan. He puts out a 2-3-2-3 formation in which Rafinha, Lahm and Alaba are the first line of midfielders with Schweinsteiger and Götze the inside-forwards in front of them. If Dortmund close Lahm when he attempts to bring the ball out it is Rafinha who takes over, and does so very well. It's all going swimmingly until Bayern fail to defend a throw-in. Dortmund produce one of their lightning-fast moves which ends up with Mjitaryán scoring. The goal seems to cloud the vision of Pep's players even before Neuer goes off with a tight calf muscle in the second half. Within a few minutes, one counter-attack and one long ball add two more goals, thus rounding off a bitter experience which has thrown up a number of weaknesses.

We are talking about much more than one or two details. The decline is more serious than that. Bayern are in freefall with only a week-and-a-half to go before they face Real Madrid in the Champions League semi-finals. There are players out through injury (Thiago, Neuer and Shaqiri), Ribéry and Götze are having problems and Schweinsteiger and Mandžukić are a bit off form, too. Team spirit has been affected and the players feel like they've lost control. The process of decompression after winning the league has led to a loss of identity at the most decisive stage of the season. The momentum has gone, that state of grace teams experience when they are on peak form.

For me it's fascinating to see how Pep behaves in the face of defeat. This is not something he has much experience of. In his 303 games as a first-division coach (four years at Barcelona and one at Bayern), he has only lost 27 games. On average, one defeat every 11 games.

These defeats add dimension to the victories and it is no accident that one of his bedside books is *Saber perder* (Knowing how to lose) by his friend, the filmmaker David Trueba. For him defeat is also a catharsis, a revelation. As the journalist Isaac Lluch explained to me one evening, referring to Bayern's defeat in the Super Cup, it is a necessity. 'Starting off with a defeat gives Pep the right element of epic drama, exactly what any hero needs as he embarks on his quest.'

There's always a fall simply because, amongst other reasons, every success is built from the ashes of previous defeat, as long as the reasons for the defeat are properly and clearly assimilated.

Bayern have lost in monumental fashion. The 3-0 trouncing in the Allianz Arena has been particularly hard to take because this time Guardiola chose not to field a weaker team. Unlike the recent defeat in Augsburg when the Bayern line-up was mainly substitutes and youth team players, this time he used his key men. And he had also worked hard on his own analysis of the opposition. All for nothing. Klopp's Dortmund has been the better team.

In the post-match press conference Pep is much more forthcoming than usual. He gets on well with Klopp and is happy to publicly congratulate him. He also accepts the errors he and his team have made and recognises that it is vital for them to regain the competitive form they displayed before winning the league. As he makes his way through the Allianz Arena's corridors he stops for every fan who asks for an autograph or a photo. He smiles, apparently completely untroubled by the defeat.

Once inside the Players' Lounge he greets his players and their families warmly but I pick up on one principal difference tonight: he eats with his wife Cristina. It may just be coincidence but I suspect it is more significant than that. Usually Pep gets to the restaurant and immediately hugs his kids, Valentina, Màrius and Maria. He kisses and cuddles them before embracing Cristina and spending a couple of minutes with her. Then he's off talking to friends and acquaintances or the players' families who want a photo with him. It is only much later that he will spend time with his family.

But today things are different. He sits down beside Cristina and, instead of champagne, orders a glass of red wine. I'm sitting at the next table but get the impression that Pep needs some time alone with his partner to process what has happened. Before he can pick himself up he needs time to mourn his loss, to withdraw for a while and share his private feelings, rather than his professional thoughts.

And so, for about 30 minutes, nobody goes near his table, as if the whole room is aware that Pep needs some quiet time. In the end it is his own children who interrupt his introspection by announcing that Barça have lost in Granada and may well have missed out on winning the Spanish league. By now the restaurant is almost empty. A frustrated Arjen Robben gives his own take on the defeat: the team needs to regain their hunger if they are to have any chance of making it to the Champions League final.

Pep's quiet time is over and Cristina has obviously helped him recharge his batteries. Glass in hand, he moves to another table and is once more the enthusiastic Pep we know so well, full of energy and chat.

'I messed up.'

Initially I assume that he's referring to a tactical error but I'm wrong. He's actually talking about his management of the team's success.

'You are nobody if you're only giving 95%. That includes me. This isn't false modesty. I am a complete nobody if I'm not performing at my very, very best. And I'll tell you another thing. I don't consider myself a good coach. I know you won't believe me and that people will think it's false modesty but it's honestly what I believe. I have so many doubts, I worry about everything and am secure about nothing. But there is one thing I am sure of. I messed up. We thought we were the greatest and our decline started that day in Berlin [when they won the Bundesliga]. It hasn't been a gentle decline, no, we've gone right off the rails.'

Màrius and Maria come over to listen to their father, interrupting occasionally to ask a question, but Pep presses on. 'Praise actually makes you weaker. It happens to us all. I went soft after Berlin. They asked me to cancel training the next day and I agreed. I wanted to avoid injuries so we stopped doing full on 11-against-11 matches in training. And we fucked it up. I was trying to stop them getting injured and what I actually did was turn my players soft. And we're nobodies if we turn soft. That's not a tactical problem. This team played 53 games without a loss, under Jupp and me, using a thousand different tactics. 53 matches, with injuries, with key players missing, using different tactics and we didn't lose a game. What we did was run. We ran ourselves into the ground. And then we stopped running. It's got nothing to do with tactics!'

Cristina now joins us, obviously anxious to support her husband in recovering his equilibrium. She suggests that perhaps some level of relaxation is inevitable after a great success.

'But Pep, it happens to us all. When I got to the stadium this evening I was really relaxed compared to other matches. All I could think was that we were playing Dortmund with the league title already in the bag.'

'I know, I know, you're right of course. I was the same today. I even managed to eat something before the game. Can you believe it?'

He had had a plate of prawns for lunch at the hotel and obviously wasn't feeling his usual nerves.

'It's true,' he continues. 'But I also prepared for this match with exactly the same attention to detail as I normally do. I went home at nine o'clock last night. I would have liked to have spent the evening with the kids but stayed on at the office analysing Dortmund and looking for ways to beat them. Carles Planchart and I were the last to leave Säbener Strasse. We had to lock up. I work very hard and today has been a total fuck-up.'

I still want to know whether there were some tactical reasons for today's heavy defeat.

'We played well to begin with and I was thinking: this is a good start, even though we're finding it hard to find Götze with the ball between the lines. If Dortmund's two *pivotes* are marking our two then it's clear that Götze is free, but we just weren't accurate enough in finding him. Still, I'm not moaning too much about the first half. With Rafinha and Alaba playing inside, how many counter-attacks did Dortmund hit us with in the first half? Not one.

'In the second half I moved the two full-backs wide, changing it, so that we could have four attackers, and Dortmund destroyed us. Okay, so, it's interesting because we'll be playing them in the final of the DFB-Pokal. But it was hard to properly analyse and assimilate what was going on during the game because I was so, so pissed off.'

His kids ask about particular players but Pep insists that there has been a change in the whole team's attitude. 'We shouldn't make the mistake of believing we are infallible. We are not super-human and need to keep running. Even when a team is on top form, it is still only hanging from a thread. All it takes is for us to stop running for the thread to break and everything to collapse on top of us.'

Whilst he talks, Guardiola is already forming his plan of action for the next few days. '*S'ha acabat el bròquil.*' It is a Catalan saying meaning 'things are going to change around here'.

'There will be no rotations in Braunschweig [next Saturday they are at home to the team in last place in the league] and if anyone gets injured, tough luck, they won't get to play at the Bernabéu. We won the Bundesliga with half the team missing after all and managed to win in difficult grounds with most of our key men out, like in Dortmund. No one could score against us and now in just three days, suddenly we're full of holes. Well, it stops here.'

Màrius, who is 11, asks his dad if he intends to say all this to his players.

'Of course! Monday morning. At training. And then on Tuesday, during the team talk. I'll tell them I messed up. Big time. But they need to run and run. They mustn't fall into the trap of believing they have some sort of special status. If we want to be good, to go on being good, we have to run. I'm paid to coach and they're paid to run. We're not paid to play beautiful football but to run. The minute players stop running, they're nobodies. If we really want to be in those two finals [the DFB-Pokal and the Champions League] we have to demand everything of ourselves.'

I make the same point as Cristina: it's normal to relax a little after great success. 'Of course, it's logical but I don't need to accept it. The same thing happened at Barça. Every time we won the league our performance dipped. But I'm not going to accept it. I'm rebelling. I am not going off on holiday thinking about this shit, this 3-0, without having done everything I can to turn things around. Have I ever been beaten 3-0 before?'

It's a rhetorical question. Pep knows only too well that he has never suffered such a bad defeat at home (although he has yet to experience an even worse result).

Bayern's next step is to make it to the DFB-Pokal final. 'Let's hope the game against Kaiserslautern [the Second Division team who will visit the Allianz Arena on Wednesday for the semi-final] makes up for today's mess. Who knows, perhaps this defeat will end up doing us some good. If we had beaten Dortmund we would have been even fuller of ourselves. Now at least if we make it to the final we won't be favourites. If we're up against Dortmund, obviously they'll be favourites. And the same applies to Real Madrid in the Champions League.'

His thoughts are already turning to Tuesday's team talk and the upcoming matches against Kaiserslautern and Real Madrid.

'Right now we need to get back to training as hard as we can, without stopping. And against Madrid our two strikers need to tie-up their entire back four, our wingers have to double up as full-backs, just as they did against United, and in the midfield we need the best players who keep and move the ball for long spells of productive possession. I won't be wasting a lot of words on our strategy against Madrid, just two main tactical ideas plus a few specific directions to some of the players and then I'll tell them all to run themselves into the ground. We just need two ideas to win: control the counter-attacks and hold on to possession. And *laufen*, a lot of *laufen*. Run like bastards…'

It's now three hours since the end of the Dortmund game. The Allianz is practically deserted and, as always, Pep carries a sleeping Valentina in his arms. It's the same scene match after match, except today he's been defeated. In these three hours he has dealt with the impact of the defeat. He has accepted it, brooded on it in private, verbalised his feelings and identified his own mistakes and those of his players. He has then started the healing process by setting out his approach for the next few days. In the end this has been a transformative process and he has found the positive in the situation; he has ended the evening revitalised.

As he goes down in the lift, he starts talking about next season. 'Lewandowski and one more. We need more competition within the team. Nobody should get too comfortable. I want them to work like bastards to earn their place. In every single training session. If we don't do that then we'll end up like some other teams. We need to use this success to reinvent ourselves. Otherwise there's a real risk of Dortmund overtaking us next season.'

And, before he leaves, Pep cannot resist mentioning something that has been on his mind for a while: the fact that his football philosophy is alien to German football culture. He doesn't say it disparagingly or in an aggressive way. For him it is just a fact of life, another opportunity to broaden his horizons.

60

'WE HAVE TO REMEMBER THAT IF WE DON'T RUN, WE'RE NOTHING.'

Madrid, April 23, 2014

BAYERN SHOW THE kind of personality in the Bernabéu that very few teams manage to summon up when they play here. They enclose Real Madrid in their own penalty box and hold on to the ball, maintaining such tight control that, after only nine minutes, the Madrid fans begin to whistle in protest at the manner in which the home side are allowing themselves to be pummelled into submission.

Guardiola's tactical talk had been brief and to the point: 'You are great players. Go out into this great, historical stadium and show it. Go out and play like you know how. This is football. You are footballers. Be footballers.'

A week ago Real Madrid won the Copa del Rey against Barcelona by playing a defensive, deep 4-4-2 formation, a strategy which allowed them to control their opponents and deliver their own counter-attacks. Himself a first-rate-tactician, coach Carlo Ancelotti has decided to approach the Bayern game in the same way. He is happy to sacrifice control of the game and the ball, opting for deep defending in the third of the pitch in front of Madrid's own goal, where Pepe and Sergio Ramos have been outstanding.

Bayern start strongly and the players do everything the coach has asked: Kroos moves the ball from wing to wing, driving Bayern's attacks down either side. Robben drives forward from a central area, the full-backs hit Mandžukić with their crosses and Bayern's positional play allows them to avoid Madrid's counter-attacks.

However, Madrid won't even need a genuine counter-attack in order to win. The only goal of the game comes from a Karim Benzema tapin in the 19th minute. It's a terrible blow for a team which has run out of steam over the last three weeks, managing to hold on only because of men like Lahm, Kroos and Robben. Even a goalkeeper as dependable as Neuer has come back full of doubts and errors after being injured 11 days ago against Borussia Dortmund.

Guardiola had tried to revitalise his men during the 10 days between the Dortmund defeat and the Madrid tie. On Tuesday, April 15, he called the squad together. Standing in the Säbener Strasse lecture theatre, with the lights off, Pep started by asking for his men's forgiveness for his poor German, 'although I think you can all understand me'. He then explained that when he gets home after training he always opens a bottle of wine to drink with his wife over dinner. The players laughed as he mimed opening an enormous bottle of wine. 'Whilst I'm doing that I'm always thinking of you guys, thinking about how to help you, what I can do to help you play even better, how I can make you more secure. I reflect on all the things I can do to support you.'

But the one thing he cannot do, he told them, is 'run for you'. He then showed them a short video which demonstrated very clearly the difference in the rhythm of their game before winning the league and after. They had obviously just stopped running full-out.

'It's completely normal and it happens to everyone after a bit of success. But we have to remember that if we don't run, we're nothing. If we start asking team-mates to send the ball to our feet instead of into the space in front of us, then we'll lose much of our excellence and we'll be a weaker opponent.'

He then turned the lights on and set up a whiteboard on which he had written the following figures:

27 games = 13 goals

3 games = 7 goals

This was the balance of goals conceded in the league thus far: only 13 in the first 27 games before winning the title, and then seven in three matches. The team had collapsed.

In their two matches preceding the first leg in Madrid his players made a huge effort to address the problem. They beat Kaiserslautern 5-1 in the semi-finals of the DFB-Pokal and then emerged with a 2-0 away win at Eintracht Braunschweig. Neither of these was a straightforward game. They may have been a second division team, but Kaiserslautern battled hard at the Allianz Arena, where Pep fielded his best team, minus Neuer. There were mixed feelings after the game. On the one hand, they were delighted to be going to the final in Berlin against no less a rival than Borussia Dortmund. On the other, the Bayern players had appeared sluggish and lacked fluidity.

It was also sadly lacking in Braunschweig, where the team fighting relegation fought tooth and nail for one last chance to save themselves. This game was possibly Bayern's worst performance of the entire season, with some players misdirecting more than half of their passes, and the team achieving a mediocre pass accuracy of 78%. Moreover, with just five days to go before facing Real Madrid, it was clear that the best player of 2013 was still blocked. Franck Ribéry was struggling to regain his form, although not through lack of effort or desire. He was pushing himself to the limit but not managing to get back to that state of grace which had allowed him to take on all-comers. The causes may well have been partly psychological, but his back problems – he had a procedure to drain bad bruising on February 6 – were badly hampering his performance. These same back problems would eventually prevent him from playing in the World Cup.

Pizarro's goal in the 75th minute sealed the win in Braunschweig and he was the team's most effective forward at this point in the season, averaging a goal every 68 minutes. Pep insisted that his contract be renewed for another season.

In Madrid, the eventual successor to Bayern as European champions awaited them. Guardiola wasn't sure whether or not to include Ribéry in his line-up, given his state of fitness. He was not feeling positive: just before leaving Munich the coach learned that Højbjerg's father had passed away. In the group that travelled to Madrid, Alaba had a cold, Neuer was just back from injury, and Götze hadn't yet reached his best. To add to their woes, Javi Martínez – who should have been a starter – was suffering from a bout of gastroenteritis which had caused him to lose almost four kilos in one weekend.

The players had undoubtedly run much more in the two matches since April 14 but, apparently, the guardian angel of the previous months had deserted them. Despite all of this, Bayern were exactly where they had aimed to be at this stage: with three titles won, the final of the DFB-Pokal to contest and just 180 minutes away from the Champions League final.

Pep decided to confront Madrid with courage and daring. He had experienced momentous victories with Barcelona in this stadium and, out of respect for Real Madrid, had been irritated by people in Munich talking about the *bête noire* (Bayern) which was about to descend on the Bernabéu. Madrid had been a great rival for Pep, as a player and coach and, regardless of their current difficulties, his team were determined to face them with valour and pride.

'We've worked very, very hard to get here,' he told me, 'and we have done it by the skin of our teeth at times. I have only had my entire squad fit for three weeks this season. Just three weeks. And we've worked like dogs to get where we are. We're not going to give up now. We need to go out there and enjoy this. I'm really looking forward to it. We're going to try to take the ball off them, bring the ball out from the back and dominate the Bernabéu.'

And, as it turns out, the ball does indeed belong to Bayern. In the first 15 minutes they have 80% of possession, most of it in the opposition's half.

Schweinsteiger gets a header on target from a corner, but Iker Casillas makes a straightforward save. Robben hits a deflected shot from outside the area.

Then Kroos hits a shot which comes off Pepe and bounces to Benzema. No Bayern player defends the move well and 19 seconds later the ball is beyond Neuer and in the net – scored at close range by Benzema, who started the move, from Fábio Coentráo's centre.

This is a tired team which has dug deep away from home. They have dominated the ball, shown bravery, but concede from what is practically the home side's first chance.

Bayern go through a dip which lasts six minutes, during which Madrid generate two moderate chances on goal as well as a Cristiano Ronaldo near miss.

The German team rally and subdue Madrid until, in the last minute of the first half, Angel di Maria goes face-to-face with Neuer, and shoots over.

Madrid have conceded nine corners in that first half, but still manage to limit Bayern's efforts on target. Pep's team has dominated the play, but rarely put themselves in a position to beat Casillas.

After the break Madrid control the ball completely for the first six minutes but the game then changes and Bayern begin to dominate. Guardiola's team has been slightly stronger in attack and has managed to reduce Madrid's counter-attacks to just one, from Gareth Bale in the 88th minute.

Müller and Götze come on for Ribéry and Mandžukić and Bayern surrender some of their control in exchange for creating more chances, culminating in the 84th minute with a shot on goal by Götze – it's a clear chance, but Casillas deflects it.

Bayern are sterile in attack. Fifteen corners, 31 crosses into the box, 94% pass accuracy and 18 shots on target (double Madrid's number) – to no effect. Götze's miss is typical. It could have been the goal *Kalle* Rummenigge had asked for the day that they were drawn against Madrid. 'If we score in the Bernabéu we'll be in the final for sure.' But Götze fluffs it, Casillas saves and the men from Munich leave the game looking down in the dumps.

Once again criticism is heaped on Pep, just as it had been after the defeats against Augsburg and Dortmund. A few papers even started predicting the demise of a certain playing style. Franz Beckenbauer had this to say on Sky Germany: 'Possession is meaningless if you give away chances. We should be happy that Madrid only managed to score one goal.'

But Pep also received messages of support, one of which, an SMS from a Barça player, reads: 'Pep, you can be very proud of your team. Very few teams could have done what you managed to do at the Bernabéu.'

Bayern had played well, but they hadn't achieved enough accuracy or efficacy in their finishing. However, in the heat of the moment, the knee-jerk reaction seemed to offer a totally different analysis and left players, press and supporters feeling depressed and pessimistic. This negativity would play a decisive role in the disastrous mistakes Guardiola would make in his strategy for the return leg.

In reality, Bayern had played extraordinarily well although their finishing had been very poor. Despite the visitors' shortcomings on the night, all the commentary focused on Benzema's goal, as well as Ronaldo and Di María's two chances. There was very little appreciation of the domination and character shown by Bayern in one of the greatest sporting theatres in the world. This was a serious error of judgment.

Simultaneously, the culture shock between Pep's game and traditional German football was becoming apparent.

'I understand that this style of game is not part of German football culture,' he explained at dinner after the match. 'People should know that I do understand. In Germany clubs like to play a style of football that's very different from my own and no doubt people prefer Madrid or Dortmund's game. But guys, Bayern chose me. I am making compromises between my ideas and German football but at the end of the day it's the players who matter. And I'll tell you something: the players support my ideas.'

You can interpret this clash of culture negatively or positively, but it is a reality. If the Bundesliga is characterised by excellent counter-attacking and direct, fast, vertical football, then Guardiola's model is indeed a complete contradiction of that. His positional play is based on unified forward movement and winning zonal superiority further up the pitch, like two Alpine climbers, roped together, moving up a mountain stage by stage and with complete co-ordination. It's a philosophy which allows you to re-start from the back again if one route forward, one movement, ends up blocked. It doesn't matter how many consecutive passes it takes to make the rival disorganised – you have to keep passing. It was inevitable and natural that comparisons were being made between this and the traditional German model.

After dinner at Madrid's Intercontinental Hotel, Rummenigge and Matthias Sammer join the technical team at their table and try to raise the coach's spirits. They are worried that he seems so low and urge him not to abandon his ideas. They have full confidence in him and his players, and in the game plan which has taken them this far. They reiterate that the club is determined to support his ideas and wants to develop them even further over the next few years.

Pep, Domènec Torrent and Carles Planchart spend the next few hours dissecting the match and discussing the best way to approach the return leg. The coach reckons it might be a good idea to start with three central defenders at the back and populate the middle of the pitch in order to dominate and reduce the chances of Madrid scoring a killer away goal. They work until 3.48am and in the end Pep asks Torrent to ensure that he doesn't change his mind, no matter what happens. Pep knows exactly how he wants to play and doesn't want to change his plans.

Guardiola is not down because of the score or as a result of the criticism. The truth is that he has just received a call from a doctor informing him of the precarious state of Tito Vilanova's health.

61

'A COMPLETE FUCK-UP.'

Munich, April 29, 2014

'I GOT IT wrong man. I got it totally wrong. It's a monumental fuck-up. A total mess. The biggest fuck-up of my life as a coach.'

Pep comes into his office in the Allianz having just done the press conference during which he has publicly assumed total responsibility for the catastrophe. Real Madrid have wiped the floor with Bayern in the Champions League semi-final, a game which will stay with Guardiola for the rest of his career. The 4-0 home defeat is the worst of his professional life and the biggest trouncing Bayern have ever received in a European competition. His team has been pummelled into submission and totally humiliated in their own stadium by the team who will take the European title from them a few weeks from now.

Bayern had conceded only two goals direct from corner kicks all season: today Sergio Ramos makes it three, rising majestically above the Bavarian defence in the 16th minute. Pep's team are on the ropes. It's the start of a debacle.

This season Bayern haven't conceded a single goal from an indirect free-kick. Not one. But in the 20th minute Di Maria delivers, Pepe flicks it on with his head and Ramos, again, beats Neuer, taking advantage of the fact that Dante is badly positioned. Fifteen minutes later Ronaldo adds another from a counter-attack which begins when Ribéry loses the ball. And then, just to round off a dark, dark night for the holders, they concede only their second goal all season from a direct free-kick. Again, it is Ronaldo who shoots hard and low whilst the Bayern wall jumps. A bitter moment. Humiliation complete.

The fact that Madrid have scored three of their four goals from set plays could give a false impression. Certainly, this is completely unexpected. Until this point Bayern have been the most reliable defenders of set plays anywhere in Europe, statistics which leave no room for doubt about the excellence of their organisation and preparation. For context, the mighty Juventus have run away with the Italian title with a Serie A record of 102 points but only after conceding 10 times from corners and free-kicks.

However, getting bogged down in an analysis of the goals fails to give a full picture of the reasons for a defeat primarily caused by serious errors of judgment on Guardiola's part. And we need to go back one week, to the previous Thursday morning, to get to the root of the problem. The scene is a private room in Madrid's Hotel Intercontinental, where Bayern have enjoyed their traditional post-match dinner. The meal has finished and all but three tables lie empty. The remaining diners include members of the club's press department, a group of Bayern's sponsors and, at the third table, Pep and his assistants.

The group has already diagnosed the problems at the root of their 1-0 defeat at the Bernabéu and are proud of the way the players have imposed themselves in this arena by sticking to the game plan. They are also, however, well aware of the fact that their men are below par and have struggled against a defensive line-up made up of well-organised, super-talented players who defend as a unit almost to perfection. Right now, Guardiola is facing one of the most common dilemmas in a football coach's life: how do you attack effectively in such tight space?

Often the suggested solution in this situation will be to shoot powerfully at goal. Bayern shot at goal 18 times at the Bernabéu – twice as many times as Madrid. Another will be to get crosses into a centre-forward in the box. Bayern put 31 crosses into the box – three times Madrid's tally.

The reality of football is that using Guardiola's type of positional play against a team which defends deep and well, demands not only high-quality preparation but also a touch of individual creativity.

In other words, in this kind of difficult, frustrating situation, it is usually down to the talent of a top player to make the breakthrough. Unfortunately, during the game, of all Bayern's forwards, only Arjen Robben has been on his game. Either they haven't managed to dribble past their markers or have failed to get the right shot away, because they are blocked by the centre-halves.

At 3am on Thursday, April 24, Pep is considering the obvious fact that Madrid will shut up shop when they visit the Allianz for the second leg and that he will be counting on all the same weapons as in the first game. These include Robben, who is in fine form, Ribéry, who is mentally blocked and pained by his loss of form, Mandžukić, who had managed to get on the end of only one of Bayern's 15 corner kicks in the Bernabéu, and Müller, with his anarchic movement. The coach also has Garry Kasparov's words ringing in his ears: 'Remember, Pep, you don't win games just because you've moved your pieces to the front.'

It is during this early-hours reflection on what he has just seen that Pep decides to play the return leg with a 3-4-3 formation. With three central defenders, two full-backs pushed up into the midfield next to the creative midfielders and Götze as one of the two strikers, so that he can add superiority in midfield by dropping back to help in the middle of the pitch. It's a 3-4-3 which can be changed to a basic 3-5-2 with minimal alteration. Theoretically good for defending against the counter-attacks which, Pep is convinced, will feature heavily in Madrid's game. But it should also allow Bayern to dominate the middle of the pitch, to keep the ball and not to get log-jammed in and around the Madrid penalty area.

It's then that I overhear Guardiola telling Torrent: 'Domè, don't let me change my mind. This is the only way to go.'

Then, on the flight back to Munich, Pep changed his mind. Reflecting on the fact that the team had last practised a three-man defence in December, the coach realised that there was very little time to prepare his players. Added to this, Javi Martínez had not only just recovered from a bad bout of gastroenteritis, but was also suffering from tendinitis in both knees. There was no way he was going to make it through 90 minutes against Madrid. The coach decided to leave the 3-4-3 for next season and by the time the plane touched down in Munich Pep had switched to a 4-2-3-1. This formation had worked well in Bundesliga games and would give his men superiority in the midfield. What's more, it was a system they were completely familiar with and would allow him to use both Ribéry and Götze. If only he could do something to get Ribéry back to his best.

On Friday, April 25, Pep addressed his squad briefly. 'I'll be eternally grateful for all you did in the Bernabéu. You showed enormous courage and played the kind of football I want to see. I'm proud of you all.'

This was also the day Tito Vilanova passed away, a desperately sad day for his family, FC Barcelona, their supporters and all his friends. The world of football shared their grief and for Pep, Torrent, Planchart, Estiarte and Buenaventura, who had been part of Tito's life over so many years, it was a devastating blow.

The home game against Werder Bremen on Saturday was tough. Bayern responded to the tragic news by taking steps to protect their coach. Releasing a statement of condolence in both German and Catalan, the club organised a minute's silence in the stadium where all the players were wearing black armbands. Pep struggled to focus on the game and jumped to his feet only in the 70th minute to hug Ribéry, and tell him how well he had done in the centre-forward position.

Although Werder Bremen managed to pull ahead on two occasions through well-executed counter-attacks, Bayern finished the game with a 5-2 victory and the happy news that Ribéry seemed to be rediscovering his form. Robben had played for only 15 minutes, but put away the fifth goal with his first touch, causing Pep to make a mental note to continue to edge the Dutch striker towards the centre-forward position and away from his normal role on the wing.

That night the coach dined out with friends but his mind was elsewhere. From time to time he pulled out photos showing himself and Tito together, his favourite having been taken in Atlético Madrid's Vicente Calderón dressing room. In the picture the two men are discussing their plans for the game. All in all it was a strange evening, during which they toasted Tito and discussed almost every subject under the sun except football. Pep had other things on his mind.

By Monday the players are fired up and eagerly anticipating their chance to take revenge on Madrid. There is a sense that this will be an encounter of epic proportions, but there is little evidence of cool, tactical analysis. Pep allows himself to be carried away and even his performance at the press conference seems out of character. It's then he makes a big mistake. He asks his men how they are feeling and they talk to him about the German talent for glorious comebacks, as well as the passion they have all felt on similarly epic nights in the Allianz Arena. All they want is to be allowed to play with their hearts and souls. They need to go out and attack hard from the first second of the game. Pep changes his mind again. The 3-4-3 had become a 4-2-3-1, but now he opts for a 4-2-4 formation. Just as he did in Dortmund in July 2013, in his debut match, he swithers between patience and passion and ends up going for passion. But it didn't work in Dortmund, and it won't work now.

Monday's training consists of *rondos*, a short session looking for explosive strength and two 11 v 11 matches of 10 minutes each. It all draws to an end with 20 minutes of crosses and finishes, with a view to what's likely to happen the following night in the match. Alaba and Ribéry have slightly raised temperatures and sore throats, and Javi's knees are bothering him. The line-up is finally agreed and Pep pulls Ribéry to one side and tells him he'll be starting.

The pre-match team talk, in the Presidential Suite of the Charles Hotel, reflects the optimism everyone in Munich is feeling: 'Lads, this is not about going out and having a good time. You are going out there to do some damage. Go for the jugular. You are German, so be German and *attack*.'

In the end, their epic story ends in disaster. Not only because of the way in which they concede the goals but most of all because this Bayern side is unrecognisable. These are not the masters of possession who have dominated at the Bernabéu, in Manchester, London and in so many other arenas. No, this is a team which appears to have been stripped of their principal asset: superiority in the centre of the field.

It's all too reminiscent of what happened in the German Super Cup, when Bayern put out a midfield of Thiago, Kroos and Müller and then changed to a 4-2-4 in an infamous game of two halves.

And yet the Allianz Arena is the perfect setting for Bayern's comeback – a breathtaking atmosphere and a fired up, emotional and very vocal home crowd. The players run on to the pitch in high spirits. They are raring to go and for the first and only time this season huddle together in a circle, looking for that last-minute boost that will propel them into the final. Before the referee has even blown his whistle to start the game the stadium is echoing to their supporters' war cry: '*Auf geht's Bayern, schießt ein Tor!*' Come on Bayern, give us a goal!

The Bayern players are running on pure adrenalin, but the first two moves are a foretaste of what is to come. Twenty seconds in, Ribéry takes the ball down the left wing and tries to shake off Carvajal, but Gareth Bale joins in and helps the right-back. Between them they snuff out the Frenchman's move. All night it remains 3 v 2 in favour of Madrid whenever Bayern try to open up the wings.

Pep will confess later that even at this early stage of the game he already knew that the team was messing up. And you can see it right from the kick off. The ref blows, Madrid move the ball back through their team while Mandžukić and Müller hare off like madmen to try to win it from them. It is courageous, ambitious, but also the first clear indication that Bayern's midfield is going to be left gaping all night, at their rival's mercy. Pep has kept Rafinha on the bench and returned Lahm to right-back. It is a crucial error. On this, the biggest night of his Bayern career, Pep has stripped his midfield of the guy who has locked all the components together and been his best midfielder all season; the man who has imposed order on the team.

Kroos, on the right, and Schweinsteiger, to the left, form the double pivote, each playing on his more natural side, but, lacking the passing finesse of Lahm, Götze and Thiago, they come off second best to their opponents. Defensively, they are outnumbered by Madrid players.

Madrid play more intelligently, albeit they don't attempt to own the ball. Bayern bring the ball out from the back, but do so badly. They often resort to a long ball, leaving their midfielders isolated and outnumbered. The team isn't moving forward in unison. In every zone they look and feel inferior and have failed to establish superiority. Every time they lose the ball they hand Madrid a huge opportunity and Luka Modric is performing majestically for the Spanish side. Bayern abandon their usual patient, intelligent approach and end up completely dislocated. Their poor defending as well as an apparent lack of tactical and emotional control result in the first two goals.

Bayern never give in, however, not even when Ronaldo puts away the third goal during a quick counter-attack, which Ribéry inadvertently starts by passing to Bale. Four passes later it's a goal. By then Martínez is warming up. The German side may have lost the game but their pride is still intact. Repeatedly they try to break through, even now, 4-0 down on aggregate. Robben's attacks down the middle help win them four corners in the space of seven minutes, but nothing comes of any of them. In the first leg Bayern had 15 corners and put seven of them on target, tonight, of the nine corners they take, only one is on target. Madrid defend splendidly and there is always a body in the way of any Bavarian shot.

Guardiola uses the break to make some changes. Martínez comes on for Mandžukić and the team moves to a 4-3-3, with Schweinsteiger at the top of a triangle ahead of Kroos and Martínez. This functions well; it helps. But it's already too late. Now Bayern are playing the ball out from the back pretty well, they begin to control the game and their team lines are better positionally. It is tempting to reflect on how different the outcome might have been had Javi Martínez been fit enough for the entirety of both home and away games. Or if Thiago had been able to play. But in the end Bayern have to face the truth. They are going to miss out on the Champions League final – by a long way.

The Bayern supporters whistle their disapproval as Götze comes on for Ribéry, despite the fact that the Frenchman is clearly on his last legs because of his lumbago. In the coming weeks he will discover just how high a price he will pay for today's efforts. But there is worse to come. The stadium rounds on Pep when he replaces Müller with Pizarro, the fans' jeers and shouts making their preference for the Bavarian striker crystal clear. The Bayern support are deeply unhappy with Pep.

Later the coach assumes all the blame for the disaster. He makes no reference to his players' requests and goes out of his way to protect them, making sure that they are left out of the post-match debate. He had abandoned the centre of the field on the very day his men were up against a pack of lions.

They've faced a formidable side in which Modric and Alonso, overall, have controlled the direction of the ball. Benzema has brought a superb sense of timing to his ball control whilst Bale and Ronaldo have performed brilliantly in open space, getting the ball and running at Bayern. Instead of putting a premium on superiority in the middle of the pitch with more midfielders and fewer forwards, Bayern have put the emphasis on 'up and at 'em', often resulting in positional inferiority.

Throughout the season Pep had often commented on the clash of cultures between his own style and the German game. After winning 3-0 in Dortmund, he said: 'If we bombard the penalty area with shots, sure, we'll score but we'll never dominate the game.' But tonight even that statement doesn't ring true. They have put the ball into Iker Casillas' penalty area 74 times across the 180 minutes and barely scraped half a dozen very moderate efforts on goal.

Pep had been more than clear. 'We dominate the play when all the good players are together in the middle. And if I end up losing it won't matter. I'll go home happy to have done it my way.' And yet, on this, the most important day of the season so far, he has betrayed his own belief system. He has failed to play the football he believes in and has not even attempted to build the kind of game he considers vital to attack and win. It's true that he was perhaps missing the men best qualified to deliver his style of high-risk football, a game that must be executed with the utmost precision. Even so, it is evident that Pep's own decision was the catalyst for this catastrophe. Today, Pep betrayed his own principles.

Several weeks before, the coach compared a football team to a glass bottle hanging by a thread. Today, the thread has broken and Bayern has come crashing down. There have been very few teams who have imploded so dramatically in such a short space of time and this defeat will mark a turning point for Guardiola. Nothing will be the same again in Germany and, if the press coverage is to be believed, in one night the Catalan has gone from national hero to a figure of scorn.

All great sportsmen have experienced monumental disasters and humiliating defeats. But the evening of April 29 is Pep's first bitter taste of such devastating failure and the scars will be a long time healing. There are those who would argue that such suffering is necessary for the renewal of energy in the life of any sports professional. Great victory always emerges from devastating defeat, after all.

Pep is still shut up in his office with Domènec Torrent, Carles Planchart and Manel Estiarte well past midnight. Ostensibly, they are there to review the match together, but in reality his assistants are trying to boost the boss's morale. They can see that tonight Pep is a broken man.

But they need to know how they're going to get out of this hole. Are they going to keep moving forward or end up taking a backward step?

'I spend the whole season refusing to use a 4-2-4. The whole season. And I decide to do it tonight, the most important night of the year. A complete fuck-up.'

62

'I SAW PEP UTTERLY BEATEN FOR THE FIRST TIME.'

Munich, May 1, 2014

AS SHE LEFT the stadium, Rummenigge's wife told Bayern's most senior director how concerned she was for Pep. The coach was obviously devastated and demoralised. Kalle was equally worried. Although obviously shaken by their disastrous defeat at Real Madrid's hands, Rummenigge was just as concerned for Pep, whom he still considered a crucial part of the club's future. For him, the relationship is not just about supporting Pep; he is also passionate about Pep's football philosophy, despite all its difficulties and fragility, and accepts that they are breaking with the tradition of direct attack at Bayern.

Just a week earlier, he had been taken aback by the reduced frequency of Bayern's passing in the Braunschweig game but, at the time, Guardiola explained that he had changed tactics after seeing the state of the pitch. Rummenigge, as an executive, had been anxious to avoid external criticism undermining Pep or causing him to doubt the club's backing for him. Of course, that was before their deadly encounter with Madrid.

This was the moment that the club's support in Pep would be put to the test. Not long after the fateful game, I met with Rummenigge in his office and asked the obvious question: 'Will Bayern continue to support Guardiola's style of play after this elimination from the Champions League and despite the fact that it is so at odds with German football?'

KHR: 'Look, when we signed Pep up we knew exactly what to expect from him. I like people who are prepared to take responsibility and Pep is responsible for the tactical decisions. He is absolutely clear about those tactics, which are based on possession of the ball. So nothing that has happened has been a big surprise. In personal terms Pep has another great advantage – he's not a complicated man. When he prepares for matches he never forgets he's in Germany and he always takes account of our cultural norms. Of course, we Germans are used to a more physical game. Fast, direct football is more common here, but we have added so many more strings to our bow this year. We've achieved high levels of possession and have performed strongly in attack. We've defended well and maintained the speed of our game. For one reason or another, our concentration has dipped over the last three weeks. Perhaps winning the league so early derailed the whole team or at least a few of our players. But I believe that Pep's credibility and his ability to fulfil his responsibilities both depend on our adherence to his philosophy. We must not ask him to be anything other than he is.'

MP: 'Surely the second leg defeat by Real Madrid was a disaster of catastrophic proportions?'

KHR: 'I don't deny it and on Tuesday I saw Pep utterly beaten for the first time ever. Essentially it happened because he changed some aspects of his approach without being 100% sure. He made some choices that were not really his and was furious with himself for failing to stick to his own ideas. He was very clear about that. He deserted the middle of the pitch and opted for much more direct football. He had allowed himself to be influenced by the result of the away game in the Bernabéu [as opposed to Bayern's performance that day]. And I'll tell you something, the criticism he received for his tactics that day were completely unfair. He played the game the same way he has done all season, looking for the ball. We just didn't manage to score and that's why people were so quick to condemn. If we had played the same way and scored in Madrid, everyone would have been calling Pep a genius. But it's true; those of us who have been around this game for a long time can't afford to be influenced too much by a goal here or there. You have to analyse the game as well. If Götze had scored in the Bernabéu, Bayern and Pep would have been praised to the hilt. But he missed and suddenly it was all a disaster. We have a problem here in Germany in that we don't focus enough on tactics. We are content to play fast, physical, direct football. But this game can be so much more than that. There's a reason for us winning the league with such an extraordinary lead. And that reason is Pep.'

MP: 'Pep has two more years on his contract. What do you expect of him during this time?'

KHR: 'I believe that he can help change German football culture, regardless of the last three weeks and the fact that people have begun to try to devalue what he has achieved. Public opinion, which has always been behind him, is suddenly dragging him down amid claims that his philosophy is just not good enough. For me, the opposite is true. I've spoken to our longest-serving players, the guys who have had between five and seven coaches in as many years and they all say the same thing: Pep stands out – in a positive way. He has brought a rich variety of new ideas. This coach has complete credibility in the eyes of his players.'

MP: 'Given the culture clash we've talked about, isn't it strange that it has been the German players who have adapted best to Pep's ideas? I'm thinking of Lahm, Kroos, Boateng, Neuer and Götze.

KHR: 'Pep has already changed German football philosophy a little. I would have loved him to win everything this year for one reason – it would have convinced the public that his is a winning philosophy. It may be that German football has been too simple until now and football certainly can't only be judged in terms of trophies. That approach can only be harmful. Two years ago we were runners-up in three competitions – the Bundesliga, the DFB-Pokal and the

Champions League, despite the fact that we played the final at home. We ended up with nothing, but even back then I was not prepared to say that Heynckes had done a bad job. And then, of course, Jupp went on to win the lot the very next season. Only then did people say that he'd done a good job, because he had won everything. So what about the year before? You know, I was lucky enough to live and play in Italy for five years and I learned a completely different kind of football there.'

MP: 'Are Bayern satisfied with Guardiola's first year?'

KHR: 'When I look back at the whole year, I am very pleased with the association between Pep and Bayern. First and foremost because I believe he is a great coach. He has clear ideas, a definite plan, his own philosophy and a range of tactics. And all those things have meant that he has achieved something we would not normally expect the year after winning the treble. The year after a successful season is always tough because the players are a bit weary and a lot less motivated. In 2001, after we had won the Champions League by beating Valencia the previous year, we really struggled. We ended up in third place in the league, were kicked out of the Champions League in the quarter-finals and didn't even make it to the Cup final. That was such a disappointing season and Pep has made sure that we have avoided the same fate this year. Usually players' motivation and desire dip after periods of great success but thanks to Pep we remained as hungry as ever. Of course, at the difficult times, like last Tuesday when we lost against Real Madrid, people are sorely disappointed and the press starts to criticise. But I don't think we should pay too much attention to all of that. It's important to maintain a global perspective on the whole season. Let's not forget that just four weeks ago when we won the league title in Berlin, the same journalists were writing that the league had become boring since Bayern had been playing so well and were out of reach as opponents. And now suddenly we're no good at all. We have certainly dipped in psychological terms and that has resulted in defeats. Obviously Tuesday's result was painful but these things happen and they are understandable.'

MP: 'Does that defeat inevitably affect your view of the whole season?'

KHR: 'There's a law in football which says that whoever won the Champions League last season cannot win it this year. Nobody knows why but that is the way it has been for 22 years now. We had hoped to change all that and rewrite the history books but it was not to be. To my mind the extent of a team's stability is seen in their game, although obviously their successes – how far they go in the competition – are also important. Barcelona, during Pep's era, and even before, were always a benchmark for me. They made it to the semis of the Champions League almost every year. And they tended to be in the finals of all the other competitions. That's what really matters. And there's something else. At the moment there are many teams performing at more or less the same level and there's a fine line between success and failure. It can be as narrow as a missed call on a penalty by the referee, the tiniest mistake or the fact that a key player is injured. So really, as long as a team consistently makes it to the semi-finals of the competitions, then you know it's a great team. Statistically speaking we've played 38 Champions League games in the last three years. We are No.1. Neither Real Madrid, nor Barcelona, nor Manchester United nor Chelsea have played more games than us.'

MP: 'During the last three years the actual stats are: Bayern 38 games, Real Madrid 37, Barcelona 34, Chelsea 29 and United 24. If we look at the last five years we see that Bayern and Barcelona are drawn on 59 games against 57 for Real Madrid and 47 each for Chelsea and United.'

KHR: 'The number of games is a good indicator of the team's solidity. And we have done well this season, too, despite the awful defeat.

Obviously the Madrid game is going to affect our judgment, but it's also important for me to look at how we played against City and United in Manchester, against Arsenal in London and in the Bernabéu against Madrid. All of that is important, too. We need to be much more rational about these things. I'm delighted to have Pep as coach. He is enormously talented. I completely understand why he was so down after the Madrid game, but he is still a great, great coach.'

MP: 'The 2015 Champions League final will be played in Germany [in Berlin]. Do you see 2014-15's main objective as the Bundesliga?'

KHR: 'Definitely. The most important trophy in any season is the league title, whether it's in Germany, Spain, Italy, England or anywhere else. You have to play 34 games in the Bundesliga, so winning it proves your true worth. With the quality of football nowadays, all it takes is one bad day and you're out of the Champions League. That's what has happened here. In the league you could lose a game 4-0, but if you're in good shape you can then go on to win the next 10 games. In the Champions League, it's much more cut-throat. It's certainly the biggest and most glamorous title, but the most relevant championship will always be the league.'

MP: 'Bayern will have to take a decision: either maintain the team which has already won everything and has gone on winning or bring in fresh blood.'

KHR: 'We need to be subtle about any changes we make. It will take sensitivity and intelligence. Sammer, our sports director, the coach and I have always tried to reach a consensus. We need to bear in mind the club's financial responsibilities and proceed with caution. It would be foolish to allow our judgment to be affected by this latest defeat. If you had asked me that question five weeks ago I would have told you that there was very little we needed to change because the team was working well. We had won the league in record-breaking style; we were defending our Champions League title and were in the DFB-Pokal final. Now after this defeat the question has changed slightly, but I have always believed that when things go wrong, it's better to go home, sleep on it and then come back to solve the problem quietly and calmly together.'

MP: 'It's clear that signing Robert Lewandowski will not be enough. You need another top-level player, a signing which will reinforce Bayern's status as a behemoth nobody else can challenge – particularly within Germany.'

KHR: 'Over the last 10 years Bayern have won half of the league titles and obviously there have been other champions. Dortmund have won it twice, Wolfsburg have won it, as has Stuttgart, a team who this year flirted with the relegation positions. Bayern are a powerful club and we work hard to maintain that strength and power in everything we do. We have a solid financial basis from which to develop and will therefore be able to make significant signings. But if a club allows a player to leave thanks to a previously-agreed clause, that's not our problem. We are a bit unusual in Germany, it's true. If we sign a Dortmund or a Schalke player or, in years gone by, a Bremen player, everyone writes the same thing: Bayern's signing policy isn't about reinforcement, it's an attempt to weaken the opposition. But that's just not true. Where else are you likely to find good players in Germany? Well, at the moment, in Dortmund and Schalke, in the teams that are strong enough to fight for the league title. It's only logical and I'm sure the same thing happens in other countries. It happens every year, but I'm not going to keep justifying it. If a player like Lewandowski becomes free, it would be madness not to sign him. Otherwise he would have left Dortmund for England, Spain or elsewhere. We managed to convince him that Bayern was the best place for him. It would have been stupid not to approach Lewandowski.'

MP: 'Is it true that Real Madrid tried to sign Lewandowski?'

KHR: 'Yes, they tried to make a deal at the end of December 2013. We heard about it and immediately moved to close our deal. He is a talented striker and will be a great addition to the squad.'

MP: 'If Bayern are shopping in the transfer market, does that mean your youth academy lacks quality players?'

KHR: 'We like our youth-development players in Germany and we have our fair share here – Lahm, Schweinsteiger, Müller, Badstuber – homegrown players whom the fans adore. Pep will always look for in-house youngsters in order to realise his philosophy of the game, but our problem is that at the moment we don't have six youth team players who are good enough to make the move up. In fact, we only have two right now. We need to improve what we're doing so that those kinds of players emerge. That would be great for the team – in financial terms, too.'

Although Guardiola would explain later that next season's planning will start after the DFB-Pokal final, he and Rummenigge met five days later, on May 6. Along with Matthias Sammer and financial director, Jan-Christian Dreesen, they would decide which players would be leaving and who they wanted to sign to continue their campaign to win as many trophies as possible.

63

MEA CULPA

Munich, May 1, 2014

VALENTINA IS PLAYING with a ball out on the grass at Säbener Strasse. It is the only light note of this Thursday afternoon. The team is back together after the disaster and, as is to be expected, all the faces are much more solemn than usual. The session is conducted with the same level of intensity as always. It's about working to build strength in reactive movements and a game of the tiring double area drill which, after what has felt like an endless recovery process, Holger Badstuber joins. Thiago trains separately, doing sprints and turns over a short distance to strengthen his knee. From a distance you could be fooled into thinking that this is just another day.

Pep's moment of fragility is over. Tuesday's demoralised coach has disappeared and he is obviously feeling much better. 'There are only two ways to react to this kind of situation. Either you let it throw you off your stride and are effectively finished, or you pick yourself up and make yourself even stronger than before. I'm going to go forward with more energy and conviction. I believe in this style of football even more now.'

He then spends the next few minutes delivering his *mea culpa*. I have told him that Tuesday's game plan was a betrayal of his own philosophy, and, throwing caution to the wind, added that the resulting criticisms had been spot-on. He had left the key centre-of-the-pitch zone too empty and played in a manner which was contradictory to his firmly held ideas.

'You're absolutely right,' he agrees. 'That's what happened and it was my fault. Instead of going with my own game plan, I went with the players' suggestion, and I was wrong. It's the second time I've done something like this. I did it in 2010 for the Barça-Inter game. I put a star player before my own game plan, thinking about the €60million he had cost us instead of following through on my own ideas. We would probably have lost to Madrid anyway because they are in peak form at the moment, but at least we would have played according to our philosophy and not produced such a mess.'

The coach takes all the responsibility and refuses to blame his players. It's true that at least seven or eight had suggested that they approach the task of overturning the first leg 1-0 deficit by playing an all-guns-blazing attack. Pep recognises that his mistake was to agree with their suggestion: he had betrayed his own philosophy. On the most important day of the year he had used a game plan he didn't believe in. 'I can't coach any other way,' he insists. 'These are my beliefs and although I don't claim that they're the best, at least they're mine. And it's my job to convince my players that we can achieve more using these ideas, as we have done this year in the league and elsewhere.'

However, as well as imposing his ideas, a coach has to take the decisions and can't afford to worry about political correctness. Pep, at times, is too politically correct. As Philipp Lahm's agent, Roman Grill said, you have to be prepared to shake up the established hierarchy in a team. You need to pick the guys who improve the whole team's performance, as opposed to the big-name stars. Pep needs to make changes now, not next year, regardless of what people outside the club might say. To bring his proposition of positional play to fruition and to achieve maximum benefit he needs his midfielders to control and pass the ball still more rapidly and avoid holding on to it. He also needs his strikers to score more regularly when the play takes them into the opponents' penalty box.

And if the club doesn't support him in achieving these specific aims then the future won't be as glittering as it had promised to be. 'Next season, not only are we not going to take a step back from the demands of positional play, there'll be even more of it,' Bayern's coach promises.

The defeat has been a disaster but it does not necessarily cast doubt on the efficacy of Pep's playing style. They didn't play like they had in Manchester and Leverkusen, nor like they had in February and March. Pep betrayed his own philosophy. He remembers how on the plane back from Madrid he had been happy with Bayern's excellent performance (although they had been dreadful in the opponents' penalty box). At that stage the plan for the return leg was to play with three central defenders and four in midfield. The 3-4-3. Then, once he had arrived in Munich, he began to think that a 4-2-3-1, which had worked well until April, would be better. And finally, on the Monday before the match, he had been carried away by all the positive energy at the club and agreed the suicidal 4-2-4 formation. The coach scribbles each plan on a piece of paper which he then rips into pieces as if he'd like it all to have been a bad dream.

'Never again. From now on, if I mess up I will at least have stayed true to my own ideas.'

Cristina and the kids are at the training session. It's a holiday and she wants to give her husband some support. Their eldest daughter, Maria leaves an affectionate message for her dad on the whiteboard in his office, writing underneath it, in English: Do not wipe off. The players are trying to put it all behind them but Robben, amongst others, is obviously still very down.

Not everyone reacted the same way to the defeat, although the majority of players were completely behind the coach and appreciated his willingness to take the blame after such a tough night. Rafinha, who hadn't actually played, burst into tears in the dressing room when the coach, breaking with tradition, came down to comfort them and accept the blame. Javi gave Pep a hug and almost all the players were clearly concerned for the boss.

After today's training session Pep and Lahm have their longest conversation of the whole year on Pitch No.2. Over 60 minutes, Pep apologises to his captain and explains why he changed his mind about playing with three at the back. He then tells Lahm that he is convinced they need to reinforce and develop the playing style that has dominated this year. Lahm listens and doesn't say much, but when he does respond it's with a definite: 'We're behind you all the way Pep. All the way.'

The captain is speaking for the vast majority of his team-mates. They believe in Pep and are equally convinced that his playing style will bring them more success in the future. The rest of the conversation remains private, but Lahm's words stay with Pep: 'We're behind you all the way.'

When he has done playing with Valentina and Màrius, who love kicking balls at a miniature goal, Guardiola reflects: 'I'm not here to change German football culture, nor even Bayern's culture. That's not my objective. But neither can I teach my players something I don't believe in. I'm sorry but I have my own ideas and that's what I'm going to use next season. I understand and accept the criticism for what happened with Madrid, but I am not some kind of Taliban, I'm not totally inflexible. I like to listen and watch. I am happy to evolve, but please don't ask me to do something I don't believe in. Otherwise Bayern would suffer and the players would stop trusting me. I know that this is Germany and I am adapting. Whilst here I've played with one, sometimes even two out-and-out strikers. I've done things I would never have done at Barcelona and I've never tried to make Bayern play like Barça. The players are just too different, as you know. But I can't plan according to the players' ideas, because every one of them would be asking for a different thing.'

'Will the club support you?'

'Look, we have had a magnificent league campaign using my ideas. And we played well in the Bernabéu, despite losing. I want the best for this club and its players. I am proud to be part of Bayern and am doing the best job I can. I will continue to give this job 100% until my very last day here, but with my own ideas. The directors? All football coaches everywhere are dependent on their results. And it's not really about whether they are convinced or not. I can't get bogged down in looking for reassurance from the directors or the players. You have to start each day afresh, particularly after a defeat. Such a dreadful defeat will stay with me forever, mentally and emotionally but, at the same time, it has also reinforced my belief in my own ideas and instincts. It hasn't knocked me off course, quite the reverse in fact. There's only one way to win and that's to play the kind of good football I understand best – over-run the middle of the pitch and pass the ball even more. Whenever we've played that way and done it well, we've almost always won.'

On Tuesday he will meet with Rummenigge, Sammer and Dreesen. They'll work out who is definitely leaving, the role of the established players and the new signings required. He'll find out then if the club is backing him in word and deed. Pep has come to a watershed moment in his career. The political correctness has to go.

64

'ALL TEAMS GO THROUGH DIFFERENT PHASES'

Munich, May 15, 2014

THEY PLAY BORUSSIA Dortmund in the DFB-Pokal final on Saturday, the last match of a season which fate has dictated should start and end with Guardiola and Jürgen Klopp contesting a final. And, just as in last July, Dortmund are currently in better shape than Bayern, although Pep's men have rallied since the Real Madrid debacle. There has been a positive shift in the group dynamic over the last two weeks and the majority of Pep's men have united even more closely around him, forming a solid block of mutual support.

Whenever I comment on this to any of the players, they all say similar things. 'We're right behind Pep.'

'We'll fight to the death with the boss.'

'We've learned our lesson.'

'We have our game plan and we're not going to deviate from it.'

But it's a majority, not the whole squad. One player is feeling overlooked and has become more of a detached observer. Another is not convinced by Pep and his ideas and is also waiting and watching. Yet another makes no attempt to hide the tension that has been simmering between himself and the coach all year. But the majority are behind him, to the death. They understand that there is no going back. But more than that, they believe that they can go far playing this kind of football. They see in front of them not only triumphs and trophies but stability, consistency and the potential to remain at the elite level of world football for a long time to come. A rough count on the training pitch yields at least 15 players who I know are completely committed to this football. Eleven of them will start the DFB-Pokal final.

Borussia Dortmund are in their best form of the entire season. Since they were beaten 3-0 by Real Madrid in the Bernabéu on April 2, they have not lost a single match and are playing mesmerisingly fast, direct football. They've played eight games in the last five weeks, winning seven and drawing one – 22 goals scored, seven conceded. Spectacular results. They've beaten Madrid 2-0 in Dortmund and trounced Bayern 3-0 at the Allianz Arena. They have twice defeated Wolfsburg (in the league and the DFB-Pokal) and put in superb performances against Mainz (4-2) and Hertha in Berlin (4-0). Dortmund come into this Cup final in peak form and as out-and-out favourites.

Pep, however, has other ideas. The hammer blow delivered by Madrid has actually made him stronger. He talks with even more conviction, as if it has convinced him to doubt himself less and believe more in his own ideas. Five days before the final, on Monday morning, he already has his team list. Robben will play down the middle, there will be three at the back, a diamond formation in the middle of the pitch and young Højbjerg will be in the starting XI. Mandžukić is dropped altogether.

Pep has had a look at all Dortmund's recent matches and his analysis is clear: 'When they beat us 3-0 in the Allianz they won only two corners. On Saturday they beat Hertha away, 4-0, and took only one corner. That's no fluke.'

It is possible to conclude that this means Dortmund aren't looking to open teams up down the wing and cross into the box. Instead they appear to be hunting for the ball, waiting for the break down and then piling forward down the inside channels in counter-attacks. What's more, they always seem to finish a move with an effort on goal. This seems to account for the fact that Dortmund are winning so few corners. Inside channels and shots on goal. Dortmund have trained repeatedly and well on this. They close ranks defensively, try to bottle the rival up in the middle of the pitch, rob possession via clusters of pressing and then erupt into a fast counter-attack and a shot on goal.

Guardiola has thought up a very clear game plan for this final: three at the back, tight together to close the inside channels and the full-backs higher up, either side of Lahm at *pivote*. Kroos, Højbjerg and Götze will form a diamond shape ahead of those three with the latter asked to work hard flitting between the wing and a No.10 position.

Robben will be centre-forward. 'Arjen must be sharp – very, very sharp. I don't want him chasing the ball and pressing and running out of energy. And I don't want any of this asking for the ball to feet – I want us running into space and demanding the ball there.'

On Monday, with his players fully recovered from their league title celebrations, Pep starts to rehearse the game plan with his men. Pizarro's goal in the last second of the Bayern-Stuttgart match ended the Bundesliga campaign with a final victory to add to their record-breaking total of 29, with three draws and two defeats. They scored 94 goals and conceded 23 for a total of 90 points, 19 more than runners-up Dortmund and 26 more than third-placed Schalke.

They celebrated the title win in Munich on May 10, although it had been won in Berlin seven weeks earlier. So much has happened since then that the Hertha Berlin game feels like a distant memory but nothing can dampen the players' euphoria as they celebrate with their traditional 'beer shower'. Guardiola is the principal victim and he has put on his favourite red top for the occasion. Jerôme Boateng is the first to spray him with beer and Pep is only too happy to be drenched in the stuff: 'I wanted us to celebrate big time. We deserved it. I loved every minute of that shower because of what it symbolised: we are the champions. No mean feat! This is my first Bundesliga and I am over the moon!'

A few minutes later, holding the trophy (just before it slips out of his hands onto the grass) Pep is drenched again, this time by Van Buyten, who has no qualms about chucking the beer at him from over two metres away.

Pep and all his players are soaked through, although Domènec Torrent somehow escapes the worst of it. Manel Estiarte manages to avoid the 'beer shower' altogether by sneakily attaching himself to Pep's three kids. David Alaba comes towards him, beer in hand, but has to stop himself for the sake of the children. Estiarte has escaped his fate today, but if Bayern win the DFB-Pokal, it will be a whole different story.

Bayern party on and thousands of fans are treated to the spectacle of their players at their most jubilant. Pep speaks briefly from the balcony of the new rathaus (council buildings): '*Ich liebe euch. Ich bin ein Münchener.*' I love you. I'm a Munich man now.

He is following no pre-arranged script. This city has welcomed Guardiola with open arms and he is speaking from the heart.

By Monday the beer has all been washed away and it is business as usual – preparing for the final. Thiago joins the squad and instantly looks brilliant in the positional drills. The technical team are planning a few minutes' match time for him.

Pep's dream ticket is this diamond composed of Lahm, Kroos, Thiago and Götze. In February and March the latter two in combination had made the team soar. But, in the last move of the last training exercise, Thiago collapses. It's his knee ligaments, which had seemed completely restored after four weeks of treatment in Barcelona followed by two weeks with the physios at Säbener Strasse. Things had been looking up for the player – he had been pre-selected by Spain for the World Cup and it looked like he could manage the last half hour of the DFB-Pokal final. But now there will be no Cup final, no World Cup for Thiago. All he has to look forward to is another operation. Behind him lies a year which had been full of possibilities, ruined by serious ankle and knee injuries caused by clashes with opponents. We have not seen the best of Thiago (he started 19 games) but the whole team has witnessed his determination not to give up and his commitment to help the team regardless of the personal consequences.

With neither Thiago nor Schweinsteiger (who has a damaged tendon in his knee), the coach picks Højbjerg to start the game against Dortmund. Ten months have passed since the pre-season training camp in Trentino, where Pep first spotted the young Dane's potential.

He has worked intensively with the player throughout the year and now his time has come. During the last 10 months Højbjerg had not disappointed him once. Some days he had even turned up unannounced at the first team's dressing room, pretending that he'd wandered over absent-mindedly. On those occasions Pep always gave him a hug and sent him out to train anyway. Fiercely loyal and desperate to learn, Højbjerg's respect and passion for the coach is obvious.

'Pep thinks about training in the now and for the future,' says Højbjerg. 'He wants to win today but he wants to keep winning tomorrow and that's why he shows so much interest in us young players. It's like he's injecting his own tactical ideas in the team's bloodstream. It's not just about this week but for the future as well. In that respect he has gone much further than Heynckes. Pep doesn't reduce his planning to mere preparation for the next game. Everything he does is underpinned by his passion and his philosophy. Heynckes was all about winning. Pep, too, wants to win today, but he wants the club to still be winning in years to come. And the team knows that we can be sure of great success over the next five years. We have the right mentality, the right character and we just need to learn to be more emotional if we want to play even better.'

In the last few weeks Højbjerg has been performing brilliantly and has been called up to play for Denmark in two friendlies, against Hungary and Sweden.

'Can you believe it? Playing against Zlatan [Ibrahimovic]! And in my home city, Copenhagen! I can't wait! And you know, there's a little chapel I used to go to with my dad [his father passed away one month ago] just behind the stadium. My mum is delighted. And she's coming to watch the Cup final in Berlin.'

At this point Højbjerg still didn't know that Pep had decided to put him in his starting line-up against Dortmund, although it was pretty evident in the training sessions. Lorenzo Buenaventura had recently introduced strength-resistance exercises, but the training sessions were focused on tactics as the final drew near.

'Pep is the best thing that could have happened to Bayern,' Højbjerg says. 'Last year the team was amazing and I was wondering how Bayern could get any better. Yet Pep has taught us new and better tactics in every training session, every day, in every video and team talk. We all knew that the team could play football, but if you improve tactically then your control of the ball gets even better. Bayern were at 99% of our full potential and Pep has added that crucial 1%.'

Pep has put lots of emphasis on defensive work, with Martínez converted back into his third centre-half, between Boateng and Dante – the Spaniard will have the specific mission of keeping Lewandowski in his pocket on Saturday.

Over and over he explains Dortmund's system of attack so that his men understand how to stop it. Javi is in top form and I say to Pep at the end: 'Javi's superb. He's worked back up to the level of fitness he needs.'

All teams experience different phases, none of which lasts an entire year. That wouldn't be possible. Bayern enjoyed a particularly fertile phase in February and March, then they went into a downturn in April but they seem to have entered another productive phase right now. There are still missing players, for one reason or another (Ribéry is out of form; Thiago and Schweinsteiger are injured and Mandžukić's only interest is his next club), but the wheels are beginning to turn smoothly again, driven by Lahm and Kroos. The captain stands with Pep, analysing the best way of dealing with Dortmund's midfielders. They both throw their arms about, discussing how their opponents will move. Lahm is a clear leader in this team, the head of operations. Tactically he is an extension of Pep on the field.

Toni Kroos is the other brain of the outfit and the coach seeks his opinion on his game plan for Saturday. It's a private conversation but I overhear some of it. 'That's great Pep. I'm very happy with that. It's the right approach for the final.'

Kroos is another Pep man through and through. He believes utterly in the coach's playing style and would die for him out on the pitch. Even in training sessions he works himself to the point of exhaustion. He's done it today, running his legs off even for those exercises where it's not really necessary. For his part, Pep has complete faith in Kroos and tells him that Robben needs to stay fresh and to be fed the ball as he's moving into space – not to his feet when he's stationary.

Suddenly Pep introduces a whole new topic: 'I was reading something this morning that your daughter posted on Twitter [it was a quote from distinguished Portuguese writer José Saramago: "Defeat can have positive outcomes and it never lasts forever. Conversely, victory can have negative outcomes, although it too never lasts forever"]. I liked it a lot and it's certainly true. Everything is temporary.'

Every team goes through different phases and none of them lasts forever. Going by their performance in training, Bayern seem to be on an upward trajectory once more, although they must still prove it on Saturday in a final which they will start as underdogs.

He has already completed his basic game plan by Tuesday. On Wednesday morning he is working on his team's defensive strategy and then after lunch works with his defenders again showing them Dortmund's likely attacking moves.

He says goodbye to Mandžukić on Thursday, highlighting one of the other visible changes in his approach. He wants to tie up all the loose ends and therefore calls the Croat into his office before training, tells him he won't be playing in Berlin and wishes him good luck at his new club.

Training has a light emphasis on explosive force and two exhausting tactical drills which are repeated over and again. First the strikers and midfielders practise how to pressurise the other team as they play the ball from the back. The seven players who are charged with carrying out this task in the final work on it time after time, without pause. When, finally, it's perfect, Pep takes the defenders and goalkeeper and works on precisely the opposite, with the same detail: bringing the ball out from the back, starting with Neuer.

The main difference, with respect to the rest of the season, is that they're playing three at the back. Under pressure from strikers, Boateng, Martínez and Dante move the ball from one side to another with Lahm's help as he drops back from his principal position of *pivote* to help. Lahm's got a hard task in front of him this weekend. Martínez is choosing all the smart moves as he practises and Pep emphasises to him that he wants his passes to curve just in front of Boateng and Dante to help them move forward on the ball, or hit a first-time forward pass, not stop to receive possession.

Robben's instructions are subtle. 'Arjen, just walk a bit. Wander from one side of the pitch to the other. Don't burn yourself out running around. I need you fresh. Walk... but when you see that you can pick up the ball on the run then – *bam*! – off you go...'

This is a very different Pep from the man we saw in April, when he sensed that his team had lost their way and was trying to get them moving again. He is more laid back, and the players' body language suggests his message is understood quickly and easily.

Thiago is going into the operating theatre just as his team-mates finish the most important part of their preparations for the final. This is their last training session of the season here at Säbener Strasse. First, it's about defending corners – zonal defending. Then it's attacking corners – to be taken short. Finally, they practise attacking throw-ins in the opposition midfield.

'Lads,' warns Pep, 'it's all in the strategic play for a final like this. We have to get this right.'

Their work is over. This has been an intense, detailed, targeted session. The coach has used all his analytical skill to ensure that his men have as many weapons as possible at their disposal. He hasn't told them the line-up, but everyone knows who will be playing. This week they have worked with intensity and focus, keen to understand and try out every move he has suggested. They are off to Berlin to finish their season, the scene of their league triumph.

This time however, faced once more with the dilemma between passion and patience, Guardiola has gone for patience, control and the orthodox approach. This time he's sticking with the plan.

65

'JAVI AND ROBBEN, IN DEFENCE AND ATTACK'

Munich, May 16, 2014

AS THEIR FANS gather outside the Regent Hotel, just beside Unten der Linden, the capital's famous Linden tree-lined boulevard, the players inside are enjoying some peace and quiet. On this, the eve of the DFB-Pokal final, they are feeling quietly confident and I grab this chance to chat about the season with the two men who tomorrow will be the the axis of the defence and the attack, respectively.

Javi Martínez has had an injury-plagued year. He has had two operations (on his groin and mouth), has twisted his ankle and suffered tendonitis in his knees, as well as two or three bouts of gastroenteritis. He has started only 19 matches, and has come off the bench in a further 14. He started 34 times in his first season at Bayern and 53 in his last season at Athletic de Bilbao. Despite such an arduous year, the Spaniard has been happy working under Pep.

JM: 'He's such a talented man, and it shows. Look at us now. Bayern is a team where you can see how much work has gone into each line of the unit. All of the coaches who have come along to watch the games or our training sessions comment on that – how everyone's following the same script, from defenders to forwards, from the goalie to the centre-forward. And he also knows exactly how to manage the dressing room – how to deal with the guys who are playing and those who are not. He knows exactly when to lighten the tone. He does all of that perfectly.'

MP: 'But he has a bit of a temper at times, doesn't he?'

JM: 'No, he's not a bad-tempered guy. Obviously there are times when he needs to be hard on us, but only if there's a good reason. You know, Heynckes was more than capable of that, too. Whenever Pep sees that we're shifting down a gear or whatever, he'll let us have it and he has no hesitation in coming down hard on even the most senior and respected of players, if he needs to. He's the boss and he's the one that lays down the law.'

MP: 'When you came back from holiday last July and Pep was in charge, did you imagine that you would end up in central defence?'

JM: 'Not at all. I had no idea what Pep expected. I knew from the press that when he was at Barça, he was interested in signing me for the defence, but I didn't know what he wanted me to do here. Pep told me straight away that he wanted me to play as a central defender, but also as *pivote* too. He reckoned that I would make a good centre-half and said that he expected me to work hard to understand his ideas. In Guardiola's football the positions of central midfielder and central defender are actually very similar. In fact the *pivote* acts as the third centre-half, particularly when we are bringing the ball out from the back. I like playing centre-half because I think that one of my best qualities is defensive concentration. It's a key characteristic of mine and it's imperative if you play in that position.'

MP: 'Guardiola has made many tactical changes since arriving.'

JM: 'Yes, we've been on a steep learning curve in terms of our playing style, as well as the role I and other players fulfil in the team. All the changes have been pretty significant. And the great thing is that we haven't yet reached our peak. There's still so much to improve. Pep works every day to help us perform even better when we compete.'

MP: 'You've won three titles so far but also fell flat on your faces in the Champions League. Had the team become too conceited and complacent after so much success?'

JM: 'It's up to each of us to keep pushing ourselves, and stay hungry. We're young guys who want to make our mark on football history and need to remember that it's all about the present, not the past. We need to stay hungry. Bayern need to keep fighting for new titles. The minute we start thinking how wonderful we are, that's when we'll stop winning.'

I now turn to Arjen Robben, who will play as the central striker tomorrow. Robben's experience has been the opposite of Javi's – he's never played so many games in any one season before. Recurrent injury was his single greatest handicap throughout his time at Real Madrid, Chelsea, PSV Eindhoven and, until now, at Bayern. But all of that is behind him now and he has appeared as a starter for Bayern on 37 occasions this season, and played a total of 45 games, in which he has scored 21 goals and given 14 assists. The best stats of his professional life.

'That's certainly true,' agrees Robben, 'although my first year here [2009/10] and last year's treble win were also good years. Working with Pep has been brilliant because he's helped me improve so much. And everything has gone well in terms of fitness, too. I have been injury-free since January 2013 and that has helped me maintain consistent levels of performance. But without a doubt the high point has been working with Pep. I love his vision of football, the way he thinks.'

MP: 'What have you changed in terms of injury prevention?'

AR: 'If you look back, you'll see that things started improving as soon as I got here and things have continued progressively from there. I started to work with an osteopath, who actually started helping me in my last year with Real Madrid. I'm still working with him. I think that in my five years in Munich, I have only had two serious injuries, everything else was just little niggles. Usually players have fewer injuries when they're younger but it has been the reverse for me and maturity and experience have helped me a lot. I am getting better and better at managing the physical side of things and am feeling great.'

MP: 'People thought that you and Guardiola wouldn't get on.'

AR: 'Yes, I was asked that a lot here in Germany and in Holland. Everyone said that I had too strong a character and that Pep liked *tiquitaca* whilst I prefer to dribble. People claimed we'd be incompatible but I knew that we would work together brilliantly. I had no doubt at all.'

MP: 'You were the star of the Champions League final which Bayern won at Wembley, but when you arrived in Trentino for the pre-season training, you didn't act like a superstar. It was a pleasant surprise for Pep, I think.'

AR: 'Look, I was looking forward to working with Pep as soon as they announced his signing and my expectations were more than confirmed when I met not just him but Domè [Torrent] and Loren [Buenaventura] too. I was totally up for his brand of football and I clearly remember our first conversation in Trentino. He said: "Enjoy your football. You scored in the Champions League final and you score in all the big games, so relax, enjoy it and take some time with your family, be happy." Those were his first words to me, on the very first day. It's a wonderful feeling when your coach speaks to you like that. It gives you such a boost. So we really started out on a high.'

MP: 'Some players have said that although Heynckes created a fantastic Bayern side, things needed to change to avoid stagnation.'

AR: 'I agree with that. That can be a real danger when you win everything. If you just go on doing the same things, following the same ideas, it can be disastrous and it is only too easy to sit back and relax after winning the treble. Bringing in a new coach with new ideas prevented the rot setting in. We needed to focus from day one.'

MP: 'Were Pep's ideas difficult to grasp?'

AR: 'The whole process has been a challenge. For the players and for Pep, too, because he had just moved to a new country, he had to learn a new language – he had worked really hard to learn German before he even got here and we were amazed by how good he was at the start. The first few months are always difficult. It's a process of adaptation for everyone, but we've improved a little every week, every month and have put on some storming performances, like the one against Manchester City. I love this style of football because it reminds me a bit of the traditional Dutch game, the football Van Gaal used to play. There's something about it, this attacking style, always playing high up the pitch without getting hemmed in defensively at the back. I loved it from day one.'

MP: 'Attacking so much and so high up the pitch is unusual nowadays and most teams pack their defences and wait for you to attack them. It will always be difficult to break down that kind of team and it must be tough mentally to keep going.'

AR: 'Obviously it's easier to defend than attack, but if you like to have the ball then you have to keep looking for new routes to do that, and building something is always harder than destroying it. In fact the *Mister* was saying only yesterday, "If you are a footballer, it must mean that you enjoy playing this game and our style of play is a lot more fulfilling". Although I do accept that going up against a very defensive team is much, much harder.'

MP: 'Are you surprised that you have scored the most goals and provided the most assists this season? Has that got something to do with this new style of game?'

AR: 'I think so, yes. There was a stage at which Pep told me not to obsess about getting goals. He said that if I just got on with playing the goals would come anyway. And that's exactly what happened. If you just focus on playing, looking for spaces, holding on to the ball and working with your team-mates then you almost always get a goal in the end. I think that in every single game I've ended up with chances to score. If you have the ball a lot and make sure that you're in the midst of the action, then you'll always get chances to score.'

MP: 'The team played very well in February and March but started to mess up in April. Was it just one of those things or were there specific reasons? Was winning the league so early a problem?'

AR: 'It wasn't just because we won the league too early, but it's hard to explain what else caused it. I still struggle to understand how we could win the league with such style and then come a cropper here. It felt like we were getting worse and worse every week. It was the combination of lots of factors. A football team is complex and at the same time, pretty fragile. Look at the injuries we suffered in April, for example. But it will take me a bit of time to reflect on everything and work out what happened to cause it.'

MP: 'The team seems to be back in top form, from the evidence of this week's training.'

AR: 'Yes, I think that too. We have a good chance of winning the Cup tomorrow despite what people think. Getting your head right is the most important thing and we are all completely focused.'

MP: 'Pep says that this football represents a bit of a culture clash in Germany. Do you think it will ever really catch on here?'

AR: 'Undoubtedly. Everyone recognised how well we played in the league and gave Pep the credit he was due. But football is about results and no matter how much we achieved this year, the minute we started losing, the praise dried up and suddenly we were rubbish. But of course that wasn't the case at all. We have played superb football with this system and have achieved great things. Next season we must, and we will, play even better. We've started down the right road and I'm looking forward to starting it all over again next season.'

MP: 'The team will be even better because you have adapted to this new system.'

AR: 'Exactly. The first year under a new coach with a different style is the toughest. And this year we've won three trophies, broken all the Bundesliga records, made it to the Champions League semi-finals and are going out to win the Cup tomorrow. That's an incredible tally for our first year. And we players know that we can make even more improvements next year because we understand everything so much better now.'

66

BLOOM IN THE GLOW OF HAPPINESS

Berlin, May 17, 2014

IT WAS THE last training session of the season in Berlin's Olympiastadion and, as he jumped for the ball, David Alaba clashed with Ribéry, injuring himself in the abdomen. Alaba would not make the final. One more major loss for the team.

After dinner, Guardiola called Rafinha and asked him: 'Rafa, can you play on the left?'

The Brazilian's reply was firm. 'Pep, you know I'll play anywhere you tell me to.'

It meant the coach already had a replacement for Alaba, but this move meant that he would need to play the full-backs more open than he had planned to. Now all he had to do was find a replacement for Rafinha on the right, but he decided to give his chosen stand-in an untroubled night's sleep.

On Saturday morning just after breakfast he shares the news with Højbjerg. He's going to start the game, not as a midfielder, but at right-back instead. The youngster tells the coach that he's happy to play wherever the team needs him.

Berlin is transformed. Thousands of *Borussers* have flooded the capital in a sea of yellow within which you can distinguish only the odd flash of red. The odds seem stacked in Dortmund's favour, and media opinion firmly is behind the in-form team.

Pep has his line-up and his game plan ready. The team he will field represents a declaration of intent for next season. He has picked the men who are most committed to his playing philosophy (injured players aside) and today's strategy will take them through one more stage in the constant tactical evolution which the Catalan has instituted and which he is determined will be an unassailable part of the DNA of his era.

Pep hums a line from the German national anthem, '*Blüh'im Glanze dieses Glückes* (Bloom in the glow of happiness)'. It's 8pm, it's raining in Berlin and there is so much more at stake right now than simply the DFB-Pokal. After their cataclysmic failure against Real Madrid, Guardiola has made one key change that goes way beyond mere tactics. It is a strategic decision that he has been working on for a long time. Reflecting on the team's strengths, Pep has concluded that they are at their best when they bring the ball out with a three-man backline; when they ensure that at least one full-back has the athletic ability and stamina to get up and down the line all game, but at the same time monitor the inside channel next to him; when they use a controlling central midfield *pivote* whose key task is to control opposition counter-attacks and who can drop back to play with the centre-halves if needs be; with a centre-forward capable of pushing the opposition back four backwards and a second striker/attacking midfielder who knows how to play in space but can also stay linked to the movements of the centre-forwards.

In preparation for the match he had noted these five principles on his whiteboard and developed his game strategy from there. Now, days later, the plan is in place, recreated out on the grass just before kick-off: a basic 3-6-1 which will become a 5-4-1 when they're defending and a 3-4-3 for the attack.

In the final Højbjerg plays right-back, Rafinha on the left, Lahm and Kroos are the two *pivotes*. Götze starts wide left, Müller wide right. Meanwhile Robben is the highest point of that forward pressing triangle. When Bayern have the ball he's free to follow his instincts. Without it, Götze and Müller must try to choke Dortmund, with Lahm and Kroos in behind that first wave of pressure. Most unusually of all, Bayern will play more conservatively, they will wait for Dortmund, and will play the back line far deeper than has been normal all season. They don't want to gift Klopp's team any space.

Yellow dominates the Olympiastadion, as do the songs and cheers of the Dortmund support. But from the start Klopp and his men are disconcerted by this all-new Bayern. This isn't the audacious side which would throw itself into bold attack, leaving itself stripped down to bare essentials at the back. Suddenly there's a role reversal. And even before anyone can make sense of this change, Müller has nearly scored, the ball deflecting off the face of the goalkeeper, Weidenfeller, and Robben has had a second chance after a long and accurate ball from Lahm.

Dortmund are at a loss. Normally, they are expert at setting traps. They allow the opposition to bring the ball forward quite happily, like a cat tempting Bayern with a tasty chunk of cheese in its paws, but when they reach a certain point the predator will react with lightning speed and tear its prey to pieces. Today, however, the mouse seems to be a good deal smarter. It has changed its routine. Guardiola stakes it all on massive superiority in the middle of the pitch. He leaves three fixed centre-halves at the back and places six of his team in midfield. In the face of this surprise Dortmund cannot find a response. The pressure they try to exert with their strikers has no effect, given the huge numerical superiority Bayern exerts in midfield. The consequence is that Pep's team has fewer attacks than normal, but almost all of them are far more dangerous.

Pep opts for less attack but more control. Robben is alone up front but he manages to tie up three defenders – both centre-halves and one full-back. When Müller is free to help him they make a formidable duo. When that happens, two Bayern forwards tie up all four Dortmund defenders, meaning that Pep's five midfielders always get the better of Dortmund's four in the centre of the pitch.

Lahm is designed to be the key in this final. He will help the back three play the ball out and will put pressure on Sahin every time Weidenfeller rolls the ball to him to re-start Dortmund's play. Those two tasks give the Bayern captain a 70-metre area to cover – his afternoon must be full of effort. But eight minutes in he takes a heavy knock on his left calf. After quarter of an hour he needs medical attention. Five minutes later, he is noticeably limping and after 28 minutes the calf muscle betrays him. It's a huge loss and looks decisive. No Lahm, no Thiago, no Schweinsteiger, no Alaba – and without Lahm, Pep's plan to dominate midfield is in jeopardy.

There are very few options on the bench but Pep goes for Ribéry, who has been struggling for weeks with serious back problems which have also affected his leg muscles.

Pep's next decision is surprising but it will, in the end, become the key to winning. Ribéry won't play as a winger but, instead, in the double *pivote* with Kroos. It's an unheard of idea, improvised on the go, under the pressure of a growing injury crisis. But it will demolish Dortmund, who take at least half an hour to come to terms with it. Until this point the Bayern play hasn't shone brilliantly, but it has been effective. Not one dangerous Dortmund counter-attack.

Despite Neuer still looking a little insecure when he kicks the ball, Bayern manage to continue imposing their plan thanks to the cleverly spaced-out positions which Martínez, Kroos and Ribéry all adopt when they begin to bring the ball out. The three of them form a fulcrum to support the wide guys, with Højbjerg growing in confidence minute by minute, and Bayern begin to operate with fluidity and simplicity. Martínez shows the tactical intelligence and defensive concentration he is famous for; Ribéry gives a formidable display in this totally new position – it seems contradictory that such an anarchic wide player can offer calm, intelligent defensive organisation in midfield. Kroos adds Lahm's workload to his own.

An hour in, after Müller has another big chance created by Robben and Ribéry, the Dortmund coach makes his first tactical change. Oliver Kirch comes on for Mjitaryán and the two teams are now man-for-man in midfield. Guardiola swaps Ribéry with Götze – meaning the German is now side-by-side with Kroos in the double *pivote*. Pep wants Ribéry nearer the Dortmund goal, but it's at the loss of the positive effect the Frenchman was having in the middle of the Bayern midfield.

Hummels gets his head to a wide free-kick and sends the ball beyond Neuer. It looks in by the time Dante clears it, but the referee doesn't give the goal. Extra time arrives without a goal, but Dortmund have managed only two efforts on target – including the Hummels header. Bayern have played with intelligence and have had five efforts on goal, even while robbing Dortmund of their main weapon, the counter.

During the extra-time team talk, out on the pitch, Pep merely reminds his players they are entering a stage where their minds, not their legs, are in charge. The emphasis is on concentration, confidence and determination. He just gives one instruction: 'Look for Mario [Götze]. Give him the ball between the lines.'

Ribéry is on his last legs. The pain in his back is unbearable and Pep and Robben discuss their options. 'Pep asked me if I could keep going,' the Dutchman tells me the next morning, 'and I said yes. I could see that Franck [Ribéry] couldn't go on any longer and Højbjerg had taken a kick to his calf. We had to keep going as best we could.'

Extra time may be, as Pep suggested, a question of mental strength rather than physical stamina and certainly, on this occasion, many of his men have nothing left in their legs. And things are about to get much worse. No sooner have they trotted on to the pitch to finish this epic battle than Kroos makes his first mistake of the night, allowing Aubameyang to get away a low, hard shot. Neuer slips on the wet grass and dislocates his right shoulder. He remains in the game, but will spend the next 30 minutes having ice applied for the pain.

Next, it's the turn of Kroos to get a kick on his calf, which leaves him limping for the rest of the match, Müller gets cramp in his hamstrings and Højbjerg has to be substituted for Van Buyten. Despite all this, Bayern somehow continue to bring the ball out from the back without too much difficulty thanks to the brilliant connection between Martínez and Kroos, and Dortmund still don't manage to mount a good counter-attack.

Pizarro is waiting on the touchline, about to replace Ribéry, when the goal arrives. Boateng switches flanks with a long ball, Ribéry gets it, holds it and lays it off to Robben, who has sprinted towards the penalty spot and shoots. Weidenfeller palms it out in the direction of Grosskreutz, but Boateng has pushed up and quickly robs the Dortmund defender. He crosses and there's Robben again, ahead of everyone, to land the definitive blow.

Guardiola's euphoria lasts about two seconds and then his thoughts turn to making the Ribéry substitution, because he is now noticeably limping. The last quarter of an hour is taken up by increasingly desperate Dortmund attacks, but they manage only one good effort, by Reus, and two more good chances on the counter.

Müller seals it in the 122nd minute thanks to a steal by Rafinha, Robben's insatiable running, a clever pass by Pizarro and Müller's own shrewd movement to escape Schmelzer and Weidenfeller before scoring.

Bayern have won the double – the league and Cup titles – becoming only the second team in history to have done so immediately after a treble-winning year (PSV Eindhoven did it in 1987/8 and 1988/9). The men from Munich have won their fourth piece of silverware of the season, having contested six competitions, and for Guardiola it's his 18th trophy out of a possible 25 in his five seasons as a top-flight coach (14 out of 19 with Barcelona and four out of six with Bayern).

Bayern go wild. Boateng hoists Guardiola into the air as if his boss weighs nothing. Then Neuer, despite his injured arm, does the same thing. The coach is enveloped in the arms of Javi, Rafinha, Götze and Kroos, and has a special hug for Robben. Once they have the trophy, Dante and Van Buyten shower the boss in beer once again and this time even Estiarte fails to escape the soaking.

During the post-match dinner the players talk about their coach in glowing terms.

'He's designed my perfect position. Finally I've got the right position in the right system which allows me to give my very best,' says Martínez.

Lahm: 'We have shown the world our true value and this has been a huge boost to our confidence.'

You can see the players are still hurting over the disaster against

Real Madrid, but their total support for Pep is clear, as is their determination to continue to follow his playing philosophy.

By 2am Rafinha decides to deliver his end-of-season message: 'Before the match I said to Domè [Torrent]: "We're going out there to die together." Half the team were in pieces, but we showed big balls. You have to have guts to put a kid of 18 out there in that position [right-back]. Or to put me at left-back.

'For Pep this is super important: if anyone has any doubts about what he's asking them to do, they just have to swallow them and do what's needed.' Robben shares similar sentiments: 'This victory is amazing, and it will have far-reaching effects. It has vindicated us and our style of play. We are more and more committed to these ideas every day. Pep's strategy has given us this victory and next year is going to be even better.'

During the party Pep spends some time tucked away with his family in a corner. He's delighted of course, but you can see how angry he still is with himself for the Madrid debacle, for having failed to play that day with this team.

At 3.30am he bids the party goers goodnight and walks off with Valentina asleep, curled up in his arms like a baby.

Outside in the street it's still raining.

67

THE KID AND THE CAPTAIN

Berlin, May 18, 2014

BAYERN SET OFF for Munich with the cup they have won in Berlin, the capital city which has become a talisman for Pep this year. Thousands of fans await the team in Marienplatz, ready to celebrate their double-winning season and, on the way, I chat to two of the players who are most symbolic of Pep's first year in charge: Højbjerg and Lahm.

Firstly, I ask Højbjerg what he has learned from Pep. 'To be a bit bolder with the ball. He's shown me how important it is to play without fear. Just to get on with playing whether you're up against Xabi Alonso or a complete amateur. Play with courage and without fear, and "show some balls", as Pep puts it. When you're young you can be a bit hesitant about things, but that gets you nowhere. You have to give it everything if you want to improve. Pep has insisted that I let go of any anxiety or hesitancy when I play. He's also taught me a huge amount about tactics and about defending. I've learned to stay when my team-mate pushes forward and to attack as high up as I can when it's my turn to push on. He's taught me all about the right tactics and shown me how to play with passion, intelligence and courage. I had some difficult times this season and Pep really helped me. He told me that I only needed to dedicate 90 minutes a day to football, but that those 90 minutes had to be full-on. If I did that, he assured me, I could stop worrying about my game.'

Højbjerg joined Bayern in 2012 when he was just 16 and initially struggled with a four-day per week training schedule.

'I was pretty small and my body couldn't cope with so much work. I was basically sore all over for an entire year. And this year with Pep has been similar. At times I've had real problems keeping up with the older guys' training schedule – six times a week.'

MP: 'For you the season has been more about learning rather than competing.'

PH: 'Of course. When I get out of my bed in the morning I always say to myself, "Today will be even better than yesterday. Today I will be a better player. I'll learn something new". I like to learn something new every day and I want to keep improving. I think Pep sees all that in me and I try to take everything he teaches me and incorporate it in my game. I like to follow my instincts and try to do the things that will help me progress. I'm not big-headed but I am very self-confident and can be a bit too quick to conclude that my solution is the best one. I have to learn that other people sometimes have better answers and with Pep that has certainly happened. He shows me much better solutions. For example, this is the first time I have really understood that you need to be on top of defensive tactics and be super-disciplined if you want to stay at the elite level. I now know how important your mental attitude is to maintain defensive order; to be aware that every sprint, every touch on the ball, every shot must be given 100%, every time.

'I have learned so much since last summer, mentally, physically and tactically and am a better player than I was before Pep arrived because I now have knowledge I didn't possess before. But I am still capable of doing five things well and then maybe messing up and losing the ball in the sixth move. Right now I am in the process of making the jump from the youth categories to professional and it's really important to get things right mentally. Some of my team-mates, like Dante, for example, remind me every day how important it is to be totally focused.'

MP: 'What has Pep been to you?'

PH: 'He is a man who puts all his emotion, all his passion, into football. He's my coach of course but he's so much more than that. He's been like a second father to me. He's a great guy who spends his days showing us how we can play even better.'

MP: 'Is there a difference this year in terms of the way the team is feeling?'

PH: 'I think that we were a bit more Germanic last year – we weren't excessively emotional. In German we would call that *gerade* [stiff upper lip]. Now everyone's a bit more emotional and I like it this way. I'm very emotional myself. I like to play with a bit of passion. But the Germans are less used to that approach than the Brazilians, the Spanish players and Pizarro and me. I'm not saying that it's better or worse to be more emotional, it's just different for them. But you can see the change in the team and I like it. A little bit of emotion will keep us hungry to win every week. And Pep himself is very emotional.'

MP: 'This lack of emotion applies to defeat as well as victory.'

PH: 'This is a very Germanic team and we are not used to expressing our emotions, to the extent that we can appear cold and arrogant at times. I prefer to be a bit more emotional and, after all, we train and play all year so that we can cut loose at the end of the season at the celebrations.'

MP: 'Are you going to be a key part of this team?'

PH: 'Sometimes it still feels like it will be very, very difficult to make it at Bayern and there are always people who say I won't do it. It's certainly a tough place to play when you're only 18 and sometimes I think that in two years I'll still only be 20, then there are other days I tell myself, "I have worked under Pep Guardiola for a year, I play for Bayern Munich, the best team in the world led by the best coach in the world and this season I have learnt more than in the rest of my life put together". And then I think, "Yes, I can develop into a good player".

'I understand that I can't play every week because the team needs to win matches. It's almost like I'm at school. The school of Pep and Bayern, and it's just great. Obviously the day will come when I'll be expected to play every week and that won't be easy. I know that, I'm not an idiot. I understand that I might go off and play for other teams in the Bundesliga. But I will always be proud of my time with Pep, of having learnt so much from him and from Bayern. Right now I need to learn as much as possible, every hour of the day. Then maybe in 10 years I'll be saying to some young kid, "I can teach you what I know". Right now I am receiving a lot. Perhaps in the future I'll give a lot back.'

MP: 'Nobody can doubt your strength of character. At 18 you played in a major final.'

PH: 'I have a big heart and always commit myself 100% to what I'm doing. That approach can have its disadvantages but it's also what makes me strong. I have inherited a very strong character from my dad and other members of the family. At times it can be too strong, but in the long run it will help me succeed. I just need to find the path that's correct for me and get the balance right.'

After my chat with the youngest member of the squad I turn to the captain, the man Pep has described as 'the guy who puts all the pieces in order', Lahm, the full-back who converted to an organising midfielder right in the middle of the UEFA Super Cup on August 30.

MP: 'Philipp, what was it like when you changed position in such a radical way?'
PL: 'The good thing was that I had played in the midfield a lot with Pep during our pre-season training. He often put me there for our

friendlies. I hadn't played in midfield for years but he decided it was the right thing to do and he knew that I could cover the requisites of the job. I like that position and playing in the midfield for the Super Cup was really special. The coach trusted me to do it well despite the fact that for so long I'd been playing in other positions.'

MP: 'Have you had any problems adjusting or are you completely comfortable as a number 6?'

PH: 'It's been great playing in this position and I think Pep saw how comfortable I was there. That's why he decided to go for it. I had almost always been a full-back and it has been great making the change to *pivote*. You need to be 100% alert when you first change to a new position. You have a lot of players around you in the midfield and I think my performance this year has shown Pep made the right decision.'

MP: 'In the future do you see yourself playing more in the midfield or as a full-back?'

PL: 'I reckon I've shown this season that I can play in either position. I love playing in the midfield, it has been a real novelty after 10 years as a full-back, but that doesn't mean I'll never be a defender again. At the end of the day, it's the coach's decision.'

MP: 'What were the biggest changes Guardiola made?'

PL: 'He's changed our positional play as well as my own position and we also go for much higher levels of possession than we did under Jupp. We dominate more. For example, last season we hung back much more waiting for a chance to counter-attack in the big matches, like the Champions League quarter and semi-finals. We played with energy, but didn't have the ball as much or dominate matches in the way we do now. The second thing which has changed dramatically is the space every player knows he must occupy. And that's related to how we immediately all press as a unit when we've lost the ball. Those are the two main areas we've improved this year compared to last season.'

MP: 'Adapting to Pep's ideas hasn't been quick or easy.'

PL: 'It has been difficult. It was all so new. But it was also necessary after we had won everything. We had won the treble and Pep wanted to teach us something new. I think a lot of the guys found it hard and a few of them initially said that our old approach had worked well. We'd won everything after all. I think Pep has also adapted to German football and it has changed the way he does things. The players have needed time to adjust and the coach has also had to adapt to us. But I reckon he's done a pretty good job.'

MP: 'Guardiola has often talked about the culture clash between his ideas and the German tradition. Do you think the two have clashed and will continue to do so? Will he be able to bridge the gap?'

PL: 'It has been a culture clash, but it's a process. Pep has often commented on the fact that so many German teams like counter-attacking. A lot of opponents play very defensively and then suddenly launch a lethal counter-attack. They're not bothered about high possession. I think it's the difference between Spanish and German football, but it's a process of learning from each other. We players have to learn from the coach, but Pep has also had to get to know German football, our opponents and how they play. But I think that the learning process is complete.'

MP: 'Only PSV Eindhoven has ever won the double after a treble-winning season. Has Pep been an important part of your success in this?'

PL: 'I'm pretty sure that he deserves a large part of the credit for ensuring that we didn't fall on our faces. Usually after winning the treble players are exhausted and it's very, very tough to win the league again, but I think that Pep, with his technical team and his new ways of thinking and doing things, kept us all on our toes. We had to concentrate hard to make sure that everything worked. We started out with the right rhythm and then went on to win the Bundesliga in fabulous style.'

MP: 'What are the best and the worst things about Pep?'

PL: 'His incredible tactical knowledge is a huge strength. He's also meticulous about everything he does and prepares us brilliantly for each opponent. He's the best and that's probably also a slight weakness because he's such a perfectionist. He wants everything, down to the last detail, to be perfect. That's great as far as it goes, but at times it goes too far and prevents him from being totally satisfied. He can never allow himself to sit back and say "this is brilliant".'

MP: 'Do you think he'll stay a long time?'

PL: 'I'm certain he will, although it will depend on the players. When a team is successful it's more likely the coach will stay for longer but if you don't keep winning in a prestigious club like Bayern, everyone starts to doubt the coach, including the players. But I think it's pretty likely that we're going to keep winning under Pep. I really enjoy working with him.'

MP: 'Your style of game means that your opponents play very defensively and wait to counter-attack. Isn't it exhausting mentally to have to keep playing like that all the time?

PL: 'I can only tell you what it's like from a player's point of view and it's so much better when you play the ball rather than defending all the time. If you defend like that you end up with just five seconds with the ball, trying to score, and then you're back to defending again. It's great to have the ball at your feet. Ok, you're likely to be facing 11 players all packed up together at the back and that's hard, very hard, but it's much better to be taking the initiative rather than standing waiting for your chance.'

MP: 'But when your attacks end with ranks of banked defenders in front of them and the goal won't come, what should the team do: shoot more, cross better? What are the solutions when you are blocked off?'

PL: 'We have to be completely focused because every pass matters. The quicker the ball moves, the less time the opposition have on the ball, the better your chance of breaking them down and of course your precision of movement is important to leave space for your team-mates to help break down the defence. What's decisive is when the team reaches the final third of the pitch, near the opposition goal. It's important how you organise and use the little space that's available. You need players who understand that, who are extremely good technically and who always want to have the ball.'

And so, I give you Højbjerg and Lahm, the symbols of Pep's philosophy, the 18-year-old midfielder who has played the DFB-Pokal final at full-back and the 30-year-old full-back who has become the undisputed midfielder of the season.

EPILOGUE

A LAST WORD FROM PEP

Munich, May 20, 2014

BY THE TIME you read this book, season 2014-2015 will be well underway and Bayern will have competed in their first competition of the new footballing year – the German Super Cup. Once again the Westfalen Stadion will have been the setting for the start of this new phase of the club's endless cycle of competition; Guardiola battling the same opponent with whom he started and ended his first season: Jürgen Klopp's Borussia Dortmund.

In Pep's first season Bayern played 56 official matches, resulting in 44 wins, 6 draws and 6 defeats. In other words, 78.5% of their games ended in victory, a figure which becomes 85.3% in Bundesliga fixtures. They scored 150 goals (an average of 2.67 per game) and conceded 44 (0.78 per game).

From set plays, Bayern scored 28 goals (14 corners, nine indirect free-kicks and five direct free-kicks). From the same situations they conceded eight (five from corners, including 'second ball' and own-goals, one from an indirect free-kick and two direct). They also played 14 friendlies as well as having completed 279 training sessions in the 326 days between June 26, 2013 and May 17, 2014. In this time they had had two weeks' holiday, which effectively meant that they completed their 349 sessions (70 matches plus 279 training sessions) in 312 days.

Most of the players had also played an average of eight games with their national teams in preparation for the World Cup. Technical development and practice was a central element in all 279 sessions and these were divided into: heavily tactical; demonstrably physically based and aimed at quantity [such as strength and resistance, or stamina]; physical but aimed more at quality of a specific component, like explosive force; preventative – focused on mobility and stretching; the remaining number were specific sessions where the squad was broken down into separate groups for a variety of reasons.

Nine players stand out for their consistent appearances across the 39 weeks of competition, of which there were only six without a midweek match. The list of players who exceeded 4000 minutes – or a figure close to that – and took part in at least 90% of training, includes: Neuer, Lahm, Boateng, Dante, Alaba, Kroos, Müller, Mandžukić and Robben. Müller is the player who missed fewest sessions through injury (just two days), followed by Alaba (three days) and Kroos (four days).

Statistics aside, several key developments epitomise Guardiola's first year: Pep's process of adaptation to German football and the Bayern players; the epidemic of injuries; his teaching of the basic concepts related to positional play (Bayern's new language); outstandingly competitive performances in all tournaments and better results than expected.

At the end of the season, a new list of priorities were being compiled: the need to evolve in tactical terms so as to avoid becoming stuck with out-of-date formulae; the importance of new players learning to speak the language of the game more fluently; the renovation and management of a group of footballers who had been at the elite levels of European football for five years and the laying of the foundations for another successful campaign.

But the last word surely belongs to Guardiola himself, and we get together for a chat in his office on Tuesday, May 20. His players pop in from time to time to say goodbye. Some of them are off to the World Cup whilst others, like Thiago, Neuer and Lahm, are still working with the physios. Pep played golf with Cristina on Monday, but today he is right on time for our appointment. The report on the Borussia Dortmund game is still lying on his desk and there on the whiteboard I can see the scribbled plans for their 3-6-1 in Berlin, Maria's sweet message and two phrases written in green. One is a quote from the film, Moneyball: 'I know that they're giving you a hard time. But the first one through the wall always gets bloody. Always.'

The other is a quote from Pep himself: 'Ego is the source of the majority of a team's problems.'

MP: 'Pep, what is your analysis of your first year? You've experienced success, defeat, drama and joy. Are you happy here?'

PG: 'I'll need a bit more time to be absolutely sure that the team is mine [he says this after a pause which at the time seemed to go on forever, but which in fact lasted only eight seconds]. We've won a lot and everyone is delighted because winning titles buys you the time you need to start building the future. But real satisfaction comes when you start to feel that the team is really yours and is playing the kind of football you want. That's why I need more time. The team isn't completely mine yet. Am I going to get that time? Truly great teams need to keep winning, but if I get the time I need, we can really plan where we want to go. I'm trying to implement something that flies in the face of the culture here. I'm from Santpedor and the players are from Munich, Greifswald, Rosenheim or Gelsenkirchen, so I have to convince them. And there has to be a mix of give and take. I can't and wouldn't want to try to persuade Beckenbauer to my way of thinking and neither would he be able to convince me. So we have to meet somewhere in the middle. It has been a clash of cultures which has taken place immediately after winning the treble and with the same basic group of players. If you win a treble and then seven new guys join the team, it's easier to change the way you play. But that's not what happened here. When I joined Barça there were eight new players in the team and the club had just had a disastrous season. Bayern were fresh from an outstanding season and there were only two new players [Thiago and Götze]. That's just the reality of the situation, but it hasn't been an easy situation to manage.'
MP: 'Have you felt disorientated at times?'

PG: 'It has certainly been challenging. At Barça I was in charge of revitalising a team which had lost the league by 18 points. Here I came in just after they won the treble. That's a huge difference. But each time I have managed to get the right results which, at the end of the day, is the litmus test for any president or director general. In that sense this year has been a success – four out of six possible trophies. We lost the Champions League, but it was the way we lost that left the bitter taste in our mouths, not the fact that we went out in the semi-finals, which was completely logical. There is no justification for the way we lost to Madrid. I just need to hold up my hands and accept it. But I did well otherwise. I had come to a new country to take charge of the treble winners, with only two new players, and all of it in a new language. That bit was tricky because it's one thing to be able to express yourself, but it's quite another to do it well enough so that you really communicate with the players, make them grasp fully what you are saying. You need a really good vocabulary for that and mine isn't quite there yet. If you can imagine, just a year ago if someone had said Guten Abend to me I would have had no idea what it meant. I wouldn't have known if they were talking about night or day. But it's not easy to improve your vocabulary quickly enough so that you are sure you can reach the players.'

MP: 'Succeeding Heynckes was a huge challenge.'

PG: 'Yes, but many of our wins were thanks to Jupp's work last year, and to the team's competitive attitude. They saw themselves as winners. That's why it was so important to win the Cup and the league. It really boosted the players' confidence. They saw that they could keep winning after having won everything already. If we had lost the Cup, the following months might have been much harder. I was in charge of Barcelona, too, just after they had won the treble, but they had done it with me on the bench and here I was taking over from Jupp. It's definitely been a challenge, but I wanted to test myself by coming to a different country, where I'd have to learn a new language and take on another coach's super-successful team. I knew it would be difficult. I've won four titles this season, but for me that's not the most important thing. The crucial thing is to create something that is genuinely mine in terms of playing style, like we did for the Telekom Cup last summer, in the City game and in Leverkusen against Bayer.'

MP: 'Surely anything you do away from Barcelona will be a clash of cultures?'

PG: 'That's true because I am a fan of positional play, hemming the other team in their penalty box and not letting them leave it. Very few teams play like that. Barça do, as does Paco Jémez [the Rayo Vallecano coach] but almost nobody else. Most teams prefer to wait for the chance to counter-attack. Positional attacking is also very difficult because your players need a large dose of humility. It means essentially that an individual player has to realise that he might not be in the heat of the action for a while but he is still helping the team by what he is doing. But when he does intervene on the ball, he alone can be decisive. To fulfil that role a player needs a highly developed sense of humility, of self-sacrifice. You have to accept that you are not always in the action, that your job is to open up space for your team-mates. If instead you play eight or nine well co-ordinated players in defence, there are other difficulties but it's more straightforward and it's also how most games are played. If you're the only one employing positional play and are working with players who have won everything using a different model, well…

'The great thing is I have guys like Thiago and Philipp who hold back and wait for their chance so that we can then have a 3 v 2 in a key area. Or great players like Robben and Ribéry who accept the fact that they won't be directly involved for 15 minutes or so because their job is to wait while we construct the play in a manner which will finalise with a dangerous attack which involves them.'

MP: 'Has there been a process of mutual adaptation between coach and players?'

PG: 'Of course. And I, too, have made an effort to show humility by adapting to the players. When we have played badly it has been because you can't adapt this playing style to individual players. The players have to adapt to positional attacking. For example, I'm a fan of wingers and here I've got two magnificent examples of that breed. But in order for them to have an advantage when they get on the ball we have to build up right from the back so that they have an advantage over the rival from the instant they receive the ball. And that's a long, complicated process. It requires patience. Then there are the central defenders, who now play 50 metres ahead of their keeper. Of course it's a risk but we conceded only 13 goals in the 27 games we needed to win the league. Xavi, Messi and Iniesta have been playing this way for 10 years, so of course it has been a clash of cultures!'

MP: 'The players have given you enormous support.'

PG: 'I particularly appreciate all the effort made by players who find this playing style difficult, who are not naturally suited to it. I think that all of them, whether or not they took to it easily, saw the value of our positional play as well as all the tactical work, our emphasis on not running for running's sake. I can't believe that anyone would not like this kind of work. And remember, it has not been easy for the players to come back from a treble-winning season and stay mentally or physically at peak.'

MP: 'Isn't it frustrating to play attacking football knowing that just one counter-attack could destroy all your work?'

PG: 'Yes, that's true. But it's also very satisfying to stop your opponent's counter-attacks. The first concept to make clear is that when you attack properly in this way you ensure you are protected against losing the ball, wherever or however that happens. That was our big mistake in the Madrid disaster. I could see it right from the start but it was too difficult to change the system on the hoof and I had to wait for the break, and by then it was too late. I changed to a 4-3-3 and in the second half the problems didn't re-occur and we didn't suffer counter-attacks. In Germany the players are accustomed to having space. Look at our second goal in the DFB-Pokal final, for example. Müller had that space which he loves. But to generate it you have to drop back because if you have the opponent corralled in their own penalty area then there'll be no space at all and it's much tougher to create dangerous football.'

MP: 'A few months ago you said to me: "We'll play better next season but we'll lose more games."'

PG: 'It was just a turn of phrase. In fact I believe that if we play better we'll lose less. I hope to have more players who are fit the whole year round, so that I have more reserves and can ensure that we play better and keep winning. I think we will play better. We won't be comparing ourselves with Jupp's treble, but with our own achievements this season. It was completely normal and natural that after all that Heynckes had done, everyone wondered why we needed to change. I thought the same thing myself at times.'

MP: 'But surely it was vital to make changes after the treble because in football if you don't evolve you stagnate.'

PG: 'I suppose we'll never know how it would have turned out if we hadn't made those changes but football is evolution and successful change depends on the kind of players you have. I had to use a style I wasn't committed to many times this season but that adaptation was also to allow the guys to regain match sharpness and tempo. You need to make mistakes if you want to make progress. And you need to know your opponents, and the league. I have now played against all our opponents here, I know their stadiums, the coaches and I know and understand my own club. And whilst I was learning all of this we managed to win four trophies, which in turn will spur us on to make more progress and keep evolving. The trophies will be a real boost for my team's confidence as they start next season. They were not easy to win, but neither did we consider it enough just to make it to the finals. You have to win. After winning there is usually a period of decompression. Kalle [Rummenigge] was always saying to me: "We always have a disappointing year after winning the league or the Champions League." But we continued to perform like champions and broke records by winning the league so early, with 25 wins and two draws. A brilliant performance.'

MP: 'Is the team moving in the right direction?'

PG: 'In the last 11 months the team has lived through enormous change and we have had moments of sheer brilliance as well as real setbacks, of which the Champions League was the worst. Some of our Champions League matches were outstanding: at the Emirates, Old Trafford and the Bernabéu, for example. And it's those games, the ones in which we played the kind of football I wanted, that are important. And in time we'll give the Bayern support a lot more of them, and then one day we'll realise that the time has come to stop.'

Guardiola's second year promises to be even more intense. Pep is going to be bolder and go deeper in terms of his playing style. And he'll be working with players who are more convinced, more committed and more fluent in his language. This will be the Pep we glimpsed at the DFB-Pokal final, a man with a whole arsenal of weapons at his fingertips who will on occasion revisit old ideas. As we have seen this season, a team is a living entity, not a frozen image. It grows and flows, retreats and advances – a team is the sum of all its successes. It is a state of mind, although it is also so much more than that. It is about tactics and work, talent and ability. It's about clear ideas and effective training, but it's also about emotions and feelings. A team is like a journey. At times it's unknown territory, full of adventure, at others it's a well-worn path full of old routines. It needs to advance as a unit with commitment and clarity in a single, clear direction, understanding all the potential danger. It is a journey which has no end, or rather it has many ends but, ultimately, no final destination.

Back in New York over dinner Garry Kasparov had looked at Guardiola and said: 'The minute I won my second World Championship in 1986, I knew who would beat me in the end.'

'Who was it?' the coach had enquired.

'It was time, Pep. Time…'